OPEN TO
DEBATE

OPEN TO DEBATE

How William F. Buckley
Put Liberal America on
THE FIRING LINE

HEATHER HENDERSHOT

BROADSIDE BOOKS
An Imprint of HarperCollinsPublishers

HarperCollins books may be purchased for educational, business, or sales promotional use. For information, please email the Special Markets Department at SPsales@harpercollins.com.

Broadside Books™ and the Broadside logo are trademarks of HarperCollins Publishers.

First Broadside hardcover published 2016

FIRST EDITION

Designed by Leah Carlson-Stanisic

Hendershot, Heather. Open to debate : how William F. Buckley put liberal America on the Firing Line / Heather Hendershot.
First edition. | New York, NY : Broadside, 2016.
LCCN 2016015903| ISBN 978-0-06-243045-8 (hardback : alkaline paper) | ISBN 9780062430465 (paperback : alkaline paper) | ISBN 9780062430472 (ebook)
Buckley, William F., Jr., 1925–2008. | Buckley, William F., Jr., 1925–2008— Political and social views. | Firing line (Television program)—History. | Journalists—United States—Biography. | Television personalities— United States—Biography. | Conservatism—United States—History— 20th century. | Political culture—United States—History—20th century. | United States—Politics and government—1945–1989. | United States— Intellectual life—20th century. | BISAC: POLITICAL SCIENCE / Political Ideologies / Conservatism & Liberalism. | POLITICAL SCIENCE / Government / General. | BIOGRAPHY & AUTOBIOGRAPHY / Political. LCC PN4874.B796 H46 2016 | DDC 070.92 [B] —dc23 LC record available at https://lccn.loc.gov/2016015903

16 17 18 19 20   RRD   10 9 8 7 6 5 4 3 2 1

CONTENTS

ACKNOWLEDGMENTS

Whittaker Chambers once told William F. Buckley Jr. that "a scenic view from one's desk is the great enemy of productivity." This sentiment may seem excessively Spartan, but there is something to it. My best moments at the keyboard occur in the dead of night, when most people are asleep, incoming email slows to a trickle, and there are no distractions out the pitch-black window. I know others who feel a similar connection with the early morning hours. These are moments when one has the impression of solitude. It is only an impression, though, because the solitary writer, or at least *this* solitary writer, ultimately produces work that depends on interactions—social, professional, intellectual—with so many others. And now is my chance to express my gratitude to those others.

Many thanks to the staffs of the Columbia University Rare Book & Manuscript Library, the Manuscripts & Archives collection at Yale University's Sterling Memorial Library, and Harvard University's Schlesinger Library. Spencer DeVilbiss, at Utah State University's Merrill-Cazier Library, went above and beyond the call of duty in gaining me access to a few *Firing Line* rarities. Nancy Rose and Ron Basich came to my rescue with technical assistance, and, at the very end, Erik Stayton tweaked and formatted the manuscript over the finish line with patience and acumen. I owe a particular debt to the staff of the Hoover Institution, especially the ever-vigilant and helpful Rachel Bauer. Rachel's assistance was absolutely invaluable to this project. How amazing, during the Boston Snowpocalypse of 2015, to have an ally determined that my precious *Firing Line* DVDs from Stanford would somehow arrive on my doorstep in Cambridge. The Massachusetts Institute of Technology provided generous funding for research and, especially, technical assistance toward the end, and my MIT colleagues and students in Comparative Media Studies/Writing have also been tremendously supportive. How lucky I am to have found a professional home where people laugh (politely?) at my *Star Trek* jokes.

For their time and insights, I am most grateful to those whom I interviewed for this book: Linda Bridges, Richard Brookhiser, Christopher Buckley, Lawrence Chickerling, Agatha Dowd, Neal Freeman, Ira Glasser, Mark Green, Jeff Greenfield, Michael Kinsley, Rich Lowry, Newton Minow, and Victor Navasky. Also, John Judis very kindly shared several unpublished interviews with me.

Chris Calhoun and Adam Bellow were terrifically gung ho about the project and were a pleasure to work with. Several folks were kind enough to read the work as it moved along, or to otherwise provide inspiration and/or intellectual support: Henri Cole, Donald Crafton, Beverly Gage, Pupa Gilbert, Elyse Graham, David Greenberg, Patrick Keating, Kevin Kruse, Diane McWhorter, Ben Miller, Erin Lee Mock, Susan Moffitt, Francesca Rossi, Casey Rothschild (thanks for explaining about Laffer and his napkin!), Meghan O'Rourke, Susan Ohmer, ZZ Packer, Mauricio Pauly, Leona Sampson, Carol Steiker, John Tasioulas, Itai Yanai, and Clark Williams. Jonathan Kirshner had total confidence in the book before anyone else, even me.

The Radcliffe Institute for Advanced Study offered a most gracious and supportive home in which to advance the project in 2014–15. There, record shindigs, Rob Roys, intellectual companionship, group dinners, movie nights, and congealed baked brie somehow all came together as the dilithium crystals that powered my warp drive. I shall always treasure my year at Radcliffe.

Buckley once (well, probably more than once) declared that "industry is the enemy of melancholy." True enough, but one needs comrades as well. I owe much to the friends who in various ways saw me through the challenging days of 2012–13: Barbara Abrash, Josh Berman, Mark Betz, Andrea Buffa, Eric Freedman, Mary Fuller, Amy Herzog, Harry Holtzman, Barb Klinger, Julie Lavelle, Lynn Love, Kevin Maher, Allison McCracken, D. N. Rodowick, Sallyann Roth, David Smith, and Buffy Summers.

Finally, my pinball wizard, Mauricio Cordero, provided light, momentum, dance breaks, pizza, martinis, and inspiration. How do you think he does it? I don't know! What makes him so good?

PREFACE

The Making of William F. Buckley Jr.

In 1951, William F. Buckley Jr. wrote a book with the weighty title *God and Man at Yale: On the Superstitions of Academic Freedom*. There was no reason to expect the book to be a great hit. It had been released by Regnery, a small conservative publisher. If practically no one had heard of Regnery—it was one of only three conservative American presses, and it was hardly thriving—absolutely no one had heard of Buckley. He was just a twenty-six-year-old kid from a wealthy Connecticut family that had made and lost a fortune in Mexican oil, then made a second fortune in the oilfields of Venezuela. In 1955 Buckley would found America's preeminent journal of conservative opinion, and in 1966 he would found America's longest-running conservative public affairs television program. He would, in short, become a public intellectual, a political movement builder, and a TV star. But in 1951 he was still an unknown quantity.

Buckley was whip-smart, and he had a lot of nerve. At the age of six, he had written a letter to the king of England demanding that the country pay the debt it owed to the United States from the Great War. Buckley had served in World War II, excelled on the Yale debate team, and edited the *Yale Daily News*. He was an accomplished young man, but with his erudite vocabulary, aristocratic manner, and archconservative politics, few in 1951 would have pegged him as an up-and-coming celebrity. In the wake of almost twenty years of New Deal liberalism, conservatism barely had a pulse. Why should anyone notice this brash young man?

In *God and Man at Yale,* Buckley laid into his alma mater for its secular humanism and, to his mind, its professors' rabid support of the New Deal, the Fair Deal, and liberal encroachments on the free market. The book would prove a minor sensation, in part because Yale went out of its way to alert everyone that they really should not read it. Perhaps out of a patrician sense of decorum, Buckley had allowed Yale president Whitney Griswold to see the manuscript in advance of publication. Soon after, a wealthy alumnus phoned Buckley to tell him that Yale was taking care of some of the professors Buckley had attacked and that there was really no longer a need for the book.

Needless to say, Buckley thought this was stuff and nonsense. Griswold rather dubiously told concerned alumni who got in touch with him that the book was the product of Buckley's "militant Catholicism." Yale graduate and Harvard professor McGeorge Bundy wrote a scathing review in the *Atlantic,* having first discussed the review's major points with Griswold. Bundy attacked Buckley's arguments as ill-founded and also noted that he had no purchase as a Catholic to attack an essentially Protestant institution. This burning criticism was topped off with a range of positive and negative reviews, an introduction by the reputable journalist John Chamberlain, and Buckley Sr.'s subsidizing of a book tour for his son—it all spelled success for the book.

The initial print run of *God and Man at Yale* in October 1951 had been 5,000. The book quickly sold 12,000 copies.[1] The bestselling nonfiction books of 1951 and 1952 included Rachel Carson's environmentalist *The Sea Around Us;* Jack Lait and Lee Mortimer's muckraking *Washington Confidential; Mr. President,* a collection of Harry Truman's papers and diaries; *Witness* by Whittaker Chambers; and Tallulah Bankhead's autobiography. Buckley's book edged in at number sixteen in November 1951. Not bad for a first book, written by a twenty-six-year-old, published by what was then a nothing press.

As a youth, Buckley had struck many as arrogant and obnoxious. He was not inclined to cut slack to those he deemed less intelligent than himself, and he disliked those whose politics or morality did not align with his own. Mostly homeschooled, in 1938 he was sent to a British boarding school for a year, while his mother endured a difficult pregnancy. Young Bill echoed the isolationist politics he had learned from his father and exhibited the American flag whenever he had the opportunity. His father, Buckley would later recount, "dispatched every fortnight a survival package comprising a case of grapefruit and a large jar of peanut butter."

Peanut butter was then, and would remain, Buckley's favorite food. Bill offered to share, and his schoolmates dove for the grapefruits "but one after another actually spit out the peanut butter. . . . No wonder they needed American help to win the war," he joked (sort of).[2] Buckley could not make friends with only grapefruits for tender; he needed goodwill. It probably didn't help that he had no interest in sports, either. He would face similar problems in the army, where his vocal opposition to President Franklin Roosevelt did not meet friendly ears, and where he again exhibited feelings of superiority that earned him low marks for character in Officer Candidate School. He once brought a training exercise to a halt so that he could pick an interesting flower.[3] It's not that he was cavalier about his training, but why should a good soldier be impervious to botanical curiosities?

Buckley never suffered fools gladly, but he did finally become a very charming and gracious man, a major—make that *the* major—conservative public intellectual of the postwar years and beyond. He would also become what many would consider a supreme oxymoron: a TV intellectual. More on this anon. Above all, he became a man comfortable with those whose viewpoints were very different from his own. It was his army experiences that pushed him to reconsider how he related to others. In a letter to his father, Buckley explained the transformation:

> When I went to the Army, I learned the importance of tolerance, and the importance of a sense of proportion about all matters—even in regard to religion, morality etc. Some friends I made whom I really prized were atheistic, even immoral. But I learned, nevertheless, that regardless of the individual's dogmas, the most important thing as far as I was concerned was the personality: would his friendship broaden your horizon and provide you with intellectual entertainment? I found that there were actually very few prerequisites to the good friend: he had to have a good sense of humor, a pleasant personality and a certain number of common interests.[4]

In short, Buckley came to realize that one could have very interesting conversations, and even become very good friends with, people whose belief systems were very different from one's own. This kind of personal realization was not strictly necessary for a political pundit, a conservative movement organizer, an editor of a journal of opinion, or a nationally syndicated right-wing columnist. You could, theoretically, perform all of these roles from within an isolated bubble filled only with your own ideological compatriots. But a willingness to engage generously with political opponents *would* make you a better host of a public affairs TV show. Of course, Buckley did not need to be friends with all of his liberal and left-wing TV guests, but it would have been boring if he had simply attacked and disdained them. He succeeded on his program *Firing Line*—for more than thirty years—because he was *open* to guests, open to their differences, open to debate.

Even before starting his TV show, Buckley had found opportunities for mediated debates with his ideological foes. Having
been pegged as the voice of respectable, not to mention *entertaining*, conservatism following the celebrity of *God and Man
at Yale* in 1951 and the founding of *National Review* magazine
in 1955, Buckley was regularly invited to represent the right in
debates at college campuses and on radio. He also appeared
on TV, but he was nowhere close to being a big star. Still, even
if he was not widely recognized by the culture at large in the
1950s, he was recognized among those who followed such
things as the face of American conservatism. Searching for
guests to mark its one-hundred-fifty-year anniversary in 1965,
the Cambridge Union debating society at Cambridge University made a provocative choice: James Baldwin and William F.
Buckley would debate the motion "The American Dream Has
Been Achieved at the Expense of the American Negro."

The debate took place on February 18, 1965. Malcolm X would
be assassinated three days later. One month after the Buckley-
Baldwin debate, participants in the Selma to Montgomery
March were teargassed and beaten with billy clubs while crossing the Edmund Pettus Bridge. Both the Voting Rights Act and
the Watts riots would take place in August 1965. And earlier, of
course, in the summer of 1964, there had been rioting in Harlem a few days after the Civil Rights Act had been signed into
law. All of which is to say, Baldwin and Buckley met for their
debate at a fraught moment, with Jim Crow laws lingering on
and the struggle for racial equality still very much a work in
progress. The debate resolution was designed to provoke a discussion as polarized as America itself.

The debate opened with remarks by two Cambridge under-
graduates, one supporting Baldwin's side, the other Buckley's.
Buckley's advocate, Jeremy Burford, noted that his purpose was
not to oppose civil rights but to oppose the motion. If progress
had been made in the advancement of "the American Dream,"

it was in spite of—not because of—the inequality and the suffering of the American Negro. He emphasized that the debate was not over whether civil rights should be extended to American Negroes; if it were, it would be a very simple motion, and the answer would be yes. Burford's comments were not well received; the crowd laughed when he observed that there were thirty-five Negro millionaires in the United States. But he had gotten at the kernel of the issue, the fact that the motion demanded that Baldwin and Buckley debate not whether Negroes were ill-treated or racist oppression must end. Instead, the motion demanded that the speakers stake a claim for the very meaning of America.

Baldwin argued passionately about how the American Negro was treated as less than human, but he also quite smartly asked the audience to consider the inner life—the absolute moral corruption—of the racist within the American system. The speech built to so many finely crafted crescendos that it is hard to pick one to typify the quality of the discourse. This one will have to do:

> I suggest that what has happened to white Southerners is in some ways much worse than what has happened to Negroes there. Because Sheriff Clark in Selma, Alabama, cannot be considered, you know, no one can be dismissed as a total monster; I am sure he loves his wife, his children. I'm sure that he likes to get drunk. He is visibly a man like me. But he doesn't know what drives him to use the club, to menace with the gun, and to use the cattle prod. Something awful must have happened to a human being to be able to put a cattle prod against a woman's breasts, for example. What happens to the woman is ghastly. What happens to the man who does it is in some ways much, much worse. This is being done, after all, not a hundred years ago, but in 1965 in a country which is blessed with what we call prosperity (a word we won't examine too

*closely), with a certain kind of social coherence, which calls
itself a civilized nation, and which espouses the notion of the
freedom of the world. . . . Any American Negro watching this,
no matter where he is—from the vantage point of Harlem, a
terrible place—he has to say to himself, in spite of what the
government says, the government says "we can't do anything
about it," [he has to say to himself] "if those were white people
being murdered in Mississippi work farms, being carried off
to jail, if those were white children running up and down the
streets, the government would find some way of doing something about it." We have a civil rights bill now. We had the
15th Amendment nearly 100 years ago. I hate to sound again
like an Old Testament prophet, but if the amendment was
not honored then, I don't have any reason to believe that the
civil rights bill will be honored now. . . . If one has got to prove
one's title to the land, isn't four hundred years enough? Four
hundred years, at least three wars? The American soil is full
of the corpses of my ancestors. Why is my freedom, my citizenship, or my right to live there, how is it conceivably a question
now? And I suggest further and in the same way that the
moral life of Alabama sheriffs and poor Alabama white ladies, their moral lives have been destroyed by the plague called
color. That the American sense of reality had been corrupted
by it. . . . What one begs the American people to do, for all our
sakes, is simply to accept our history.*

Baldwin had unequivocally won the sympathies of the room.
Fifty years later, it is still a powerful and convincing piece of
oratory.

Buckley came back with equal passion. He conceded that
the situation in the United States was dire. He cited several
examples of racist incidents from Baldwin's *The Fire Next Time*
and stated, "I know from your faces that you share with me a
feeling of compassion and a feeling of outrage that this kind

of thing should have happened. How are we going to avoid the
kind of humiliations which are visited perpetually upon members of the minority race?" That he found American racism
to be unjust and immoral was clear from his comments. That
his solutions were both conservative and patriotic was to be expected, as illustrated in his closing comments:

*We must reach through to the Negro people and tell them that
their best chances are in a mobile society, and the most mobile
society in the world today my friends is the United States of
America. . . . And it is precisely that mobility which will give
opportunities to the Negroes, which they must be encouraged
to take. But they must not in the course of their ordeal be
encouraged to adopt the kind of cynicism, the kind of despair,
the kind of iconoclasm that is urged upon them by Mr. Baldwin in his recent works. Because of one thing, I can tell you, I
believe with absolute authority that where the United States
is concerned if it ever becomes a confrontation between a
continuation of our own sort of idealism, the private stock of
which granted like most people in the world we tend to lavish
only every now and then for public enterprises, reserving it
so often for our own irritations and pleasures, but the fundamental friend of the Negro people in the United States is
the good nature, and is the generosity, and is the good wishes,
is the fundamental decency that do lie at the reserves of the
spirit of the American people. These must not be laughed at* [a
reference to the audience's outbursts of derisive laughter
during both Buckley's and Burford's comments], *under
no circumstances must they be laughed at, and under no circumstances must America be addressed and told that the only
alternative to the status quo is to overthrow a vast civilization which we consider to be the faith of our fathers, the faith
indeed of your fathers. This is what must animate whatever
meliorism must come, because if it finally does come to a rad-*

ical confrontation between giving up what we understand to be the best features of the American way of life . . . then we will fight the issue. And we will fight the issue not only in the Cambridge Union, but we will fight it as you were once recently called to do on beaches, and on hills, and on mountains, and on landing grounds. And we will be convinced that just as you won the war against a particular threat to civilization, you were nevertheless waging a war in favor of and for the benefit of Germans, your own enemies, just as we are convinced that if it should ever come to that kind of a confrontation our own determination to win the struggle will be a determination to wage a war not only for whites, but also for Negroes.

Buckley believed in the inherent goodness at the root of the American dream, even as he frankly acknowledged that the country had not always lived up to those ideals. His great fear was that the American racial crisis would end in revolution. As a conservative, of course, his objective was to work within the system, to fix what was broken. Where Baldwin was pessimistic, Buckley was hopeful.

Watching the debate today, most conclude that Baldwin won (as he indeed did by an overwhelming vote of Cambridge students at the time) and that Buckley was simply out-argued. One historian has gone so far as to say that "when Buckley stood up to speak, rather than listen to Baldwin's arguments and push back, he stepped directly into the role of the Alabama Sheriff who just couldn't understand what Baldwin was saying. In a flash, Buckley morphed into Bull Connor."[5] Connor had turned fire hoses and attack dogs on little children. He was exactly the kind of cruel and violent racist whom Baldwin had gone to great pains to describe as not a "total monster," and as someone we should attempt to understand. It is difficult to imagine that Connor was not abhorrent to Buckley or that he had as little understanding of the racism Baldwin decried as Connor did.

But it is true that Buckley had made several errors. First, he had opened his comments by suggesting that Baldwin protested his continual subjugation as a Negro, and that Buckley would instead respond to his *arguments* rather than to his skin color. The problem was, Buckley stated that he would treat Baldwin exactly as if he were white. The implication was that white signified neutral racelessness. It was a tasteless and unkind notion that disregarded all that Baldwin had described as very specific to what the Negro experiences in America, an experience that whites had great difficulty understanding. Buckley seemed in that moment to be confirming exactly that difficulty.

Second, he ended with a somewhat befuddling return to World War II. He did so, presumably in part, to tap into passions he thought would be animated specifically in a room full of Brits. But the fighting-for-the-Germans material was somewhat difficult to decipher. What Buckley seemed to be indicating was that the Allies had fought not just against the Nazis but for the liberation of the Germans from their Nazi oppressors and that, by analogy, if there was a racial revolution in the United States, Americans would fight for both whites and Negroes against the totalitarian forces seeking to overthrow America. Were the revolutionary leaders of the Negro movement really being rhetorically aligned with the Nazis here? Perhaps some conservatives at the time would have been comfortable with the analogy, but at the very least Buckley had lost the room.

Third, Buckley argued that Negroes were simply not seizing the opportunities available to them as other ethnic groups had. If there were 3,500 Negro doctors in 1900 and only 400 more in 1960, the fault lay with Negroes, since medical schools were bending over backward to help them. This conveyed a basic incomprehension of the realities of the struggle for upward mobility faced by American Negroes. Notably, Buckley indicated elsewhere that the disadvantages faced by blacks could not compare to those of groups such as the Irish, Italians, and

Jews, and that there was a *"special* burden [his emphasis] that the white man must discharge as he seeks some kind of a law of expiation."[6] He also stated, "I think there's a very good argument for voting for a Negro because he's a Negro—until such time as it becomes simply redundant to make such a demonstration" and that it was right for an employer to give preference to applications from black candidates.[7] His feeling was that the error lay not in extending special assistance to blacks but in mandating such assistance by law. But this was not aptly conveyed at the Baldwin debate.

Fourth, Buckley did something he generally avoided at all costs in an argumentative situation: he got personal. He opened by declaring, "It seems to me that of all the indictments Mr. Baldwin has made of America here tonight, and in his copious literature of protest, the one that is most striking involves, in effect, the refusal of the American community to treat him other than as a Negro. The American community has refused to do this. The American community, almost everywhere he goes, treats him with the kind of unction, with the kind of satisfaction that a posturing hero gets for his flagellations of our civilization, so that he quite properly commands the contempt he so eloquently showers upon us."

The idea here was that Baldwin was having one over on us. He protested ill-treatment but was treated in a princely manner, a star of the intellectual side of the American Negro movement. Further, Buckley did not simply respond to the material presented that afternoon by Baldwin. He also drew from *The Fire Next Time*, a work that he judged deeply cynical and counterproductive. Buckley even went so far as to accuse Baldwin of playing the crowd by putting on a fake British accent. At this, Baldwin's eyes widened in disbelief (we are treated here to one of only a small number of reaction shots at an event shot flat-footedly for American educational television), and the crowd loudly guffawed. There was simply nothing British in

Baldwin's intonations, and one is hard-pressed to explain Buckley's bizarre accusation, but we can discern that it was another personal attack, a game that Buckley did not usually play in public forums.

In sum, everything about Baldwin rubbed Buckley the wrong way. Obviously, plenty of radicals rubbed Buckley the wrong way. But there were also plenty of radicals he strongly disagreed with whom he also admired and respected as intellectual forces, such as (some years later) the Marxist *Nation* columnist Christopher Hitchens. Baldwin, by contrast, would serve as a negative example of radicalism for the rest of Buckley's career.

So, was the debate with Baldwin a hit or a miss for Buckley? The whole event certainly highlighted the limits of formal debate. In a nutshell: Baldwin made a speech, Buckley made a speech, attendees voted. The speeches were riveting, but there was no room for conversation built into the format. The fact that Buckley had mastered the art of formal debate at Yale would serve him well on *Firing Line*, but *Firing Line* would also serve Buckley well by allowing for genuine engagement, exchange, and even mistakes, on both sides. So the Baldwin debate was a failure for Buckley to the extent that it revealed the real limitations of this rigid mode of discourse.

But notwithstanding the missteps Buckley made, the judgment of many sympathetic to the civil rights movement—then and now—that Baldwin had slam-dunked it, and the indisputably negative outcome of the debate based on votes at the end, there is one level on which the debate was *hugely successful* for Buckley. He had been introduced at the outset by the British TV announcer as a supporter of Barry Goldwater's recently failed presidential campaign. The connotations were clear: to most viewers, "Goldwater" would convey extremism and the specter of a twitchy finger on the nuclear button. The Goldwater movement—and, by extension, American conservatism—

was at that time understood to be teeming with racist, ignorant nuts.

But in debating Baldwin, Buckley had shown a temperate and intellectual version of conservatism. He was passionate, but not unhinged. He had gestured intently with his hands, addressing the crowd personally, referring to the hard work of Cambridge students and their grandparents, referring to them as "my friends," using all the tools of the seasoned debater. Buckley wore a tuxedo, the favored costume for Cambridge debates. He also spoke directly to the chairman, which was part of the accepted protocol. It was a polished and sophisticated presentation. Further, he acknowledged the immorality of racism and rejected its practice in America. He fought what he saw as pure cynicism (what Baldwin and his supporters surely saw as realism, *tout court*) with patriotic optimism and panache, without reverting to conspiratorial arguments or the extremist's default argument that everything related to fighting racism in America was a communist conspiracy.

Whether you agreed with him or not, everything in his rhetoric and self-presentation conveyed that conservatism was not the last refuge of raving lunatics, and that criticism of the tactics of the Negro movement need not be based in a hatred of Negroes and fear of "race mixing," the hysterical default notion of so many, especially in the deep South. He didn't agree with the ways that many people wanted to fix the "race problem," but he did agree that racism was a real crisis with deeply unsettling moral ramifications. Even as one might quite reasonably, from a liberal perspective, attack Buckley's patrician notions of the meaning of "the faith of our fathers," viewed objectively Buckley had offered a performance of modern conservatism that conveyed unequivocally "to hell with the KKK, the White Citizens' Councils, the John Birch Society, and George Wallace."

Now, the next question is, to whom exactly was this message conveyed, beyond an overflow crowd at Cambridge University?

In 1965, the television networks had scant interest in airing one-off intellectual debates about Negroes and the American dream. But National Educational Television (NET) had taped the event, and a few months later it would be shown by NET in New York City, and then distributed by NET to other educational stations around the country. NET had a reputation for exceedingly dry adult educational programming. The Baldwin-Buckley debate was anything but dry, but it was adult, intellectual, and utterly lacking in visual dynamism. This was hardly the TV event of the year. But its biggest audience—the intelligentsia and the political junkies of New York City—was also exactly the right audience, for the program would air just as Buckley was gearing up for his famous, symbolic run for mayor. If Buckley's first moment in the spotlight had come with *God and Man at Yale,* and the Baldwin debate had made a smaller blip on the mass media radar, the mayoral campaign would lift him up to the next level.

In 1965, Buckley ran for mayor of New York City on the Conservative Party line. His objective was to protest that "Republican" John Lindsay was no such thing—and, more generally, to demonstrate that conservatism was in sad shape and needed a swift kick in the pants if it were to rally. There was also a Democratic mayoral candidate in the mix, Abraham Beame. Beame and Lindsay were career politicians who, naturally, gave themselves over to *campaigning,* for that is, of course, what you are supposed to do. Buckley, by contrast, sandwiched speeches and interviews into his busy schedule. Just because he was running for mayor didn't mean he'd stop writing his column or editing his magazine. In effect, he ran for mayor part-time.

It is difficult to imagine that Buckley deliberately ran the campaign as an avant-garde performance piece, but there was a delicious absurdity to the whole thing. As Norman Mailer wrote at the time, no one was more "majestically unsuited" for the job of mayor, for "it is possible Old Bill has never been in a subway in his life. To be fair, it must also be said that no one could have been more majestically suited for spoiling Lindsay's campaign. Buckley's personality is the highest Camp we are ever going to find in a mayoralty. No other actor on earth can project simultaneous hints that he is in the act of playing commodore of the Yacht Club, Joseph Goebbels, Robert Mitchum, Maverick, Savonarola, the nice prep-school kid next door, and the snows of yesteryear. If he didn't talk about politics—if he was just the most Camp gun ever to walk into Gunsmoke—I'd give up Saturday nights to watch him."[8]

Of course, there were liberals who assumed he was some kind of a crazed-fascist-Goldwater-manqué. But conservative, liberal, or apolitical, all New Yorkers appreciate chutzpah. Buckley was putting on a terrific show. He was deadly serious about his politics but never lost sight of the inherent absurdity and humor of politics. The performance was half Milton Friedman, half Rufus T. Firefly. Asked what he would do first if elected, he replied, "demand a recount." The press ate it up with a spoon. As Neal Freeman, who assisted in the campaign, would later observe, "Bill was good copy. . . . Beame and Lindsay seemed to be quotable only when quoting Bill, usually in high theatrical dudgeon."[9]

Most shockingly, when asked questions, Buckley answered with complete candor. For example, during the campaign he suggested that a viable way to tame the city's traffic congestion problem would be to stagger the days on which truck deliveries were permitted. Off camera, Buckley claimed, the other candidates confided that they thought this was a great idea. On camera, in debates, they said his idea was ludicrous. Explaining the discrepancy was easy: no politician could publicly support a plan that would infuriate the Teamsters. (Buckley's opponents would have been better off sticking to rebutting his dubious proposal to forcibly relocate drug addicts to treatment centers outside the city. Buckley said it was simply a public health issue;

the other candidates screamed "fascist!" but could have toned
down the histrionics and simply focused on the civil rights violations that the plan would have necessitated.) Buckley rejected
the kinds of public relations strategies that real politicians understood as a matter of course.

His campaign ran few ads not only because it was on a very
tight budget but also because Buckley was uncomfortable with
bumper sticker politics. His slogans included "Buckley for
Mayor" and, slightly more catchy, "He has the guts to tell the
truth: will you listen?" This was frustrating to those who actually wanted him to win. In fact, one month before the election, a sympathetic New York City advertising agency had even
offered its services to Buckley at cost, submitting a detailed
plan of action. Apparently suffering from some delusion that
Buckley could be won over by alliterative purple prose, the report sycophantically praised Buckley for his "scathing saber of
sarcastic syllogism" and "darting dirk of devilish dissection."

The advertisers suggested that Buckley needed to tone down
his rhetoric: "To speak only in the Buckley idiom excludes tens
of thousands of important voters. . . . Undeniably, we all enjoy
pheasant and wild rice occasionally but the facts are that hamburgers, pork chops, and beef stew are far more popular—and
much more easily digested. So let's not talk down—à la carte—
let's make the menu as appetizing, understandable, and familiar as we can." Adding insult to injury, the agency offered
idiotic sample radio spots. One consisted mostly of the sound
of a dripping faucet: "Let's turn off the tap at the top. Elect Bill
Buckley mayor—and let's get rid of the waste and worries. And
get rid of all the drips." A spot focusing on the crime problem
featured a woman's high heels clacking on the pavement, going faster and faster, until she screams twice, "Oh please, no!"[10]

Could anyone really imagine this nonsense as suitable Buckley promotional material? An earnest citizen wrote to Buckley
that the star of the silent 1915 French film serial *Les Vampires*

looked exactly like Buckley; he suggested that Buckley's staff could insert new intertitles into the film to create clever campaign ads. Buckley wrote back to thank him for his "pixilated suggestion."[11] None of these proposals came to fruition, but the wacky silent film idea—real pheasant and wild rice–type stuff—must have been more appealing to Buckley than the ridiculous hamburgers, pork chops, and beef stew ideas issuing from the admen.

Throughout the campaign he talked the way he had always talked, drawing from a deep well of vocabulary that would send a Ph.D. in English rushing to the dictionary. (A supporter from the Bronx who described herself as "a normal girl" of "*some* intelligence" wrote Buckley to complain that she got muddled listening to Beame and Lindsay but that she "got the gist" of what Buckley was saying, even though he used "50 cent words.")[12] This was as clear an indicator as any that he knew his campaign was symbolic and that he had no chance of winning. Lindsay's speeches, which he mostly wrote himself, overflowed with "remorseless clichés . . . ear-clanging phrases . . . irretrievable syntax," as Buckley put it.[13] He was appalled that this somehow passed for cogent political discourse in New York City.

Ironically, though, it was Buckley's own appealing televisual presence that ultimately enabled him to show how truly shallow Lindsay was. In a tremendous stroke of good luck for Buckley, there was a newspaper strike in the middle of the campaign. Suddenly, the number of candidates' TV appearances increased to compensate for the lacking newspaper coverage. No political candidate ever dared to look so bored and above-it-all as Buckley did on TV. By rejecting the notion that it was appearances that mattered in political campaigning, Buckley won the war of appearances. He was thus perfectly positioned to continue his war against liberalism—and moderate conservatism—when *Firing Line* premiered a year later.

Buckley deplored the "photo op" and, fully realizing that his

No political candidate ever dared to look so bored and above-it-all as
Buckley did on TV when he ran for mayor of New York City in 1965.
CREDIT: *Cornell Capa © International Center of Photography/Magnum
Photos*

campaign was symbolic, he was dismissive of foolish hand-
shaking events that candidates engaged in purely to ingratiate
themselves with this or that special interest group. He disparaged such party players as "goo-goos" ("good government
boys") and "blintz munchers." Buckley was not anti-Semitic,
but the blintz did come to symbolize for him the empty sym-
bolism of politicking; eating blintzes at Jewish delis was like
kissing babies at parades. Buckley made news by skipping an
opportunity to march in the Pulaski Day parade. How could
he slight the Poles of New York? And they were Catholics like
him! Was he mad? He didn't see what all the fuss was about, as
he had no interest in courting each of the ethnic, religious, and
racial subgroups of New York City. There would be no opportu-

nity to share political ideas while participating in a parade, and such nonsense would divert him from more productive work.

When it was all over, Buckley had pulled in 13 percent of the vote. Not too shabby in a city where Democrats outnumber Republicans five-to-one. He even wrote a lively book about the race, *The Unmaking of a Mayor.* Of Lindsay's Upper East Side neighborhood, the "Silk Stocking" district, Buckley wrote, "it shelters not only just about all the resident financial, social, and artistic elite of New York but also probably the densest national concentration of vegetarians, pacifists, hermaphrodites, junkies, Communists, Randites, clam-juice-and-betel-nut eaters; plus, also, a sprinkling of quite normal people."[14] Take that, *Atlas Shrugged* . . . and Clamato!

The campaign was a crucial stage in Buckley's creation of himself as a celebrity persona and, thus, as a likely success as a talk show host. Many private citizens who wrote to Buckley during the campaign noted that they were already familiar with him from the televised debate with Baldwin. (They also mentioned his appearances on *Meet the Press* and David Susskind's *Open End.*) Buckley might have overwhelmingly lost the Baldwin debate by the vote of the Cambridge students, but he apparently won as far as many US TV viewers were concerned, and they wrote fan mail to him to tell him as much.

Others wrote during the mayoral campaign just to tell him that they appreciated his having the guts to challenge party machine politics. Journalist Ken Auletta wrote Buckley a letter complimenting him on his "candor and fairness," though he noted that he would not dream of voting for him: "I trust that you will not win . . . yet I hope and believe that the political 'pros' who sit on this city will run a little more scared because William F. Buckley Jr. had the temerity to kick them swiftly in the fat of their butt."[15] CBS newsman Fred Friendly—Edward R. Murrow's old colleague—was charmed by Buckley's charis-

matic televisual presence during the mayoral campaign, and
wrote him to ask for a meeting to discuss his future in the TV
business.

The mayoral campaign resurfaced throughout Buckley's career, and it will resurface in the pages ahead. For now, suffice it
to say that it was a key moment in Buckley's transition from successful conservative writer and editor to hugely successful conservative celebrity and media pundit. As Freeman would later
explain, before the mayoral run Buckley "was an obscure talented young man. *National Review* was a fringe publication, and
Bill was not even a fixture on the outer circle of talk shows and
lecture circles. . . . Both the column and radio-television projects were a very hard sell in 1964."[16] But after the campaign, the
column took off, as did Buckley's new TV show. His TV show,
Firing Line, could have easily fizzled after a short run had Buckley's national profile not been elevated by the New York City race.

If we take the mayoral campaign as a sort of warm-up for
Firing Line we can handily suss out Buckley's own attitudes toward mass media. In short, he was wary of it, and having been
egregiously misquoted by a number of newspapers early in the
campaign, he began bringing both a stenographer and a reel-
to-reel tape recorder to all his public events. The campaign had
taught Buckley that media was difficult to use: one was more
often used by it. The solution was to create your own TV show
on which you called all the shots. Hence, *Firing Line*. For more
than thirty years, the show served as a vehicle conveying Buckley's notion of what conservatism really was. And throughout
it all, even as Buckley was unshakable in his conservatism, he
remained open to debating with the other side and resistant to
tearing into any aspect of the private lives of his opponents. He
valued the precise use of language to advance arguments, especially if that precision came with a sense of humor. If you were
fun to argue with, Buckley was interested in mixing things up,
whether you were a liberal or a conservative.

One *Firing Line* episode illustrates this particularly well. In 1984, Christopher Hitchens and R. Emmett Tyrrell Jr. appeared on the show to answer the question "Is There a Liberal Crack-Up?" Tyrrell, editor of the *American Spectator*, had just written a book advancing an affirmative answer to that question. Hitchens has read Tyrrell's book quite closely and takes issue not only with his central arguments but also with his tone and style. Tyrrell argues that the liberal decline began with Richard Nixon's election; Hitchens sees Nixon's election as disastrous, but not because it was the beginning of a "liberal crack-up." The Nixon administration was, he explains, disastrous not only for Cambodia and Vietnam but also for Americans because Nixon had propagated "appalling corruption amounting practically to a coup against the Constitution in Washington." It would have been better for America had George McGovern been elected. Buckley agrees! But he agrees because Nixon let South Vietnam down, and he would have preferred that to have happened on McGovern's watch. The lively dispute continues, and one soon realizes that Tyrrell is in over his head.

HITCHENS: His book is an attack on the left, with which I am prepared to associate myself, and I think we have—though this may be intensely boring for everyone to watch—I think we have cleared the ground in a sense. I mean, he's not really attacking Lyndon Johnson in this book. He's attacking the left, the—

BUCKLEY: Obviously he is attacking Lyndon Johnson.

HITCHENS:—attacking the left that survived and came out of the civil rights movement, the women's movement, and the movement against the Vietnam War.

BUCKLEY: You say it, Mr. Tyrrell, whom you're attacking.

TYRRELL: Well, I mean, I don't— See, I don't— See, I'm a much more *peaceful* man than you are, Christopher. I'm not

attacking anyone. I'm merely describing what happened in
the 1970s. What happened in the 1970s was the breakdown
of American liberalism into a riot of enthusiasms, and if
you would like to read [aloud from the book, which Hitchens
holds in his hands], perhaps we have some organ [music].
Bill, did you bring your harpsichord? Christopher is about to
read.

HITCHENS: I don't—

BUCKLEY: The harpsichord makes very poor organ music.

HITCHENS: I don't think that "peaceful"—"peaceful" isn't
the word I'm in search of. But if you say you don't attack
anyone, how come you say, "the vast majority of feminists
were disagreeable misanthropes, horrible to behold, uncouth
and unlovely. They were inferior women, contemptuous of
the superior women, who, through their charm and intellect
have so often been able to establish such enviable lives for
themselves"? I could go on. I mean, I will if you like.

TYRRELL: Go on. It's beautiful.

HITCHENS: Why don't you plug your own book? I would say
that was a "critical" use of language.

TYRRELL: I would say that was my opinion. It's a clinical
description.

BUCKLEY: You were just being facetious, though, weren't
you?

HITCHENS: Not elegant. Not elegant, but certainly not
peaceful.

TYRRELL: I know the difference between agreeable women
and disagreeable women.

HITCHENS: Well, yes, you have a number of roguish asides
about yourself on this point, but you have a certain want
of gallantry when you discuss the women's movement in

general, one that I'm surprised at in someone who is so fond of conservative affectations about—

TYRRELL: Here we go.

HITCHENS: —the good old stylish days.

TYRRELL: Here we are again.

BUCKLEY: Mr. Tyrrell, why are you so anxious to say that you don't attack people? Because you do.[17]

Hitchens goes on to show exactly how Tyrrell attacks people, pointing to his rude gender-based insults, and observing that he himself disagrees with many women on the right, such as Jeane Kirkpatrick and Midge Decter, but—thanks to lessons taught by the feminist movement—he would never disparage one of them as an "old bitch" or "old bag" or "old douche bag" in his column. Tyrrell flounders and comes up with this feeble retort: "Billingsgate I will not . . . stoop to." Hitchens is simply better at making arguments than Tyrrell, and at various points in the show Buckley ignores Tyrrell altogether and strikes up a separate conversation with Hitchens.

As a liberal watching this episode of *Firing Line*, my own assessment is that Hitchens prevails in his arguments with Buckley. A conservative would probably conclude the reverse. But anyone would have to concur that Tyrrell loses quite miserably. As Buckley's son, Christopher, would later observe, "Tyrrell was left limp and bleeding by the end of the show." It was a "delicious evisceration."[18]

Tyrrell appeared on *Firing Line* once, Hitchens five times. Hitchens was an avowed Marxist and atheist who wrote a bestseller titled *God is Not Great: How Religion Poisons Everything*. He even wrote a book taking down Mother Teresa titled (brace yourself) *The Missionary Position*. You would not expect Buckley to enjoy Hitchens's company. Indeed, after the Mother Teresa book he wrote a note to *Firing Line* producer Warren

Steibel saying, "I never want to lay eyes on this guy again."[19] Yet there Hitchens was, back on the show a few years later. Buckley could not resist him; he was simply too clever.

Looking back from today's world of shrieking pundits—a world in which TV talking heads deliberately strike up personality-based feuds with their ideological foes—the Buckley approach seems positively mind-blowing. How have we allowed our political discourse to become so coarsened and polarized? Frankly, there could not be a better time to revisit *Firing Line*. Even if—like me—you disagree with most of Buckley's political positions, it is impossible not to find value in a program that offers such a compelling model of gracious and rigorous political engagement.

Once or twice a year, Buckley even hosted "turning-the-tables" episodes in which he would put himself on the firing line, as it were, allowing a panel of liberal guests to interrogate him, with an occasional conservative thrown in for pepper. Guests for these shows included Nat Hentoff, Ed Koch, Morton Kondracke, Gabe Pressman, Jeff Greenfield, Joseph Sobran, Michael Kinsley, and Mark Green. In 1981, Buckley opened one such episode by explaining that for these reversed shows, "three dragons are selected as executioners, and, traditionally, they have done their job with obscene zest," but his words were patently hyperbolic. These were not gimmicky shouting matches but, rather, genuine efforts to let the other side have a go at Buckley. Kondracke would later be a regular on *The Mc-Laughlin Group*, a show he described as "the beginning of the end of civil discourse in this country, if not the beginning of the end of Western Civilization."[20] The turning-the-tables episodes served the opposite purpose, staking a claim for civil discourse, which, of course, Buckley saw as the very cornerstone of Western Civilization.

Firing Line's approach is perhaps incomprehensible to a younger generation who grew up in the world of Fox News,

MSNBC, and one-sided opinion blogs, and who have no memory of what media was like in the three-channel days. In the network era, viewers chose from a very limited menu, and the industry sought to produce the least offensive programming that would attract the widest possible audience. CBS, ABC, and NBC fought the rise of cable tooth and nail. Scripted TV is significantly better (or at least more diverse) today precisely because they lost that battle and there are now niche options available. If you like lowbrow stuff, you can watch vituperative housewives weaving plots against each other or drunken twenty-somethings hooking up in hot tubs. If you like highbrow stuff, you can find a sociological drama about the inner-city drug trade or finely crafted satire about Beltway politics. It's the triumph of the free market!

But where does this leave news and public affairs programming? In our splintered American mediascape, conservatives tend to seek out news media that they agree with, and liberals do the same. There seems to be very little space for political opponents to sit down and talk, without interrupting, shouting insults, or hurling chairs at each other. Restoring genteel notions of civility to TV will not provide a magic cure for all that ails us politically today. But *Firing Line* offers a model for what smart political TV once was. And could be again?

INTRODUCTION

The Making of *Firing Line*:
A "Bare Knuckled Intellectual Brawl"
with "No Production Values!"

In 1966, Buckley was producing two newspaper columns a week, editing a magazine, giving speeches on college campuses, hobnobbing with intellectuals and politicians, and sailing and playing the harpsichord in his spare time. He more than had his hands full without taking on a weekly TV show, and it certainly was not a profitable endeavor, so why bother?

At the most basic level, *Firing Line* offered Buckley a chance to present conservative views to a mass audience that otherwise might never have encountered them. Whereas in *National Review* Buckley could speak "institutionally," Neal Freeman explains, in the column and on *Firing Line* "he could be more playful, he could be more adventurous."[1] Such ludic possibilities made the show and column more inviting venues for selling conservatism to newcomers than the magazine. Readers were likely to come to *National Review* as subscribing conservatives hoping to have their worldviews confirmed, or to learn more.

Current *National Review* editor Rich Lowry wonderfully describes his youthful encounter with Buckley's work: "Discovering *Firing Line* . . . prompted me to seek out . . . *National Review*. I coveted a copy. I remember excitedly walking to the local drugstore and finding only the *New Republic*. I chafed at the injustice of it. It was in my high school library that I finally found copies of *NR*, stuck in those hard plastic binders that libraries used to have."²

Reagan and Bush speechwriter Peggy Noonan tells a similar story of observing her friend's mother enthusiastically rooting for Buckley on TV and hurling epithets at left-wing Harvard economist John Kenneth Galbraith ("facile jackass!"). Her friend lent her copies of her mom's favorite magazine: "I started reading *NR*, and it sang to me. . . . Later I found that half the people in the Reagan administration had as their first conservative friend that little magazine."³ The magazine was niche media; you had to seek it out.

Buckley's TV show, conversely, existed in the mass media sphere and was easier to encounter casually. You came to it as a liberal, conservative, or moderate flipping channels, and you might stop to consider the message, or you might move on, if such heady stuff was not to your liking. If you stuck around, you might even become more liberal from watching the show, depending on the debating skills of the guest. This was a risk Buckley was clearly willing to take. Today we are accustomed to Fox's Bill O'Reilly hectoring his guests and yelling "shut off his mic!" when they offend him. This kind of bluster was alien to Buckley, who wanted to take a deep dive into the ideological currents of his opponents.

Firing Line was only one tool of several that Buckley used to articulate the conservative perspective, and, while we cannot ascribe direct causality to the show—it alone did not push the Republican Party right, for example, or help it recover from Nixon's flameout—the show offered a consistent articulation of what right-wing conservatism was, or of what it should be according to Buckley, for more than thirty years. If it was less than a steering wheel of the postwar conservative movement, it was more than a compass.

There is no doubt that liberalism seemed to have won when *Firing Line* premiered, and on into the 1970s. *Seemed* is the

operative word here. The antiwar movement and the counterculture thrived in the 1960s; the feminist and gay rights movements accelerated in the 1970s; and even TV became "relevant,"
as they said in the industry, and vaguely liberal, with the rise
of shows like *All in the Family* and *The Mary Tyler Moore Show*.

At the same time, a conservative insurgency was growing,
coming to a head with Ronald Reagan's election to the presidency in 1980. *Firing Line* did not create the Reagan Revolution, but it did function as an intellectual barometer of the
social upheaval of the sixties and seventies, showing how one
very smart conservative reacted to and made sense of that
upheaval. In those same years, conservative activists such as
Richard Viguerie and Paul Weyrich were building social movements on the ground; they were motivating conservatives to
open their wallets and go to the voting booth. Their strategies
worked, and this way of telling the story of the growth of the
American conservative movement is not incorrect.

But Buckley's work with *Firing Line* was of a different timbre.
He was asking how conservative theory could be translated into
practice. How could theories of conservative economists such
as Friedrich von Hayek be manifested as supply-side economics? Buckley's questions were practical, but also *intellectual*. As
popular conservatism took off—fueled by Weyrich, Viguerie,
Jerry Falwell, and others—activists hit the streets to canvass
for votes, circulate petitions, and picket women's health clinics.
But Buckley remained planted behind his portable blue Olivetti
Lettera 32 typewriter, pounding out copy on deregulation for
National Review, or behind his clipboard, on *Firing Line,* debating cerebral topics.

When *Firing Line* premiered, conservatism was either on the
ropes or down for the count, depending on who you talked to.
Buckley had guested on other TV and radio shows as the token
conservative, but now he could pick his own guests and stage-
manage discussion. He could, at last, use TV to be proactive

Buckley was always cranking out copy. Here, he works on his portable blue Olivetti Lettera 32 in the backseat of his limo, flanked by phone and dog.

CREDIT: ©*Jan Lukas*

rather than reactive in articulating the conservative viewpoint. He probably did not have a masterful long-term plan—who knew the show would last thirty-three years?—but taking a helicopter view decades later, starting in the liberal 1960s and continuing through the conservative 1980s, we can see how *Firing Line* engaged with the key issues and personalities that undergirded America's dramatic shift from left to right in those years.

As we follow the trajectory of the show over the years, we will see Buckley support Goldwater, oppose the extremists, and craft a new, stylish brand of conservatism; stand up for Joe McCarthy and disparage those on the blacklist; interrogate the feminists, civil rights activists, and Black Power advocates; forge a conservative response to the Nixon crisis; and both pave the wave for and bask in the glory of Reagan's election. Buckley, the gentleman pugilist, will jab, bob, weave, and duck. Sometimes he will knock an opponent flat, sometimes he will help an opponent up, sometimes he himself will be on the ropes. We will see *Firing Line* display Buckley at his best, and occasionally at his worst.

* * *

In the earliest years of the show, Buckley was still sorting through the ins and outs of *Firing Line*. What would the format be? Was there a large enough conservative American TV audience to support Buckley's endeavor? Was it possible that liberals would watch, too? Would liberal guests even want to appear on such a show? Robert Kennedy declined to appear, and when Buckley was asked why he responded, "Why does baloney reject the grinder?" Was this just a smart-aleck rejoinder, or would *Firing Line* really be a rough-and-tumble experience for Buckley's opponents?

The founding concept of *Firing Line* in 1966 had been that liberals would be "on the firing line," and that a very entertaining "bare knuckled intellectual brawl," as Neal Freeman, one of the show's early producers described it, would inevitably ensue. Guests ranged from big names (Noam Chomsky on the futility of continuing in Vietnam) to then-unknowns (twenty-seven-year-old Captain Oliver North on the absence of war crimes in Vietnam). The show pitted Buckley against liberals to discuss topics such as: "How Goes It with the Black Movement?" with Huey P. Newton; "How Should Ex-Communists Cooperate?" with Victor Navasky; "Armies of the Night" with Norman Mailer; "The Black Panthers" with Eldridge Cleaver; and, one of the all-time worst episodes of Firing Line, "Is the World Funny?" with Groucho Marx. (Buckley was much better at debating the other kind of Marxists.)

This debate format embodied thoughtful "two-sided programming"—a rigorous enactment of the Fairness Doctrine conceived by someone who thought the doctrine (which mandated balance in TV coverage of controversial issues) should be eliminated, yet who also recognized that smart political discussions (and smart political TV) benefited from ideological conflict.[4] The show also featured musicians, novelists, filmmakers, poets, and theologians. But notwithstanding Buckley's range of interests—his passion for the arts, his obsession with Bach, his religious devotion—politics were the show's home base.

Firing Line began airing only two years after Barry Goldwater's blowout defeat by Lyndon Johnson, as conservative activists and politicians were engineering America's tectonic shift right. Conservatives felt the change as gradual, laborious. To many liberals, it was more like a car crash, sudden and unexpected. They had assumed that the triumph of liberalism was simply a fait accompli.

This is amply illustrated by the seventh episode of the show, featuring liberal talk show host David Susskind, who was invited to discuss "The Prevailing Bias." Buckley's contention was that the dominant thrust of the mainstream media was a liberal one. He introduced Susskind by describing him as a "staunch liberal. If there were a contest for the title 'Mr. Eleanor Roosevelt,' he would unquestionably win it." The short-tempered Susskind was seething with anger from the get-go: "I regard that introduction as somewhat rude and insulting, Mr. Buckley. I'd hoped that on the occasion of your having your own television program you'd abandon your traditional penchant for personal bitchiness and stick to facts and issues, but evidently your rude behavior is congenital and compulsive, and so I forgive you." Buckley smiled and noted his appreciation of "the generosity of [Mr. Susskind's] broad spirit." The gloves were off.

The sparring that followed was energetic, aggressive, and just plain fun, whether you were in Buckley's or Susskind's corner. At one point, Susskind references something potentially damning that Buckley has said, and Buckley retorts, with rhetorical bare knuckles, "Yes, yes, do you care to read the context, or shall I cram it down your throat?" This elicits hearty laughter from the studio audience; Susskind takes it in stride and then reads aloud the entire quotation, about Jews and their attitude toward communism. The two disagree about how to interpret what Buckley has said, but they agree that Susskind will send the text of Buckley's comments to Louis Finkelstein of the Jewish Theological Seminary, and based on Finkelstein's judgment, Susskind or Buckley will send a thousand dollars to the other's favorite charity. They obviously can't stand each other, but there is a strained gentility underpinning the exchange.

Buckley was smiling and unflappable. Susskind, speaking through clenched teeth, was utterly flappable. But he also spoke from a position of supreme confidence. He insisted that there was a diversity of opinion expressed in American media, running the gamut from the *Daily Worker* on the left to the *National Review* on the right, but he also maintained that a liberal center ultimately dominated: "The entire thrust of our country

in the last forty years has been a liberal thrust. In our legislation, in our churches, in our schools, in our communications
media. There's nothing sinister or evil [about that]. We call that
progress." Other *Firing Line* guests would confirm Susskind's
thesis. Yet Buckley plugged on, assuming his side would win,
until it finally did.

It took a good five years to sort out what the best format for
the show should be—whether there should be a moderator,
whether there should be open questions from the audience,
how exactly the audience should be shot, and so on, and there
seemed to be quite a bit of trial and error involved.

Early on, Buckley had experimented with adding a moderator
into the mix, *National Review* lawyer C. Dickerman Williams.
The show's producer, Warren Steibel, explained that "Bill loved
C. Dickerman Williams, and in Bill's mind C. Dickerman Williams was a sort of 'Welch' from the McCarthy hearings . . . he
saw him as a conservative [Joseph] Welch. That was an idea so
that Bill didn't have to be polite, he could be more antagonistic."[5] Steibel also explains that he got rid of Williams because he
felt the moderator detracted attention from Buckley. While that
may have been the reasoning from Steibel's perspective, any
viewer could see that Williams slowed down the pace. When a
show wasn't clicking, Williams only made things worse.

When Groucho Marx appeared in the second year of the
show, for example, Williams stood between the two discussants, anchored behind a large podium, a gigantic potted plant
to his right, with nondescript paintings hanging on either side
on the wood-paneled, fake studio walls. The idea seemed to be
to host a humorless debate about comedy in a studio designed
to look like the den of a suburban home. Williams awkwardly
referred to Groucho as "Mr. Marx," and neither he nor Buckley
could grasp Groucho's jokes. Groucho pokes fun at Williams,
calling him "Judge" throughout the show. Williams remains
utterly oblivious to the fact that he is playing the straight man.

National Review lawyer C. Dickerman Williams was the awkward moderator in early episodes. Podiums did little to improve interpersonal dynamics, and guests perched on barstools like birds.
CREDIT: *Hoover Institution*

On the topic of Jewish jokes, Groucho asks Williams, "How do you feel, Judge? You have no animosity toward we people, do you?" Williams says, "no," and Groucho deadpans to Buckley, "Isn't he a character? You're crazy if you ever lose him. He's a big asset to your show, Willy." Williams insists on interrupting for commercial breaks by interjecting, "Gentlemen!," which amuses Groucho no end.

WILLIAMS: Gentlemen, I'm sorry . . .

GROUCHO: Gentlemen? Who are you referring to?

WILLIAMS: We must take another break. I am referring to you.

GROUCHO: Thank you, Judge. You're a real cutie and will go far. . . .

Poor Groucho is milking every joke he can squeeze out of the situation (at one point he candidly acknowledges that he is really only there because he's got a new book to plug), but he's not getting any traction from Buckley and Williams, and he can't play off of energy from the rest of the room since, atypically, there is no studio audience assembled for this episode. Groucho is reduced to cracking jokes about cracking jokes to a bunch of empty chairs and the show's makeup lady. Buckley attempts a serious discussion about comedy, and at one point even goes so far as to rebuke Groucho for his suggestion that Federal Communications Commission (FCC) chairman Newton Minow had cribbed the notion of "the vast wasteland" from T. S. Eliot. Perhaps Williams's presence did enable Buckley to be extra antagonistic, as Steibel had noted, but why be so aggressive with Groucho in the first place? It turns out that Buckley could be funny—or at least wry—conversing on any topic, except comedy.

Williams was an unmitigated disaster, and numerous viewers sent letters to Buckley to tell him as much. One viewer in Miami wrote, "we do not like the idea of the gentleman sitting between Mr. Buckley and his guest—he adds nothing to the show and interrupts the speakers at the end of a comma to tell us the show will be back shortly. . . . This week a very loud voice came on from somewhere behind Mr. Buckley to tell us the same thing—and it seemed to startle Mr. Buckley also." Another viewer noted that a show shot in Spain looked like it had been "filmed through a badly-worn pair of cheap nylons!"[6]

People were picking up on the program's myriad technical glitches, and Buckley, perhaps out of disdain for (or simply disinterest in) the very medium within which he was performing, did not seem to mind. Finally, he came around to making a few improvements upon receiving a two-page critique of the show's format from literary critic Hugh Kenner. Kenner mainly suggested a structure for the show—how the moderator should be properly introduced (the moderator is known as "Plato McReaganwater," in Kenner's gentle parody), how the moderator should sum up at the end, and so on. The points were all obvious: "The normal visual effect is DREADFUL: in a long shot, [the] bottom of [the] field [of vision is] occupied by lecterns, [and the] top by [a] blank wall." The best part of the letter, in fact, was not the technical notes but Kenner's spot-on parody of Buckley's introduction to the show: "'The stature of Casimir Sewage as a national, not to say nationalized, ideologue has never been negligible in the opinion of Mr. Sewage; but until the initiation of FLUSH—Federal Legislation of Utterly Stupendous Happenings—he gurgled, so far as the majority of us were concerned, down a fairly remote pipe. Since then, however, . . .' (etc.)."[7]

Buckley would eventually address the concerns of Kenner and other viewers who were perplexed by the show's gaffes. He would also tone down his "baloney grinder" approach, but in the first few years there were some truly bitter exchanges. Consider the very first episode, for example, with Norman Thomas. As Buckley recounted twenty years later, "Thomas had become the grand old man of the American left. It was a hot-tempered exchange. I had several times debated with Mr. Thomas on the college circuit, and he was progressively displeased with everything I said, and the positions I took. In retrospect, I regret I dealt with him so outspokenly. If he had been a younger man, he'd have resented it if I had been less blunt: Norman Thomas was a veteran of the rhetorical street brawling in which he delighted. But he was now an old man, and a valiant figure, even as his causes were surrealistic."[8] The topic was "Vietnam: Pull

Out? Stay In? Escalate?" Thomas is nearly blind, and he disconcertingly displays his contempt for Buckley by not making even a token gesture of eye contact. He simply will not turn his head in Buckley's direction.

What is remarkable are not the ideas of the show, for they are about what you would expect. Thomas is against continuing the war; Buckley is for it. What makes the strongest impression is the snarling tone of the discussants. Buckley's introduction is an odd potpourri worth citing in its entirety:

Mr. Norman Thomas has run six times for President of the United States. And six times the American people, in their infinite wisdom, have declined to elect him. But they did something for him which I suspect he prefers even more than the exercise of great power. They returned their affection, because he is a grand old man, a monument to physical stamina and good heartedness. If I were asked what has been his specialty in the course of a long career, I guess I would say "being wrong." But somehow it doesn't seem to matter anymore than it matters that Don Quixote specialized in like-minded activity, yet emerged as probably the greatest anti-hero in literary history. Mr. Thomas is a socialist and a pacifist, and his newest crusade is to save Vietnam from the United States Marines. Or perhaps to save the world from the costly displeasures of the Communists, who tend to stand in the way of anyone whose aggressions are directed toward them and to treat the Communists like the slightly excessive radicals at the University of California, who if given just half a chance would succumb to Mr. Thomas' overwhelming charm. But Mr. Thomas is a man of militant idealism and outspokenness. And it's therefore lucky for the entire world that he was not born in Russia. The charm which wins over practically everyone, would not, I fear, greatly have affected the Bolsheviks.

It is the highest tribute to Mr. Thomas that he would have been bloodily executed in the very first purge conducted by the Soviet Union. Mr. Thomas has written a thousand books and made a million speeches. I hope he will live to write another thousand and speak another million times, always provided his audiences continue to love him but patiently and determinedly reject his counsel, as they have done so often in the past, particularly in the realm of foreign policy. He has said that he likes the human race and is very glad to be a member of it. The human race, for whom I presume to speak just this one time, reciprocates the compliment to Mr. Thomas.

Thomas is apoplectic and reciprocates thusly:

THOMAS: I thought we were going to debate Vietnam, not to discuss me and my life and work and miracles.

BUCKLEY: You've been brilliantly introduced.

THOMAS: As a matter of—I doubt it, but I would point out that while I have not achieved many of the things I cared most about, I'll come nearer hitting the nail on the head of what the people would adopt later than most candidates for president or other office. I'm no Don Quixote tilting at windmills, when I was the pioneer on so much social legislation as the country now has.

Thomas goes on to accuse Buckley of using the old debater's tactic of killing an opponent with kindness, and Buckley retorts, "Are you quite dead?" He's joking, but still, it is really stinging, and things spiral from there.

Of course, this was the premiere episode, and over time Buckley would work up a solid formula for his introductions. Mercifully, he did not always reference the guest's mortality quite so forcefully. But the Thomas introduction was typical in

that Buckley consistently made an effort to find both negative
and positive qualities in his guests. Indeed, he did not care for
Freeman's "bare-knuckled" comment and retorts that his show
always avoided the "plain personal rudeness" exhibited by Joe
Pyne and Morton Downey Jr. types.[9] In the main, that is quite
true, but there is no denying that in that first year Buckley was
still finding his TV voice, both literally and figuratively, and a
snarling tone did creep in and out of some of the early shows.

A striking counterexample to the Thomas episode is the
nineteenth episode of 1966, "The Role of the Church Militant,"
with guest William Sloane Coffin. Buckley finds Coffin quite
lunatic for his liberal activism, but he seeks not so much to
win an argument about Vietnam or civil rights with Coffin as
to discuss whether clergy should urge their political feelings
on their congregations. As he puts it to Coffin, "I'm wondering
whether you're as concerned as some people—myself for instance—at an increasing tendency among certain churchmen
to gospelize their entire social and economic weltanschauung
so as to, in effect, meet their communions on Sundays and tell
them how to vote and how to think on all kinds of particular
issues, about which there is very live moral controversy. Don't
they run the risk of undercutting their own authority to speak
concerning such matters about which there clearly is a right
and wrong?" Coffin speaks on an entirely different rhetorical
plane than Buckley—although he lets "weltanschauung" slide,
he does later in the show ask Buckley to define *asymptotic.*

Buckley and Coffin had both been born into wealth and had
attended Yale. Both had been in the Skull and Bones secret
society (Coffin was brought into the society by his old friend
George H. W. Bush), and both had briefly worked for the CIA.
Yet they were like night and day—politically, rhetorically, theo-
logically. Speaking in a most un-Buckley mode, Coffin at one
point even says, for example, "the Church ought to be like a
movable crap game. Every morning the members ought to

wake up and ask: where's the action today?" Most centrally, Coffin makes an impassioned argument for the duty of churchmen to act according to the dictates of their consciences:

> Now there is a nice statement in the Book of Acts where Peter is guilty of civil disobedience, and he gives a very simple, straightforward statement, we must obey God rather than man. Now that's the kind of statement that sort of takes wings to the church. On the other hand, it's very dangerous because it can be twisted into moral demagoguery, and one could always say, I am obeying God rather than man. On the other hand, as we told the Germans at Nuremberg, and as every Christian should have very clear in his own mind, no Christian is under an invariable obligation at all times to obey the national will. His conscience . . . has to come first. Now he has to take the consequences. Civil disobedience can be a very honorable thing. Thoreau was in the mainstream of American life. . . . I think it's much too simple to say we must never disturb the peace by committing civil disobedience.

The Coffin episode offers viewers an engaging intellectual brawl, but not exactly of the bare-knuckled variety. For one thing, the reverend is relentlessly cheerful and even-tempered, and Buckley respects him for his religious faith, even if he finds his theology more than a little bit screwball. (At one point Buckley pointedly observes that James Baldwin has rejected the church and despises Coffin, notwithstanding the reverend's support for the civil rights movement; Coffin defends Baldwin, in effect turning the other cheek.) For another, Buckley sets the tone with an introduction that is as affable as his Norman Thomas introduction had been hostile.

> The Reverend William Sloane Coffin Jr. is the University Chaplain at Yale University, and ordained minister in the

Presbyterian Church, known throughout the country as a militant in the cause of civil rights. He has frequently been arrested, has sat-in in many states in the South proclaiming that his cause is not peace but justice. And recently he has turned his attention to Far Eastern affairs, as a co-founder, with other prominent liberals, of a National Conference for New Politics, which calls for pulling out of South Vietnam, apparently in the cause of peace if not justice. Doctor Coffin is marvelously gifted. He is a great rhetorician with a booming voice, perfectly suited to his stentorian convictions. He was an accomplished pianist—we once played a duet together, and I struggled unsuccessfully to keep up with him, as no doubt I will this afternoon—and an accomplished linguist, who could carry on today's discussion as easily in French or in Russian. We hope to discuss here the role of the churches and their ministers in the social order, to discuss some of the ramifications of the tendency to more and more explicit social policies by the churches. Doctor Coffin's views on the matter are highly elaborated, and I'll begin by asking him for a word or two on his own position on the matter of the militant divine. Doctor Coffin, you are most welcome.

The format details were still a work in progress at this point in the first year of the show (indeed, the problem of awkward commercial interruptions would be solved only by moving to PBS and eliminating commercials), but Buckley had already nailed down the tone of his introductions of liberal guests: provide background information, make a bit of arch critique, include some friendly words, and don't go on for too long. In sum, in 1966 the show had ups and downs, while still offering the best political discussion on American television.

Although the program was undeniably *his* for thirty-three years, *Firing Line* was not Buckley's idea to begin with. This is not altogether surprising: it is hard to imagine a TV star less interested in TV than Buckley. He won an Emmy for *Firing Line* in 1969, and it was the longest-running public affairs show with a single host in US history, but Buckley remained a TV industry outsider.

It would be somewhat unfair—even uncouth—to describe Buckley as a snob. He *did* write a fun novel about Elvis Presley, after all. And if he failed to understand how anyone could consider Mick Jagger a good singer—"his voice couldn't be better than that of, say, every fourth person listed in the telephone directory"—he did at least listen to the Beatles during his weekly sessions with his personal trainer.[10] (This was perhaps a masochistic choice, as he really could not stand the Beatles.) In 1970 he consented to be interviewed by *Playboy* magazine. This made him practically hip. That same year he appeared on the NBC comedy show *Rowan & Martin's Laugh-In*, explaining that "I did an interview with *Playboy* because I decided it was the only way to communicate my views to my son" and noting that he had only agreed to appear on *Laugh-In* because the producers offered to fly him out to California on "an airplane with two right-wings."

Laugh-In staged a sort of press conference for Buckley, where cast member Henry Gibson queried, "Mr. Buckley, I've noticed that whenever you appear on television you're always seated. Does this mean you can't think on your feet?" Buckley cannily responded, "It's very hard to stand up carrying the weight of what I know." Asked his opinion about nudity in entertainment, he tersely replied, "It's excessive." And asked, finally, whose image would be more harmed by his appearance on *Laugh-In*, his or the show's, he laughed and said, "Well, I suppose it will make you more respectable [coy wink inserted here] and me less so. And both of those are probably to be desired."

He had managed to play along and be a good sport while remaining the dignified face of conservatism. It's doubtful he had ever watched an entire episode of *Laugh-In*, but he did admit to a real fondness for *All in the Family*. "Archie Bunker," he noted on a 1979 *Firing Line* episode with Ben Stein, "is the greatest anti-conservative rip-off in the history of modern offensives. I mean, you don't need Karl Marx. All you need is Archie Bunker. He's despicable, but he's kind of endearing in a way." Buckley was once late for a dinner party hosted by Nelson Rockefeller because he was at home watching *All in the Family*.[11]

Conveying a startling openness to television viewing, Buckley once acknowledged that "anybody who wants effectively to understand what's going on has got to watch TV. . . . The most bookish man I ever knew, Whittaker Chambers, watched television *un*interruptedly from about seven until eleven every single night of his life."[12] Yet Buckley also noted that he was too busy to watch TV very much himself. He honestly had no idea who Jabba the Hutt was, he admitted to never watching professional football, and, during his run for mayor of New York City, he was stumped by a reference to Mickey Mantle.[13]

Buckley finally agreed to appear on *Laugh-In*, if they would fly him out to California "on a plane with two right-wings."
CREDIT: ©*NBC Universal/Getty Images*

All of which is to say, Buckley was neither unaware of the importance of mass culture, nor deeply plugged into it himself. He was a devoted yachtsman and harpsichordist who got his kicks listening to Bach. In a TV world of expository theme songs issuing from the Sherwood Schwartz school of music ("here's the story of a lovely lady, who was bringing up three very lovely girls . . .") how audacious it was for Buckley to choose an excerpt from the Brandenburg Concertos as his own program's theme song.

Although he occasionally settled down to watch an old movie on TV, what Buckley loved was the power to click from show to show. (In fact, his family saw fit to slip not only a jar of peanut butter into his casket but also a remote control.) Individual programs were of fleeting interest to the founder and editor of America's most important conservative journal of opinion, a man who took vacations with the Reagans at Claudette Colbert's beach house in Barbados, thought that a peanut butter and bacon sandwich could only be improved by a lovely bottle of 1949 Lafite Rothschild, and traveled annually to Gstaad, Switzerland, to write a book, taking daily ski breaks with David Niven and John Kenneth Galbraith.[14] Given his high culture bona fides, it would have been odd if Buckley had actually originated the idea of hosting a TV show, even a political one.

In his 1989 book on *Firing Line*, Buckley says that the idea for the show was pitched to him in 1965 by "a young entrepreneur."[15] Buckley was agreeable to the notion but deferred production until 1966 so that he could complete his symbolic run for mayor of New York. It was only in his posthumous book on Ronald Reagan that Buckley publicly revealed that *Firing Line* was the brainchild of conservative businessman Tom O'Neil. O'Neil's company, RKO, produced and syndicated the show from 1966 until 1971, when *Firing Line* left the commercial syndication market behind for the comparative stability of PBS. It's unclear exactly how or why O'Neil expected his involvement in *Firing Line* to remain hush-hush, given that the program closed with the RKO logo, and it was no secret who owned RKO; in New York City the show even aired on WOR-TV, a station owned by O'Neil. Perhaps his politics were simply not generally known and he hoped to keep it that way. Buckley did note that some of O'Neil's corporate associates were dismayed by his involvement with the program.[16]

O'Neil appears to have limited much of his political engagement to behind-the-scenes financial support of conservative causes. In a 1970 memo to his brother James, who was then running for senator of New York on the Conservative Party ticket, Bill Buckley advises, "When you write to Tom O'Neil to thank him for his enormous contribution please bear in mind that he is the silent originator and sponsor of *Firing Line* and that I am very devoted to him personally. His contribution to you is I think probably the largest he has ever made to anybody."[17] The allusion to O'Neil as "sponsor" of *Firing Line* certainly indicates investment in the program that went beyond producing and distributing it for Buckley.

Financing aside, with no experience in TV production, Buckley needed more than just an idea for a show from O'Neil: he needed his showbiz expertise. If O'Neil had not decided as a young man that he was more interested in broadcasting than rubber, *Firing Line* might never have come to fruition. O'Neil's father had founded General Tire and Rubber Company, and in 1948 his son had expanded the company's holdings to include General Teleradio, which in turn owned several independent (not ABC, CBS, or NBC affiliated) TV stations, including the aforementioned WOR-TV. O'Neil invented the *Million Dollar Movie*, a program on which he aired the same Hollywood film sixteen times a week. The *Million Dollar Movie* was profitable, but O'Neil had leased the rights to only thirty films, and the program could only function for so long, especially once General Teleradio started to acquire more stations and needed more product.[18] The solution? O'Neil would purchase RKO Pictures—its studio lots and library of 740 films—for $25 million.[19]

But how to get eccentric billionaire Howard Hughes to sell RKO? For some time, the story goes, O'Neil had been pressuring Hughes to sell. In 1954, O'Neil followed Hughes into a men's room at the Beverly Hills Hotel, and Hughes finally agreed to the transaction. It was a brave move on O'Neil's part. At this point, Hughes, in the thrall of obsessive-compulsive disorder and apparently suffering from a painful skin condition that made him averse to bathing—or even wearing clothing—was not known for his close attention to personal hygiene, or for his nuanced interpersonal communication skills. Hughes had acquired controlling interest of RKO in 1948, at least partly motivated by the desire to promote the pneumatic Jane Russell, who had starred in Hughes's scandalous 1943 production of *The Outlaw*. Tapping into his aeronautical engineering expertise, Hughes had famously designed a cantilevered foundation garment for Russell to wear in the film. O'Neil's motivations for business decisions were less eccentric: he wanted to make a lot of money. And so he did. But not off *Firing Line*. *Firing Line* needed RKO more than RKO needed *Firing Line*.

Firing Line was initially imagined as a thirteen-episode series, but ultimately ran for almost 1,500 episodes. To understand how impressive these numbers are for a weekly show, consider that today a very successful program typically runs seven seasons, for a total of 154 episodes. There were 635 episodes of the long-running *Gunsmoke* and 456 episodes of *Law & Order*. Buckley claimed from the beginning, perhaps with some pride, that his ratings were "exiguous." Freeman, conversely, claims that before the show switched to PBS in 1971 it had no problem finding advertisers and had high ratings. While this may have been true at some point in the show's early life, the cold, hard Nielsen data reveal a different story: *Firing*

Line's ratings were quite often abysmal. In 1967, for example, the show aired in New York City from 10:30 to 11:30 p.m. In the 10:30 to 11 p.m. slot, the highest-rated shows, in order, were *What's My Line?* (with 27 percent of the market tuning in), *Andy Williams, David Susskind*, an unnamed ABC movie, *Firing Line* (with 3 percent of the market watching), and, finally, in last place, *Guest Shot* (with 1 percent).[20]

To be sure, 3 percent of New York City TV viewers was really a lot of people—certainly more people than subscribed to *National Review* at the time—but 10:30 p.m. was already not a hot spot for ad sales. Add poor ratings on top of that, and you had a truly unprofitable program. The archival documents at the Hoover Institution reveal a show that was getting by in syndication (sometimes with high ratings) but not absolutely thriving. The problem was not just advertising but also complications in working with RKO.

And viewer numbers did not swerve dramatically upward after the switch to PBS. PBS was technically not driven by the need to garner high numbers in order to sell advertising, but the Corporation for Public Broadcasting (CPB) did hire Nielsen to gather ratings for internal use, and one 1975 Nielsen report to CPB offers some interesting concrete figures. Numbers were generally low across the board, but *Upstairs, Downstairs* was the strongest PBS show at the time, pulling in 10.6 percent of all women over fifty watching TV in the 8–11 p.m. time slot in the markets assessed (New York, Chicago, Philadelphia, Boston, and San Francisco) and 6 percent of women 18–49, this being the demographic most highly coveted at the time in the commercial market. *Monty Python's Flying Circus* came in second, drawing only 1.9 percent of the 50+ women, 3.9 percent of the 18–49 women, and a strong (for PBS!) 6 percent of men 18–49. Lumped together, the PBS public affairs shows (listed as including *Washington Week in Review, Wall Street Week*, and *Firing Line*) brought in 5.4 percent of the women 50+, 1.4 percent of the 18–49 women, and 1.9 percent of the 18–49 men. As for men 50+, *Monty Python* drew 0.8 percent, *Upstairs, Downstairs* 6.8 percent, and public affairs 4.3 percent.

Since PBS generally skewed toward older viewers, CPB was particularly happy with *Monty Python*, their only show that drew younger viewers outside of the *Sesame Street* demographic.[21] Buckley was more than a little bit disgruntled by *Monty Python*'s success; such silliness did not constitute worthy competition, in his book. How it must have vexed him when Margaret Thatcher parodied the Monty Python dead parrot sketch in a 1990 speech to the Conservative Party!

In sum, Buckley would never turn a profit on *Firing Line*, or *National Review* for that matter. These were labors of love, and also, of course, ideological dedication. Buckley, the supreme free market capitalist, observed that "there are enterprises in life that simply aren't devised to generate profits. We accept them as institutions that need to be patronized, because they do vital work."[22]

Of course, Buckley wouldn't have *minded* if *Firing Line* had been lucrative, but the show had originated at a moment when news and public affairs shows were considered loss leaders or, to put it less cynically, public service. Broadcasters aired such unprofitable programming because they were expected to serve "the public interest" in exchange for their FCC licenses. While syndicated in the pre-PBS days, *Firing Line* had had inconsistent ratings and struggled with being slotted into the late night or early morning programming ghettos.

Buckley noted his frustration in a 1969 letter to RKO: "In May, RKO–New York unilaterally pulled *Firing Line* away from its prime time position on Sunday night and slugged it into an hour on Sunday morning when civilized people, i.e. those who watch *Firing Line*, are either asleep, at church, or on the golf links. The effect has been serious. . . . Returns from advertising bring in only about twenty percent of what they did during the evening hour. . . . The show was moved by an ironic master-stroke, to its present ignominious position, approximately one week after winning an Emmy."²³ With this erratic scheduling, in an age before YouTube, DVRs, VHS, and DVD, keeping up with *Firing Line* demanded real devotion. Once on PBS, *Firing Line* did not draw more viewers, but at least it was easier for viewers to find the show.

At its best, *Firing Line* was a spirited, entertaining discussion show. At its worst, host and guest failed to connect intellectually or interpersonally. Either way, even a putatively sexy topic (*"Deep Throat* and the First Amendment" with lawyer Alan Dershowitz and porn star Harry Reems) demanded cerebration beyond the ken of the casual TV viewer. The show appealed to a small, special interest audience. Compared to *National Review*, it was "mass" media (it was distributed far and wide), but within the TV environment it was, in effect, niche programming *avant la lettre*.

President Reagan's deregulation of the communications industry in the 1980s would later finally open up the market for cable, paving the way for the rise of Fox, MTV, and HBO. At the same time, Reagan's deregulation destroyed long-standing notions of public service, wiped out the Fairness Doctrine, which had sought to keep political speech on TV genuinely "fair and balanced," and eliminated regulatory checks and balances against overcommercialization. Many years before deregulation brought these big changes to the media industry, Buckley was a proponent of what used to be called "pay TV," that is, cable.

Given his relative disengagement from the ins and outs of the TV business, one rather suspects that Buckley was initially tutored in the hypothetical merits of pay TV by O'Neil. Buckley had no delusions that TV would ever foster politically astute programming appealing to large audiences. But he did understand that pay TV would allow for a range of more specialized content, and that government regulation limited free market innovation in TV content.[24] While the idea of producing *original* pay TV content was still far away, as early as the 1950s there had been efforts to get home viewers to pay for previously released Hollywood films, and O'Neil got in on the bottom floor of these efforts.[25]

As an ardent advocate for pay TV, O'Neil was, in sum, a perfect match with Buckley, at least politically. *Firing Line* was not the only unprofitable public affairs–type talk show on TV—there was also David Susskind's *Open End*, for example, as well as the *Mike Wallace Interview*, and the long-running *Meet the Press*—but *Firing Line* was the only specifically *conservative* example of such programming. Broadcasters lumped all of these types of shows together conceptually as serving a "public service" function. In terms of ad sales, or lack thereof, they were all the same. But *Firing Line* was the only such show on the air advocating for conservative reforms that would, among other things, kill the notion that the government should foster broadcasting as a public service.

If *Firing Line* was unique as a specifically conservative public affairs program, it did mirror the dull aesthetic of other public affairs shows. As Buckley described it, "My television program, *Firing Line*, was modestly designed—'No production values!' exclaimed one horrified TV executive. . . ."[26] What is fascinating here is that Buckley was comfortable hosting such a drab-looking affair. As a writer and editor, Buckley had flair. You might not care for his heavy-handed dropping of Latinates, or for his politics, but no one could accuse his work of sloppiness or imprecision.

While not exactly technically incompetent, *Firing Line* was not slick. The show appeared to be produced using a conventional three-camera setup. Episodes would often, but not always, open with a moving shot across the assembled audience. Throughout the sixties and seventies, the audience typically consisted of high school or college students. Students would occasionally be seated on folding chairs, but they were often scattered on the floor, with pillows if they were lucky. Buckley was keen on converting youth to the conservative cause, and there was something charming—if haphazard—about the seating arrangements. Such minimalism also made it easier when the show traveled and was shot outside of New York City, and even abroad. But there's no denying that the audience setup looked *cheap*.

Following the opening shot, there would be a master shot of host and guest(s), and then shots would ping-pong back and forth between talking heads, with an occasionally repeated

The *Firing Line* set evolved little over the years, but in the 1960s audience members were lucky if they even got pillows to sit on. The questioners (Jeff Greenfield, right) had the luxury of a couch.
CREDIT: *Hoover Institution*

master shot of discussants. Reaction shots of the audience were rare, though the very earliest episodes the show did conclude with questions from the audience. (At the end of *Firing Line*'s third episode, on school prayer with Bishop James Pike as guest, the first audience question came from a young man named George Gilder who was concerned about religious justifications for civil disobedience.) By 1968, two years into the life of the show, audience Q&A had been replaced by questions from a preselected guest panel, usually consisting of college students and/or professors, and by the 1980s, the panel had been replaced by a single examiner at a podium.

Frequently, Jeff Greenfield was included among the questioners. Greenfield had written a *Yale Alumni Magazine* essay on a Buckley debate at Yale with Rev. Coffin.[27] Buckley described the essay, with some pleasure, as "withering."[28] Greenfield had later interviewed Buckley for *Eye* magazine, and he had worked for both Senator Robert Kennedy and Mayor John Lindsay. Buckley thought he was a very bright young liberal, and he brought him on board the show in 1968.

Greenfield was a total unknown, but he suited Buckley's purposes, precisely because he was clever and young. Buckley was always particularly keen on converting youth to his cause—he had, in fact, helped Young Americans for Freedom get off the ground in 1960 as a sort of right-wing alternative to Students for a Democratic Society—and one feels this interest in younger viewers particularly in the *Firing Line* episodes of the late 1960s and early 1970s, at the peak moment of campus activism and the antiwar movement.

Now, Buckley did not go out of his way to target a youthful audience by booking cool young guests. On the contrary. He would book difficult guests to discuss complex issues, and younger viewers would simply have to do their best to keep up. That Buckley did hope to exhibit the virtues of conservatism specifically to impressionable youth was demonstrated by the

˒ did, quite consistently throughout the early years, ˒e audience almost exclusively with college or high school ˒dents. Obviously, issues such as Vietnam and the counterculture were inherently of interest to that demographic, and the show took pains to address the issue of campus radicalism on numerous occasions.

One of the earliest episodes featuring a conservative guest (though this one only recently turned right) was "The Campus Destroyers" (1969) with cartoonist Al Capp. The episode notably includes more audience reaction shots than usual, as Capp's one-liners attacking student radicals are a hit with the kids from Morristown High School. Buckley politely smiles along, but Capp's insults (the Harvard dean is a "fathead," student protestors are "vermin carriers") don't lend any clarity to understanding the crisis of campus unrest. Buckley's follow-up questions fail to push Capp to a deeper analysis. He goes so far as to articulate the argument from the other side, asking Capp what the proper response should be.

BUCKLEY: If in fact the faculty at Harvard University believes that we must almost encourage, or if not encourage at least endure vicious retaliation from a minority group which over the years we have persecuted, then in effect it is being supine in tending to prove some moral point, right? If one of those Harvard faculty members . . . was sitting here right now, presumably what he would say is, "Look, can't you understand impatience among a people which has had difficulties that you haven't had?" To which you would reply what?

CAPP: I would reply that to select a black student and say, "You are not man enough to obey rules," is to degrade him. To select a black student and say, "I don't respect you enough to expect you to be as good a citizen as the next one," is to detest him. I have a vastly greater respect for blacks.

BUCKLEY: Suppose the black student says, "But you detest me anyway, and I care less that you detest me than that I should force you to do what I want you to do"? Remember that Jimmy Baldwin said, "The only thing the white man has that the black man *should* want is power." Now, isn't this really an expression of the philosophy of *The Fire Next Time?*

CAPP: This is like my saying the only thing that Chase Manhattan Bank has got that I haven't got is several billion dollars, so I can go in and take it.

Capp is not completely dense; he hears what Buckley is saying, but he refuses to engage. Questioners Jeff Greenfield and Frances FitzGerald (whose Pulitzer Prize–winning book on the Vietnam War, *Fire in the Lake,* would appear just three years later) are less patient than Buckley with Capp's bullying demeanor. Greenfield asks him to drop the invective and engage in a serious argument about police brutality, to which Capp responds that Greenfield has made an ass of himself. FitzGerald accuses him of reveling in recounting brutality without making any clear arguments about the situation, ultimately rather like "the people who are so much against pornography that they have to examine it terribly closely to find out how much they're against it." Capp brushes off FitzGerald by saying, "This is your own reaction, and it's fascinating [by which he means exactly the opposite], but you're not going to rub any of it off on me."

Buckley jumps in to answer cogently a few questions that Capp cannot, or will not. Overall, it is a fascinating show precisely because Capp is so patently nasty and—an even worse crime on *Firing Line*—such a shallow thinker. At a moment in American popular culture when a common negative response to student protestors was something along the lines of "get a haircut and get a job!" *Firing Line* consistently strove to demon-

.nere were much smarter and better ways to con-
.e issue of campus unrest.

ₐn even earlier episode that dealt directly with issues of direct and obvious concern to the youth audience was "The Hippies," from 1968. The show's opening title is still up and the
theme song still playing when we hear a gruntlike exclamation,
something along the lines of "bang!," though it is impossible to
be sure. This alarming noise has issued from guest Jack Kerouac, who, bleary-eyed, beet red, and absolutely hammered (visually evoking Jerry Lewis at hour twenty of a telethon), makes
strange outbursts throughout the show, even going out of his
way to insult audience member Allen Ginsberg, who responds
with good humor by holding up his hands like Nixon but giving a double-Om sign instead of a V-for-Victory.

The other guests are sociologist Lewis Yablonsky, author of
The Hippie Trip, and Ed Sanders, cofounder of the band the
Fugs and founder of *Fuck You: A Magazine of the Arts* (which
he censors as *Gutter Expletive: A Magazine of the Arts* for the
benefit of the TV audience). Yablonsky provides a largely sympathetic explanation of the hippie worldview and its rejection
of middle-class "plastic" experience; Sanders points to socie-
tal bias against alternative ways of thinking and suggests that
hippie is a shallow, narrow descriptor; and Kerouac mostly provides harrowing sound effects and ineptly corrects the pronun-
ciation of the other guests. The whole show is a trip.

BUCKLEY: Now, Jack, Mr. Kerouac, what I want to ask is
this, to what extent do you believe that the Beat generation is
related to the hippies? What do they have in common? Was
this an evolution from the one to the other?

KEROUAC: Just the older ones. See I'm forty-six years old, and
these kids are eighteen, but it's the same movement, which is
apparently some kind of *Dionysian* [his emphasis] movement

in late civilization. And which I did not intend any more than I suppose Dionysus did or whatever his name was. Although I'm not Dionysus to your Areopagite ["Eh-oo-ROPE-a-jite"]. I should have been.

BUCKLEY: Yeah, that's a point, yeah.

KEROUAC: No, it's just a movement which is supposed to be licentious ["lie-sent-chee-ouse"], but it isn't really.

BUCKLEY: Well, now licentious in what respect? . . . Your point was that a movement which you conceived as relatively pure has become ideologized and misanthropic, and generally objectionable?

KEROUAC: Yes, it was pure in my heart.

BUCKLEY: What about that, Mr. Yablonsky, do you see that [transformation] as having happened somewhere between the Beats and the hippies?

YABLONSKY: I think there's in early '67 and going back to I suppose '64 or '65—

KEROUAC: [muffled horse sound]

YABLONSKY: —there were a lot of people kind of trying to return to sort of an Indian style of life or relate to the land differently—

KEROUAC: oo-oo-oo-oo-oo-oo-oo-oo [perhaps an attempt at Native American war cry but sounds like 1950s sci-fi movie special effect]

BUCKLEY: Shush!

YABLONSKY: —trying to love each other and communicate, be more open with each other, and I think recently it's taken a turn in a violent direction. A lot of responsibility I think is due to drugs like methedrine, amphetamines, and perhaps the overuse . . . of drugs like LSD.

How about herring?

LEY: What is herring, is that a kind of a drug?

SANDERS: Cherry Heering! [Danish liqueur]

KEROUAC: Sour cream and herring!

YABLONSKY: Kerouac is out of style, he's still on alcohol—

KEROUAC: I'm on alcohol and other drugs!

BUCKLEY: What about that, Mr. Sanders, is alcohol out of style?

SANDERS: Well, you mentioned "misanthropic" and objectionable—

KEROUAC: "Miz-AN-thrrrrrr-o-pick"!

Sanders goes on to discuss the feelings that the hippies have about Vietnam. At first glance, this show seems like a hot mess. Buckley is weaving his questions in and out, trying to hold it all together. The guests are at their very best (and it follows that one would not want to see Kerouac at his very worst), and the ideas are flying, but the energy has spiraled out of control, with Buckley remaining affable as the others seem to get more and more steamed with each other. You have to watch the show a few times to get a handle on it. Really, it's a bit like watching Jackson Pollock at work: it seems like madness, but then it's done, and you step back and see that it coheres.

By the early 1970s, Nixon had won reelection, the Summer of Love and Woodstock were receding in America's rearview mirror, and Buckley and his conservative compatriots were less worried about hippies and insurrection on college campuses than they had been a few years earlier. A perfect illustration of this shift is "The Young" (1972), in which *A Clockwork Orange* author Anthony Burgess despairs of the poor language and reasoning skills of students he is teaching as a guest professor at City College of New York. Buckley presses hard for specifics, and Burgess says, "I don't know how far I'm able to quote words on this program, but when a student comes to my office, as one did the other day, and says, 'Why did you write that fucked-up article in the *New York Times?*' I have to say, 'Well, what precisely do you mean by 'fucked-up'? Do you mean it was badly written? Do you mean it was ill-considered? Or do you mean you merely don't like it?' And he has to conclude that he merely doesn't like it."

I may be wrong, but I do believe that this may be the very first use of this particular profanity on American television. In any case, Buckley concurs with Burgess that the educational system is failing, and the two men putter along griping about declining standards. The anxiety over student militants had dissipated and the millennial anxiety of earlier *Firing Line* episodes is quite lacking. Buckley would still hope to attract young converts to conservatism via *Firing Line*, but youth qua youth would resurface only sporadically as a show topic in the years to come.

By this point, the show's style and format were more or less settled, and the permanent production team was in place. *Firing Line* initially had been produced by Neal Freeman (who procured guests), with Robert Klein, an RKO employee, doing the technical heavy lifting. Freeman and Klein were succeeded in 1967 by Warren Steibel. Outside of his *Firing Line* work, Steibel was best known as the producer of the cult exploitation film *The Honeymoon Killers* (1969). Written and directed by his romantic partner, Leonard Kastle, the only appeal this rough film about serial killers could have possibly held for Buckley lay in its inventive Mahler soundtrack. Steibel had also, before *Firing Line*, served as associate producer on *Hootenanny*, a folk music show shot on college campuses.

How on earth could this confirmed liberal end up producing America's most well-known conservative TV show for thirty years? His qualifications for the position were acceptable but not stellar, and he didn't get the job the first time he inter-

agent persisted, and Buckley needed a new pro-
Steibel finally came on board and immediately wowed
new boss by explaining that when the show cut for a commercial (as it did before the move to PBS in 1971), Buckley and
his guest only had to pause for ten seconds rather than for the
entire length of the commercial break. The show was taped,
after all, not broadcast live.

That Buckley was surprised reveals how little he really knew
about TV production. And that this sealed the deal for Steibel
reveals much about Buckley's persona and priorities. He was
a damn busy man. As Steibel explained in an interview in the
mid-1980s, "that cemented our love affair, which has lasted
twenty years, because I saved him two and a half minutes. Any
man who can do it two and a half minutes faster [is] under Bill's
real scale of priorities . . . a good man."[29] When letters arrived
complaining about technical glitches, Buckley would drop Steibel a note, but he was not terribly concerned, and there was no
possibility that Steibel would be fired, for the simple reason
that Buckley really liked him.

Firing Line was, to say the least, not a good-looking show. The
carpeted dais was drab, the lighting never varied, and many of
the guests were men in suits, their legs crossed, trousers riding up above black socks revealing an inch or two of pale white
skin. The exceptions—Black Power spokesmen wearing dramatic dashikis, feminists sporting smart plaid pantsuits, antifeminists flaunting Ann Landers–style hairdos—brought only
occasional visual relief. One could also count on the distraction
of Buckley's distinctive mannerisms, his almost-British accent,
his inclination to dart his tongue out like a lizard. Jeff Greenfield, who emceed a twenty-year anniversary celebration program, noted that "television is said to be a visual medium. . . .
The only element of visual interest on *Firing Line* I have ever
been able to detect is whether Mr. Buckley would someday part
his hair with his tongue."[30]

One viewer wrote to complain that an episode looked like it had been "filmed through a badly-worn pair of cheap nylons!" but Buckley liked working with producer Warren Steibel and rarely fretted over technical glitches.
CREDIT: *Hoover Institution*

But it really didn't matter. Viewers came for the words and the ideas, and also perhaps, when the show premiered in 1966, for the sheer novelty of seeing an articulate right-wing conservative explain his position. Whether you watched the show as a liberal or conservative viewer, you would find your politics both defended and challenged. In 1964, Richard Hofstadter had famously attributed right-wing political thinking to paranoia, anti-intellectualism, and "status anxiety."[31] Whether you thought his politics were brilliant or abhorrent, Buckley seemed to be walking, talking proof of the insufficiency of Hofstadter's claims.

As if to drive the point home, one of *Firing Line*'s earliest guests was Barry Goldwater. To many Americans, Goldwater's landslide defeat confirmed Susskind's confident claims about the triumph of liberalism and the waning of the "extremism" that Hofstadter had described. Buckley was determined to show the world that conservatism was alive and well—if struggling for the foothold it needed in order to dominate American politics—and that paranoid conspiracy theorists of the John Birch Society variety should not be taken as synecdochic for the conservative movement.

To truly understand *Firing Line*, then, we must consider how Buckley used the show to stake a claim for Goldwater—and, by extension, to stake a claim for what then seemed a pipe dream, the possibility of a thriving conservative movement purged of the conspiracy theorists, the extremists, and the kooks. These were the folks who seemed to have a stranglehold on American conservatism when *Firing Line* began in 1966. Buckley would have to forge a new image for conservatism, virtually from scratch.

OPEN TO
DEBATE

CHAPTER ONE

FORGING A NEW IMAGE FOR THE RIGHT

Goldwater, Extremism, and Stylish Conservatism

*Bill's contribution is making conservatism
not only respectable but stylish. That was the meaning of the
mayoral campaign. That was the meaning of* Firing Line.
That was the meaning of National Review *and its political
triumph with Reagan. Other people could have
made it respectable. Nobody else could have made it stylish.
When Bill ran for mayor, the establishment's idea
of political style was John Lindsay. And Bill
made John Lindsay look tired intellectually.*

—NEAL FREEMAN, ASSISTANT MANAGER OF BUCKLEY
MAYORAL CAMPAIGN AND EARLY *FIRING LINE* PRODUCER[1]

He is fresh and everyone else is tired.

—CAMPAIGN SLOGAN FOR NEW YORK CITY MAYORAL
CANDIDATE JOHN LINDSAY, 1965

When *Firing Line* premiered in 1966, Goldwater's defeat still
loomed large, apparently confirming the eternal triumph

of American liberalism. Conservatism had a practical problem that the movement strategists would have to address: how
could conservative Republican candidates get elected? This
was a long-term conundrum. But conservatism also had an
image problem that could, with patience and persistence, be
addressed and solved more immediately. In the popular imagination of the mid-1960s, American conservatives were largely
identified with the conspiracy theorists of the John Birch Society (JBS), violent groups like the Ku Klux Klan (KKK), and a variety of nutty broadcast operations run by anticommunists like
H. L. Hunt and fundamentalists such as Billy James Hargis
and Carl McIntire.[2] To most people at the time, the idea of an
intellectual or urbane conservative would have seemed pretty
far-fetched. Buckley would take the bull by the horns on both
Firing Line and in the pages of *National Review* to demonstrate
the legitimate status of conservatism. He would push the extremists out, argue that Goldwater could not be categorized in
that camp, and, by example, show that conservatism could be
not only upright but also stylish.

As Hugh Kenner summarized, "Bill was responsible for rejecting the John Birch Society and the other kooks. . . . [W]ith-
out him, there probably would be no respectable conservative
movement in this country."[3] What is left unsaid here is that
Buckley began as a Birch Society supporter. Like Barry Goldwater, he maintained for some time that many Birchers held
legitimate conservative notions; it was only their fearless leader,
Robert Welch, who had gone off the deep end, diving into a
conspiratorial morass, even calling President Eisenhower a
"dedicated conscious agent of the Communist conspiracy." *National Review* wryly countered that Ike was not a communist;
he was a golfer.

Rejecting Welch meant losing *National Review* subscribers,
which was no small thing, as *National Review* was persistently
in the red, like all journals of opinion. But Buckley bit the bul-

let and officially rejected Welch in the pages of his magazine. A bit later, Buckley realized that he had not gone far enough. The JBS rank and file was not merely held captive by Welch's personality—perhaps a far-fetched notion to anyone who had ever heard Welch deliver one of his decidedly unscintillating lectures on the dangers of communism; Birchers were in and of themselves of a die-hard and disreputable conspiratorial bent. Buckley's rather commonsensical insight was that such extremists had to be cut loose for the conservative movement to move forward. *Firing Line* would become a useful, high-profile platform for his efforts to create distance from the extremists.

An episode that aptly illustrated the challenge of shifting the conservative image away from extremism was "The Decline of Anti-Communism" (1967) with guest Fred C. Schwarz. Schwarz was the man behind the Christian Anti-Communism Crusade; he traveled across the United States hosting daylong anticommunist "schools," published a newsletter, and authored the bestselling *You Can Trust the Communists (to Be Communists)* in 1960. He even pioneered conservative folk singing with his discovery of Janet Greene, the "anti-Baez." (Inexplicably, her tunes "Fascist Threat," "Commie Lies," and "Comrades Lament" never hit the big time.) This was a man who ate, drank, and slept anticommunism. He was bespectacled and tidy, with an Australian accent, always in dark suit and tie, his short hair slicked back.

Buckley never had any of the out-and-out anticommunist nuts on his show—people like Hargis, McIntire, or Hunt—and he was at pains to demonstrate that Schwarz did not fit in that camp of political operatives. Introducing him, Buckley emphasized that "Dr. Schwarz has never made it easy for his critics. He has not, for instance, uttered any memorable inanity—not that Eisenhower is a Communist, or that Communism is a Jewish plot, or that the United Nations was conceived by the Third Internationale."

That Schwarz was not anti-Semitic or conspiratorial was enough for Buckley to place him in the nonextremist camp. Yet Schwarz's own self-presentation made it difficult to cling to the notion that he was a regular Joe, just an ardent, God-fearing anticommunist. Schwarz had made a close study of Marxist-Leninist doctrine. So close, in fact, that it was at several points rather difficult for Buckley to have a genuine exchange with him. Buckley wonders how changes in the economy of the Soviet Union might change the communist situation, for example.

BUCKLEY: It might just be possible for people to argue plausibly that a strong economy in the Soviet Union is one which necessarily would augment the power of the people vis-à-vis the power of its leaders and cause them to be a more considerable restraining influence than they are in situations in which they are in perpetual penury.

SCHWARZ: You know why I discount that argument, Bill. . . . This argument, that the changes within the Soviet Union in which the people become more economically well-to-do and that they get certain basic advantages will moderate communism and change it, reminded me of the Marxist argument in *The Communist Manifesto* that capitalism was creating its own grave diggers. Now we are reversing it and saying that communism is creating its own grave diggers: in order to industrialize, they have had to educate their people, they have to give them certain economic advantages, that freedom is an appetite—

BUCKLEY: But might that not be true? That is to say, as I understand it, at least this is my own position, that the greatest friend of conservatism is realism. The reason I am a conservative is because I understand it to be realistic. Now, if the greatest enemy, therefore, of fantasy is circumstance, then

don't we have a lot to gain by trying to put the Soviet Union
in situations where it finds out how jejune and misleading its
own axioms are?

SCHWARZ: I doubt if it's true, Bill. It was certainly not true
for Marx—the argument that capitalism was creating its own
gravediggers. . . .

Buckley is looking for nuances and trying to tease out hy-
potheticals. Granted, it seemed unlikely that the Soviet Union
would realize its axioms were jejune, but what if? Schwarz can
only go back to *The Communist Manifesto* again and again, like
a hack *Pravda* journalist.

Interestingly, Buckley does not seem frustrated that he
keeps hitting this brick wall. He's convinced that Schwarz is a
respectable anticommunist, and Schwarz's performance more
or less confirms this, but there is at the very least, if not a nut-
tiness, a, shall we say, limited quality to his articulation of the
dangers of communism. He even argues that his work is simply "Christian and anticommunist" but categorically could not
be labeled "conservative." Buckley pushes back that there is a
"natural correspondence" between anticommunism and conservatism, but Schwarz will not budge: he is not part of the
conservative movement. Buckley finally says, not unkindly,
"I'm aware that that has been your rubric, and I won't embarrass you by probing it." Schwarz laughs, and they move on.

Schwarz could not satisfactorily talk through the ways that
communism had changed since the Russian Revolution, consider the nuances of the hostility between Russia and China,
or ponder how differences between Stalin and later Soviet pre-
mier Alexei Kosygin affected the global communist movement.
He had a plethora of facts and figures at his fingertips, but, like
a broken record, it all came back to the Marxist-Leninist doctrine of unilateral communist conquest. He was a friendly, per-

petually smiling man who projected exactly the opposite image of anticommunism as that projected by Senator McCarthy, and to that extent he was a good *Firing Line* guest for demonstrating that the right need not be alarming.

Buckley also had Schwarz on the show specifically as part of his ongoing effort to debunk *Danger on the Right*, a book in which Schwarz featured prominently. The 1964 exposé was written by Arnold Forster and Benjamin R. Epstein under the aegis of the Anti-Defamation League of B'nai B'rith, and its objective was to expose the "radical right" and the somewhat less dangerous "extreme conservatives." Forster and Epstein identified Schwarz with the former camp, Buckley with the latter. The book described Schwarz as a "professional anticommunist," implying that he was in the business of attacking the Reds to turn a quick buck. The authors correctly noted that Schwarz himself was not anti-Semitic and that he "avoid[ed] the extremes, relatively speaking, of Welch and the Birchites."[4] They also noted his scare tactics; in his traveling lectures, Schwarz would elaborate in grueling detail what the communists would do when they took over America (he predicted their goal was to accomplish this feat in 1973). They would take San Francisco as world headquarters, for example, and dump its people into the bay, or cast them into the Nevada desert. A color comic book that the Christian Anti-Communism Crusade distributed to Mexican children showed "communist soldiers prodding a priest with a bayonet; a woman with a hammer and sickle on her uniform flourishing a whip threateningly over helpless little children; [and] a group of slave laborers, one of whom was being lashed by a guard."[5]

The *Danger on the Right* authors speculated that Schwarz's scare tactics softened people up and made them more open to conversion by the John Birch Society and other far-right groups. They also noted that he had gotten a bit dumpy since beginning his anticommunist work in 1950, that he rarely smiled, and that he was nervous and insecure and bit his fingernails or cracked his knuckles when feeling unsure of himself.[6] That such tacky comments added a bit of dash to a book that was otherwise a dull list of facts and figures was indisputable. But the gratuitous insults also undercut the book's authority as neutral reportage.

Buckley resented *Danger on the Right*'s attack on both him and his magazine. If the authors had stuck to the facts—as when they quoted Buckley saying, in 1964, "I believe in pot-holing, rather than broadening, the highway to the voting booth"[7]—they would have had sufficient fodder to brand him an "extreme conservative." (Buckley and his associates were comfortable describing their position as "right-wing"; it was the notion that there was anything "extreme" in this position that rankled them.[8]) Why then call him "the aging Boy Wonder of the American Right" (he was an old man of thirty-nine at the time) and suggest that, "if his propaganda strength were not so useful to the Radical Right, he would be very amusing and harmless"?[9]

Buckley disparaged the book repeatedly in the early years of *Firing Line*, and in 1966 he even devoted an episode to the topic "Extremism" and invited Dore Schary—former president of MGM and current national chairman of the Anti-Defamation League—onto the show in order to drive home his arguments against the book. Buckley said in his introduction to the show that the thesis of the book was "that America suffers from a terrible affliction, namely the conservative movement. The book makes, if only for the record, a distinction between what it calls the 'rabble rousing right,' for instance Gerald L. K. Smith, or the radical right, for instance Robert Welch, and the extreme conservatives, for instance me. But somehow the distinctions have a way of blurring, and the reader emerges with the impression that what might roughly be called the 'Gold-water Right' is a collection of radicals and extremists, whose exposure and resistance it is the sublime historical duty of the Anti-Defamation League to effect."

Today, *Danger on the Right*'s labels might not seem so egregious, but at the Goldwater moment the fascist connotations of *extremist* were unambiguous. Schary attempts to moderate the book's message, arguing that it had said that some who supported Goldwater "happened to be members of the radical right, in the same way that sometimes very liberal candidates will attract the support of those much further to the left than they are. I understood, from what I've been told, that what we were really going to discuss was extremism in the United States today, and I think it would be helpful and perhaps a little bit more purposeful if we were to avoid going back to books that were written two years ago, and discuss what the perils might be in terms of extremism in the United States today." In what is perhaps an all-time first, Schary actually declines to engage in book promotion on TV. Undeterred, Buckley maintains that *Danger on the Right* is still being sold and merchandised and is still relevant. He goes on to attack a number of details in the book. On the book's notion that "the new extremism, it appeared as the Coughlin movement, and flowered into the reactionary 'America First' movement," Buckley says "that's the kind of thing that sends me up a tree." Here's the exchange that ensues.

BUCKLEY: I know an awful lot of people who were in the "America First" movement. Jessup was there; Chester Bowles was a member; Norman Thomas was very, very close to it; it had the largest membership of any organization—any recent organization—in American history, but all of a sudden, I read in your text that I'm supposed to consider it as a flowering of the radical right extremism of the thirties. Heaven only knows what you're going to do to the Goldwater movement in your next book, dealing with it historically at this rate.

You do understand why people are a little bit edgy about your organization?

SCHARY: Yes, I can understand why they're a little bit edgy, and I think some people are edgy with perhaps—in good conscience. Perhaps yourself. But I think there are some people who are edgy who have no reason to be edgy, except the fact that they have been exposed. You are concentrating, in your attacks on the book, in the areas that might very appropriately be called gray. You are not concentrating on the areas in the book which deal very specifically with people who ally themselves—

BUCKLEY: Certainly not. Why should I criticize things that shouldn't be criticized?

SCHARY: I don't know why you should. But you're not making the point—

BUCKLEY: I don't say to you, Mr. Schary, "You concentrate only on the weaknesses of the John Birch Society. You never mention its strengths."

SCHARY: I don't think it has any strengths.

BUCKLEY: Aha! I was hoping you'd say that. . . . You say that the John Birch Society has no strengths?

SCHARY: No, not in my opinion.

BUCKLEY: Well, what objection would you have, for instance, to the leadership of the John Birch Society saying, "You should familiarize yourself with your congressman, your senator, and find out how he votes"? There's nothing wrong with that, is there?

SCHARY: No, nothing at all.

BUCKLEY: If your organization did that, we'd have to call it "civic-mindedness," wouldn't we?

SCHARY: Not if our organization had as the starting point

a program as the John Birch Society appears to be, [as] articulated by its leaders. I think an organization such as the John Birch organization, that attacks every recent president we've had, that attacks Justice Warren, that attacks our congressmen, that attacks an administration and the clergy, and the military as being part of a communist conspiracy—I think this organization is an irresponsible organization.

BUCKLEY: Positively. I think it's criminal. At least, I think Mr. Welch is cuckoo. But that really wasn't what I was talking about. On the one hand, the making of distinctions when they are convenient, on the other, not making distinctions—

SCHARY: No, it isn't a question of inconvenience—

BUCKLEY: You knocked me a moment ago for not mentioning those chapters in your book devoted to the conventional scurrilities of the KKK, and Gerald L. K. Smith, and so on. The answer is, I don't mention them because I agree with them [that is, with those negative chapters on the KKK, etc.]; I think anybody agrees with them. But I find myself uncomfortable between the same covers of the book that includes me and [the racist anti-Semite] Gerald L. K. Smith.

Here and throughout, Schary gives careful, arid responses. Buckley is frustrated at the difference between Schary's published remarks and his *Firing Line* performance; he says "here's one of the reasons why it's awfully hard to discuss these questions, Mr. Schary, because you have been [on the show], I think, so amiable and so reasonable, and so soft-spoken; but when you get on the typewriter, it sort of comes out different." This gets a big laugh from the studio audience, but Schary still refuses to let his feathers be ruffled. This was a tactic that worked well for some guests, such as Noam Chomsky, but not for Schary. He just seemed milquetoast. Why not take a stand and debate specific points? Yes, there had been plenty of liberal members

of the antiwar, noninterventionist America First Committee—
even a young Gore Vidal—and also right-wingers, such as the
pro-Hitler Charles Lindbergh. Why not just acknowledge that
Danger on the Right could have explained some things better
and then make a case for the book's value?

Ultimately, Schary either needed to rally and find a way to
defend the notion that "extreme conservatives" such as Buckley
were in the book because they were on a political continuum
with far rightists like Smith, or he needed to back down and—
either with his tail between his legs, or, if he could muster it,
with his chin up—explain why maybe the "extreme conservatives" should not have been included, but the other 90 percent
of the book was spot-on. Really, as soon as Buckley said, "Aha!
I was hoping you'd say that," it was clear that Schary was in
trouble. Buckley had laid a simple rhetorical trap to show that
Schary was insufficiently precise in his thinking, and it had
snapped tight. The show closed with Buckley saying, "Thank
you very much, Mr. Schary. I appreciate your coming, and I
hope you will keep me and my twenty-seven million friends
out of your next book." He was, of course, referring to the number of Americans who had voted for Goldwater. Goldwater had
been slammed hard in the presidential election. Winning only
six states, he received 39 percent of the popular vote. But could
27 million Americans really be categorized as "extremists"
rather than simply extremely conservative? Buckley clearly
thought not.

Moving away from the extremists was an expression of a
principled stance against paranoid and conspiratorial thinking.
But it was also a straight-up practical move. Buckley realized
that the Cold War right-wing extremists were not good movement strategizers and were generally better at complaining
than at getting things done. High-profile right-wing broadcasters like Dan Smoot would advise their listeners not to vote in
presidential elections, for example, feeling that there were no

truly conservative candidates. Eccentric right-wing broadcaster
H. L. Hunt even imagined a perfect world in which rich people
had extra votes; Buckley's association with him as a guest on
his TV show *Answers for Americans* was short-lived.[10]

Buckley understood that to move right-wing conservatism
forward you needed someone worth voting for, but you also
needed to break from those who could not understand that
it was better to vote for a dissatisfying candidate like Eisenhower, while continuing the search for Republican candidates
further to the right, than to retreat from the voting booth altogether. That said, it is worth noting that the extremists and
Buckley were aligned on numerous political fronts in the 1950s
and '60s; they concurred in their opposition to the civil rights
movement and in their opposition to federal spending on social welfare programs, for example. Buckley accepted many of
the *ideas* promoted by the nuts; he just didn't like how they
expressed and justified them.

The kooks made conservatism look bad, but what was the
practical value of increased respectability? Certainly, you could
be disrespectable, not disavow the nuts, and still get elected
to public office. Lester Maddox—the owner of a fried chicken
restaurant who famously chased out black customers while
waving an ax handle, and who was later elected governor of
Georgia—was perhaps the most extreme example of that. Not
only did he not disavow the nuts, he was one himself. Alabama
governor George Wallace was respectable by comparison,
though he had, of course, implicitly counted on the White Citizens' Councils, Ku Klux Klan, and Birchers for votes, all the
while maintaining that there was no race problem in the state
at all ("we don't have segregation in Alabama," he said on *Firing Line* in 1968). Wallace's handlers knew that the right-wing
extremists were on his side, but they kept critical discussion of
the nuts internal so as not to alienate them.

It became tricky, though, when Wallace ran for *national*

office in 1968, gave a speech at Madison Square Garden, and found that Klansmen had driven up from Louisiana and were rallying in support across the street, along with American Nazi Party members wearing "I like Eich" buttons, in memory of Adolf Eichmann.[11] Buckley agreed with Wallace that federally induced desegregation was an unconstitutional violation of states' rights. But "I like Eich" buttons? This was not the kind of nonsense that Buckley wanted associated with the conservative movement as it grew in the Goldwater years and beyond. Indeed, he had Wallace on *Firing Line* in 1968 in order to debunk any notion that Wallace counted as a "conservative" at all. After all, he had a "New Dealer" background and supported government pensions for the elderly. "I've never been in favor of necessarily increasing the franchise, I've simply been against its being denied on the basis of color," he told Wallace on the show.

Crafting a respectable conservative movement entailed more than creating distance from the extremists. It was also crucial to forge alliances across different conservative positions. Historians of American conservatism agree that Buckley was vital for creating the modern movement, first and foremost, via the "fusionism" embodied by *National Review.* That is to say, Buckley found a way to bring together in the same pages (and, eventually, the same movement) traditionalism, libertarianism, and, as *Nation* editor Victor Navasky put it, "good old-fashioned anti-Communism, the Elmer's Glue of the Cold War years."[12]

It was, to put it mildly, difficult to wrangle the different politics and personalities appearing in the *National Review.* In their book celebrating Buckley, Linda Bridges and John R. Coyne note that "the only categories excluded were racists, anti-Semites, and 'kooks,'"[13] an assessment that is mostly on the mark, though much has been made of the publication's 1957 editorial "Why the South Must Prevail," in which Buckley noted that whites were, "for the time being," the "advanced

race" in the South; he contended that "it is more important for
any community, anywhere in the world, to affirm and live by
civilized standards than to bow to the demands of the numer-
ical majority."[14]

While conservatives looking back have tended to describe
this famous editorial as anomalous, this was not the last time
that the magazine would make troubling statements about
southern blacks. A 1960 editorial (this one not authored by
Buckley) noted, for example, that, "in the Deep South the Negroes are, by comparison with the Whites, retarded. . . ."[15] This
was appalling stuff. In later years, Buckley's stance on the civil
rights movement did shift, as we shall see in examining *Firing Line*'s engagement with both that movement and the Black
Power movement.

What is important to emphasize here, in terms of thinking through Buckley's remaking of the conservative image, is
that he and his team truly *saw themselves* as operating from
a reasoned and fair position in opposition to the racists, anti-
Semites, and kooks.[16] *National Review* authors and editors positioned themselves as emphatically different from the kinds of
folks who insisted that the fluoridation of drinking water was a
communist conspiracy. Indeed, it is telling that as late as 1978,
in a *Firing Line* debate with Ronald Reagan on the Panama Canal, Buckley attacked certain notions advanced by Reagan as
"the kind of talk that belongs in Belmont, Massachusetts" (the
home base of the JBS), and in a 1985 *Firing Line* episode with
Norman Mailer and Kurt Vonnegut, Buckley playfully accused
Mailer of being a "grassy knoller." Conspiratorial thinking,
whether emerging from the left or right, was simply nonsense
in Buckley's book.

If the "grassy knollers"—JFK assassination obsessives—
were the ultimate conspiracy theorists, the Birchers came in a
very close second. Two episodes of *Firing Line* were specifically
devoted to dressing down the JBS. In 1968 ex-Bircher Slobodan

Draskovich appeared on the show and disappointed Buckley by being very negative—but not quite negative enough—about Welch and the society. He implied that it was the *communist* press (not the mainstream press, not to mention the *National Review*) that had been responsible for taking Welch down a notch for his conspiratorial thinking. He even indicated that if Welch had done his work properly, the JBS really could have done something about communism—more than a mere magazine like *National Review* could.

Draskovich is looking for conservative anticommunist *action*, not just *ideas*. Buckley is not too dismayed by his slighting of *National Review*, but he is perplexed by the fact that it took Draskovich seven years to discern the folly of the society: "What I think is continuously fascinating is that so many people who are anticommunist, like yourself, continue for so long to refuse to understand that Mr. Welch's analysis of what has happened during the past twenty or thirty years, is not only perverse but is almost certain to contribute to anti-anticommunism. As [conservative political theorist] Russell Kirk said, except for the fact that this would sound as though he, himself, had swallowed Birchite poisoning, he would be very anxious to make a demonstration to the effect that the Communist Party subsidizes the Welch Society in an effort to make anticommunism ridiculous."

Draskovich had long held out hope that he could reform the society from within. Buckley questions how he could be so naïve, and Draskovich can only convey his despair that things did not work out. The episode was a chance for Buckley to reinforce his distance from the Birchers but also to display how conservatives could voice disagreements about anticommunist tactics without losing sight of their common cause.

Much more lively was the 1971 episode on the JBS featuring two guests, Peter Koltypin and Gerald Schomp. Koltypin was in the society and was also an anticommunist writer and lecturer in his own right. Schomp had been the Florida state co-ordinator for the JBS but had defected and written an insider's account, *Birchism Was My Business.* Schomp offers information about the inner workings of the society, a real rarity given how secretive Welch was. (Welch himself had been invited to be on the show but had declined and had instructed his followers to do the same.) Koltypin, by contrast, offers a picture of JBS indoctrination in action. Buckley affects an almost saintly patience with the man, politely asking him a range of questions and always getting the same response, a list of informative books "proving" Welch's conspiratorial arguments. Koltypin explains how he traveled to Belmont to meet in person with Welch, was convinced by their conversation, and joined the society, at which Buckley asks, "Did he confide to you that Eisenhower was a member of the Communist Party?" In response, Koltypin reviews grave mistakes that Eisenhower made, including Operation Keelhaul, whereby Soviets held by the Nazis as POWs were forcibly repatriated after the war, and then sent to gulags or slaughtered. The implication is that no one could do such a thing without being in league with the communists, but, as is JBS policy, Koltypin avoids saying this directly.

KOLTYPIN: Well my opinion is—personal opinion, of course—that Mr. Eisenhower was being told what to do because I can't conceive that so many mistakes that had been happening thereafter and before concerning, for instance, Hungary or Tibet or even stopping Patton, as came out very recently—

BUCKLEY: Being told what to do by whom? Other than the president?

KOLTYPIN: Some other people of interest who are to a great extent—

BUCKLEY: I don't think you should be coy. Are you saying that he was taking orders from the communists?

KOLTYPIN: Well, not exactly communists. I don't agree in that respect, but there are people in this world who are financing and helping the communist conspiracy.

Koltypin then turns to facts and figures about the financing of the Russian Revolution, all material that, as Jeff Greenfield points out during the Q&A later in the show, dates right back to Father Coughlin's anti-Semitic radio shows of the 1930s. At this point, Schomp jumps in and notes that one of the things that turned him off the JBS was that Welch avoided naming the shady financiers so that Birchites were free to interpret his theory as they liked, and many of them assumed that it was the Jews who were behind everything. Koltypin denies that there is anything specifically anti-Semitic about the conspiracy that Welch has identified and then again launches into a list of informative books, such as John Robison's Freemason-smashing *The Proofs of Conspiracy* (1798), and more recent publications such as Dan Smoot's *The Invisible Government* and W. Cleon Skousen's *The Naked Capitalist*. If this conspiracy has been so patently *proved*, Buckley pointedly asks, "Why doesn't Edgar Hoover tell us about it?" Koltypin responds, "Excellent thought!" pushing the notion that if people such as Hoover and others only *knew* the facts they would take action.

Obviously, Buckley's implicit point—which completely eludes Koltypin—is that FBI director J. Edgar Hoover is about as informed about communist subversion in the United States as anyone could be. Of course, most to the left of Buckley would argue that Hoover had cast his net much too wide. But whether you were for or against Hoover, no one in his or her right mind could claim the problem was that he hadn't gathered enough information.

Back in 1966 with Dore Schary, in 1967 with Fred Schwarz, and in 1968 with Slobodan Draskovich, Buckley had clearly still been on edge about the "extremist" label being indiscriminately pinned to the right. So the 1971 Koltypin and Schomp episode—titled "The John Birch Society and the American Right"—is particularly striking because Buckley is so even-tempered and composed on the topic. His work has been effective, and the slur has receded. Ten years earlier, the John Birch Society *was* the American right, in the public imagination. Now this is not the case. In fact, after Buckley's introduction the show never quite fully circles back to the second half of the title.

Welch himself had shifted tactics in a way that inadvertently confirmed Buckley's victory. In earlier years, Welch had accused generals, politicians, even the president himself of being communist agents or at least pawns. But now he had his new explanatory schema in place, as indicated by Koltypin above. Over the Communist Party itself were the puppet masters, the wealthy and powerful elite who directed and funded the communists in world domination. Although Welch generally avoided naming names, it turned out that he believed this sinister cabal—"the Insiders"—included the Rockefellers, the Rothschilds, the Council on Foreign Relations, the Trilateral Commission, and, of course, William F. Buckley Jr. No one could accuse the "respectable right," as Buckley often referred to himself and his circle, as being in league with the nuts if the nuts had actually accused them of financing the international communist conspiracy!

So, Buckley used *Firing Line* to make conservatism "respectable." But Neal Freeman, who was the assistant manager of Buckley's mayoral campaign and also an early *Firing Line* producer, provides a different angle from which to approach our understanding of Buckley's—and, by extension, *Firing Line*'s—contribution to the movement. Other people could have made conservatism "respectable," he notes. But "nobody else could have made it stylish." Of course, Freeman fully understood the tactical political importance of fusionism; he did not think that

Buckley's contribution was *purely* stylistic. But his stylishness was extremely important. What did it mean to make conservatism not just respectable but also stylish? And what role did *Firing Line* play in this elaborate makeover?

Via his performance on *Firing Line* Buckley showed that conservatives could be witty, urbane, and eloquent. If you came to the show as a liberal viewer, you might find him snide and condescending, especially in some of the early shows. But even when he was at his most disdainful, there was no denying his panache. The extremists were deeply offended by his cerebral verbal maneuvers; that he was wealthy and had attended Yale was enough to alienate the conspiratorial yahoos. In offering his stylish intellectualism, Buckley was, in a sense, *advertising* his nonextremist version of right-wing conservatism on *Firing Line*. (Today we might even crassly describe his efforts as "rebranding.") By rhetorically sparring with liberal after liberal on the show, Buckley would demonstrate that right-wing conservatism had not died with Goldwater's 1964 defeat. Goldwater's campaign had not been an *aberration*, then, that confirmed the triumph of liberalism and the death of all but the moderate and liberal wings of the Republican Party. Rather, Goldwater had set a *precedent*: a right-wing conservative could be nominated and run for the presidency.

How could this failed effort be promoted by Buckley (and *Firing Line*) precisely as a precedent—a first step toward an eventual conservative electoral triumph—rather than as an abject failure? Goldwater staffer Ted Humes argued that "conservative truths" per se had not been rejected by voters in 1964; those truths simply had not been properly hyped. Goldwater "was charismatic but not anywhere near profound enough to carry a campaign," and what was needed was better "salesmen for conservatism."[17] Buckley would be one of the very best of those salesmen, and *Firing Line*, Buckley's nationally syndicated newspaper column, and, of course, *National Review* would be his main venues for making the pitch.

Notwithstanding his inclination toward the ideological deep dive, there was also a surface quality to Buckley's style on *Firing Line*—the quick quips, the condescension (to Wallace: "You're telling me something I knew when I was three years old"), the cutting smile accompanying verbal expressions of disbelief. This is not to say that Buckley wanted to bring viewers to the conservative side simply by virtue of his verbal dexterity, close shave, and fine dress shirts. He knew that the image of conservatism he was creating was not merely one of surfaces. After all, a frequent reference point for him was the infamous first Kennedy-Nixon debate of 1960; radio listeners felt the debaters did equally well or that Nixon had won, while TV viewers felt Kennedy had won. JFK was more handsome and did not suffer from the five o'clock shadow that apparently sprouted on Nixon shortly after breakfast. (Edging out of the harsh studio lights during a break from filming his 1968 campaign ads, Nixon bluntly stated the obvious: "I sweat too much."[18])

As the liberal Theodore White succinctly notes in his Pulitzer Prize–winning *The Making of the President 1960*, "television had won the nation away from sound to images, and that was that."[19] With his "Checkers" address in 1952, Nixon had proved that he understood how to use TV to sway public opinion, but in his first debate with Kennedy, White argues, he had fatally erred by addressing *Kennedy*: "He was concerned with the cool and undisturbed man who sat across the platform from him, with the personal adversary in the studio, not with the mind of America."[20]

In other words, Nixon acted like he was engaged in a debate with an individual, not in a *televisual* debate viewed by millions. When the race began, Nixon had been seen as the seasoned professional, the obvious winner, while JFK was the inexperienced upstart. The day after the election, Kennedy observed, "it was TV more than anything else that turned the tide."[21]

As Joe McGinniss recounts in *The Selling of the President 1968*, by the time Nixon's next presidential campaign came along he had procured a crew of media-savvy handlers such as Roger Ailes—now known first and foremost as the creator of Fox News. Ailes was the kind of man who would visit a studio set designed for a Nixon TV special and immediately assess a threat looming over his boss's image: "Those stupid bastards on the set designing crew put turquoise curtains in the background. Nixon wouldn't look right unless he was carrying a pocketbook." Ailes replaced the curtains with wood that, as he described it, had "clean, solid, masculine lines."[22] The "new Nixon" poached TV industry people—Ailes from the *Mike Douglas Show*, a *Laugh-In* producer, even a makeup man from Johnny Carson—to make sure the gaffes of 1960 would not be repeated.

Buckley was more than *troubled* by the notion that JFK had beat Nixon in 1960 because of the power of the televisual image. He was *offended*. Indeed, on a 1967 *Firing Line* episode with moderate Republican senator Mark Hatfield of Oregon, in which Hatfield advocated for nationwide presidential primaries and shorter congressional terms (in effect, arguing for increased power in the hands of voters), Buckley expressed concern that voters could be easily swayed by propaganda into irresponsible recalls and so on. He noted that a hundred years ago, literacy rates were very low compared to 1967, "but then you examine the relative difference between, let's say, the debates between Lincoln and Douglas, and the debate between Nixon and Kennedy, and ask yourself, are we a more mature nation?" Buckley even, on the same program, implied that Republican Party players had not supported Robert Taft over Eisenhower in 1952 because the latter was "so successful on television."

Buckley was critiquing TV's image-crafting capability but

was also well aware that Hatfield himself was using *Firing Line* to convey his own image of moderate conservatism. This was the very man who had inveighed against extremism at the Republican convention where Goldwater was nominated, and who was now gunning to be Nixon's running mate in 1968. When queried about this during the show's Q&A session, Hatfield began to unfold a coy, strategic response, but he was backed into a corner:

QUESTIONER: Would you accept a vice presidential nomination with someone like Richard Nixon whose view on Vietnam is so diametrically opposed to yours?

HATFIELD: I haven't been invited.

QUESTIONER: If you were. [audience laughter]

BUCKLEY: [laughing] Ah—poor politician.

HATFIELD: Er—this is a very [laughing]—did you ever get questions like this when you ran for mayor?

BUCKLEY: Yeah, but I didn't *care*, you see. [big audience laughter]

HATFIELD: Didn't you want to win?

Buckley's "Ah—poor politician!" says so much about his stance toward realpolitik. If you held, or aspired to hold, public office, you simply couldn't say what you thought or even knew to be true half the time. Hatfield patently wanted to be the vice presidential candidate, but he had to squirm about without actually saying as much, while also conveying an image of himself that would look good to Nixon and his team if they ever caught wind of the exchange with Buckley. Buckley was good at drawing out his guests, but with politicians there was always this kind of phony song-and-dance to contend with.

As we have already seen, when Buckley had run for mayor

of New York City he knew he would lose not simply because the city would not elect an archconservative but also because he wouldn't engage in nonsense such as commissioning promotional slogans designed to appeal to emotion rather than intellect. Lindsay, by contrast, had run against Buckley with the slogan "He is fresh and everyone else is tired." This was on a par with, or perhaps even more foolish than, Timex's famous "takes a licking and keeps on ticking." Lindsay had even commissioned a hokey campaign song, "Oh, It's Great to Be the Mayor of New York," sung by a pre–*Brady Bunch* Florence Henderson.* By rejecting all such nonsense, Buckley had signaled his rejection of politics as usual.

This was, of course, frustrating to those who actually wanted (or even naïvely expected) him to win. In fact, voters had written him saying that they wished he would take the whole thing more seriously, and Freeman sent him a memo shortly before the election observing, "you have been frighteningly effective in communicating an indifference to your campaign. Now is the time to radically change that impression; and it can be done by using some transitional device as: 'I have been tremendously encouraged by the hundreds of letters from people giving me their support and their energies in this campaign.' Whore yourself, and hold out the possibility of an electoral miracle." He added, perhaps with a bit of desperation, "try a short sentence once in awhile."[23] Buckley was not amenable to these suggestions.

All of which is to say, yes, we can see in retrospect that *Firing Line* made a hard sell for a new kind of conservatism, but Buckley was plainly never comfortable with sloganeering and other Madison Avenue advertising methods. The *National Review*'s

---

* No good deed goes unpunished: Lindsay gave Henderson crabs, she revealed in her autobiography, confirming that the 1968 garbage strike was not Lindsay's only hygiene crisis.

catchy tagline was "Don't immanentize the eschaton." As we
might infer from this tongue-in-cheek "slogan," Buckley ran a
magazine for forty years and hosted a TV show for thirty-three
years, while feigning to be above mass culture. If his magazine
targeted a niche market of hard-line conservatives, his TV show
cast a broader net and could be widely enjoyed by all political
camps. Yet by using arcane language and labyrinthine gram-
matical constructions, Buckley conveyed that he was above the
simplicity that infused the rest of TV. He was on TV, *and* he
was "better" than TV.

If Buckley was to seal the deal on his right-wingers-are-not-
extremists gambit, one *Firing Line* guest was crucial above all
others: Barry Goldwater. Goldwater appeared on the show for
the first time in 1966 to discuss "The Future of Conservatism." Lacking the aggressive edge that often characterized the
show at the time, the episode was, frankly, a bit dull. Both men
agreed that the Republican Party needed to become more conservative, that Nixon had a good shot at being the presidential
nominee in 1968, and that Reagan had a great political future
ahead of him. Lest this sound too crystal ball–ish, Goldwater
did also predict that Vietnam would not be a particularly divi-
sive issue in the 1968 election.

Oddly enough, it may well be that the most interesting thing
about the 1966 Goldwater show was exactly the fact that it was
so boring. Buckley observed in his introduction that Goldwater
was "indisputably the best-known and perhaps for that reason
the most maligned conservative in the world. During the campaign in 1964 he was maligned by his professional detractors,
painted into a bogeyman, which amply attests to the imaginative ingenuity of the public relations industry." Well, if he
were really the bogeyman that the PR people had imagined,
he would have said all kinds of outlandish things. Instead he
upheld certain conservative notions (he believed that aspects of
the civil rights bill he had voted against were unconstitutional),

said a few things proving he was not the extremist monster many had imagined (he agreed with Dr. Martin Luther King Jr. that the nonenforcement of civil rights laws was an egregious problem), and confirmed that he was a hawk (he regretted we had not preemptively attacked China and destroyed her atomic capability, and now it was too late).

Notably, and this was the only area in which there was a contrast between the two, Buckley expressed frustration that Goldwater had been misrepresented during the 1964 campaign, while Goldwater ignored that issue completely and was instead vexed that numerous Republican politicians had not been team players and supported his campaign. Buckley was the pundit concerned about liberal media bias. Goldwater was the politician concerned about party solidarity.

The issue of "extremism" was submerged during the senator's visit until near the end of the program, when Buckley

Appearing on *Firing Line*, Barry Goldwater was a symbol for liberals that conservatism had been defeated, and a symbol for conservatives that the right-wing would triumph.
CREDIT: *Hoover Institution*

declared that the notion that Goldwater's platform was "extremist" rather than "truly conservative" was "patently invalid," the delusion of those who understood the campaign "as it was painted by [the liberal political cartoonist] Herblock." Buckley had noted in his book on the 1965 mayoral campaign that "the Establishment's hard hold over . . . rhetorical categories is, in political discourse, its most important weapon." The *New York Times* never seemed to call anyone an "extreme liberal," he griped, preferring to reserve the word *extreme* (or the prefix *ultra-*) "for the unfashionable right (e.g. the Goldwaterites)."[24]

Both Goldwater and Buckley knew that the extremist charge still hung in the air from the 1964 presidential election, but they also thought it was balderdash. There was no reason, then, to give the accusation more publicity on *Firing Line* in 1966. Goldwater himself had rhetorically blown it two years earlier by defending the notion of extremism in accepting the Republican nomination: "I would remind you that extremism in the defense of liberty is no vice. And let me remind you also that moderation in the pursuit of justice is no virtue." "Goldwater had learned too late the lesson that one must guard against any use of a word which, for many, amounted to a call to immoral ends," Buckley observed in his 2008 book on Goldwater. "It was so in 1964 with the word 'extremism.' It could not be hygienically used in any affirmative context."[25]

In the pages of *Danger on the Right*, Goldwater had been pegged as someone who attracted radical right-wingers. Even his devoted speechwriter Karl Hess—who would later join the New Left, participate in Students for a Democratic Society, go libertarian, become an infamous tax evader, embrace outright anarchism, and publish a survivalist newsletter—conceded in his 1967 book that right-wing extremists were drawn to Goldwater. While Hess insisted rather excessively that Goldwater represented "the strong center" of the Republican Party,[26] he did reasonably observe that "the undesirables of the left will—no matter *who* the Democrats run or what they run for or from—always gravitate toward the Democrats. The undesirables of the right will do the same with the Republicans."[27]

Fair enough. But what Hess did not do was push harder and ask what it was about Goldwater that drew so many "undesirables." After all, the Communist Party USA was not bending over backward to campaign for LBJ's election. While the mass media surely overplayed Goldwater's bloodlust for the annihilation of Vietnam (not to mention his monstrous urge to annihilate pretty American children plucking the petals off daisies), and his supporters said that Goldwater was speaking temperately and hypothetically, he *had* suggested that the use of nuclear bombs in Southeast Asia would be reasonable. Again discussing heavy bombing strategies on a 1969 *Firing Line* appearance, even Goldwater himself admitted, "I'm probably a little more of a hawk than the average hawk."

Goldwater did not seek out the nut vote, but he nonetheless won it handily. Theodore White summed up the situation quite ably: there was a striking "contrast between the Goldwater movement and the Goldwater organization." No one "in the organizational structure of the Goldwater campaign . . . [even] remotely qualified for the title 'kook.' Nor was there evident any 'kook' on the floor. But the 'kooks' dominated the galleries [at the nominating convention], hating and screaming and reveling in their own frenzy."[28]

Ultimately, Goldwater had lost terribly, but he had rallied a devoted base of grassroots activists—the "Goldwater movement," as White put it, which included both kooks and less alarming right-wing conservatives—that would long outlive his campaign. The Goldwater base would, in fact, provide the financial backbone of the conservative movement. Richard Viguerie, the direct-mail fundraising innovator, started up his master list of conservative donors by hand-copying 12,500 names and addresses of Goldwater supporters who had given fifty dollars or more to the campaign.[29] Buckley supporters also played a part in Viguerie's fundraising; a few years later, Viguerie filled the trunk of his car with 50,000 metal address printing plates purchased from Marvin Liebman, who had raised funds for both the Goldwater presidential and Buckley mayoral campaigns, each a failure in its own interesting way.

In 1995, some thirty years after Goldwater's defeat, Buckley hosted a *Firing Line* episode titled "Goldwater, Old and New." His guests were fellow conservatives Lee Edwards and Richard Brookhiser. Edwards was a founding member of Young Americans for Freedom and had worked in the Goldwater campaign. Brookhiser was a senior editor at *National Review*; he would release a book on George Washington the next year and was already emerging as a specialist in presidential history. The program began with expressions of mutual befuddlement. Goldwater had opposed abortion and gay rights legislation in the past, but now he had reversed direction on both issues. What on earth was going on?

One hypothesis advanced was that he had shifted allegiance from old-fashioned conservatism to more or less amoral libertarianism. Another theory was that his shift sprang from personal investment in the issues: he had supported his own daughter's choice to abort in the fifties, and he had a gay, HIV-positive grandson. A third theory was that he had run for president before the Christian Right had emerged. In effect, the social issues that the evangelicals had made hot simply hadn't been on the table at the height of Goldwater's political career, so there had been no reason to take a stand in those days.

But then discussion shifted back to the 1964 election, and to how Goldwater had been bamboozled by the mainstream media. The famous LBJ "Daisy" campaign ad, which clearly indicated that, if elected, Goldwater would blow everyone to kingdom come, had only aired once as an ad before being pulled. But then it had aired repeatedly (at no cost to the Democrats) as a news story. Further, *Fact* magazine had published an article titled "1,189 Psychiatrists Say Barry Goldwater is Unfit for the Presidency." Buckley and his guests failed to mention that *Fact* was a satirical magazine published by Ralph Ginzburg, best known for his 1963 conviction on federal obscenity charges. Other Ginzburg publications included *The Housewife's Handbook on Selective Promiscuity* and *An Unhurried View of Erotica*. Goldwater sued him and eventually won one dollar in damages.

The point, really, is that Ralph Ginzburg's work was hardly in the journalistic ballpark with *Time* magazine or the *New York Times*. The interesting thing about the psychiatrist story is not so much its reckless attack on Goldwater as the fact that such a story could actually gain traction and receive wide attention in 1964. You could argue that it was deliberately deceptive, but you could also argue that it simply struck a nerve. If the so-called liberal media was unsympathetic to Goldwater, it was picking up on wide public anxiety about both extremism and, a notch down from that in intensity, the extreme conservatism embodied by Goldwater.

It's true that the mainstream media implied that he would eliminate Social Security and Medicare if elected, even though he had clearly indicated that he would not. But he *had* clearly indicated that he had serious reservations about these programs. Further, even if he made some very strong speeches, his improvised comments were often too candid, and the press covered the latter more than the former. As White put it, "if he insisted on speaking thus in public, how could one resist quoting him?"[30]

Decades later, after Reagan had been elected and the Republican Party had shifted right, Buckley and his *Firing Line* guests were still reluctant to admit that Americans really had voted against right-wing conservatism in 1964; the implication was that this had been the outcome of the election because people had been misinformed and had therefore misperceived Gold-water as an "extremist." (Or, as some liberals had put it in 1964, countering the Goldwater campaign slogan "in your heart, you know he's right": "in your gut, you know he's nuts.") Goldwater had set a precedent not only by virtue of showing that a deeply conservative Republican could be nominated for president but also by virtue of the accusations of "liberal media bias" that bubbled up around him, accusations that continue in conservative circles today.

Liberals counter that the accusations of a liberal media monopoly seem thin in light of the current strength of not only Fox News but also, of course, conservative talk radio, not to mention the perennial appearance of books by Bill O'Reilly, Ann Coulter, Rush Limbaugh, and Dinesh D'Souza on the bestseller lists. But conservatives and liberals can agree on one front. As Edwards put it on *Firing Line*, Goldwater proved to be "the most important loser in American politics."

Few could have predicted this in 1964. Democrats confidently declared liberalism forever triumphant, and the big players in the Republican Party also assumed that the election had been a referendum on hard-right conservatism. Indeed, before the convention, moderate Republican senators Thomas Kuchel of California and Jacob Javits of New York had predicted that nominating Goldwater would be downright suicide for the party. As Rick Perlstein notes in his definitive study of Goldwater, "the New York Republican chair lamented the party's having paid a 'shattering price for the erratic deviation from our soundly moderate, twentieth-century course.'"[31] Buckley and his compatriots were in a minuscule minority who believed that Goldwater augured the eventual triumph of hard-right conservatism. Buckley's hosting of a *Firing Line* episode with Goldwater titled "The Future of Conservatism" in 1966, at a moment when all assumed that Goldwater symbolized exactly what the future of conservatism would *not* be, must have seemed positively lunatic to, well, virtually *everyone* but Buckley and his confederates.

Thirty years later, Buckley et al. had been proved correct, and this made "Goldwater Old and New" a particularly difficult episode of *Firing Line*. Buckley and his guests could make neither head nor tail of the "new" Goldwater. A man who was honored by Planned Parenthood for persistently voting to uphold *Roe v. Wade*. A man who referred to the Christian Right–wingers who seemed to have stolen the Republican Party in 1989 as "a bunch of kooks." A man who reacted to Jerry Falwell's admonition that "good Christians" should be worried about the nomination of Sandra Day O'Connor to the Supreme Court by saying, "I think every good Christian ought to kick Falwell right in the ass."[32] A man who, responding in 1982 to the rise of the "New Right," as embodied by Senator Jesse Helms of North Carolina, said, "I don't like being called the New Right; I'm an old, old son-of-a-bitch. I'm a conservative."[33]

The "extremist" label had been *Firing Line*'s bugaboo in the 1960s, and Buckley had particularly taken offense when it was applied to Goldwater, himself, or his "twenty-seven million friends." By the time "Goldwater Old and New" aired in 1995, *extremist* would have seemed like a terribly dated pejorative. But "old son-of-a-bitch conservative," well, that was both apt, and timeless.

Goldwater had gone soft on social issues, Buckley's show was on its last legs, and the Clinton years had deflated some of the exuberance conservatives had felt during the Reagan years. But, still, Buckley had every reason to believe he had definitively won the battle against the "extremist" label that had clung so tenaciously to the conservative image in the 1960s. How fitting that Buckley's penultimate posthumous publication would be a tribute to Goldwater, the man who emboldened the Cold War right, at last, to go to the polls and vote for a real conservative presidential candidate. He lost the election, of course, but a conservative movement blossomed in his wake. Or, as Buckley put it in introducing Goldwater when he appeared on *Firing Line* in 1989, quoting George Will, "Barry Goldwater ran for the White House in 1964 and won it in 1980."

CHAPTER TWO

"APODICTIC ALL THE WAY THROUGH"

Firing Line Takes On Communism

As *Firing Line* charted and promoted America's turn from left to right, from the 1960s into the Reagan years, its host's unbending anticommunism was steadfast. Buckley kept a level head on *Firing Line* most of the time, but an argument about communism was the thing most likely to make him lose his cool. As his son, Christopher, explains, Buckley "viewed the struggle against communism as the great struggle of his day. And he frankly viewed it as a struggle between Christianity and Godless atheism. . . . He grew up in a household where FDR was referred to as *that man* and Eleanor Roosevelt was referred to as *that woman*. Above all, he grew up in a world that was to a large degree dominated by Joseph Stalin. When my dad's political consciousness was forming the show trials were going on in Moscow. So this is the world that he inhabited and in which his worldview was formed."[1]

Buckley expressed this worldview in intellectual terms in his columns, in the pages of *National Review*, and on *Firing Line*, and in the 1960s and '70s this put him out of step with most of the American mediascape, where anticommunism was rarely expressed with any kind of analytical, intellectual precision.

In the 1950s and into the early 1960s, American film and TV producers churned out a seemingly endless stream of alarming anticommunist media. Schoolchildren were subjected to informative cartoons advising what to do should our enemies strike first with an A-bomb (quick, cover your head, "even a newspaper can save you from a bad burn!" one film instructed), and films of the decidedly B variety included titles like *Invasion U.S.A.* and *Red Nightmare,* alternate title—seriously—*The Commies Are Coming! The Commies Are Coming!* The sixties may have brought miniskirts and sanitized countercultural affectation to TV—love beads and beards without the pot and free love—but an apocalyptic "imagination of disaster," as Susan Sontag once put it, persevered in Cold War films. It was not all schlock and not all politically homogeneous, but, at its worst, this stuff was heavy with clichés and simplistically right-wing in its anticommunist fervor, with giant irradiated marauding ants (*Them!*) or totalitarian alien invaders (*Earth vs. the Flying Saucers*) standing in for the Red Menace.

The appearance of Stanley Kubrick's brilliant black comedy *Dr. Strangelove or: How I Learned to Stop Worrying and Love the Bomb* in 1964 could be read as an early indicator that hard-core anticommunism was on its way out as the default setting of mainstream American media. Kubrick's film was absolutely bracing. There was Sterling Hayden, who had been a friendly witness before the House Un-American Activities Committee (HUAC) in 1951, and who had been racked with guilt for over a decade, up on the screen portraying a flipped out air force general ranting about communist subversion, fluoridation, and precious bodily fluids, like a John Birch Society recruiter on acid. There's nothing like good satire to take the piss out of a movement.

To be sure, the Cold War continued to rage in the late sixties and all the way into the Reagan years, and this would continue to be reflected in our mass media. But by the time *Firing Line* premiered in 1966, representations of anticommunism had solidified along three axes: liberals were understood to see the communist threat as primarily external (foreign), conservatives to see it as both external and internal (domestic), and paranoid right-wingers to see it as entirely *too* internal. It was now considered, shall we say, excessive to seek signs of subversion under every rock, or inside every pumpkin.

For many on the right, Senator Joe McCarthy remained a hero, and his crusade to ferret out domestic subversives had ended much too soon, but this wasn't an attitude one still saw expressed frequently on the big screen, or the little one, notwithstanding the archly conservative 1960s incarnation of Jack Webb's *Dragnet* and spy shows like *The Man from U.N.C.L.E.* and *Mission: Impossible*, with their Manichean battles between upright Americans and despicable communists.[2]

The news media went with the flow. When anticommunism had brought high ratings, it had been covered. Likewise, antianticommunism. In 1971, CBS News went so far as to air *The Selling of the Pentagon*, a controversial special criticizing the $12 million a year that the Pentagon was spending on propaganda directed to Americans. Host Roger Mudd noted, "It has been more than a decade since the national policy of peaceful coexistence replaced the harsher rhetoric of the early Cold War years."[3] "Get *with* it," CBS seemed to be saying to the conservative viewers; "anxiety about internal subversion went out with poodle skirts." The Birchers stubbornly maintained "it ain't necessarily so," but Buckley was more realistic. In 1967, he opened his Fred Schwarz *Firing Line* episode—"The Decline of Anticommunism"—by noting that "anticommunism is greatly out of fashion these days."

Yet here he was hosting a TV series that would devote much of its energy to the putatively unfashionable. In the ongoing effort to bring a mainstream, nonextremist image to right-wing conservatism, *Firing Line*'s strategic tackling of communism would be very productive for Buckley. For example, on the show

he would be aggressively suspicious of the power and effica-
ciousness of unions, without branding them as "subversive."
He would also debate socialists, whose objectives he saw as
bonkers, and whose occasional inroads in the realm of federal
spending he saw as dangerous, but who, he recognized, were in
no serious position to topple American capitalism.

In effect, the socialist guest became the alternative to the
communist guest. Buckley also enjoyed having ex-communists
as guests, and many were his personal friends. All of this
marked *Firing Line* as far removed from the ethos of the anticommunist crackpots. At the same time, Buckley's advocacy
of hard-line anticommunist foreign policy on *Firing Line*, his
relentless support of HUAC, and his steadfast lack of sympathy
for blacklisted Hollywood leftists marked him as a man of the
far right. Through it all he showed by example that you could
be an intellectual anticommunist. Buckley was setting a new
tone for anticommunism, illustrating that you could be anticommunist without being conspiratorial. You could be "out of
fashion" in attacking communism, yet still be awfully stylish.

Assessing how opposition to communism infused *Firing Line*
is complicated. On the one hand, the specter of Adam Smith so
thoroughly haunted the show, rattling his chains either explicitly
or implicitly, that even when a particular episode really seemed
to have *nothing* to do with support of a capitalist, unregulated
free market—Timothy Leary rhapsodizing about "The World of
LSD," Tom Wolfe sharing his thoughts on "Radical Chic," or
Hugh Hefner expounding on "The Playboy Philosophy"—one
knew that a bon mot about the demerits of collectivism and the
merits of individual achievement unfettered by governmental
interference might materialize at anytime.

On the other hand, so many of the anticommunist clichés
that permeated American media in the Cold War years were
in short supply on *Firing Line*. In the early shows Buckley was
quick to observe, a bit unfairly, that a left-wing guest obviously

"hated America," but he was rather less likely to crudely accuse a left-wing guest of being a communist or fellow traveler. While Cold War wingnuts of that era like fundamentalist radio broadcaster Carl McIntire insisted that Communist Party USA (CPUSA) leader Gus Hall was conspiring with Russia, the National Council of Churches, the Federal Communications Commission, and the United Nations to bring America to its knees, Buckley was attuned to the reality that by the late 1960s CPUSA rolls were not only thin but also heavily infiltrated with FBI agents.

Buckley made his first public foray into anticommunism some twelve years before the premiere of *Firing Line*. While he is widely remembered for his first book—*God and Man at Yale*—Buckley's second book is less often recalled today. *McCarthy and His Enemies: The Record and Its Meaning*, published in 1954 and coauthored with his brother-in-law L. Brent Bozell, offered a rigorous defense of McCarthyism, though the authors did criticize excesses of the man himself. "His conduct was sometimes objectionable . . . but his activating premise was not," they note impersonally in their prologue, absolutely avoiding the lure of psychobiography to explain why McCarthy was the man he was.[4] The book was, you might say, pro-McCarthyism without being definitively pro-McCarthy.

McCarthy and His Enemies was published the same month that Edward R. Murrow's famous anti-McCarthy *See It Now* episode aired on CBS. Murrow gave McCarthy a black eye by compiling clips revealing his cold cruelty, crude humor, and bullying ignorance. In effect, rather than cold-cocking him with his own fists, Murrow allowed McCarthy to bring *himself* down, *Fight Club*–style. As one media historian aptly puts it, "Milton Berle may have been the first superstar made by television, but Joseph McCarthy was the first superstar undone by television."[5] Offered response time, McCarthy asked CBS to allow Buckley to stand in for him. CBS said he had to speak for himself, and

McCarthy did, but rather than actually rebutting any details of the *See It Now* episode, McCarthy attacked Murrow and accused him of spreading Soviet propaganda and being a member of various "terrorist" organizations such as the Industrial Workers of the World. Much of this was twisted or simply made up. Murrow had never been in the IWW, for example. So it was easy for Murrow to rebut the senator in the next episode.

The bottom line was that McCarthy's own angry and vilifying rebuttal had confirmed much of what Murrow had shown in the initial episode. Soon thereafter, the televised Army-McCarthy hearings brought the fatal deathblow to the senator, according to popular wisdom, though the networks actually showed only excerpts from the hearings after prime time, sensing that they were not huge ratings grabbers. Running between twenty-five minutes and an hour, these excerpts were hastily edited, and at moments the sound even cut out. Viewed today, they seem remarkably sloppy, but the rawness of the footage also conveys the dire urgency of the "breaking news" story.

Buckley had sought to set the record straight about McCarthy in his 1954 book by affirming his anticommunist objectives, but McCarthy was his own worst enemy, and no book could provide sufficient ballast to compensate. As an ardent anticommunist, Buckley was a logical defender of McCarthy. At the same time, even as Buckley and the senator were in many ways ideologically aligned, McCarthy could not measure up to Buckley as a thinker. Shown the galleys of *McCarthy and His Enemies*, as a courtesy, by Buckley and Bozell, McCarthy simply couldn't get through the manuscript: "I don't understand the book. It is too intellectual for me," he told Bozell's wife (Buckley's sister), Patricia.[6]

In sum, some twelve years before *Firing Line* premiered, Buckley had established himself as an expert on anticommunism and McCarthyism, but he had written a dense thicket of a book that could not even be deciphered by its own subject. Could he hope to convey his anticommunist, conservative perspective to a general audience of TV viewers? He would start by speaking to a narrower audience of magazine readers.

One year after the release of the McCarthy book, Buckley explained in his introduction to the premiere issue of *National Review*: "We begin publishing . . . with a considerable stock of experience with the irresponsible Right, and a despair of the intransigence of the liberals, who run this country; and all this in a world dominated by the jubilant singlemindedness of the practicing Communist, with his inside track to History. All this would not appear to augur well for *National Review*. Yet we start with a considerable—and considered—optimism."[7] Naturally, the *National Review*'s masthead and contributors included former communists: converts are a particularly ardent lot, and ex-communists are likely to advocate for the free market as hardily as ex-atheists advocate for religious redemption.

In a rather charming 1982 episode of *Firing Line* in which guests Jeffrey Hart (conservative) and John Leonard (liberal) ask, "Have We Misread the '50s?," Leonard, then an editor at the *New York Times* and some years later the literary editor of the *Nation*, revisits his early days as an editorial assistant at *NR* in the 1950s (Joan Didion and Gary Wills had also been involved with the magazine in those years). He notes in particular that, while the *majority* of the magazine's editorial board did not consist of ex-communists, there was certainly a "heavy proportion of people" who had been involved in communism on an organizational and/or intellectual level. Leonard tells Buckley that "the books that you gave me to read, the books that you grew up on and I grew up on as children of the fifties, were books by people who had been communists. It would be impossible for me to understand even the romance of communism without an Arthur Koestler . . . without a Gustav Regler, without a Victor Serge. . . ."

Something about the phrase "the books that you gave me to read" resonates here. One imagines Buckley dropping a copy of Whittaker Chambers's *Witness* off on the young *National Review* initiate's desk, adding with his signature wink, "If you liked F. A. Hayek's *The Road to Serfdom* you'll love this!" Leonard would quit *NR* after a year to become a union organizer, anti–Vietnam War activist, and all-around lefty. And when Victor Navasky asked him to write a piece for his satirical "leisurely quarterly" *Monocle* (it came out twice a year) titled "Confessions of a *National Review* Contributor," Leonard took the assignment, submitting the piece in the form of a parody of Chambers's foreword to *Witness*.[8] So the books that Buckley gave Leonard to read did not exactly stick in the way Buckley must have intended.*

Still, as a young man who had "flunked out of Harvard just before it was completely fashionable to do so," as Buckley wisecracked in his 1982 *Firing Line* introduction, Leonard had studied at the feet of ardent anticommunists at *National Review*. The editorial cast may have changed over the years, but the anticommunist ethos was permanent.

National Review was a small journal of opinion pitched to a niche audience. Authors writing for the magazine knew that readers had different ideas about how best to tackle the communist menace, and about whether that threat to the United States was more an internal or an external one, but they could be confident that their readers were conservative and, by exten-

---

* One cannot imagine Buckley recoiling from Leonard's parody of his friend Chambers, if it was *good* parody. It is worth adding that Buckley himself had agreed to write for *Monocle* in the early 1960s. Journalist Murray Kempton had poked fun at Buckley, and Buckley struck back with a satirical piece written in diary form and centering on "two weeks in the life of Murray Kempton" (Navasky, interview with the author, May 4, 2012). As Buckley liked to say with some glee when a particularly good retort was made on *Firing Line*, "Put that in your pipe and smoke it!"

sion, anticommunist. Television, by contrast, was a mass medium: unlike the narrowly targeted *National Review*, the whole point of *Firing Line* was to speak to a wider audience of both liberals and conservatives. Buckley may have disagreed with liberals about virtually everything, but he judged them *particularly* naïve about communism.

Firing Line featured avowed progressives, ex-communists, socialists, and other radicals in order to debate ideas, not to victimize in the McCarthy mode. This meant, for one thing, avoiding excessive vilification of trade unions. Or, to be more precise, avoiding the stigmatizing of trade unions as inherently communistic in orientation. *Firing Line*'s host disagreed with every single perspective put forth by James B. Carey of the AFL-CIO on "Labor Unions and American Freedom" (1969), but Carey was an exemplary citizen on one front: when the United Electrical Workers union had been taken over by communists and other radicals, Carey had fought them, and when that failed, he had cofounded the International Union of Electrical Workers, which grew to a membership of 300,000, even as the membership of the more radical union had dropped to 50,000. From Buckley's perspective, Carey was wrong about pretty much everything except the dangers of communist agitators.

He had more patience with newspaperman Victor Riesel—who appeared in 1966 to answer the question "Should Labor Power Be Reduced?"—even though Riesel fully approved of the right to strike and was rather nonplussed by the notion that one should be put out by inconveniences caused by striking workers. Their debate was lively and revealed not only Buckley's skepticism about the minimum wage, mandatory union membership, and the right to strike but also his opposition to monopolies. Further, it showed how much more *fun* journalists could be on the show than politicians, who tended to be extremely image conscious and, therefore, potentially dull. Riesel had nothing to lose by letting his sense of humor and ink-stained wretchedness show.

> RIESEL: . . . we have a stalwart ally in fighting the mob in [AFL-CIO president] George Meany. We have—

> BUCKLEY: Mr. Riesel, you're really suggesting that it's metaphysically impossible to pass a series of laws seeking to control labor unions in the same way that big businesses were controlled. Would you, in 1890, in arguing with somebody who wanted to control the big monopoly companies, tell them that it was impossible to do so, that they have to go into another world and address themselves to this crusade?

> RIESEL: Bill, the whole business of using the word *metaphysical* with George Meany has so discombobulated me, I'm going to have to recollect all my thoughts. But, no, seriously, the fact is that when you're talking about new laws, I mean the Sherman Act, the Clayton Act, antitrust and all that, we're talking—you're going back eighty-five years to an era when, true, I mean, the robber baron had the power, the huge tycoon, businessmen, vast railroads, etc. Sure, you have a parallel now, there's enormous industrial power in the trade union movement, but we have *laws* and I say enforce the laws. . . .

> BUCKLEY: What laws are there that could've done something to save the nation from the nationwide airplane strike last summer?

> RIESEL: Well, you know, that always amuses me, I remember we had a ball, Bill [during the airline strike]. We would get on a train and we would get to Chicago at three o'clock, you know, at nine o'clock we'd go to the Ambassador East, and if you'll forgive me, we had an extra drink or two, or three or five at the Pump Room, and then we'd pour ourselves back down and we'd go across to Los Angeles, and, you know, we covered

great stories. The motion picture industry survived, California grew, I didn't know there was any great crisis in the airline strike. But where I say you should have used presidential emergency powers [to shut down a strike] was when the same machinist union struck a ball powder [artillery] plant. The same machinist union struck the McDonnell Aircraft, and ended the production for a while of the wing sweptback Phantom jets. And so on. So that you have to be able to draw a line, not at the strike of the airplanes, but where the health, the welfare, and the security of the land is involved, and you have those laws [covering that contingency]. . . .

BUCKLEY: Well, Mr. Riesel, one man's inconvenience can be another man's necessity. As I understand it, your advice is to simply head for a bar the next time the labor union inconveniences you and wait there until it's all over. In this case this would have been quite a binge, thirty-three or four days in the bar. This, I think, probably outclasses Marie Antoinette's suggestion of what to do under certain kinds of inconveniences. . . .

RIESEL: I'm sure there'll be so many violent protests from your millions of viewers about my suggestion that somebody take four drinks at the Pump Room.

BUCKLEY: No, I think it's a very good idea, and every time I think of George Meany that's exactly what I'm driven to do.

RIESEL: Just think of the effect you have on *him*. . . .

Tippling aside, Riesel's specialty was ferreting out union corruption, and Buckley approved of anyone willing to take some heat from the Teamsters. With just a few seconds left in the program, Buckley asked Riesel if there was "still a racketeering problem, or for that matter, a communist problem in the labor unions." Riesel responded: "Well, for the most part, the communist problem I think has been wiped out, except for one union in the West, but as for organized crime, that's not just a television [drama] scenario. The Mafia, or the Cosa Nostra, call it what you will, is there, it's still on some sections on the waterfront, it's still hovering around . . . and I think that the AF of L, CIO would do well to revive its ethical practices committee and once more look into it. . . ."

This was an issue Riesel had reported on for years. Indeed, ten years earlier a gangster had retaliated by throwing acid in his face, permanently blinding him. It is telling that Buckley tacked on the communism question at the end, just as the announcer said they were out of time. It was an important issue to acknowledge, but Buckley had no illusions that American unions were a vast Marxist conspiracy, even if some of their attempts to improve wages amounted to "redistribution" (a socialistic if not communistic impulse) in his considered opinion.

Of course, Buckley approved of right-to-work laws. He claimed not to disapprove of trade unions across the board, in principle, but he generally felt that they promoted exactly the wrong policies. Demanding raises, for example, could work, but it could also put companies out of business, so that while some workers might enjoy a higher income, others would find themselves unemployed. In short, he considered himself to be rooting for labor insofar as he saw unions as tamping down individual freedoms of laborers—forcing them to join unions and pay dues, requiring them to produce certain amounts of goods (no more, no less), and discouraging individualism in favor of collectivism. If he saw as positive the historical roots of unionism in the fight against monopolistic exploitation at the turn of the century, he also felt that by the postwar years unions had gained so much power that they were the exploiter rather than the exploited. Overall, as one might expect from a wealthy and successful conservative, the scales of his empathy tilted toward management more than labor. And let us not forget that, as the editor of *National Review*, Buckley *was* management.

In a gently comic turn of events, however, he found himself considered *labor* as a performer on *Firing Line*. In 1966 he had told Riesel, "I belong to two labor unions, one I was forced into, otherwise all the lights would turn off here and bombs would explode and sand would go into the machine, or whatever." The union whose revenge he anticipated was the American Federation of Television and Radio Artists (AFTRA). And he was *very* cranky about his forced membership. (His voluntary membership was in the Authors League, and with that he was pleased: "They tell me how to sue my publishers, give me lots of good technical advice.") RKO, who produced *Firing Line* until it moved to PBS in 1971, had a contract with AFTRA requiring all of its film and TV employees to join the union. Naturally, Buckley dropped his membership when he parted ways with RKO.

Trouble began brewing shortly thereafter. As Buckley tells it, he was exiting a TV studio in 1972 after appearing on *The Merv Griffin Show* when he was approached by "a man in his forties, rather seedy in appearance and just a little menacing in manner" who told him that unless he joined AFTRA he "would be prohibited from appearing on television." Buckley filed a lawsuit (even receiving support from the American Civil Liberties Union) and finally won in 1978, insofar as a court of appeals ruled that "anyone regularly appearing on TV had to pay AFTRA dues" but did not have "to join AFTRA or to obey its instructions." AFTRA could not punish Buckley for crossing a picket line, for example, and could not order him to strike.[9] AFTRA saw themselves as winning because the US Supreme Court had declined to review the case in 1974. Now, it had been the case all along that, according to the law, entertainment workers did not *have* to join AFTRA; the problem was that AFTRA did not choose to share this fact, preferring to tell everyone that they had to join, though presumably not sending out seedy men in trench coats to track down all malfeasants.[10]

Notably, Buckley resented AFTRA's impingement on his individual rights, but his response to their activities reads much more as libertarian than anticommunist in tone.

Similarly, he would deflect any "extremist" Cold War anticommunist inflection from *Firing Line* by inviting socialist guests such as Norman Thomas and Michael Harrington, who were, you might say, "light communists." Tellingly, the episodes with Thomas and Harrington were the first and second aired in 1966—he was not starting out with softball guests! Buckley could debate the pros and cons of the free market with these two without the specter of the CPUSA and a looming conspiracy to overthrow the US government hanging heavily over proceedings. The 1966 Thomas episode, as we have seen, is purely hostile, with Thomas (who had run for president six times on the Socialist Party ticket) enraged by Buckley's support of the Vietnam War.

The second episode of *Firing Line* featured Harrington—who would cofound the Democratic Socialists of America in 1982—making an even-tempered argument for the federal government's War on Poverty. Buckley insists that there is suffering and psychological despair at all income levels and that the government's poverty program doesn't get at the metaphysical roots of unhappiness: "You may very well find, after you have run out of any complaints about the nutritional dereliction of any members of the American society, that you will walk into an unhappier society than ever existed before." The subtext here is that Harrington, whose book *The Other America* had provided motivation for Johnson's War on Poverty, is not only a socialist but also, more specifically, an *atheist*. In light of his aspiritual worldview, any action Harrington would advocate to improve people's lives, such as ending hunger, cannot, from Buckley's perspective, be considered sufficient.

Still, Harrington ends with a rhetorically strong rebuttal: "There is a profound psychological problem among the poor.

That's one of the terrible things about being poor. But not having enough to eat, living in a miserable tenement in Harlem or in Watts . . . these things, although they cause psychic misery, are not psychological. And these are the proper objects of federal and government policy. And I think, if we can get at them, then after people have something to eat, they can start to think about being happy." Buckley gives his all to discrediting Harrington's ideas, but Harrington's very basic arguments about the need to alleviate hunger and about the difficulties in major cities caused by a lower tax base produced by suburbanization (white flight) are powerful. Where Thomas's hostility had been alarming, Harrington's levelheadedness blunts the radical socialist edge that Buckley might have wished to reveal. The image of the socialist is done no harm here, though no love is lost between host and guest.

In a memorial episode twenty-three years later, Buckley pointed to Harrington, who had appeared on *Firing Line* four times, as "a marvelous example . . . of the extent to which the rhetoric of social gentility tends to help the left-winger. He reaches to Adam Smith for a quote that says, in effect, even the father of modern conservatism can care for people." Here Buckley conveys that he is taken with Harrington because he is rhetorically canny. He immediately adds, to set the record straight, "conservatives have never, I think, said that people should not care for other people, with the possible exception of Ayn Rand, with her war on altruism." As a dedicated socialist, Harrington rubbed Buckley the wrong way, but he liked having him on the show because he was, Buckley said, "a formidable polemicist."[11] Harrington had enabled Buckley to set the anticommunist tone that he was searching for; he could use the socialist guest to attack collectivist ideas, without tapping into "Red Scare" paranoia.

Notably, over *Firing Line*'s thirty-three-year run, Buckley ran only five memorial episodes devoted to favorite guests who had passed away. That he paid tribute to fellow conservatives Clare Boothe Luce, Barry Goldwater, and Malcolm Muggeridge comes as no surprise, but the episodes devoted to the socialist Harrington and the liberal Democrat Allard Lowenstein tug at the heartstrings in a different way, indicating as they do the kinds of relationships that can exist as bridges across massive political differences.

Lowenstein, who appeared nine times on *Firing Line*, had begun his life in politics by serving as a congressional aide in the 1950s. (It was in this role that he met his good friend Donald Rumsfeld.) He had been active in the civil rights movement, traveling to Mississippi during the "Freedom Summer" of 1964. As a vocal opponent of the Vietnam War, Lowenstein was probably best known as the man behind the "Dump Johnson" movement, a campaign that was at least in part responsible for LBJ's decision not to run for reelection in 1968. Lowenstein had served one term in the House of Representatives, from 1969 to 1971. Like Harrington, Lowenstein was on Nixon's "Enemies" list. (Harrington once said, "I was in good company. It would have been terrible to be left off it."[12]) Lowenstein was a left-wing Democrat committed to working within the system, and Buckley was particularly devoted to him.

In the context of *Firing Line*'s advocacy of opposition to communism, our particular interest here, Lowenstein stands out as one of the strongly anticommunist liberals who repeatedly appeared on the show. As Buckley observed years later, "on one matter, Lowenstein was not typical: His opposition to the Soviet Union was always explicit and unbending."[13] Buckley's affection for Lowenstein reached new heights in 1977 when, as he later recounted, "Lowenstein was made the American delegate to the Human Rights Commission of the United Nations, which meets every year in Geneva. For the first time in the twenty-five year history of that commission—thanks to Allard Lowenstein—there was public US criticism of the suppression

of human rights in the Soviet Union; specifically of persecu-
tion of dissidents."[14] Buckley himself had been a UN delegate
in 1973, and like Lowenstein had found the experience of trying
to address human rights issues in that venue frustrating. In his
book on the experience, Buckley went so far as to describe his
aspirations heading into the UN experience as "pure, undiluted
Walter Mittyism."[15]

Lowenstein was shot down in 1980 by a deranged assassin. Buckley noted in his book on *Firing Line* that both Bobby
and Teddy Kennedy had declined to appear on *Firing Line*. But
Teddy delivered a eulogy at Lowenstein's funeral service, and it
would be aired shortly thereafter in the opening moments of
"Allard Lowenstein on *Firing Line*: A Retrospective." The show
is jarring, as well it should be. It opens with no music or titles,
at the funeral, showing Kennedy from overhead, shot with a
single camera held by a not altogether steady hand. Kennedy
opens by referencing Lowenstein's pro–civil rights and anti–
Vietnam War activism, and then praising his taking a stand in
the UN regarding Soviet political prisoners.

We then cut to Buckley—a month later—atypically alone
in the *Firing Line* studio, introducing clips from all of Lowenstein's appearances on the show. We see Lowenstein agree
with Buckley about the death penalty, disagree about the Equal
Rights Amendment, agree about human rights issues, disagree
about Eugene McCarthy, and so on. Finally, we cut back to the
memorial service, where Buckley delivers his own eulogy, and
then singer Harry Chapin performs. Chapin was best known
for "Cat's in the Cradle," but here he performs "Circle." The
show closes out with this song rather than the familiar strains
of Bach with which it normally ends.

Another archliberal Buckley favorite was Murray Kempton.
Kempton was more eloquent on the page than on TV, but he
appeared on five *Firing Line* episodes because Buckley liked
him. He had a sharp sense of humor, a taste for neat suits, and

a gentlemanly demeanor. Plus, he could write the hell out of a sentence.* ("We are all addicts in various stages of degradation where I live on the Upper West Side, some to heroin, some to small dogs, and some to the *New York Times*. The heroin is cut, the dogs are paranoid, and the *Times* cheats by skimping on the West Coast ball scores. No matter; each of us goes upon the street solely in pursuit of his own particular curse."[16]) Kempton had at one time been a communist, and then a member of the Socialist Party, at that time under the leadership of Norman Thomas. By the time *Firing Line* appeared on the scene, he technically fit in the "ex-communist" category, a well from which Buckley had drawn many friends, and *Firing Line* guests, over the years.

Underplaying his youthful political convictions, Kempton would later recount, "I didn't read anything closely in those days [the 1930s] except Lenin and Trotsky. Ahhh, well. You read that shit for absolute truth. But I suppose my Marxism-Leninism was an affectation, like everything else."[17] Buckley described Kempton fondly as a "socialist—sworn enemy of all anticommunist legislation, sworn friend of militant unionism" and "the finest writer in the newspaper profession . . . a great artist and a great friend."[18] Kempton's last book contained this dedication: "For William F. Buckley, Jr., genius at friendships that surpass all understanding."

The multiple appearances of a single exemplary guest—John Kenneth Galbraith—perhaps best convey the timbre of Buckley's interactions with the socialist-but-not-communist *Firing Line* guests who were his ideological foes but personal favorites. Galbraith was an ultraliberal Harvard economist, a

---

* Kempton also had a talent for *over*writing, to such an extent that he once won a libel suit that had been brought against him when the court ruled, in effect, that the offending prose had been so confusing that the charge could not be substantiated.

long-standing friend of Buckley, a wit, and, apparently, a very poor skier. Buckley once characterized the lanky and clunky Galbraith on skis as "like Charles De Gaulle, in an elevator."[19] And Galbraith once blurbed one of Buckley's novels with these kind words: "Mr. Buckley has a great talent for fiction, as readers of his columns know."[20]

An ardent Keynesian and critic of advertising, of the power of large corporations, and of the selfishness of the wealthy, Galbraith could not have been more politically opposed to Buckley. In 1981's "John Kenneth Galbraith Looks Back," Buckley's guest described Reaganomics and the whole notion that the poor would benefit from tax cuts to the wealthy ("trickle-down economics") thusly: "if you feed enough oats to the horses, there will be some left over on the road for the sparrows." Buckley, of course, favored tax breaks for the affluent and thought Milton Friedman was the bee's knees. Interviewed for the 60 Minutes profile of Buckley, which aired two days before Reagan's first inauguration, Galbraith noted lightly that "he's as good at taking it as he is at giving it." In brief, these two did not seem to agree on anything except that it was terribly fun to insult each other.

Galbraith and Buckley's first major media co-appearance was at a Cambridge Union debate in 1970, which was crewed in part by *Firing Line* staff and aired on WNET, the New York City educational station.[21] Buckley's previous Cambridge debate had been the one he had lost to James Baldwin five years earlier, and he was clearly determined to seize the day this time around. The 1970 debate topic was: "Resolved: The Market Is a Snare and a Delusion."

Now, the debate with Baldwin had had some real meat to it, but the Cambridge house style was flexible: sometimes there was less emphasis on heavy argumentation than on clever put-downs. Galbraith opens at Cambridge with a light volley, noting that Buckley is "the editor of an excellent journal. It is perhaps the only conservative journal in what has until recently been referred to as the free world which has some semblance of a sense of humor. It has always been a matter of great regret to me that it doesn't have readers." This draws a good chuckle from the audience. The heaviest point he makes is that a putative conservative (Nixon) is finally in the White House but has done very little to create the kind of unregulated market that Buckley desires.

Buckley speaks next, sporting double cowlicks, his bow tie askew. (Both gentlemen are in tuxedos.) He points out that Congress is dominated by Democrats, so Nixon cannot simply do whatever he wants. Retaliating against Galbraith's belief that corporations control the market, Buckley runs through the tumbling stock offerings of numerous companies that once seemed invincible. It being acceptable for the audience to occasionally cut in during these formal presentations, an unidentified, striking young woman in a long white satin gown and impressive beaded belt asks a muddled question in a heavy Greek accent: is Buckley using the stock market to prove his argument because he has "failed to prove his argument in all other markets"? Buckley responds, "Madame, I don't know what markets you patronize," drawing wild applause. (Arianna Stassinopoulos is among the minority who finally vote for Galbraith; she would have better luck as a debater when she next appeared on *Firing Line* twenty-four years later, now as Arianna Huffington.)

Buckley allows that Galbraith has no "totalitarian instincts" and that "he believes that dissent has its place, properly situated and properly modulated. But there is one thing about the free marketplace that he has never been able to understand, and that is that it is a mechanism by which people can come to conclusions different from his own." Buckley wins handily, the vote being 200 to 118, with 45 abstentions.

When Galbraith was a guest on *Firing Line* proper (he ap-

peared fifteen times), the one-upmanship was relentless. Remember those *Dean Martin Celebrity Roasts*, where panelists
on a dais—Phyllis Diller, Don Rickles—rose to the mic to hurl
comic insults at the honoree, and everyone seemed tanked on
bourbon? It was fast, improvisational, fun, and occasionally
disturbing in its viciousness. Galbraith and Buckley together
on *Firing Line* were like that, but with more brain power and
(usually) without the booze. Galbraith declines the socialist
label, even as Buckley relentlessly pins it on him. Galbraith
insists that Buckley is derailing discussion with overwrought
metaphors and digressions. Buckley says that "digression is
your synonym for confutation." At one point in a 1996 episode
about Galbraith's newest book, *The Good Society*, Galbraith
asks, "You would not like to live on the minimum wage, would
you?" To which Buckley retorts, "Well, I wouldn't like to have
syphilis, either."

The astounded Galbraith asks what the connection is between syphilis and the minimum wage; Buckley's point is that
whether or not one "likes" the minimum wage is irrelevant. "It's
a bad economic idea," Buckley states, having long maintained
that economists oppose it and that it causes unemployment.
Galbraith states that "in all probability the higher minimum
wage and the higher purchasing power that goes with it adds
employment in the system, and that squeezing wages down to
below a starvation level does not influence the aggregate flow of
demand in the economy. I'm sorry to be slightly technical here,
Bill, but—" Buckley interrupts to say, "You're not being very
technical, you're being very rhetorical. We're not talking about
starving people."

The economic debate rolls on, with Buckley predictably arguing for an unfettered free market and Galbraith arguing for
increased taxes on the wealthy, his goal being "to equalize or improve the equality of income distribution." As always, Galbraith
avoids the straight-up communist line; he sees capitalism as

cruelly Darwinian, but he is looking to manage and regulate its excesses, not eliminate it. (He had elsewhere quipped: "Under capitalism man exploits man. And under communism it's just the reverse."[22]) Things get quite warm, but they turn white hot when Buckley incredulously quotes Galbraith as writing, "In the years of communism, it is not clear that one would wisely have exchanged the restraints on freedom of the resident of East Berlin for those imposed by poverty in the South Bronx of New York." Galbraith counters that he was being deliberately provocative by suggesting that a person facing extreme poverty and racial discrimination in the United States might be better off in "a more fortunate country in Europe."

If this were a Tex Avery cartoon, steam would be shooting out of Buckley's ears at this point. Time is up, but Galbraith slips in one last put-down: "Bill, you're the living expression of my greatest need, and that is to make patently true points patently obvious. Otherwise, I lose you. I sometimes lose you anyway." At this, Buckley grins like a Cheshire Cat.

Only a handful of guests dared to call Buckley "Bill" on the show, as it violated the show's formality, especially in its first two decades. (Theodore White pulled it off with particular charm and affability, and in a light unguarded moment Buckley even called him "Teddy.") First names were used on *interview* shows, a key element of their phony banter. Looking back in 1999 as the series neared expiration, Buckley recalled his dismay when an audience member had asked Woodward and Bernstein how fame had changed their lives. "Save it for Mike Douglas!" he might have shouted, if he had actually known who Mike Douglas was.

"No interview questions," he proclaimed, was the *sine qua non* of *Firing Line*. First names were similarly discouraged, though they crept in here and there. How discombobulating it had been in 1967 when Groucho—whom Buckley preferred to call "Mr. Marx"—asked if he could address Buckley as "Willy," adding, "It was good enough for Somerset Maugham." Buckley responded, rather uncharitably, "I wouldn't want you to start being polite on my show." Yet Galbraith had the nerve to address his host informally over and over again. As much as Galbraith's "Bill"—delivered with the lilt of the scolding schoolmarm—pushed against the *Firing Line* rules, it also added to the fun of observing Galbraith and Buckley go at it like an old married couple, offering viewers a sort of Mensa Punch-and-Judy show. If they were good at getting a rise out of one another on TV, it was because they had spent so much time together when the cameras were not rolling.

At a 1978 *Firing Line* debate hosted by Pepperdine University ("Resolved: That the Price of Oil and Natural Gas Should be Regulated by the Federal Government"), Buckley deviates from form by opening with a *personal* story about Galbraith as a teenager: "John Kenneth accompanied a lovely young girl of a literal turn of mind out into the Canadian pastures, where he paused to observe a bull serving a young cow. 'I think it would be fun to do that,' said John Kenneth. His girlfriend replied matter-of-factly, 'Well, go ahead. It's your cow.' For years we've been trying to remind Professor Galbraith that America is our cow. To no avail, he persists in serving us."

Phew, it was just a joke! This is as blue as Buckley ever got on *Firing Line*, and one has to imagine that it was a result of, first, his inspiration to really tear down his old friend for his endless advocacy of tampering with the free market (Galbraith is right on track in this episode, however, insofar as he notes that it is a bit late to simply stop regulating oil prices), and, second, the fact that this Pepperdine event is a black-tie fundraiser, and by the time they rise to the podium to entertain the crowd, Buckley and Galbraith have not only eaten heavily but have also indulged, one presumes, in a bit of drink.

The old pros are smooth as always, but slightly lubricated. The audience laps it all up, though one critical, very liberal question comes from the eminent historian Ariel Durant, who asks, "Mr. Buckley, in the history of the human race, reliance upon the accidental workings of the free marketplace has done little to mitigate the suffering caused by gross human inequality. What does your position say to the poor, the hungry, the homeless, and the despairing?" To which Buckley answers, "Mrs. Durant, as an admirer of your seventeen books, I hope you will go on to write an eighteenth in which you will record that the greatest benefactions ever performed for the poor and for the hungry have been in those societies that have encouraged the free economic enterprise of human beings." Durant probably found little satisfaction in this decorous-yet-contrarian response, but the crowd of wealthy donors applauds rigorously. She may have been the only one besides Galbraith in the swank crowd who was really amenable to the notion that there was anything not to like about the notion of an unfettered free market.

Our disputatious gents conclude the debate with one last sparring match. The Pepperdine president and debate moderator tells Galbraith he has seven minutes to cross-examine Mr. Buckley.

GALBRAITH: Well, I shall make my questions appropriately brief. My first is whether, Bill, you would be willing to join with me to bring Adam Smith back to the next meeting of the Pepperdine Associates [crowd laughter]—under appropriate circumstances, Mr. President—to explain and affirm a point that I think would be met both by you and some of the audience with some discontent: namely, his feeling that a world in which corporations, or "joint stock companies" as he [Smith] called them, existed would be inconsistent with his system, and that they should be prohibited, and to allow him to express his concern over one in which the development of these great private planning organizations, which he would have excluded, whether he would not feel that these had destroyed his system?

BUCKLEY: The questions that Adam Smith raised about private stock companies had to do with the regulation by that mechanism—it seems to me that if Adam Smith were here today he would be satisfied by the rise and fall of great industries that sought to frustrate the consumer—[by that mechanism] that, in fact, the consumer exercises, and continues to exercise, that leverage that justifies the laissez-faire with which Adam Smith is identified. I would remind you that most of the mammoth corporations you pointed to in one of your books as dominating us as though we were mere puppets are either at this point bankrupt or living off the government.

GALBRAITH: Could I pursue that point and ask which?

BUCKLEY: Well, I exaggerated a little bit. [crowd laughter] The thesis of one of Mr. Galbraith's books was that the huge companies in America have become so important, so vital, and so domineering, that in fact they can regulate their own worth by causing people, for instance, to consume their products, by causing the legislature to pass congenial laws and so on and so forth. Unhappily, his book was published just when the market slid the value of most of these corporations by about eighty-five percent, but this is a datum that Mr. Galbraith, with characteristic savoir faire, has simply transcended. [crowd laughter]

GALBRAITH: I certainly don't want to suggest that Mr. Buckley ever exaggerates. [crowd laughter] What year was it that the market declined by eighty-five percent?

BUCKLEY: No, some of the companies that you mentioned. As a matter of fact, I think Litton Industries was one of them, wasn't it?

GALBRAITH: Was that an exaggeration? What?

BUCKLEY: I think Litton Industries was one of them. One of those radio companies was one of them, too. I had a long list. In fact, I recited it to you at Cambridge on one occasion [referencing the 1970 debate that Galbraith lost].

GALBRAITH: Oh, but you said the stock market in general.

BUCKLEY: What's that?

GALBRAITH: Oh, I certainly allow for—

BUCKLEY: Well, the stock market in general went down forty to fifty percent in the most recent—

GALBRAITH: I certainly allow for exceptions, but I dined earlier this evening with [Litton CEO] Mr. Tex Thornton, and I didn't ask him, but I could see from the charmed look on his face that Litton Industries has recovered from that temporary misfortune. [crowd laughter]

BUCKLEY: Coincidental with your book going out of print. [crowd laughter]

GALBRAITH: One of the marvelous good fortunes of being an author that I share with William Buckley—there are some things that we do have in common—is that authors, unlike automobile companies, are not yet required to recall their defective works. [crowd laughter and applause] The difference between us is that I have this inner sense of security coming from a long record of valid interpretation which allows me to make confessions of that sort, and Bill does not. Am I supposed to pursue these questions further, Mr. Chairman?

MODERATOR: You have two more minutes, Mr. Galbraith.

GALBRAITH: Oh, I have lots more. Bill, where did you get those figures on the elasticity of demand? Is that another exaggeration?

BUCKLEY: I got them from a study published by your colleagues in Harvard.

GALBRAITH: It's not an absolute assurance of accuracy. [crowd laughter and applause]

BUCKLEY: Are you referring to your former students? [Bam!]

Buckley punctuates this last comeback by grinning from ear to ear. Talk about singing for your supper. Messrs. Galbraith and Buckley exhibit impeccable timing, laughing at each other's punch lines as much as they laugh at their own. This was all catnip to the Pepperdine crowd decked out in formal wear, seated at banquet tables, with waiters occasionally weaving in and out—quite a break from the usual *Firing Line* studio audience of Catholic high school boys imported from Yonkers.

We know from his introductory comments at the 1970 Cambridge debate that Buckley did not see Galbraith as patently "totalitarian" in inclination. Indeed, it is hard to imagine Buckley debating a genuine Stalinist. With his radical ideas about curbing corporate power, Galbraith would have to stand in for the militant communist hard-liners. Where then did explicitly anticommunist sentiment most prominently reside on *Firing Line*? The anticommunist line may have subtly underpinned most episodes, at least through the 1980s, but we see it most clearly and overtly in episodes focused on foreign affairs and on HUAC and the blacklist. Let's start with foreign affairs.

Over and over again on *Firing Line*, Buckley alludes to the horrors of Stalin's Gulag and Mao's atrocities, with such references serving as trump cards to rebut liberal criticisms of US anticommunist policy. Thus, when Noam Chomsky appears on the show in 1969 and argues, in effect, that America is not helping other countries, such as Vietnam and Greece, but rather imposing its will on them in an imperialistic manner, Buckley loses his cool and insists on the horrors abroad. The discussants find no common

Noam Chomsky appears in 1969 and calmly argues that America is
not helping other countries, such as Vietnam and Greece, but rather
imposing its will on them in an imperialistic manner; Buckley loses
his cool and insists on the horrors of communism abroad.
CREDIT: *Hoover Institution*

ground. Chomsky comes out ahead insofar as he calmly sticks to
his guns, arguing for the immorality of even arguing about Vietnam (it's rather like arguing about Auschwitz to his mind, as it is
a military engagement so patently wrong), aptly conveying a leftist
critique of the Truman Doctrine, and opposing both violence and
imperialism on all sides, not just on the communist side.* A short
excerpt conveys the tenor of the conversation.

  BUCKLEY: The grand fact of the postwar world is that the
  communists, the communist imperialists, by the use of

----

* Almost fifty years later Chomsky vividly recalled that "by the end Buckley
was pretty angry. When the program ended he was in a fury, stormed off
the set, and as he left shouted at me that he'd have me back again and teach
me a thing or two. I said something polite, which seemed to anger him
even more. Naturally, I never heard from him again" (email to the author,
June 19, 2014).

terrorism, by the use of, by deprivation of freedom, have contributed to the continuing bloodshed, and the sad thing about it is not only the bloodshed but the fact that they seem to dispossess you of the power of rationalization.

CHOMSKY: May I say something?

BUCKLEY: Sure.

CHOMSKY: I think that's about five percent true. And about or maybe ten percent true. It certainly is—

BUCKLEY: Why do you give that?

CHOMSKY: May I complete a sentence?

BUCKLEY: Sure.

CHOMSKY: It's perfectly true that there were areas of the world, and in particular Eastern Europe, where Stalinist imperialism very brutally took control and still maintains control. But there are also very vast areas of the world where we were doing the same thing. And there's quite an interplay in the Cold War. You see they, what you just described is I believe a mythology about the Cold War, which might have been tenable ten years ago, but which is quite inconsistent with contemporary scholars—

BUCKLEY: Ask a Czech.

CHOMSKY: Ask a Guatemalan, ask a Dominican, ask the president of the Dominican Republic, ask, you know, ask a person from South Vietnam, ask a—

BUCKLEY: Well, I would say, if you can't distinguish between the nature of our venture in Guatemala and the nature of the Soviet Union's in Prague, then we have real difficulty.

It's golden age Chomsky and well worth watching today. For his part, Buckley scores points insofar as several of the facts he states and that Chomsky disputes are now so clearly not a matter of opinion. For example, Chomsky acknowledges repression and authoritarianism in China but also notes that "one has to recognize a great deal of spontaneous democratic structure of a sort which never existed in Asia before and . . . doesn't even exist in our society" and that "starvation has been very largely overcome in China." We now know that Mao induced a famine that wiped out some 36–45 million of his own people.

To Buckley's horror, as the American left became increasingly disaffected by Soviet communism in the 1960s it was concomitantly drawn to the ideas of Mao Zedong, Che Guevara, and Fidel Castro. When Huey P. Newton appeared on *Firing Line* in 1973, he was eager to talk about his trip to China and to share what he had learned about the dialectical approach to revolution and social progress. Early in the conversation, which rather quickly veered toward soliloquy, Newton declared, "I think that one of my principles is that contradiction is the ruling principle of the universe and phenomena, whether it's the physical world or the biological world or the social world, [they] have this internal contradiction that gives motion to things, that internal strain. Much of the time we *Homo sapiens* don't realize that no matter what sort of conditions we establish at this point, there also will be that internal contradiction that will have to be resolved and resolved in a rational and just way."

Buckley clearly thought this was nonsense, and he declared that he understood none of it, but he let Newton have his say. It's a rather interesting moment in that we can be certain that Buckley did understand the notion of Marxist dialectics. The problem, however, was not strictly an ideological one. It was also stylistic. When Newton talked, one simply could not cut in, which was antithetical to Buckley's notion of political conversation.

Finding that he could not rein in Newton discursively, Buckley finally more or less threw in the towel, putting down his clipboard and giving up on the idea that Newton would say anything he judged coherent. Interestingly, during the Q&A toward the end of the show, it is clear that the crowd is completely with Newton. One Mr. Sinkin, from Trinity College, responds to Buckley's befuddlement by telling Newton, "I thought what you said was quite clear in the concepts you were exploring." Newton jokes, "Well, it seems that Mr. Buckley is the only dunce around here, so far. I'm only kidding."

Asked by Sinkin about social policies in the American inner city, Newton observes that ethnic minorities in China have community control. Asked, then, about Tibet by Buckley, Newton first says they too are self-governed. "Genocide?" Buckley responds. Newton then acknowledges that if the Chinese did wrong by the people of Tibet, they are no worse than citizens of the Western world, with their genocide of blacks. Asked about the Cultural Revolution by Buckley, Newton redirects to the issue of community control and notes that "the ethnic minorities I observed [on the China visit] control their whole thing and they have a right to have a representative on the Chinese Communist Party. . . . You cannot in China vote to organize an opposition to reinstate private ownership, any more than you can here organize an opposition to take away private ownership in this country. So, it's what do you choose? I happen to choose the way they go about it, all right?" To this, Buckley gets a laugh from the audience by sarcastically intoning, "Thank you, Mr. Sinkin, for eliciting a lucid reply to the problems of the inner city." Newton is earnest, charming, and endlessly frustrating in his insistence that everything is going *great* in China.

Theodore White offers a quite different, compelling articulation of the liberal understanding of China in his 1978 appearance to discuss "What Should Our China Policy Be?" White is today best remembered for his "Making of the President" books, centered on the elections of 1960, 1964, and 1968. But he began his career as a Sinologist, and his first book, in 1946, was the bestselling *Thunder Out of China*, which was very critical of the Chinese Nationalist Party and Chiang Kai-shek. This was not precisely the same thing as being procommunist, but the bottom line was that White could see why those suffering in China as it was under Chiang would look for alternatives. In his 1986 *National Review* obituary, Buckley wrote, "Theodore H. White made one grave strategic mistake in his journalistic lifetime. Like so many disgusted with Chiang Kai-shek, he imputed to the opposition to Chiang thaumaturgical social and political powers. He overrated the revolutionists' ideals, and underrated their capacity for totalitarian sadism."[23]

White admitted as much on the 1978 *Firing Line* episode, though he fleshed out the story, too, showing how and why the communist revolutionaries were so appealing to him as a young man in China in the 1930s and '40s. How charming Chou En-lai was, how festive the Saturday night dances (harmonicas blowing, drums thumping) at communist headquarters in Yenan were: "To see these men in that lyrical period when they were the underdogs, when they were fighting the Japanese, when they were behind the Japanese lines and risking their lives every day, to see their comradeship and their brilliance and their camaraderie, was to be carried away by it." He later understood that he was wrong, looking back and seeing how many of those comrades had been purged, their throats cut by their compatriots.

As Buckley noted in his obituary, White learned twenty-six years after writing *Thunder Out of China* that "the nature of the thunder that had hit China was not exuberant, rather it was convulsive. As was his custom, he integrated his new knowledge into his writing, and all his readers profited from the quality of revised insights."[24] Buckley's respect for White is obvious; he offers his highest praise for a humility and ability for self-reflection that we should all strive for. Faced with proof that we are wrong about something we are really sure about, how many of us could, like White, concede as much, revise our insights, and successfully move forward?

Still, in 1978, even as White rejected the horrors of Communist China on *Firing Line*, he remained adamant about the horrors of pre-communist China. White had broken the story of the Henan Famine of 1942–43, and he had never quite recovered from what he had seen: "babies clutching dead mothers . . . cannibalism and dogs eating bodies on the road." Thirty-five years later on *Firing Line*, White suggested that it would be productive for the United States to have a "cordial relationship with Red China." Buckley strongly disagreed.

This episode is riveting in large part because White is an animated storyteller. He brings passion to his disagreements with Buckley, but not animosity. The two had first met when White interviewed him during the 1965 mayoral campaign. They quickly hit it off, and White followed up with a letter in which he despaired of having taken too few notes as the wine consumed over their lunch did its work. He concludes that "if you're dealing with a man of goodwill, then, no matter how much you disagree with him, and [*sic*] can develop and must seek a continuing relationship. Basically, that was my purpose in our meeting and thus, however meager my notes, it was a good meeting."[25]

That these men of goodwill liked each other was clear— White smiles elfishly as Buckley pronounces his generous introduction at the beginning of the 1978 program—and this makes their disputatious exchange about China all the more engaging. White is critical of China, but also a confirmed liberal. Having seen others on the left, like Newton, unwilling to tackle tough questions about China, the *Firing Line* viewer has to appreciate White's thoughtfulness.

But the real zinger of the episode comes at the end, when Jeff Greenfield kicks off the Q&A with this: "Mr. White, you mention in the book [his recently released memoir *In Search of History*] that after your brush with the blacklist, seeing friends of yours driven out of employment, yourself denied a passport for a while and finally coming close to being labeled a subversive, that it caused you to avoid discussion of China and the Far East in your writings." Greenfield notes that White had turned to strictly domestic journalism with the "Making of the President" series, and he wonders if White and other informed journalists could have made a difference in America's China and Southeast Asia policy if they had been able to continue their work in the direction it was heading before the blacklist derailed them. White responds that the question *torments* him, that he should have written more about China, that he was "scared stiff" right up into the 1960s, and that he did not report about Vietnam as he could have and should have.

Next, Greenfield turns to Buckley and observes that White was an accomplished journalist, a Pulitzer Prize winner, yet some ten years after McCarthy's peak he had been scared, still worried about his passport status and the possibility of losing his livelihood. Is it possible that Buckley and his compatriots were wrong in their McCarthyite passion, that they had done something harmful? Greenfield is always very clever on *Firing Line*—on the Hayek episode his bold questions provide an absolutely crackerjack defense of liberalism—but here he outdoes himself. It was one thing for Buckley to reject the notion that a bunch of Hollywood types had grievously suffered at the hands of HUAC, but would he really defend suppression of a political journalist like White, a man whom he clearly respected? No matter how Buckley answered the question, Greenfield had scored a touchdown.

Now, no one would really expect Bill Buckley to have an epiphany at this moment and realize that he had been wrong about McCarthy, HUAC, and the nature of blacklisting. His tone of voice is measured, but there is vehemence in his diction: "Well, in the first place, conservatives in the United States, having been the intellectual niggers of the intellectual community for so long, find absolutely workaday the kind of pressures that terrified Mr. White. That is to say, it was much, much more dangerous to say a kind word for Joseph McCarthy than to say an unkind word about him. The only person I know who was ostracized during the McCarthy period at Yale was the one professor who said that McCarthy wasn't altogether wrong." He also quotes Richard Rovere as saying, "Attacking McCarthy is about as dangerous as drinking my early morning cup of coffee." Greenfield is shocked: "You can't be allowed to let that stand. Mr. White almost lost his livelihood." Buckley counters, "He didn't almost lose his livelihood."

Now White jumps in and says, "Come on, Bill, a foreign correspondent without a passport cannot leave the USA, and a lot of people gave up journalism. Have you ever stood in line and been told that your passport would not be returned to you because you fall under the legislation and then spend three months clearing yourself? No conservative had to go down to a court or a hidden trial to clear himself of charges of subversion. I did." Buckley doesn't buy a word of it and states, "I doubt if there were six noncommunists whose passports were taken away from them during that entire period, and if you were one of them I think it is outrageous that it should have happened," but he also adds that White's books had been received with "wild enthusiasm during that whole period."

This was mostly true; the book on the 1968 campaign was thrashed by many liberals bitterly disappointed by Nixon's election—a thrashing that White accounted for, in part, as their blaming the messenger. Buckley's point that White ultimately pulled through just fine is well and good, but his hardheaded insistence that it was the pro-McCarthy contingency that truly suffered in the 1950s, coupled with his use of what we now most inelegantly call "the N-word," is disconcerting, to say the least. Buckley simply did not use this kind of language on *Firing Line*. That he did in this instance speaks, for better or for worse, to the depth of his reaction against the notion that the American left was ill-treated in the McCarthy years.

I will allow the Chomsky, Newton, and White episodes to stand in for so many of the debates that Buckley had with liberals/leftists that were focused specifically on communism and foreign policy. For, really, one could spill endless ink parsing the ins and outs of the arguments of these fiercely provocative shows. Certainly, in *Firing Line* discussions of foreign policy, there was no viable counterargument to Buckley's default references to the torment suffered in the Gulag by Aleksandr Solzhenitsyn—the Russian dissident who became a ready synecdoche for the cruel realities of communist societies. Solzhenitsyn inspired awe in Buckley, who, his son Christopher observed, saw him as a "secular saint."[26]

But in the context of discussion of domestic politics and anticommunism, liberal guests did have to wonder aloud if Buckley was missing the point that huge numbers of liberals who joined the CPUSA or organizations sympathetic to the CPUSA in the 1930s and '40s were not seeking to install a dictatorship of the proletariat in the United States but, rather, to end lynching in the South, to promote voting rights for blacks, and to support union activism. As actor Larry Parks had put it, stammering as a "friendly" witness before HUAC in 1951, in the 1940s "being a member of the Communist Party fulfilled certain needs of a young man that was liberal in thought, idealistic, who was for the underprivileged, the underdog."

Buckley did not believe that HUAC and the broader anticommunist ethos that came to be shorthanded as "McCarthyism" had led to any significant, unfair victimization of communists, ex-communists, and fellow travelers, or, as they were sometimes contemptuously referred to in the Cold War years, "comsymps." He acknowledged that all congressional committees undoubtedly made mistakes, but he was steadfast in believing that HUAC's intentions were honorable and, further, that its methods were fair and constitutional.

For example, Buckley asks *Nation* magazine editor Victor

Navasky in 1980—shortly after the publication of his now-classic book about the blacklist and the ethics of informing, *Naming Names*—whether it would be reasonable for a congressional committee to interrogate Klansmen and ask them for names of fellow members. Navasky chafes at the implied analogy between the CPUSA and the KKK. People like Larry Parks and Zero Mostel did not join the CPUSA in order to engage in espionage, but people did join the KKK in order to join in lynching parties, Navasky retorts. Buckley states that comedian Zero Mostel was a "dear friend" of his and that it was very unlikely that he'd engage in espionage. However, he continues, "if my job were to serve as a member of a congressional committee at a time when the Soviet Union, among other things, got the atomic bomb through the exercise of one of their spies in America, I would think it was delinquent of me not to try to find out beyond reasonable doubt whether the Communists were active in some kind of psychological terrorist operation in Hollywood."

The revelation that Buckley was friends with Mostel—a blacklisted, confirmed leftist—is no small surprise. Mostel had bravely stood up to HUAC, and in the course of his testimony had famously admitted that he had once provided entertainment at a fundraiser for a communist magazine by giving his impression of "a butterfly at rest." "There is no crime in making anybody laugh," he had boldly declared before the committee, and perhaps Buckley appreciated the sheer moxie of the declaration. It is certainly difficult to imagine Buckley being friends with someone without a keen sense of humor. This is, after all, a man who, in one of his books on sailing, complained of scuba diving that "it is impossible to smile. If you smile, alas, you drown; so that nothing is permitted to be wrenchingly funny, or wry."[27]

In any case, Buckley's notion that a member of a congressional committee could seriously imagine a "psychological terrorist operation at work in Hollywood" is, if not wrenchingly funny, at least uninformed by the realities of the filmmaking process. Navasky explains in *Naming Names* that leadership of the Hollywood communists had "quickly understood that the collective process of moviemaking precluded the screenwriter, low man on the creative totem pole, from influencing the content of movies." In 1946, the Party's national chairman announced at a meeting at screenwriter Dalton Trumbo's house that "we can't expect to put any propaganda in the films, but we can try to keep anti-Soviet agitprop out."[28] Even this meager goal had lost all traction by the early postwar years. In fact, from hundreds of hours of inquiries HUAC had little luck finding procommunist material in Hollywood films.

On the light side, character actor Lionel Stander had whistled a few bars from "The Internationale" while waiting for an elevator in what he described as a "mindless comedy" from 1938. He had done it as a gag, assuming the director would remove it from the final cut, "but they were so apolitical in Hollywood at the time that nobody recognized the tune, and they left it in the film."[29] On the heavier side, during World War II the studios had made pro-Russia movies, and they would regret it in the McCarthy years, but, of course, the Russians had been our allies, and the government's Office of War Information had encouraged productions like *Mission to Moscow* and *Song of Russia*.[30] The Screen Writers Guild in particular had included many communist members in the thirties and forties, and it was not unreasonable for a congressional subcommittee to find this alarming and to ask questions, but was "psychological terrorism" at work in Hollywood? Or was it HUAC itself that specialized in psychological terrorism, as Navasky contended?[31]

When Navasky appeared on *Firing Line* a second time in 1999, to discuss McCarthyism with conservative art critic Hilton Kramer, he resisted the conservative line that just because the leadership of the CPUSA took orders from Moscow the rank-and-file were looking to overthrow the US government: "At the membership level, which was ninety-nine percent of the people who passed through it, they were people in Harlem who were fighting rent strikes and making common cause with the local merchants, regardless of what was said in Moscow."

In Navasky's 1980 appearance, he had similarly noted that the Hollywood workers he interviewed for *Naming Names* were not involved in a conspiracy to overthrow the government but, rather, that they joined a party that "they believed was the best way to fight racism in the South at a time when lynching was legal . . . and the best way to fight the depression at home." Buckley countered that they were awfully naïve. When did they discover that they were in error? Navasky: "Some discovered it at the time of the Nazi-Soviet pact. Others discovered it before that at the time of the purge trials. Others discovered it at the time of Khrushchev's speech—his exposing the crimes of Stalin. Others discovered it at the time of Hungary. Others discovered it at the time of Czechoslovakia."

Buckley interjects that "others discovered it as the result of the legislative and investigative activity of Congress." Navasky agrees, but argues that such activity was a violation of the rights of those under attack. It was rather straightforward: in a court of law, you are innocent until proven guilty, you have a right to see the evidence assembled against you, and you are allowed cross-examination. HUAC hearings respected none of this. Throughout the 1980 show, which had been titled "How Should Ex-Communists Cooperate?" (a weird sort of "when-did-you-stop-beating-your-wife?" kind of title), Navasky reiterates a key argument of his book, namely that HUAC engaged in elaborate "degradation rituals" whereby witnesses were forced to name names that the committee already had in hand.

This was more about punishment than investigation. Buckley states, "You have a point, and you have a nice technique of presenting your points, at first nonapodictically, but then, before the reader knows it, he's been completely ambushed and you have jumped to very hard conclusions." Navasky retorts, "Are you describing me or yourself there?" It's a somewhat weak rejoinder, but Buckley comes right back with "No, I'm apodictic all the way through."

A careful *Firing Line* viewer notes an important detail in this exchange: Buckley specifically references Navasky's skillful "technique" for presenting his arguments before jumping to conclusions that Buckley finds excessive. Buckley refers pejoratively to the "technique" of the anti-anticommunists repeatedly over the years. For WFB, "technique" is the flashiness that one reverts to when one does not have substantive winning arguments.

One first spots Buckley singling out anti-anticommunist "technique" on *Firing Line* in "The Ghost of the Army-McCarthy Hearings Part I," a 1968 episode with Roy M. Cohn, Leo Cherne, James St. Clair, and filmmaker Emile de Antonio, who four years earlier had released his now classic anti-McCarthy documentary *Point of Order*. The episode followed shortly on the heels of an *Esquire* article on McCarthy by Cohn, who had served as the senator's senior counsel during the Army-McCarthy hearings. Buckley opens with an excerpt from the film, a real rarity on a show that generally eschewed visual aids of any kind.* The clip shows a moment in the 1954 Army-McCarthy hearings in which a cropped photo used as evidence is under debate. Buckley feels the point is irrelevant, whereas the McCarthy opponents on the program feel that it is very important, but they never fully convey exactly why. Their intended point was that McCarthy was prone to fabulation. Set-

---

* Another exception: a 1970 episode on "The New Realism in Movies" opens with clips from *Women in Love* and *The Honeymoon Killers*, great raunchy pictures in their own right, but excerpted on the genteel *Firing Line*? It was a bit like farting in church.

ting aside the laborious details of the debate, the bottom line for Buckley is a critique of Joseph Welch (lead counsel for the US Army) on the same grounds that he often attacked the anti-anticommunists in general: Welch's performance illustrated the triumph of "technique" over substance, showy rhetoric over true counterargument.

The point is driven home even harder in "The Ghost of the Army-McCarthy Hearings Part II." In the *Point of Order* clip that opens this episode, the senator singles out one Fred Fisher, an attorney in Welch's firm, as having been affiliated with the National Lawyers Guild, an organization that was seen by some, including J. Edgar Hoover, as a communist front organization. In a dramatic moment thereafter marked as the tipping point for McCarthy's downfall, Welch passionately intoned, "Senator, may we not drop this? We know he belonged to the Lawyers Guild. Let us not assassinate this lad further, Senator. You've

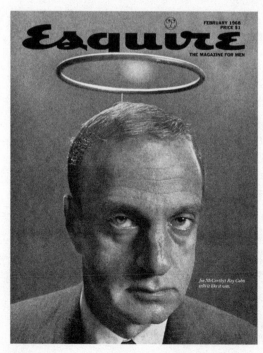

Roy M. Cohn's 1968 *Esquire* cover story inspires a *Firing Line* two-parter on the McCarthy years. CREDIT: *George Lois/ Esquire Magazine*

done enough. Have you no sense of decency, sir? At long last, have you left no sense of decency?" The show cuts back to host and guests in the studio, and Buckley asserts that Welch was being insincere, although he adds that this is not altogether an insult: "a successful lawyer needs to deploy his emotions successfully." "Mr. Welch," Buckley concludes, "was running out of a little bit of steam, and he thought he could make important emotional points, which, indeed, he proceeded to do. . . . Under the circumstances, his outrage was phony." Buckley doubts that Fisher was harmed in anyway by being singled out by McCarthy.

Now, in point of fact, Fisher came out all right compared to, say, any number of blacklisted small-time character actors who lost their livelihood when it was revealed that they had joined the CPUSA, however briefly, twenty years earlier. St. Clair, who had been a partner in Welch's firm, makes the point that Fisher initially endured a great deal of harassment—letters, phone calls, derision—but he misses an opportunity here. That Fisher was not ruined is probably less important than the fact that McCarthy chose to attack him out of sheer meanness. Fisher had been assigned to work with Welch at the hearings, but Welch sent him home, realizing it would be better if he did not participate because of the Lawyers Guild issue. There was no reason on earth for McCarthy to mention him. If Welch's reaction was not "phony" it was because he was making a genuine point: McCarthy *was* illustrating a lack of decency in targeting this young man, who was irrelevant to the hearings. Buckley dodges the critique of the senator's character by returning to his contention that no one was truly harmed by McCarthy or HUAC, at least no one who didn't deserve it.

Buckley succinctly puts his cards on the table in a 1978 episode on "The 1950s Communist Purge" with British author David Caute, stating, "As an American citizen, I want certain people to lose their jobs if there is reason to believe that they are working not for the best interest of my country, but for the best interest of somebody else's country, particularly a country that has atom bombs and imperialist designs on my freedom. I believe certain people should lose their jobs." Buckley then asks Caute if he believes that the British double agent Kim Philby should have been fired, and Caute answers "sure."

Of course, most people would agree that it is a good idea to punish enemy spies, and Buckley is speaking in the specific context of a discussion about government workers. Still, it leaves one wondering about the HUAC attack on Hollywood leftists who weren't in any kind of position to be sharing military secrets with the enemy. The bottom line was that Buckley was disinclined to discuss the suffering of those who had been blacklisted. Christopher Buckley summarized: "He was measuring their suffering against those that suffered in the Gulag, and whose political views were favorable toward those who *ran* the Gulag. . . . I think that his lack of empathy was perhaps a function of the disproportion of suffering between the two. Pup was the most empathetic man I've known, but he was not particularly put out by what they went through."[32]

Now, if there was any single *Firing Line* guest who *was* emphatically put out by what those blacklisted Hollywood workers went through it was the aforementioned Victor Navasky. And if any single figure besides McCarthy embodied the phenomenon that was McCarthyism it was Roy Cohn. How fitting, then, that Cohn was the examiner asking Navasky questions on the 1980 episode "How Should Ex-Communists Cooperate?" Navasky received no advance warning that he would be interrogated by Cohn. It was a "big surprise," he recounted later. It must have felt something like showing up at the gym for a light workout and learning your sparring partner would be Mike Tyson. Navasky had appeared on radio with Cohn before, so at least he already knew what he was like in the ring: "his strategy was to pause only between syllables, so that it was very hard to

interrupt him . . . you couldn't jump in."[33] Cohn opens with an
uppercut to the jaw.

COHN: Mr. Navasky, you've been very frank, and I hope you
won't mind my being very frank. First of all, I question the
whole basic premise of your book. You write a book which
comes out in the year 1980 which is a bleeding-heart,
pleading, sympathetic book about a bunch of communists
who, in Hollywood and other places, willingly joined a party
which has as its aim the destruction of freedom throughout
the world. You come out with that book now in a year when
there are fifty-two hostages sitting over in Iran, when your
Soviet Union has invaded Afghanistan, violated every
canon of human decency, is persecuting Jews, minorities,
trying to wipe Israel off the face of the earth; and instead
of addressing yourself to those subjects, you ask us to come
forward with some kind of bleeding-heart support for these
poor people in Hollywood who have been nurturing, with
thousands—hundreds of thousands—of dollars this very
movement which has done these things to this country,
this movement which makes it possible for somebody like a
Jane Fonda to be having lunch with Ho Chi Minh in North
Vietnam while American men are in dungeons a couple of
miles away—and that wasn't twenty years ago or during the
House committee. Now, I therefore question the timeliness
and the purpose of this whole book, and the second thing I
question—

BUCKLEY: Well, one at a time. One at a time.

COHN: All right. The next one's for you anyway, Bill.

NAVASKY: Okay. That's a long list of books I might have
written, and it would be interesting to write a book about—
I'll take one of them for example. It would be interesting
for me to write a book about the hostages that were taken

in Iran because I believe that the hostages were taken by
a band of terrorists in an inexcusable and unjustifiable
act largely because of their hatred for the United States.
And their hatred for the United States comes from our
installing the Shah as ruler in their country because of our
own anticommunist obsessions during the very Cold War
years that we're talking about now. The question is: what
relevance does *Naming Names*, which is about something
that happened thirty years ago, have to the 1980s? Well,
you know, the funny thing is, when I started going around
talking about this book, I was asked that question until the
election. The day after the election, I started being asked,
"How did you know seven years ago when you started writing
this book that it would be so timely?" And I think what
people mean is, you know, shortly after Reagan was elected,
the Heritage Foundation in Pennsylvania came out with
a report—a three-thousand-page report, nine volumes—
recommending the reinstitution of the House Committee on
Un-American Activities, the legalization of illegal break-ins,
the placement of informers in antinuke and other dissident
organizations, and a set of other procedures which seem to
me to be fundamentally antidemocratic and to violate the
civil liberties of all of our citizens. Now, I think the lesson
of the blacklist years is a simple one in a way . . . and that is
that people like Lillian Hellman and Ring Lardner Jr. and
the others who invoked the Fifth Amendment or the First
Amendment but refused to go along when there was great
pressure, at personal risk, and lived as outcasts and some of
them went to prison and some of them couldn't make a living
for ten, fifteen years, and then came back and prevailed, won
their Academy Awards and their honors . . . that they taught
us how to behave; and that makes it more difficult for it to
happen again. So I'd hope that more people study and learn
about that period for that reason.

COHN: Well, maybe they taught you how to behave, but I don't
think it taught the millions of people who are living in the
world under communist slavery how to behave. . . .

The conversation here is gripping, though in some ways it
is less a conversation than a series of alternating monologues.
Cohn is attacking Navasky for being a leftist and, thus, supporting virtually every evil in the world, even Jane Fonda. In effect,
he is being stereotypically "McCarthyite," portraying Navasky
as a nasty subversive who condones tyranny in the 1980s by
virtue of supporting the notion that political radicals (and
suspected radicals) of the 1950s had been ill-treated. Navasky
stands up for himself but basically just wants to stick to the issues raised in the book. Cohn even digs into *Buckley* for daring
to use the word *meticulous* to describe Navasky's book. Buckley explains to Cohn that he admires the "ethical taxonomy"
that Navasky has constructed. Then the show swerves into a
discussion about Alger Hiss, although Navasky contends, quite
reasonably, that his book is not about Alger Hiss.

Throughout, Navasky stays on track, acknowledging that the
questions that Buckley and Cohn are asking are perfectly interesting, but that they don't speak to his own substantive questions: is it right for a congressional committee to demand that
people inform on their friends, not to provide new or useful
information, but, rather, in order to prove their loyalty to their
country? Is it right to force people to "name names" as a test
of "good citizenship, of their civic virtue"? Navasky's performance is strong because he keeps coming back to the meat of
the book. Okay, granted, he's there not just to talk politics but
also to sell books, but still, it's an intrepid performance, and the
twist of having Cohn as examiner elevates the show from good
to great. Most viewers will come to this show seeing Buckley as
villain and Navasky as hero, or exactly the reverse—few people
are on the fence about the ethics of the blacklist. But the pug-

nacious Cohn is sure to induce a "yikes!" from viewers of any political persuasion.

Even conservatives who believe that McCarthy was right in the long run—that we had good reason to be deeply concerned about communist spies in the 1950s—acknowledge his difficult personality. But Cohn was loyal to the very end. In his 1968 book on McCarthy, Cohn attempts to convey the softer side of McCarthy, informing readers that the senator "genuinely liked people" and that "he had simple tastes and a horror of the fancy life." Cohn offers as evidence of McCarthy's simple integrity the fact that at restaurants he tended to go for "cheeseburgers and tea, occasionally roast beef or steak." The meat order is credible, the choice of tea over bourbon less so. Cohn contends that McCarthy's "broad-brush technique," as when he charged that "the Democratic party was guilty of 'twenty years of treason,'" was "meant to shock, to awaken," and that such statements were not to be taken at "face value."[34]

There is a strangely vanilla-clean quality to all of this. It reads like a *Reader's Digest* puff piece, impossibly written by a pit bull of a lawyer who did not himself "genuinely like people" and who, unlike his hero McCarthy, had no horror of the fancy life. Cohn dressed in fine silk ties, and was, according to his biographer, a "congenital partygoer" often spotted at the disco Studio 54.[35] Cohn even makes a cameo appearance in Andy Warhol's diaries. He drove a Rolls-Royce with an "RMC" vanity plate and impressed royal clients with lunch at Le Cirque. He went so far as to allow 60 Minutes to film him on the floor of his bedroom—china and stuffed frog collection assembled nearby on his massive console TV—as he did his two hundred daily sit-ups, while giving dictation to his male secretary. To say the least, Cohn was decidedly *not* camera-shy, although he had a forced smile that would shatter a thousand mirrors. Given his historical association with McCarthy, his anticommunist bona fides, and his appetite for

media appearances, it might seem odd that he was not on
Firing Line more often.

This absence was perhaps a product of the fact that Buckley found him disconcerting. Cohn was not only mean but
also humorless. When he lunges into Navasky for being a
"bleeding-heart liberal," Navasky remains unfazed, but one
can feel Buckley subtly masking a wince. In the 1979 *60 Minutes* profile, one of Cohn's clients bluntly states, "I hired Roy
Cohn because he is a tough son of a bitch." Cohn was just not
a *polite* person. Further, in his private life Cohn was, as is well
known, ragingly libidinous, which was off-putting to Buckley.
One anecdote will suffice. Crossing the Atlantic in 1975 in his
vessel *Cyrano*, Buckley and his crew landed in Bermuda, where
they found Cohn awaiting them on the dock, clad in immodest
briefs and a T-shirt that read "Superjew." His young, muscular
companion wore a T-shirt picturing an orgy. A dinner invitation was artfully declined, though two luncheons with the couple were unavoidable.[36] Buckley and his wife had once gone to a
gay bar with Truman Capote, without any apparent embarrass-
ment, but Cohn was simply too immodest for Buckley.

Cohn did appear five times on *Firing Line*, though, three
times as a regular guest and twice as an examiner.* Of Cohn's
1976 appearance with former FBI agent Mark Felt (a.k.a. Watergate's "Deep Throat") on "Subversion and the Law," Buckley
writes at some length in his book on *Firing Line*. These are his
only fleshed out public thoughts on Cohn and worth citing in
detail. Having quoted a "fine cross section of Roy Cohn at bat,"
in which Cohn stands up for the FBI's right to do pretty much
whatever it wants, Buckley moves on to dissect Cohn's perfor-

---

* *Firing Line* episodes were shot two at a time, and Cohn clearly served his
role as examiner on episodes shot back-to-back. In both he sports a double-
breasted linen suit, sky-blue tie, dress shirt with rock-hard starched club
collar, and an alarming, leathery tan.

mance and to offer an assessment of his winning personality: "He shows his adamant loyalty to the FBI, well-sheltered contempt for the character of M. L. King, and scorn for hypocritical comparative judgments, he accuses the accuser, and he ends with a mom-and-pop defense of a favorite government agency. I say this, by the way, invidiously. I cherish Roy Cohn's partner Tom Bolan's unforgettable quotation. It was the manager of Sonny Liston, the gargantuan prizefighter, who said to Bolan at a moment when Liston was being accused of a half-dozen or so felonies and misdemeanors, 'You know, Sonny has a lot of good points. It's his bad points that aren't so good.'"[37]

There's no doubt that inviting McCarthy's old right-hand man on *Firing Line* more regularly would have added fire to Buckley's recurrent anticommunist arguments, but at a certain point, Cohn's "bad points" (felonies, for example) probably became a bit much for Buckley, the scrupulously law-abiding citizen who had happily ridden a motor scooter from his Upper East Side apartment to the *National Review* office for years, until helmet laws came into effect. Buckley the libertarian chafed at the new restriction. Buckley the conservative couldn't break the law. Cohn, by contrast, was infamously lawbreaking and unethical, and he was eventually disbarred. Buckley had had convicted felons on the show, like his old friend E. Howard Hunt, but one intuits that he knew someone with Cohn's reputation might well make the conservative side look bad. Thus, Cohn would never become *Firing Line*'s go-to anticommunist, though he fit the bill in theory.

In his own book on McCarthy, Buckley had pointed out eighty-nine instances in which the senator had lied, or at least, shall we say, gotten things wrong. Whittaker Chambers himself had advised his friend Buckley that "for the Right to tie itself in anyway to Senator McCarthy is suicide. He is a raven of disaster."[38] Buckley even acknowledged toward the end of the two-part "Ghost of the Army-McCarthy Hearings" (and on a

number of other *Firing Line* episodes) that McCarthy had ultimately done more harm than good for the anticommunist
cause, though he blamed this on the anti-anticommunists.

Here's how he puts it: "My own feeling, Mr. Cohn, is that
what ended up being important was not McCarthy, but the critics of McCarthy. And that when they mobilized their strength,
they came *back* at McCarthy so ferociously that they ended us
up back before we were when we started—with the result that
I think it is safe to say that McCarthy did us [the anticommunist cause] *net* damage." Buckley was blaming McCarthy's opponents rather than McCarthy himself for the blight that was
McCarthyism. Any liberal would, of course, dispute this conclusion. On the other hand, at least Buckley was realistic about
the fact that, ultimately, McCarthy and his ism had hurt the
image of the conservative cause.

Liberal or conservative, it is hard to contest this conclusion,
though the two ends of the political spectrum agree about little else when it comes to assessing the legacy of the senator
from Wisconsin—or of the Cold War years more generally. The
aforementioned "Have We Misread the '50s?" episode from
1982 points provocatively to the ongoing argument between
left and right as to how to correctly interpret the meaning of
those years. This particular show is devoted to discussing Jeffrey Hart's book on the decade, and discussion ranges from
Owen Lattimore (accused of Soviet espionage by Senator Mc-
Carthy) to changes in professional sports—a subject so dull to
Buckley that he actually switches to the topic of sex to escape it.

John Leonard, who has noted the clumsiness involved in trying to correctly characterize decades (a somewhat random way
to subdivide history, he notes, and Buckley and Hart agree),
concludes the episode by citing Turgenev. This is not as random a choice as it might seem, for the show had earlier made a
detour back to the 1850s to determine if that decade had been
better characterized, in retrospect, than the 1950s.

LEONARD: This is from *Fathers and Sons*, and according to Ralph Matlaw's translation on page 91 of the Norton Critical Edition: "And now I hope, Arina Vlasyevna, you will turn your thoughts to satisfying the appetites of our dear guests, because, as you are aware, even nightingales can't be fed on fairy tales." Whereas in Neal Burroughs' translation of the same passage on page 122 of the Washington Square Press Edition: "And now, Arina Vlasyevna, I hope that your maternal heart has had its fill and you will see about filling our dear guests, for, you know, fair words butter no parsnips."

BUCKLEY: Oh, dear.

LEONARD: I think that every decade—not century, but every decade—is a dialectic (I hate to use the word) between parsnips and nightingales, and I think the 1950s did all right—

BUCKLEY: Sure.

LEONARD: —did all right on that. Then we ran out of parsnips—the economy and scarcity is coming back—and then we start worrying about the nightingales. But that's a lovely dialectic, unlike most of them.

BUCKLEY: Yes, but the question of a collective emphasis is, I think, distracting, isn't it? When we "worry about the nightingales," there is somebody always there worrying about the other.

LEONARD: Because they will worry about—*Time* magazine will worry about the nightingales this week, then next week it will worry about parsnips; or if it doesn't, *Newsweek* will. None of which is indicated in this [Hart's] book . . . and we haven't [even] gotten [to HUAC's coverage in the book]. . . . Lucille Ball was not a Red, and you were able to say that. You didn't ever go into, you know, was Larry Adler, the subversive harmonica player, did he deserve to be blacklisted? All that's left out. But you did say television was terribly important. Mass communications speed up this process of parsnips and nightingales; they speed up the process of our disagreements. They also dispose of them quicker than disagreements would have been disposed of earlier.

At this heady moment, time runs out, and Buckley thanks his guests.

In this far-reaching show, guests had asked, was Eisenhower a terribly dull man (the bitter parsnip) or "cold and manipulative and calculating" (the provocative nightingale)? Was the fifties the era of Audrey Hepburn or Marilyn Monroe—each a nightingale in her own right, but each representing quite different ways of remembering and mythologizing the decade? Was McCarthy "the worst man who ever lived in American history," as Buckley asked, clearly finding the notion preposterous, or should we be more concerned about the very real Soviet espionage that indisputably took place during that era? The episode did not definitively settle all these questions, but it did point to the errors in translation, as it were, that we can all feasibly make as we look back on a historical moment and declare it the best or worst of times. It also illustrated by counterexample that television by its very nature need not "speed up the process of our disagreements" and "dispose of them quicker than disagreements would have been disposed of earlier." TV could, instead, provide a place to slow down the disagreements, to tease out our parsnip and nightingale interpretations of the past.

At the end of the day, Buckley had shown on *Firing Line* that opposition to communism did not have to be extremist or conspiratorial in tone, and that there was room for intellectual anticommunism. Further, he had staked a claim for the ongoing political relevance and necessity of opposition to communism at a moment when the culture had swung toward the left, and he would hang on to this claim until it became "mainstream" again following Reagan's election.

Was Buckley ever humorless and strident about the cause? Absolutely. Buckley was always stylish and eloquent on *Firing Line*, but the passion of his anticommunism was strong, and there was no issue that made him pop his cork more quickly. This made it difficult for him to discuss the ins and outs of domestic anticommunist policy without veering away from the finer details of that policy and into attacks on communism abroad.

To his credit, though, he heard out a range of radical perspectives, from the pro–War on Poverty Michael Harrington to the pro–Mao Huey P. Newton. In 1968 he even had Eldridge Cleaver on the show, another vociferous critic of the ravages of capitalism on the black underclass. Cleaver jumped bail shortly thereafter and fled to Canada, Cuba, Algeria, North Korea, and finally France, making *Firing Line* his last US media appearance for some time.

In 1977, Eldridge Cleaver was back in America, and back on *Firing Line*. By this time he had converted to born-again Christianity, and he had come to favor democracy over communism. If early Cleaver is cool, left-wing, and macho, late Cleaver is perplexing, perplexing, and perplexing. Both versions of Cleaver, though, are undeniably spotlight grabbing. On the 1977 show he told Buckley, "I used to read your articles each time they'd come out in the *International Herald Tribune*, and I was really happy when you finally came around to the position I had, and you cut Richard Nixon loose." Buckley got laughs from the studio audience by responding, "And I welcome you on the way toward my position."

Sure enough, a few years later, Cleaver found a new calling as a Republican. In a 1998 interview with Henry Louis Gates Jr., Cleaver said, "I had a chance to witness Marxism up close in action, and so in my travels around the world I saw that it wasn't working, and I saw that the dictatorship of the proletariat was the last thing I wanted to have, and that's when I began to see that with all of our problems in the United States we had the best form of government in the world, we had the freest and most democratic procedure, and I'm telling you, after I ran into the Egyptian police and the Algerian police and the North Korean police and Nigerian police and Idi Amin's police in Uganda, I began to miss the Oakland police."[39]

As Buckley himself had done so many times over the course of the Cold War, Cleaver had highlighted the virtues of American democracy by critiquing the vices found abroad. Buckley had been quite unsympathetic to the politics of Cleaver and his compatriots over the years, as we shall see shortly, but he must have taken some small pleasure in noting that one of the all-time heroes of Black Power had joined what Buckley saw as "the right side." It was by no means a momentous moment compared to, say, the bringing down of the Berlin Wall or the collapse of the Soviet Union, but it did confirm for Buckley that he had, indeed, been apodictic all the way through.

CHAPTER THREE

FROM "WE SHALL OVERCOME" TO "SHOOT, DON'T LOOT"

Firing Line Confronts Civil Rights and Black Power

In its first ten years on the air, *Firing Line* focused often on the civil rights and Black Power movements. As a right-wing conservative, Buckley was, of course, concerned about the kinds of systemic upheaval called for by both approaches to the problem of American racism. But it would be much too simplistic to reduce his approach to one of unalloyed resistance. He did not oppose, for example, the elimination of racial discrimination, the encouragement of black personal and economic empowerment, the existence of integrated schools, or the preferential treatment of blacks in hiring decisions. But he did oppose most federal government intervention in these issues.

It was one thing to express his convictions about these issues in his columns and books and quite another to deal with them in dialogue with advocates of civil rights and Black Power, or, on the other side, with advocates for the maintenance of the racist and segregated status quo. This is what makes *Firing Line* so unique. On paper, for example, Buckley might have seemed comfortably aligned with the segregationist South Carolina senator Strom Thurmond on almost every issue, whereas in person disjunctures quickly became apparent. It was in *conversation* about racial issues with conservatives and liberals that many of the subtleties of Buckley's positions were revealed.

For example, in 1976 Roy Cohn and Mark Felt appeared on the aforementioned *Firing Line* episode "Subversion and the Law." At first, it didn't seem like the episode had much to say about the civil rights movement. Bear with me as I take you on a short detour. The question on the table for Cohn and Felt was, how far could government agencies go without violating civil liberties, or at least without being punished for such violations? Could a case be made that surreptitious entry and wiretapping were simply the right of the FBI, operating on the assumption put forward by Buckley's guests that the FBI would not act abusively or irresponsibly? Were search warrants and the like always imperative?

Cohn, snarling and defensive, upheld the FBI and his hero J. Edgar Hoover as pillars of goodness: "He's a champ to me. . . . I remember what he has done for the protection of civil rights and liberties, and I think to the American people Mr. J. Edgar Hoover is still a pretty darned good name." Cohn had been at Senator McCarthy's side during the Army-McCarthy hearings and had been on the prosecution team that had sent Ethel and Julius Rosenberg to the electric chair as spies. There was no reason to expect that he'd be anything less than worshipful of the FBI.

Felt's performance was more mild-mannered; he defended the bureau with all the flair and confidence of a highly accomplished (and finely coiffed) accountant. A thirty-year veteran of the FBI, Felt served as number three beneath Hoover, and he became second in command following Hoover's demise in 1972. Three decades after his *Firing Line* appearance, Felt would reveal himself as Woodward and Bernstein's famous informant, Deep Throat, but he did not blink when Watergate came up during the *Firing Line* Q&A. Cohn and Felt were company men. Each stuck to his script, resulting in a *Firing Line* episode that is not quite as juicy as one might expect.

Still, it was not a show without surprises. Foremost among them was Buckley's skepticism about the legality of certain FBI activities. Now, as a law-and-order type of conservative, he generally felt great confidence in the FBI. Let us not forget that he himself had been a CIA man, in 1951 in Mexico, where his supervisor was E. Howard Hunt, who was later one of Nixon's "plumbers" and who went to jail for conspiracy, burglary, and wiretapping.[1] In 1980, while on a ski vacation, Buckley found himself seated at dinner next to Miguel Alemán Valdés, former president of Mexico. Asked casually what he had done while living in Mexico, Buckley suavely responded, "I tried to undermine your regime, Mr. President."[2] Buckley was, shall we say, comfortable with the ethics of covert operations.

Yet early in "Subversion and the Law," he questioned the legality of Nixon's plumbers breaking in to the office of Dr. Lewis Fielding, Daniel Ellsberg's psychiatrist. Why would Buckley stand up for Ellsberg? There was certainly no love lost between the two of them. Buckley was irate that Ellsberg had photocopied the Pentagon Papers and turned them over to the newspapers, and when Ellsberg had appeared on *Firing Line* in 1972, Buckley had gone so far as to instruct him that the executive branch had the right to make foreign policy, wryly suggesting that Ellsberg might be informed on such things if he would Xerox the Constitution. But his psychiatric files? That was *private* stuff—or it would have been if Ellsberg's files had actually been in the office and had been successfully stolen by Nixon's men. Is this why Buckley mentions the incident to Felt and Cohn? It is unclear. His query is too brief.

More definitive—and germane to understanding *Firing Line*'s stance on the civil rights movement—are Buckley's comments to Felt and Cohn about FBI surveillance of Martin Luther King. Buckley states categorically that "finding out about the sex life" of Dr. King was "an abuse." Felt and Cohn are defensive and disingenuous. Buckley pushes back:

BUCKLEY: Okay, suppose he [Hoover] said to you, "Felt, go over and tell LBJ about the fun that Martin Luther King had at the motel last night"?

FELT: If he had told me to do just that I would have argued with him, but I think that had I not won the argument I would have done it. It seems to me that the president of the United States has a right to know of the—

BUCKLEY: Come on!

FELT: Yes, I think I would have.

COHN: Well, it's an issue that never arose.

BUCKLEY: Well, I think this is really shocking, the notion that the president of the United States has the right to know about the sex life of anybody.

COHN: Well, apparently Mr. Woodward and Mr. Bernstein think we should all know about the sex life of the president of the United States [referring to their book *The Final Days*], so—

BUCKLEY: Now wait a minute, now wait a minute. They were acting as gossip columnists; they were not acting as people who authorized surreptitious entry. I'm sorry you made that point, because I think it weakens your case. The right of Woodward and Bernstein or Truman Capote publicly to engage in thoughts about the sexual antics of anybody is a First Amendment problem, but it's very different from telling somebody to break in, record, transcribe, and then circulate information. . . . Mr. Felt believes that the president of the United States has rights which I certainly don't think he has. I don't know who voted the president of the United States the right to act as Peeping Tom.

FELT: But you're not defining this properly. The president of the United States had a very great interest. In fact, he called Martin Luther King and they had a long talk in the Rose Garden, and the president told him to discontinue his associations with suspected Communist Party members. King didn't pay any attention to that and the president was very interested in it, and I think that the president had a right to know any phase of the investigation. Now, the mic was put in because there was an expected meeting between a member of the Communist Party and Martin Luther King. It didn't turn out that way. The meeting was substantially different from that. But I think that you're saying that it was solely for sex purposes. It was for—

BUCKLEY: No, I'm not.

FELT: Well.

BUCKLEY: I'm not saying what it was that was the motive for placing the mic there. I'm saying that the mic was placed there; it picked up extrinsic information of no national concern which is now part of the national patrimony.

Perhaps Felt and Cohn are telling the truth about how the surveillance was kick-started. They just don't follow up by mentioning that once Hoover had identified King as "a tom cat with obsessive degenerate sexual urges," the bureau went straight to the press hoping to discredit him.[3] Buckley does not delve into whether the investigation was legit. The problem as far as he is concerned was the fallout: everyone knew about King's private life, and the FBI had clearly chosen to allow that information out. This is not the most important discussion point raised in "Subversion and the Law." In fact, it is a bit of a conversational dead end so far as the episode goes.

But any Buckleyologist has to be fascinated on several counts by the concerns he expressed about King and the FBI. First there

was the question of propriety. While Buckley was rather polite
to Felt and Cohn, he was quite concerned about the question of
the right of government agencies to violate personal liberties,
as he clearly felt had been done in the case of Dr. King. Sure,
Buckley had conceded in a number of Watergate-centered episodes that Nixon lied, that all presidents lied, that all politicians
lied, and that no one should be surprised about governmental
corruption. He would not be so naïve as to argue that the FBI
and CIA never played dirty pool, though he was confident that
the higher goals in the name of which they operated were just.

Indeed, he would write a whole series of spy novels to counter
the left-wing notion that American and Russian covert operations were equally immoral and corrupt; the Blackford Oakes
books, the first of which was published in 1977, were to serve as
an antidote to the post-Watergate, cynical antiheroes of American popular culture, the ethically rudderless spies of the John
le Carré ilk.

Spooks and G-men did what they had to do to get the job
done, Buckley the realist believed. But Buckley the libertarian
could not stomach the FBI getting mixed up in people's private affairs.* Such prurient nonsense keenly violated not only
his dictates regarding personal freedoms but also his sense of
decorum. It is telling that he expresses disappointment when
Cohn brings up Woodward and Bernstein. Buckley *wants* his
conservative guests to make stronger arguments and to acknowledge where Hoover or the president may have erred. He
is pushing for an intellectually honest exchange in which Cohn
and Felt—conservatives and FBI boosters, theoretically on his
side—are reluctant to engage.

---

* Buckley comfortably described himself as a "conservative libertarian" on
"The Libertarian Credo" episode of *Firing Line* in 1982. While a fierce indi-
vidualist, who would eventually align with many libertarians in his support
for drug legalization, he was also strongly in favor of government spending
on military defense, unlike many libertarians.

The second element that really resonates in this confronta-tion between Buckley and Felt and Cohn, and which takes us straight to the issue of the civil rights movement, is the fact that Buckley doesn't take the bait repeatedly dangled before him by his guests regarding King's alleged communist con-nections. Felt and Cohn fully expect that Buckley will jump on the notion that all the prurient stuff was circumstantial to the bigger issue of fighting communism. For some time, of course, the conspiratorial right wing had regarded the civil rights movement as a commie operation, and this sentiment was not limited to the hard right. In the 1960s, a poll had found that half of all Americans believed the CPUSA had played a "significant" role in both the racially motivated, post-Watts ri-ots and demonstrations, and that another 25 percent believed that communists had played at least "some" role in such distur-bances.[4] The difference between these folks and the right-wing extremists was simply one of certainty and degree. Buckley had numerous concerns about civil rights activism, but that it was all a front for communism was not among them.

For instance, in discussing "Civil Rights and Foreign Pol-icy" in 1966 with Floyd McKissick, then national director of the radical Congress of Racial Equality (CORE), Buckley asked McKissick if he regretted his role as an organizer for Youth for Wallace in 1948. The Henry Wallace presidential campaign had had the support of the Communist Party USA and had been disavowed by numerous liberals, even radical socialist Norman Thomas. McKissick had never abjured Wallace, and Buckley wondered if his poor judgment might make CORE vulnerable to expressing procommunist ideas. In the South, supporters of segregation often claimed that integration was a communist plot, and the catchphrase "outside agitators" was often code for "communist." But this was not at all what Buckley had in mind; he was concerned specifically about what *positions* civil rights groups might express on foreign policy, not about any potential espionage. That is, McKissick had just come back from a fact-finding trip to Cambodia and had declared that the country was not aiding the Viet Cong and that therefore the United States should not bomb the country. Further, CORE was offering legal support to draft evaders. The exchange quickly turns hostile, on both sides.

BUCKLEY: Your judgment is a matter of national concern, which is why so many people hope and pray that it will prove sufficient to keep the civil rights movement, or at least that part of it which you control, from deteriorating into simply another, in effect, procommunist movement. And that's why, when for instance, you go to Cambodia, a lot of people think, "Oh, my God, there's Floyd McKissick, going to Cambodia. He's going, in effect, to be given a Potemkin tour of a few jungles and forests, then he's going to meet the press, then his picture's going to be shown all over the world," and the Pentagon becomes [perceived as] a liar, you see. . . .

MCKISSICK: Now let me tell you one thing about the trip to Cambodia. We went to Cambodia simply because we wanted to know the truth about what was happening over there. And we didn't intend to go over there and let anybody sell us a bill of goods, and I really resent the inference that I could be sold a bill of goods.

BUCKLEY: Well, you certainly were by Henry Wallace's movement.

MCKISSICK: Now, I don't think Henry Wallace sold me a bill of goods.

BUCKLEY: Are you—

MCKISSICK: And I think that's a poor example—

BUCKLEY: Uh-huh.

MCKISSICK: —that to say he sold me a bill of goods. I think he was a good man. And nobody can deny that Henry Wallace didn't serve this country very well, and that he—

BUCKLEY: I don't know—

MCKISSICK: —wasn't an adequate man. Do you know the farmers right now plant that hybrid corn that he got—

BUCKLEY: Now—

MCKISSICK: Yeah, but I mean, let's get down to some of the things—

BUCKLEY: That's like saying that Adolf Hitler was a good wallpaper hanger. We're not talking about what he did. We're talking about—

MCKISSICK: I don't think, I don't think it's historically—

BUCKLEY: —when he ran for president of the United States—

MCKISSICK: I don't think it's historically correct to put Henry Wallace in the campaign—put him on a comparison to Adolf Hitler. Now, Wallace never committed the crimes or the atrocities—

BUCKLEY: I didn't say he did.

MCKISSICK: —that Hitler did. Yes, you did.

BUCKLEY: I'm not saying—now wait a minute. I'm not saying anything about Henry Wallace, in the first place, that hasn't been said by liberals, that hasn't been said by the most left liberals. All you have to do is to talk to people in the Liberal Party of New York. Talk to people like Sidney Hook, a liberal anticommunist who despaired over the success that Henry Wallace had, including people like you, into backing him. Now you say this is past history, and we should forget about it, but it—

MCKISSICK: No.

BUCKLEY: I maintain that it continues to be relevant. . . .

Buckley's full-court press set McKissick on edge, but he wasn't trying to prove that his guest was a communist, but, rather, that if even a radical lefty like Norman Thomas had seen clear to disavow Wallace, but McKissick would not, it did not augur well for how he might lead CORE.

In fact, the group had flown the flag of nonviolent civil disobedience under previous leader James Farmer (also a *Firing Line* guest in that first year), and it did turn more militant, with a Black Power orientation, under McKissick's leadership, though it did not go communist. (Notably, Farmer would break with the group a decade later over its support for a Marxist faction in Angola.) Buckley goes so far as to show that, notwithstanding his concerns about McKissick's poor judgment, he does not presume him to be part of a wider Soviet-inspired agenda.

> BUCKLEY: I happen to think that the Negro people in the twentieth century have shown a higher degree of political intelligence and resistance to the communist movement than people of my own faith.
>
> MCKISSICK: You know, I really didn't know that you knew that.
>
> BUCKLEY: Well, I—it's obvious. There was a tremendous effort made by the communists, by Paul Robeson, for instance, who felt that Negro support—
>
> MCKISSICK: And how many did they actually get?
>
> BUCKLEY: Practically none. I say they have a superb record.

To many hard-right conservatives in 1968, these words would have been quite shocking.

Firing Line guests who took the opposite point of view from Buckley regarding the communist underpinnings of black activism—white southerners like Senator Strom Thurmond and Louisiana judge Leander Perez—confirmed Buckley's own conviction that although there were many problems with the civil rights movement and the Black Power movement that would follow, concern about communist influence was irrelevant to a conservative stance on the former, and only tangential to a conservative stance on the latter. In acknowledging black activists' "superb record" in resisting communist advances, and in pushing Felt and Cohn about the King surveillance, Buckley showed not just his standard opposition to conspiratorial thinking but also, by extension, that he would not go along with conventional conservative thinking simply because it was conventional. *Idées reçues* had no place on *Firing Line.*

The skepticism exhibited in "Subversion and the Law" was textbook Buckley. When debating liberals, he could be charming or ungenerous, depending on his evaluation of the intellectual caliber of his guests. With Norman Mailer it was a spirited contest of wits.

MAILER: . . . [T]here is, you know, there's a physical, spiritual, and probably a philosophical difference between scatological matters and acts of micturation.

BUCKLEY: Well, I can see you're a student of the subject, but I—

MAILER: Well, I'm glad you can keep up with me.

BUCKLEY: I didn't say I could. I said I can see you're a student of the subject. Let's try to refocus the discussion.

With Woodward and Bernstein, Buckley was perturbed but cordial. ("You know, if you have misgivings about revealing what your own conclusions [about Nixon's guilt] are on the grounds that your own conclusions may be tendentious, I don't mind you saying that.") With Robert Vaughn, a liberal actor best known in 1967 as the star of *The Man from U.N.C.L.E.,*

he was dismissive. ("Shortly before his great success in television and in the movies, Mr. Vaughn announced after devoting
a full year's thought to the subject that 'the war in Vietnam
cannot be rationalized by moral men.' A judgment he makes,
one gathers, in behalf of himself and Plato and Aristotle.") He
went so far as to introduce Vaughn by mentioning that he ran
two miles and took forty-eight vitamins daily. Such silly personal details, generally verboten on *Firing Line*, could only be
included on this episode because Vaughn was an intellectual
lightweight whose opposition to the war Buckley perceived as
nothing short of dim-witted. How could anyone take *liberal
joggers* seriously? The only people more frivolous in Buckley's
book were vegetarians (liberal by default).

When conservatives were on the *Firing Line* dais, by contrast,
one might presume that Buckley would be more uniformly re-
spectful and in agreement with them, but this was certainly
not the case in the 1960s and '70s, even if in the years following Reagan's election there was a somewhat heightened sense
of consensus on the show. Freed from the niceties required of
the politician or the professional activist, Buckley could freely
speak his mind, even when that meant disagreeing strongly
with fellow conservatives. In light of this, he certainly wasn't
going to toe the standard conspiratorial line on the civil rights
movement. When the unrepentant bigot Judge Leander Perez
insisted that communists had authored America's civil rights
legislation, Buckley told him that his "hobgoblinized analysis
of what's going on in the United States" was "an affront to reason." As Perez goes on to attack the communists behind *Brown
v. Board of Education*, Buckley exclaims, "Your ignorance is *stag-
gering!*" By now, the conversation had degenerated into comedy,
with Buckley as jokester and Perez as unwitting straight man.

BUCKLEY: It looks as though [following from Perez's
analysis] . . . the communists are running this country, in

which case why does George Wallace bother to run because the communists will simply forbid his making any headway, so why should he make this futile effort?

PEREZ: Well, sir, would you be surprised to know that a former Red revolutionist actually controlled the election in New York and gave Jack Kennedy forty-five votes—electoral votes—which elected him to the office of President?

BUCKLEY: Judge Perez, you know so much less than I know about New York politics that I'm encouraging you to go on.

At this, the audience cracks up and applauds so much that Perez protests, with his Foghorn Leghorn accent, "No, I'm not trying to be funny, sir! I'm only speaking from the record." His notion that Negroes, notwithstanding their utter lacking of morality, have enjoyed fine treatment in his home state of Louisiana is preposterous, while his conspiracy theories are downright farcical. We'll return to Perez shortly, but for now suffice it to say that Buckley cannot stomach the notion that his "hobgoblinized analysis" adds up to a "conservative" political stance.

What is fascinating about *Firing Line*'s approach to civil rights is precisely Buckley's complicated resistance to toeing the line, a resistance to articulating an argument in perfect agreement with some unified notion of what most so-called conservatives might believe. In general, to state the obvious, conservatives opposed the civil rights movement in the 1950s and '60s, and liberals supported it. Buckley was clearly a conservative. Yet when he had opponents of civil rights on *Firing Line*, it was not unusual for him to disagree with them on numerous fronts. And when he had supporters on the show, he often revealed unexpected sympathies about certain aspects of their arguments.

Buckley spoke of the need for reconciliation between whites and blacks, and he strongly believed that racism was immoral, yet he insisted that the changing of men's consciences could not be easily enforced by law, and he opposed most forms of civil disobedience: boycotts were legal, effective, and tactically acceptable, to his mind, but sit-ins were not. Further, he did not feel that the federal government had the right to mandate how states would manage their schools or their elections. This made him a booster for "states' rights," but this statement is somewhat misleading in that "states' rights" was a descriptor widely used as a cover for racism during the civil rights years. That is, those who supported white supremacy in the South quite often did so in full or in part under the banner of states' rights.

This was endlessly frustrating to Buckley, who noted on the *Firing Line* episode with Perez that "one of the reasons why there is such a high impatience in other parts of the United States with the doctrine of states' rights, which happens to be a doctrine that I believe in very fervently, is because they hear it abused so by people like yourself and Mr. [George] Wallace." Many whites may have earnestly believed that the federal government had no constitutional right to manage their affairs and disrupt their "customs" (practically a mantra for Thurmond during his 1970 *Firing Line* appearance). But "customs" quickly became a tired euphemism. What whites identified as proud tradition blacks understood as vicious subjugation. Literacy tests and poll taxes were "customs" or "violations of civil rights," depending on who was making the case.

Buckley himself had no problem with the notion that states could make literacy a requirement for suffrage. Of course, literacy tests in the Jim Crow years were not administered out of an earnest attempt to keep the illiterate from voting. They were designed to keep blacks from voting, and this was not Buckley's objective. So Buckley was really only defending the *abstract* notion that literacy could be a criterion for voting. Those fighting on the ground for voting rights could only be discouraged by this defense of a platonic antidemocratic ideal. Notably, in his 1965 debate with James Baldwin at Cambridge, Buckley had scored only one positive response from the audience, when he said, "I think actually what is wrong in Mississippi is not that not enough Negroes have the vote but that too many white people are voting." Buckley's ungenerous attitude toward expanding the franchise made him an awkward opponent of federal intervention insofar as it differed from the standard bigoted states' rights stance put forward by organizations such as the White Citizens' Councils and the Ku Klux Klan, and by individuals such as *Firing Line* guests Strom Thurmond, George Wallace, and Leander Perez.

Now, we've already seen how Buckley pushed the extremists out of the conservative movement and forged a more mainstream image for the right, by rejecting the John Birch Society, for example. Obviously, not everyone who opposed civil rights was a nut, but so many of the most high-profile political figures were impenitent scoundrels. Who to invite on *Firing Line?* Buckley frequently pointed to the KKK as the embodiment of barbarism; he wasn't going to have a grand wizard on his show to debate the pros and cons of lynching. Sensationalist racists were to be avoided. (Even physicist William Shockley, who appeared on the show in 1974 to explain his plan for voluntary sterilization for the genetically inferior—viz., poor black people—wasn't quite a total fruitcake. He was just an idiot.)

Buckley's guests were quite often elected officials, so there was some polish and authority to their rhetoric compared to what one might expect from a roughneck Klansman. Yet opposition to civil rights was the *sine qua non* of being elected to public office in the South in the 1950s, and on into the early 1970s. Who could succeed who did not have some kind of connection with groups such as the White Citizens' Councils, the putatively upscale kissing cousins of the Klan? Jesse Helms, for instance, before his first campaign for senate in 1972, had written articles for the Citizens' Councils' newspaper and had delivered TV editorials in which he referred to the University of North Carolina at Chapel Hill as the "University of Negroes and Communists."

Buckley found himself in the odd situation of hosting a TV show on which he wanted to promote the notion of states' rights without advocating an underlying racism, a position that many southern politicians proclaimed but few, it appeared, actually sincerely believed in. To be sure, it was ideal to invite *Firing Line* guests who were not on the same page as Buckley. Without conflict, the shows might fall flat. On the other hand, in order to confirm the political viability of his position Buckley needed to find more states' rights advocates who were in tune with his perspective, and that simply wasn't going to happen.

If opponents of civil rights legislation arrived on *Firing Line* only to find that the conservative host was less receptive than they had anticipated, liberals had a better idea of what they were up against: *National Review* had a rather checkered history when it came to racial politics. As noted earlier, in 1957 Buckley himself had famously penned a *National Review* editorial titled "Why the South Must Prevail," in which he argued against the universal extension of voting rights to southern Negroes. His stance at this time was that allowing the ill-educated Negro to vote would be a ghastly mistake: "The central question . . . is whether the White community in the South is entitled to take such measures as are necessary to prevail, politically and culturally, in areas in which it does not predominate numerically? The sobering answer is *Yes*—the White community is so entitled because, for the time being, it is the advanced race." Conservatives looking back have tended to point to this as an anomalous moment for the magazine. Jeffrey Hart went so far as to note that he was repelled by the editorial, but that "everyone has a bad day." Law professor Carl T. Bogus, who has made very close study of the magazine, observes that "when it came to race and civil rights . . . *National Review* repeatedly had bad days."[5]

Bogus also rather severely argues that "[j]ust as *Playboy* thrived by packaging naked women together with serious articles by respected authors, *National Review* thrived by wrapping racism with ostensibly highbrow arguments about constitutional law and political theory, thereby appealing not only to self-confessed racists but also to those who disliked the civil rights movement but believed themselves to be untainted by racist impulses."[6] Bogus cites some damning stuff, and anyone supporting civil rights for blacks would have found the magazine quite discouraging, although, as Buckley expert Sam Tanenhaus has noted, *National Review* did not take provoking this kind of discouragement as the heart of its mission: "the magazine was founded to promote anticommunism and the free market and also to defend congressional Red-hunting inquiries of the kind led by Sen. Joseph McCarthy. The magazine did take a pro-segregationist stand, but this did not figure importantly in its core ideology."[7]

Core ideology or not, the anti–civil rights stance was there, yet the magazine never *sought* to appeal to "self-confessed racists," and, contra Bogus, racism was not the magazine's dirty centerfold, surrounded by a thin pretense of intellectual justification. Further, self-confessed racists were likely to have felt most unwelcome as *Firing Line* viewers in the 1960s and '70s. Any missteps the magazine may have made do not negate the nuanced and complicated conservative approach to racial issues that one finds on *Firing Line*.

Of course, notwithstanding Klansmen and members of the American Nazi Party, the "self-confessed racist" is a relative rarity. Judge Perez's 1968 appearance on *Firing Line* offers a case in point. Scowling and adenoidal, Perez categorically denies being a racist; he is merely "against the federal government using its coercive power to force racial integration upon

an unwilling free people" because he is "a fundamental Consti-
tutionalist." Buckley asks, then, if he has been misquoted, since
he is on record as saying, "The Negro is inherently immoral.
Yes, I think it's the brain capacity." Perez responds that not only
has he not been misquoted, but also that he was speaking the
truth: "We have a number of Negroes in our community, and
I know that basically and mentally they are immoral." Buckley
responds that it has been said of Perez that "you can grudg-
ingly admire his blunt talk—he is honest about his bigotry," to
which Perez responds that he is not a bigot. At this Buckley can
only respond, "But, look—whatever you are, Judge Perez, and
I'm sure you're a great many things, but you don't have sover-
eign power over the English language." The line gets another
big laugh from the studio audience, though Perez, predictably,
is unresponsive to the notion that if you say that Negroes are inherently immoral you are, by rudimentary deduction, a racist.

Buckley takes Perez down quite handily. Granted, this is not
particularly arduous, as Perez is so startlingly overt in expressing his prejudice, while also insisting that Negroes are treated
very well in Louisiana. He even hires large numbers of them to
work in his parish. ("Cheap labor," Buckley interjects.) An audience member inquires as to the race of not the hard laborers
but the foremen. Perez evades answering, and Buckley presses,
until the judge notes that foremen have to be able to read blue-
prints. "They must be *qualified*," he adds, casting a knowing,
nauseating smile in Buckley's direction. Buckley has already
shown himself to be Perez's enemy, and one suspects the smile
is somewhat instinctive, as if to say, "You pretend not to be on
my side, but we white folks know what I mean by 'qualified,'
don't we?" Sucking on a large greenish cigar—a southern bigot
right out of Central Casting—Perez periodically punctuates
his statements by expelling thick smoke from his nostrils. One
suspects that the studio air reeks less of tobacco than of sulfur.

Judge Perez was seventy-seven years old when he appeared

on *Firing Line*, an old man symbolizing the Old South, not to mention old-school corruption—he had twice been impeached and had so viciously opposed desegregation that he had devised a plan to get people fired from their jobs if they sent their children to integrated private Catholic schools. He was excommunicated for his efforts.

A more modern and image-savvy politician appearing on *Firing Line* would have better grasped the nuances of putting a convincing states' rights spin on his arguments. In his study of resistance to civil rights in Atlanta and the attendant "white flight" to the suburbs, historian Kevin Kruse explains that, "[b]ecause of their confrontation with the civil rights movement, white southern conservatives were forced to abandon their traditional, populist, and often starkly racist demagoguery and instead craft a new conservatism predicated on a language of rights, freedoms, and individualism." It was a strategy that worked for the long term, he concludes: "This modern conservatism proved to be both subtler and stronger than the politics that preceded it and helped southern conservatives dominate the Republican Party, and, through it, national politics as well."[8]

It was a complicated process to drop starkly racist demagoguery in favor of a language of rights and individualism. Perez didn't even try. Clearly, some politicians were better at making this transition than others. On this front, it is instructive to compare George Wallace's *Firing Line* performance with Strom Thurmond's.

"The Wallace Crusade" aired in 1968, as the Alabama governor was gearing up to announce that he was running for president. Buckley went into the show fully aware that Wallace was a racist, and not particularly concerned about belaboring the point. This, to his mind, was surely common knowledge. What irked Buckley was the notion that Wallace was a *conservative*, and his objective was to reveal that this was simply not the case.

Thus, Buckley goes after Wallace as a residual New Dealer who is pleased to take federal money for all kinds of state projects and who sinks money into pensions for the elderly. Predictably, Wallace tries to paint Buckley as a sadist who would have the destitute die of starvation; Buckley's actual stance was that charities and families should care for the aged, but that when such private care was not available the government should step in. (Unlike the hard-line libertarians, Buckley always acknowledged that state and federal agencies were obliged to help the poor, sick, and weak when no one else could or would do so.)

Watching the Wallace show keenly attuned to Buckley's motivations, one easily gleans his agenda to disprove Wallace's conservatism. But, really, it is hard to imagine many people watching this episode out of deep concern that perhaps George Wallace—stop the presses!—was not the conservative he pretended to be. Why tune in? Because Buckley was a sophisticated and intelligent conservative, and Wallace was an infamous racist. Buckley would argue with Ivy League finesse, Wallace with good ol' boy bluster. In other words, this promised to be a damn good fight, a thrilla in Manila for debate team nerds.

Everyone knew that Wallace was the populist demagogue par excellence. In his 1963 inaugural speech, the governor had famously declared, "Segregation now, segregation tomorrow, segregation forever." Buckley opens "The Wallace Crusade" by referencing a different famous quotation, noting that *Time* had quoted Wallace after losing the 1958 gubernatorial race as saying he would never be "out-segged again." Wallace is filled with barely contained rage, and he begins by condemning the scurrilous lies with which Buckley has opened the show: "There's no such expression as 'seg' in the vocabulary of southerners. I have never heard the word 'seg' or 'segged' until it was written in the *Time* magazine, which they are real good at rewriting what is written on the local scene. In fact, recently they wrote, I think, that I made a succulent sound on my teeth when I ate because they wrote the story that the writer had eaten with me. So when they then sent it to New York, they rewrote it. They rewrote in the *Newsweek* or the *Time* recently, when the writer said he ate lunch with Governor Wallace, then they, in New York, rewrote the story and said Governor Wallace picks his teeth with a dirty toothpick."

Transcribed on the page, these defensive remarks may merely seem inarticulate. But in order to decipher the full import of what is happening here you must factor in not only Wallace's indignation and heavy southern accent but also his keen sense of strategy. It's true that *seg* is not "in the vocabulary of southerners." Wallace's 1958 opponent had had Klan support, whereas Wallace had been endorsed by the National Association for the Advancement of Colored People (NAACP), and after losing the race Wallace had privately declared that he would never be "out-niggered" again. Rather than correcting Buckley by pointing out that he had actually said something *much* worse than what "the *Time* magazine" claimed, he jumps on an opportunity to attack the elite East Coast media: New York City journalists have no scruples and look down on southern folks. Wallace spends much of the episode situating Buckley like one of those mendacious, East Coast journalist sons of bitches. To Wallace, Buckley was an Ivy League Yankee who invited him onto his show only to be predictably discourteous and elitist.*

To Buckley fans, the governor surely sounded like some kind of hick. Though wearing a neatly cut suit and fine wristwatch, he might as well have been in overalls. But Wallace was play-

---

* A Yankee? Buckley's family hailed from Texas, their fortune initially made (and lost) in Mexican oil, and Buckley liked to inform his southern guests that he had lost two grandfathers fighting for the Confederacy during the Civil War. Of course, with his patrician accent and highbrow vocabulary, this got him nowhere with his segregationist guests. And any southern patriot knew that the "Civil War" was properly called "the war between the states."

ing his own constituents like a fiddle, and, in the process, with later comments about law and order in Alabama (no riots down there, he tells Buckley), he made a play to steal voters away from Nixon. The show was a total win for Wallace. He played his role of indignant and beleaguered southerner perfectly, as he had done many times before, triumphing in the mass media precisely at the moment he claimed victimization by the mass media. In her monumental history of civil rights in Birmingham, Alabama, Diane McWhorter notes that Wallace had "emerged swaggering from his first national TV forum" on *Meet the Press* in 1963. "All they wanted to know about was niggers, and I'm the expert."9 Faced with Buckley, who wanted to talk about what it meant to be a conservative, Wallace just reverted to the topics he preferred to discuss.

Buckley surely thought he was using Wallace to show that his own brand of conservative opposition to federal intervention was preferable to Wallace's explicitly racist pseudo-conservatism. Wallace, conversely, had used his *Firing Line* appearance to show himself standing up for the underdog, even colored folks ("We are proud we're helping the elderly destitute Negro citizens of our state"), and slamming the elite establishment. Getting back to Kruse's observation about southern conservatives' strategic shift from demagoguery to a language of rights and individualism, it appears that Wallace had not received the memo. Of course, he denied that there was any racial trouble in Alabama, but he didn't candy-coat his comments in the language of states' rights and "strict constitutionalism." This was not a man who was working on tempering his rhetoric in order to help southern conservatives take over the Republican Party. Wallace was always more interested in the Wallace Strategy than the Southern Strategy.

The Southern Strategy would eventually result in the overall drift of white southerners into the Republican Party, but it started with one particular Republican: Nixon. Senator Strom

Thurmond was the linchpin of Nixon's plan. When southern Democrats had broken with Harry Truman over civil rights in 1948, forming the short-lived States' Rights Democratic Party (the "Dixiecrats"), Thurmond had been their presidential candidate. He was a ruthlessly self-serving politician who left the Democratic Party for good in 1964. The senator was, in short, the obvious choice for collaboration with Nixon. Their off-the-record deal was straightforward: Thurmond would pull the South to Nixon (and away from Wallace), and once elected Nixon would go slow on integration and appoint some southerners to the Supreme Court. Nixon and Thurmond were a nicely matched Machiavellian duo. Both denied that anything called a "Southern Strategy" had been forged in 1968.

Cut to 1970, when Strom Thurmond appeared on a *Firing Line* episode titled "The Southern Strategy." The exchange was remarkably cordial, even bordering on torpid at times. Thurmond insists that the South has been repeatedly victimized by the federal government and should be treated fairly. He will not admit that the South has terrorized its black citizens, and he states as a matter of fact that most people would prefer to attend school with people of their own race. His default line is that everyone should be free to go to school wherever he or she desires. He slathers on a dubious rhetoric of "choice" with a very heavy hand. Thurmond has a handle on the southern victimization line so heavily hammered home by Wallace, but he can also speak in the more tempered tones of rights and individualism. Buckley tries in various ways, with no success, to get Thurmond to admit that he and Nixon had cut a deal regarding both integration and Supreme Court appointees.

BUCKLEY: We're here to discuss the so-called Southern Strategy, and I should like to begin by asking Senator Thurmond to what extent is that strategy based on racial prejudice?

THURMOND: Well, in the first place, I don't think there's any particular Southern Strategy. When I talked to Mr. Nixon about supporting him for president, I told him I would like to see the South treated as the rest of the nation, no favoritism, but just equal treatment. He said he favored that. . . . There's certainly no racial angle that enters into it at all. . . .

BUCKLEY: The reason I want to dwell on this is because it is widely alleged that there is a thing called the Southern Strategy and that the point of the Southern Strategy is, in effect, to devise a politics that appeals to the white people in the South, but doesn't appeal to the colored people, and that particular strategy would have the effect of greatly increasing the political strength of the Republican Party, but would do so at the expense of black people. That's why if, for instance, you have in mind a black jurist, who believes in those principles [of strict constitutional constructionism], as you just finished outlining them, it would be interesting to hear his name.

THURMOND: Well, I think Mr. Nixon wants to be fair to all peoples, and I don't think he will attempt to discriminate against any particular class. I do feel that he also doesn't want to play favoritism.

BUCKLEY: But you just said he wants to favor the South.

THURMOND: No, I don't think he necessarily wants to favor the South. . . .

Buckley has asked about the possibility of a black nominee for the Supreme Court to push Thurmond to consider the racial dimension of the Southern Strategy, but if he won't acknowledge that such a strategy actually exists, he certainly is not prepared to admit that the nonexistent strategy has a racial angle to it. The exchange wanders on but arrives nowhere. Buckley finally asks point-blank if Thurmond will allow that there is a "racial problem" in the South. Of course, he will not.

THURMOND: Well, uh, there's no question that down South we have a larger proportion of black people than they have in other parts of the country. And it does make it a problem, of course, because I think people of the same color generally prefer to associate together, go to church together, and if they had their choice, I think they'd prefer to go to school together, generally speaking. And, on the other hand, the people in the South, I think, have gotten along remarkably well, in most of the states of the South, there's been very little trouble; there have been less, fewer demonstrations on the part of black people or white people in the South, on college campuses or universities. There has been less disorder and lawlessness in the South than in other parts of the country. I think the crime rate would show that it's less in the South than in some other states.

Wallace had made the very same argument, but with imperious bluster. That show was a real shouting match. This one is more like an awkward poker game, in which Buckley refuses to bluff and Thurmond refuses to do anything else.

Buckley answers Thurmond's claim about law and order in the South with the exact same analogy he had used with Wallace.

BUCKLEY: Senator, you were talking about the progress in the South and the relative stability there. Mightn't some people feel that this was a little like a famous American industrialist who came back from the Soviet Union and said, "Wonderful! No labor problems!" That is to say, mightn't they say that the reason there is this kind of stability is because, or so it is widely thought throughout the country, there is a considerable tyrannizing by the South against its Negro people? How would you answer that question?

THURMOND: Well, you've been down in South Carolina, your mother lives down there. Have you found it that way?

BUCKLEY: Well, I've never lived there, but, uh, I've never been attacked actually in New York, either, but I know there's a lot of crime there, I do live there.

THURMOND: Well, you'd better watch out, from what I hear.

BUCKLEY: Yeah. I do, I do. I don't doubt that there's a lot of instability in New York—I write about it, in fact—but what I'm asking you is what about the charge that the stability in the South has had to do primarily with the vigilante justice that takes place there?

THURMOND: Well, do you know of any vigilante justice down there?

BUCKLEY: Well, there's been, for instance, six churches bombed in the last three weeks.

Thurmond was as slick and even-tempered as Wallace had been rough and explosive, but their messages had much in common: violence and racial unrest was a northern problem, and there was no such thing as vigilantism in the South. Buckley even says that J. Edgar Hoover states categorically that an FBI informant saw the white civil rights activist Viola Liuzzo murdered by vigilantes, adding, "Now, you know, just as I believe J. Edgar Hoover on Alger Hiss, I'm prepared to believe him on that." Thurmond evasively responds, "I have great regard for Mr. Hoover." Could Medgar Evers's murderer be convicted today in the South? Thurmond: "I just don't know. I don't know all the facts about the case."

As with Wallace, Buckley clearly agrees with Thurmond that the federal government should generally keep its nose out of the affairs of the states and that *Brown v. Board of Education* was a poor Supreme Court decision. He just wants to have an honest discussion about the real problem of violence and racism in the South. This was impossible with guests who would not acknowledge that any such thing existed. At one point,

Thurmond having redirected to the *northern* race problem for the umpteenth time, Buckley scolds him: "You're gonna lose your credibility here in a moment!"

Buckley gives it one last go. Was there really *no* racial injustice in the South? Thurmond responds by proudly pointing to the fact that as governor he had had a lynch mob arrested in 1947, an all-time first. Buckley did not miss a beat. If this was an all-time first, that meant that *before* Thurmond had been governor blacks had not been treated fairly? Thurmond gives this astounding, absolutely deadpan response: "Well, I couldn't say what the situation was beforehand. I was told that that was the case; and that may have been in error or it may not have been. I just don't know." This was like Buzz Aldrin equivocating over whether the earth was flat or round.

Buckley plunges forward and asks if the lynch mob was convicted. Thurmond starts to say that he does not recall, and then, as if realizing that this would seem utterly absurd to his constituents—it was a very famous case, after all—he admits that the accused were not convicted but that he did not really know the details and that justice had undoubtedly been served. The details were that thirty-five white men had forcibly seized from jail a black man accused of murdering a white man. The mob carved part of his face off with a knife and stabbed him repeatedly in the chest, finally shooting him in the head three times. It was vigilante justice, pure and simple. The senator was widely praised for having the villains arrested; with federal pressures mounting, the South needed to show that it could maintain law and order on its own.[10]

Making the arrests was obviously the right thing to do, and Thurmond was praised by both the American Civil Liberties Union (ACLU) and the NAACP at the time, but this was also a public relations gambit. And clearly, just as important as Thurmond's taking action was the fact that the criminals were let off scot-free. Regrettably, *Firing Line* viewers remained unenlight-

ened, as Buckley apparently did not know the full story, and
Thurmond had nothing to gain by telling it. By the end of the
episode, Buckley is casting rhetorical butterfly nets; Thurmond
artfully dodges, citing his political script like a robot. Where
Wallace had played the enraged populist, Thurmond was the
unflappable politico.

Perhaps the finest moment in the Thurmond episode occurs
at the end when a young woman in the audience, Miss Sienkiewicz, recounts the story of a black man who was terrorized
in North Carolina in 1969 by thugs who burned down his business and signed their real names to their hate mail. How, she
asks, can Thurmond claim that there is no unjust treatment
of blacks in the South? Incredibly, he asks if the abusers were
black, and cites unrelated incidents of black-on-black violence
in the North. No, they were white, she responds. Then he asks
what *she* did to bring them to justice. She wrote letters to her
city councilman. He then asks why she did not swear out a
warrant for their arrest, and he explains how the voting rights
bill was designed to punish southerners who voted for Goldwater and that he feels safer in South Carolina than he does
anywhere in the North.

At this point, we have left Kafkaesque counter-examination
behind and fallen down the rabbit hole into a Mad Tea Party.
Miss Sienkiewicz wisely states, "I think by answering my question that way, you're saying something like well, we can't talk
about the war in Vietnam because there's pollution in the country. You're taking the question that I asked you and answering it
completely different." She then observes that perhaps he would
not feel so safe in South Carolina if he were black. Thurmond
has spoken to this young woman dismissively, even offering a
wan half smile of contempt that is alarming in large part because he has been so utterly cold and affectless throughout the
show. The senator has, in sum, responded to Miss Sienkiewicz
as if she were a complete nothing, but she steals the show in

the end.* Buckley had revealed Thurmond as a standard-issue politician, sticking to script no matter what. Miss Sienkiewicz had revealed the man behind the curtain. If it was something of a loss for Buckley himself, it was nonetheless a win for *Firing Line*'s coverage of racial politics.

Of course, it was never the show's agenda to provide good "coverage," per se. As a public affairs show, *Firing Line*'s mission was to present conversations about current issues (or sometimes about art or literature or philosophy), with no obligation to link guests or topics to specific and timely news hooks. This gave the show tremendous leeway, in sharp contrast to the mainstream news media, which covered the "race problem" in an entirely different manner. The national evening news had amply reported on civil rights, and the network newsmen of that era saw such coverage as creating a kind of golden age for TV news, advancing the profession from merely reporting facts to investigating and shaping news.[11] King had emerged as the dominant civil rights spokesman. The networks were largely tone deaf to different constituencies within the movement, and to tensions between King's group, the Southern Christian Leadership Conference (SCLC), and the Student Nonviolent Coordinating Committee (SNCC), whose chairmen had included Stokely Carmichael and H. Rap Brown, both later active in the Black Power movement. If they had been paying closer attention, the mainstream media might have seen the latter movement coming. As it was, though, the radicals seemed to come out of nowhere, as if a coin toss had produced a lack of faith in the power of nonviolent resistance.

---

* It's hard to read Thurmond's condescension as gender-neutral. While upholding separation between the races in the name of protecting white southern womanhood, this was a man of a certain generation who thought it was quite acceptable to grope any keister he found to his liking. Women in the Capitol Building—from lowly secretaries to US senators—quickly learned to decline riding in the elevator with him.

Black Power radicals did not fare as well on TV as the civil rights activists had. A handful of black public affairs shows created by blacks for blacks, and generally sympathetic to the radicals—and, more broadly, promoting not only political empowerment but also racial and cultural pride—did emerge right after the King assassination,[12] but Black Power leaders were covered by mainstream TV news as crazed radicals, and to many viewers—white, black, conservative, liberal, or otherwise—the sensationalism was alarming. Sound bites like H. Rap Brown's "Shoot, don't loot!" carried the day, and "the Black Panthers clearly did not receive positive or even fair press coverage from mainstream media sources."[13] How stunning, given the widespread mass media reluctance to cover Black Power in a nonsensational manner, to encounter Black Panthers like Eldridge Cleaver and Huey P. Newton advancing their arguments in full—peppered with skeptical questions from Buckley, to be sure—on *Firing Line*.

The Black Power movement was a particularly good topic for *Firing Line*. At its worst, for Buckley it was the very epitome of left-wing radicalism. He rejected the cynicism and despair of the militants, who did not believe that change could come from within the system without revolutionary upheaval. Writing for *Look* magazine in 1970, he complained that "these militants . . . bamboozle a lot of Americans, most typically those Americans who are happiest believing the worst about America."[14] In that same article he also expressed fervent hope that a black man would be elected president by 1980. This was rather astonishing, a pie-in-the-sky notion guaranteed to win over neither black radicals, who were generally not trying to work within the electoral process, nor Strom Thurmond et al., the racist politicians most ardently fighting integration and "race mixing." Thus, in one fell swoop Buckley neatly alienated both left and right.

At its best, from Buckley's perspective, Black Power promoted self-determination and capitalism. Certainly, many Black Power advocates were fervent Marxists, but there was also a strain advocating for the power of black-owned businesses, etc. Thus, although he was more attuned to the efforts of civil rights activists attempting to work within the system, and although he condemned the black radicals as categorically racist against whites, the Black Power call for *empowerment* was inherently more appealing to him than the civil rights call for *equality*. An exchange toward the end of the otherwise thoroughly hostile episode with Floyd McKissick makes this quite clear.

ANNOUNCER: It is time for our question period on *Firing Line*. This first question is addressed to Mr. McKissick. Mr. McKissick, do you feel that the Black Power concept will obliterate the advances and contributions that Negroes made before riots, demonstrations, and Black Power?

MCKISSICK: Gee. That's a question that you can't answer yes or no. The question really has to be answered by saying first of all, and attempting to define what the Congress of Racial Equality means by Black Power, and I'll answer that by saying, first of all, we mean that black people have simply got to determine for themselves the rate of progress, the direction of that progress, and there are six basic ingredients to the accomplishment of Black Power, and Black Power is a direction through which you can obtain total equality, and those six points are as follows: One, black people have got to secure for themselves political power. Two, black people have to secure for themselves economic power. Three, black people have got to develop an improved self-image of themselves, and everybody always asks what do you mean by that? I mean that the history books fail to record the fact that Dr. Charles Drew invented blood plasma, or that the peanut was actually popularized and made famous by a black man, Dr. George

Washington Carver, that black people first smelted iron in
Africa, that Napoleon, for instance, was defeated by a black
general named Toussaint L'Ouverture in Haiti. All of these
things relate to our image that we do not know anything about
ourselves, and they have purposely been left out of the history
books. Leaving that particular point and going to point four,
we'll have to develop militant leadership. And five, we seek
enforcement of federal laws, the abolition of police state
tactics such as in the South, and six, and last, and what we
mean by Black Power, is the building and acquiring of the
black consumer block. . . . We believe that while we can talk
about one, political power, [but] that just as important is point
six, the consumer power, because, in reality, black people
vote every time they put a dollar on the counter, because we
are in an economic society, and if we do not have all basic
ingredients that we have talked about, we'll never achieve the
road to total equality.

ANNOUNCER: Mr. Buckley, is there any comment you wish to
make on that answer?

BUCKLEY: No. Just that I endorse all six of those objectives.

It is unlikely that Buckley was actually wild about point number four, regarding the acquisition of militant leadership, but,
still, his positive response is remarkable, especially coming at
the end of such a contentious episode. Buckley had expressed
huge reservations about McKissick's politics, but he was not
going to hold a grudge and be dismissive when McKissick ultimately expressed ideas that he agreed with. Buckley's support
of the six-point plan makes perfect sense when you think about
it, but these sporadic moments of appreciation of aspects of
Black Power are fleeting, their importance not immediately obvious to the casual *Firing Line* viewer.

In fact, I only began to spot the subtext when I spoke with Lawrence Chickering, who was hired as a young man in the spring of 1968 to be an assistant to Buckley at both *National Review* and *Firing Line*. Chickering was acquainted with several radical black intellectuals who were advising Stokely Carmichael, H. Rap Brown, and others. In November 1968, he arranged for a daylong meeting to take place between the intellectuals, Buckley, *National Review* writers such as James Burnham, Senator James L. Buckley (William's brother), lawyers Jean and Edgar Cahn, and even a crew of Nixon's men—who surely saw their remit as sucking up to Buckley, not forging a coalition with Black Power radicals. It was a meeting of minds with no direct and obvious outcomes, more interesting for the very strange fact that it happened than for its results. But Chickering would explain years later that a key revelation emerging from the meeting was that there were a number of shared values among the participants, a feeling that the fight for "equality" often presumed the need to help a repressed victim, whereas a fight for "empowerment" assumed greater possibility of an individual controlling his or her own life.[15]

Setting aside deeper philosophical examination of the notions of equality and empowerment, the story of the meeting does much to help us understand the underpinnings of Buckley's approach to racial politics on *Firing Line*. He invited more civil rights advocates than Black Power advocates onto the show, seeing the former as flawed in many ways but also more acceptable by virtue of being more moderate. Yet Black Power militants, advocating not federal government intervention but self-determination, could not help but appeal in a north-by-northwest way when read via Buckley's libertarian conservative lens.

Although the intention was to debunk many of the principles of Black Power, *Firing Line* provided an uncensored window onto the movement that was difficult to find elsewhere on TV. In fact, the show ultimately offers much raw material supporting the liberal and far-left perspectives. If you weren't convinced by Buckley's counterarguments, what you came away with from the show's Black Power spokesmen was a justification for (or, at least, a basic understanding of) the movement. *Firing Line* was thus perhaps the single venue in the "mainstream" American mass media where Black Power got a fair shake in the late 1960s and early 1970s. Notwithstanding their initial gravitation toward the sensational, by the end of 1968 CBS, NBC, and ABC had decided to focus on the moderate antiwar movement rather than the more radical side, and militants in general were to be censored from coverage. At NBC, one investigative journalist observed, "stories which showed black militant leaders threatening violent acts against society were not desirable [and] Stokely Carmichael and H. Rap Brown had been 'banned.'"[16]

By the time *Firing Line* premiered in 1966, Black Power was beginning its advance, as the civil rights movement began to recede. The show would feature a range of black activists and spokesmen, ranging in political orientation from liberal to far left. The 1968 *Firing Line* episode with actor Godfrey Cambridge is nicely illustrative of the space that the program allowed for black liberalism. Cambridge spoke of ongoing injustice against black Americans—including himself—not so much looking for a fight as proving the point that the civil rights movement (and its accompanying legislation) could not be seen as successful: something more needed to be done. Implicit here was Cambridge's sympathy (if not affiliation) with Black Power. Cambridge said he understood why people turned to Black Power, which he defined not as militant black nationalism (that is, separatism) but more simply as "self-realization."

Cambridge gave a strong performance by being suave, elo-

quent, and, in a word, cool. Above all, he was playful, attempting to pull Buckley to his side via his humor and his display of
cultural sophistication. McKissick's feathers had been ruffled
when the crowd laughed at Buckley's comments—he assumed
that the joke was on him—and he had been flustered when he
was unable to keep up with Buckley's vocabulary ("I don't know
whether I can answer the question with all the adjectives . . .").
Cambridge, by contrast, kept his grip on the conversation by
telling Buckley, "You're a marvelous person with compound
sentences. Every time you ask a question I start to think of the
last chapter in *Ulysses*." He injected a number of personal anec-
dotes that revealed the tenaciousness of racism. There were few
openings for counterarguments from Buckley on that front.

When Adam Clayton Powell came up, as he often did in these
years of the show, Cambridge offered a canny response. Powell had been in the US House of Representatives, representing
Harlem, from 1945 to 1971. He had been a strong civil rights
advocate, but, later, he had also been accused of a number of
financial improprieties. When Buckley was critical of Powell
on *Firing Line*, the standard hard-left ideological response was
that he would not have been singled out and treated so severely
if he had been white.

Cambridge eventually voices this line of argument, but he
warms up to it slowly, avoiding stridency and instead poking
fun: "Adam Powell is a folk hero to the black community, and
if there's one thing I believe in it's equality of opportunity. We
must have our chance at corruption. You can't expect us to come
out unscathed. We learned it from you. There's very little corruption in tribal government, so we must have learned it from
your Greek or Romans. . . . Everybody steals, white hands, black
hands, yellow hands, I want equality of opportunity." Next, he
stands up for the right of the people to elect Powell; at least
they can vote in Harlem, unlike in Mississippi. Buckley count-

ers that 40 percent of blacks had voted for Wallace in the last Alabama election, that they had erred, and that access to the vote didn't guarantee sound voting decisions. It's an interesting conversation that works in large part because Cambridge is so good at bringing up liberal arguments, then ratcheting down the tension with jokes and a casual manner. He offered a brilliant less-is-more performance.

Cambridge was what one might describe as a "soft" guest— politically opposed to Buckley, but not presenting himself as an activist or movement spokesman. These kinds of *Firing Line* guests were often the best, offering just enough conflict for an interesting conversation without pressure for either side to flat-out win the debate.* Jesse Jackson offers a clear counterexample. Speaking from a moderate-progressive perspective, he took a tempered stance in 1971, obviously aware of his need to carefully spin his image. He was unwilling to criticize other black perspectives, stating that he was more interested in seeking economic solutions than "in arguing about who best states our pain . . . Huey describes the pain and agony one way. Roy Wilkins describes it another way. Ralph Abernathy describes it another way. Julian Bond describes it another way."

Jackson is so bland and careful that things don't heat up until the end of the show, when one Mr. Hart, an angry young white man, first attacks Buckley as a hypocrite for defending Robert Kennedy (he had not so much defended RFK as attacked the Black Panthers for publishing a cartoon picturing Kennedy as a dead pig shortly after his murder) and then attacks Buckley for calling Jackson "Mister" instead of

---

* There were apolitical, conflict-free episodes, however, that were completely charming. In "Why Are They Afraid of Bach?" (1970), a crash course in Buckley's favorite composer is provided by virtuoso Rosalyn Tureck. Our usually confident and all-knowing host melts before her greatness.

"Reverend." Buckley is affronted on both counts, refers to the Kennedy question as "fatuous," and retorts that Jackson had specifically requested to be called "Mister." The questioner says, "Well, we're all 'niggers' in front of 'Big Bill.'" He then goes on to ask about the Panthers, a question that Jackson mostly dodges, once again seeking the moderate path without offending. The N-word was infrequently uttered on *Firing Line*—with exceptions generally being citational, such as a reference to Dick Gregory's autobiography, *Nigger*—and this was a truly disarming moment.

Black Power and civil rights leaders tried hard to keep a lid on hostility and to take advantage of Buckley's program as a venue in which to air their positions. Indeed, one does get a subtle sense that the black radicals most opposed to Buckley felt they were *using* his program to air ideas in full, away from the sound bite culture that pervaded the rest of the media. Elsewhere, their comments would be edited; on *Firing Line*, they had to put up with a right-wing white guy asking hostile questions, but they could, on national television, express full-blown anti-establishment, revolutionary, and even Marxist arguments that usually only saw the light of day in underground newspapers and newsletters cranked out by hand on mimeograph machines.

Given this context, the radicals generally avoided invective. There was more than self-restraint in play here. Producer Warren Steibel, a large, blustery man with a perpetually untucked shirt, gave red-flagged guests a stern lecture before they appeared on the show: blue language was strictly off-limits. He had so irked Allen Ginsberg by forbidding "dirty words" that Ginsberg complained that he would have to censor his "thought patterns." There was extra concern about Eldridge Cleaver, and Buckley made a point of following up Steibel's lecture by suggesting to Cleaver before they started shooting that the FCC fee for cursing would cancel out his payment for appearing on the show.

If there was any guest who did not need coaching in how not to incur the wrath of the FCC it was civil rights maverick James Farmer, who was the very picture of decorum. In "Where Does the Civil Rights Movement Go Now?" (1966), Buckley made some of his boilerplate libertarian arguments about parents having the right to send their children to any school they wanted. He complained that people kept discovering "new rights." And he argued that James Baldwin was all wet. Baldwin was, Buckley judged, too pessimistic about what could be accomplished in America.[17] CORE cofounder Farmer cut a striking figure, radiating dignity and composure as he defended Baldwin. But he also conveyed a mounting frustration and anger that he seemed to try to tamp down with each new cigarette he lit. In his entrancing baritone (shades of James Earl Jones), Farmer counters that Baldwin's concerns about northern Negro ghettos are very important.

> FARMER: The fact of the matter is, most of our victories, legislatively, have spoken to the South and not to the North. And the seventeen-year-old drop-out youth in a Harlem street couldn't care less if his second cousin in Mississippi can buy a hot dog. He says, man, what about the rats that bite me? What about the cockroaches?

> BUCKLEY: Why don't they kill those rats? Is there a law that says you can't kill the rats? I'm so tired of that argument. I've got rats, and I put traps all over the place. They're still there; I've never been able to get rid of them.

> FARMER: You know, in Harlem if you kill one rat, two more come back to carry his carcass away.

> BUCKLEY: Well, why doesn't that happen in other cities? Is there special refuse there [in Harlem]? Why don't they do away

with the refuse? It's a municipal function to get rid of the refuse, isn't it?

FARMER: When you have an entire family—that's the state['s duty to remove the garbage], isn't it?

BUCKLEY: Look, I'm not suggesting demunicipalizing the garbage collection.

FARMER: Oh, you're in favor of garbage collection then?

BUCKLEY: I'm in favor of socialized garbage.

Everyone laughs, including Farmer, and the tension is briefly eased. But Buckley won't let go of his insistence that there is nothing special about the ghetto garbage problem. When Farmer asks if rats have bitten his children, Buckley suggests that he is being melodramatic. There are more rhetorically refined moments in this program, as when Buckley and Farmer discuss the nature of the goals of the civil rights movement, but their discussion of the tenacious rat problem in the ghetto is the most memorable part of the show because, first, one cannot imagine such a conversation on a news or public affairs show today, decades after the War on Poverty has receded from view, when we rarely see the crisis of poverty addressed in the mass media and, second, because Buckley is so earnest and yet so very incapable of comprehending the daily crises faced by those living in urban squalor. That the rat problem was worse in Harlem than Stamford, Connecticut, was simply implausible to him.

Farmer's organization, CORE, had been one of the key civil rights organizations—with the NAACP, SNCC, the Urban League, and SCLC. After Farmer left CORE in 1966, the organization would veer more strongly in the direction of Black Power. That same year Stokely Carmichael had used the phrase "Black Power" in a speech, and it stuck. (He would have guested on *Firing Line* that year if the SNCC central committee had not nixed the appearance.[18]) How Black Power would evolve was still unclear at that point. Although Buckley would eventually oppose the militant, separatist side of the movement, at this early moment, when it was not altogether apparent to him what *Black Power* meant—or would come to mean, or that it would displace the nonviolent ethos of the civil rights movement—Buckley was remarkably open to it. Again, the self-empowerment and, in some quarters, the celebration of the potential of black capitalism tapped exactly into Buckley's sensibilities.

In 1967 he invited white journalist Nat Hentoff to discuss the meaning of Black Power. Hentoff was known primarily as a leftist music journalist specializing in jazz, but he had also written a book about the failure of New York City public schools. Buckley was interested to hear that Hentoff agreed that liberals had bungled public education in New York City. If Black Power could bring with it community control of the schools, maybe it could redress the crisis facing New York City's black schoolchildren.

HENTOFF: If you are a Negro parent in Bedford-Stuyvesant or Central Harlem, [you will find that] the schools are just as bad, if not worse, than they were ten years ago. The sense of urgency becomes very acute, indeed, so if you can do something to change those schools, it really doesn't matter what the white man outside of your neighborhood thinks, because the real priority is the possibility of changing your kid's life.

BUCKLEY: Correct.

HENTOFF: And that is where Black Power is really at. . . .

BUCKLEY: Let's suppose the conservatives are useless because it is fashionable to suppose they don't care about these matters. But New York has been run by liberals sort of forever, right?

HENTOFF: Uh-huh.

BUCKLEY: Why do they deny people in Harlem the help that people in Harlem need in order to have the best kind of schools for Negro children? Why? What's their motivation? Are they blind, misanthropic, secretly hateful, or what?

HENTOFF: I think liberals, by and large, tend to get bemused by their own rhetoric and believe that the rhetoric has led to some action. [New York City mayor] Robert Wagner was a prime example of that, a decent man, who actually thought that he had had a decent administration.

BUCKLEY: And it was dreadful, wasn't it?

HENTOFF: Yeah. . . .

MODERATOR: Do you really maintain that the Board of Education of the City of New York has not done its best for the schools of Harlem and Bedford-Stuyvesant?

HENTOFF: My God, go look at the schools!

There is no doubt in Hentoff's mind that the white liberals have utterly failed New York City's black schoolchildren. It's obvious that one reason Buckley had so many leftists on the show was that they rivaled him in their negative feelings about liberals. If white liberals weren't fixing the New York City public schools, could blacks themselves do a better job for the kids in their communities? Hentoff serenely offered his take on Black Power as something that did not yet exist, but which he defined as "the hope that Negroes in this country can first organize themselves and thereby utilize their capacities, their resources in terms of numbers, in terms of economic potential and the like, so that finally they can have some decision-making power in terms of the society at large and . . . [in] the neighborhoods in which they live and the schools in which they are miseducated." Hentoff also notes the need to generate a "feeling of pride" in being black.

Hentoff's definition of Black Power does not evoke armed self-defense; he is an advocate of autonomy and self-determination rather than militancy or separatism per se. These are not particularly revolutionary notions. And, in fact, Buckley is in agreement with him on many points. Once again, we see Buckley agree with the Black Power goals of improving black education, self-image, and economic opportunity.

In "The Ghetto" (1967), sociologist Kenneth Clark offers a more centrist perspective than Hentoff insofar as he rejects black separatism altogether. But like Hentoff he is particularly concerned about the poor quality of black education. He notes an "increasing sense of hopelessness or despair among an increasing proportion of people in the Negro community that America has the capacity to move toward a truly raceless democratic society." This has resulted in black nationalism and the call for an all-black school system in Harlem. Clark is black himself and offered supporting documentation used in *Brown v. Board of Education*. Having fought for integration for years, he cannot support what he sees as segregation proposed by blacks. He goes on to argue that integration has not so much *failed* as it has not even been *attempted*; America is sacrificing its black children by condemning them to a "criminally inferior education."

While Buckley is confident that his program can help shape opinions and do good, Clark dejectedly observes that "Negroes on TV" have become "a substitute for real power. For example, any time that Stokely Carmichael or Rap Brown want to be on TV they can be, but you use Negroes one way in society—you give them pseudo-power. . . . I feel that I should never get on another television program because I think that one of the devices that America is now using for dealing with the real problems of race is having a number of Negroes who are projected on the media, particularly television, as spokesmen. The more they talk, the less white society has to do."

Contrary to what Clark implies here, Carmichael and Brown did not have carte blanche access to mainstream media, but when they did appear they were generally covered in a sensationalist manner. Clark, of course, was an old-school civil rights advocate who would not have been terribly keen on any type of Black Power coverage. Still, the general point stands that by the late sixties black spokesmen had proliferated at a greater rate than social change. Buckley responds, "Well, I don't think you're casting universal rules because I've turned down Rap Brown for this program . . . and last year, LeRoi Jones." Clark gives credit to Buckley for his "sensitivity," but goes on to despair of real progress being made. All the TV talking was getting us nowhere.

No quotation on the written page could fully convey Clark's despair regarding white indifference to the plight of black children. It is one of the saddest hours of television I have ever seen.

Less sad but certainly disconcerting is the 1968 *Firing Line* episode with Eldridge Cleaver. In "The Black Panthers," Cleaver takes a radical line in opposition to the "pigs" who control America, singling out the Democrats (including black politicians such as Julian Bond) for disenfranchising blacks and for waging war in Vietnam. He calls for the dissolution of America's power structure and for the creation of a socialist state. Now, keep in mind that at this moment Nixon was particularly concerned about PBS liberalism and even had the Corporation for Public Broadcasting defer funding for public affairs programs.[19] The president was hoping to eliminate white-produced PBS shows that sought to radicalize "the silent majority" of white middle-class Americans.[20]

Firing Line, of course, sought to radicalize America by making it more conservative, but Nixon felt—in what one might phrase as a reversal of Louis B. Mayer's famous dictum—that there was "no such thing as *good* publicity" where the TV presentation of liberals or radicals was concerned. So this episode was radical by virtue of even existing at a moment when the president was pulling out all the dirty tricks up his sleeve to limit the broadcasting of radical perspectives. Buckley may have adequately disputed Cleaver's arguments—while actually supporting some liberal-sounding ideas about reconciliation between blacks and whites—but this could not cancel out the fact that Cleaver boldly declared on the show, "I would say that if Richard Nixon was assassinated it would only result in having another pig in line who possibly would need to be assassinated.... I don't see any reason for having Richard Nixon alive today."

Buckley had not waged much of a counteroffensive against Hentoff and Clark, but he pushes Cleaver hard, noting that his support is strongest among white liberals and questioning his "Marcusian" assumptions.[21] In essence, Buckley attacks the notion of false consciousness that underpins Cleaver's belief that blacks who do not support the Panthers have not made a rational judgment but, rather, have been deceived by the manipulative pigs of the mass media; by this logic, if properly educated, all blacks would support the Panthers and want to barbecue the pigs.

Buckley is, in effect, contending that Cleaver's arguments are flawed because they are not falsifiable. Each man is on the edge of blowing his top throughout the show, but it's not a shouting match like the Wallace episode had been. Rather, a simmering tension is consistently maintained. Which man would lose his cool first? (Answer: Cleaver, who finally refers to his endurance of Buckley's questions as "putting up with this shit.") It was damn good TV.

Buckley emphasizes in particular that Cleaver has more radical white supporters than black and that some leaders of the

Black Panther Eldridge Cleaver takes a radical line in opposition to the "pigs" who control America, singling out the Democrats (including black politicians such as Julian Bond) for disenfranchising blacks and for waging war in Vietnam. He calls for the dissolution of America's power structure and for the creation of a socialist state.
CREDIT: *Hoover Institution*

Negro movement feel that Cleaver has "set that movement back more than any man in the last ten years." Cleaver responds, "The Negro movement, they said that I would set it back ten years, and it's my desire to eliminate it totally." Buckley is eager to show how strongly opposed Cleaver is to those Negroes working for civil rights within the system, like Julian Bond, about whom, Buckley notes, Cleaver had said elsewhere, "He is becoming a pig and just might end up being barbecued with the rest of the pigs."

Cleaver does not deny the statement but also tries to explain where he is coming from in attacking Bond, who had been one of the founders of the SNCC in 1960 and who was elected to the Georgia House of Representatives in 1965, in the first wave of blacks elected to office in the wake of the Civil Rights Act and Voting Rights Act: "We feel that Julian Bond as a member of the Democratic Party is part and parcel of the machinery of oppression. We feel that the Democratic Party and the Republican Party are criminal conspiracies against the people, and we show that anyone who affiliates with them, supports them, speaks good about them, writes good about them, are aiding and abetting this criminality." Regarding Dr. King, Cleaver is somewhat more generous:

BUCKLEY: Martin Luther King advocated three specific pieces of national legislation, all of which were enacted into law, so if he were here mightn't he say that in fact his agitation did help?

CLEAVER: Well, he was here, you see, and he was agitating and he had a particular approach to the situation, namely nonviolent, and he died by violence at the hands of an assassin, you see? Someone who opposed his program very actively. . . . We don't consider Martin Luther King to be one of the pigs of the power structure. He was moving against the power structure, but in a manner that we feel was not calculated to bring the power structure down.

BUCKLEY: Why?

CLEAVER: Well, because essentially it helped to strengthen the power structure.

BUCKLEY: Why?

CLEAVER: Because of functioning within the channels that the power structure can deal with.

BUCKLEY: In other words, anything that doesn't actually require a dissolution of the power structure is simply a form of perpetuation of tyranny?

CLEAVER: Well, it's helping it to function because Martin

Luther King when he first started his nonviolent tactics, uh, they were new to the American scene, and because they were new the pigs didn't really know how to deal with them, so that some gains could be made, but after a repetition of his process over the months and over the years, the pigs had programmed it so that they were perfectly capable of containing it, and limiting its effect.

Needless to say, Buckley is not amenable to the notion that the power structure needs to be brought down. He wonders how black empowerment could serve constructive rather than destructive objectives.

BUCKLEY: In New York, there are a lot of people who nowadays are saying what only the right wing was saying a while ago, which is that the labor unions effectively block black people from entering construction trade unions. There are those who are calling for black capitalism. There are those who have enough faith in the Negro people to subscribe to the doctrines of a Nathan Glazer and Patrick Moynihan that they must be given a chance to exercise black power. Now all of that is in motion, and many of these tactics are new, and many discoveries are being made which directly benefit people in very concrete ways: education, jobs, housing, medicine, and the rest of it. But you simply want to reject the whole of it as pig hypocrisy.

CLEAVER: Well, I think it is hypocrisy. I don't see any prospect of these people who, on the one hand, are willing to drop bombs on the Vietnamese people—who are struggling to control their country—and then coming here with their wars on poverty, trying to turn black people into black capitalists, when in fact it's the capitalistic system that has to be destroyed, because it is the mother of all this oppression. The same situation that your people found themselves in when they came here, and that other ethnic groups have found themselves in, uh, we find ourself in that position. Plus, we find the descendents of those ethnic groups who first came here, now are part of the power structure, and actively involved in oppressing us. And they united against us, they closed the doors to the melting pot against us. . . .

Cleaver sticks to his guns, as it were, disagreeing that any genuine progress can come for blacks within the context of a capitalist system. Things finally come to a head during the Q&A at the end. The crowd is full of Cleaver supporters, who not only applaud his comments but also hiss at some of Buckley's comments. Cleaver has been mostly sticking to expressing the Panther platform throughout the exchange, but now he turns to a more direct attack on Buckley himself.

CLEAVER: I think that your following, the people in the Republican Party who worship you, and who read your disgusting magazine, the *National Review*, I think that they're the ones who are alienated from reality. I read some of your stuff this morning, you know, and well it was just, it seems to me that it's criminal, and I think that's far more worse than rape. I think that you're raping the future, and you're murdering the future, and everything that the Republican Party is involved in and everything in the *National Review*, I think is detrimental to the people of this country.

BUCKLEY: This is music to my ears, Mr. Cleaver. There is no higher ambition I have than to represent exactly the opposite of what you represent, and I think that I've achieved it.

CLEAVER: Well, I'm glad to be of service to you.

In objecting to the patent radicalism of Cleaver's strain of Black Power, Buckley begins to come across as a strong advocate for the more moderate civil rights movement, notwithstanding the reservations he had expressed elsewhere—in *National Review*, in his newspaper column, and on *Firing Line* itself—about certain aspects of civil rights legislation and many of the tactics of civil disobedience.

In many ways, Buckley's reaction was perfectly typical. Historian Peniel E. Joseph observes that Black Power "provoked a visceral reaction in white Americans who could more easily identify with civil rights activists than with Black Power militants."[22] Buckley could identify with elements of the less radical civil rights movement even as Black Power offered a notion of self-determination that appealed, at least in theory. Years later, it would become common for many conservatives to note that they had erred regarding civil rights. For example, in his modestly titled 1990 book, *Right from the Beginning*, paleo-conservative Patrick Buchanan writes, "the civil rights movement was liberalism's finest hour. . . . If they have stumbled and blundered terribly since, they knew what they were doing then. And what they were doing was right."[23]

In rejecting Black Power as articulated by Cleaver, Buckley was hardly moved to call civil rights liberalism's finest hour, but it is true that the opponents of civil rights that he encountered on *Firing Line*, whether unrepentant right-wing racists or fired-up left-wing radicals, reinforced his support for the objectives (and ethical underpinnings) of the civil rights movement, even as he clung tenaciously to his states' rights position.

If the newspapers and the nightly news tended to reduce Black Power spokesmen to their slogans, Buckley had taken the opposite tack by allowing them to talk themselves into a corner. This is particularly clear in "The Republic of New Africa," a 1968 episode in which Milton Henry, the vice president of said hypothetical republic, makes a radical plea for black separatism. The republic would be a separate all-black state existing in place of Alabama, Georgia, Mississippi, South Carolina,

Louisiana, and possibly Florida. Henry's radicalism is different from Cleaver's in that he is calling for separation as a solution to black problems rather than for a revolutionary defeat of the existing system. Further, though he has some good things to say about Cuba, he does not seem to oppose capitalism per se. Rather, he emphasizes that white America helped Korea establish a manufacturing economy after the war, but has not done the same for blacks; he thus implicitly advocates a separatist black capitalism.

Henry proclaims, "I'm not interested in white people. I'm interested in the realization of freedom for black people, period. . . . I'm not worried about anything other than the elevation of black men, and if that means the fall of white men, fine. . . . If that meant even the slavery of white men, so be it." He even acknowledges, "I'm a good black racist." Unlike Cleaver and the Panthers, he is unwilling to accept whites in his movement. Responding to Henry's insistence that all contemporary American whites continue to benefit from slavery, Buckley asks about a hypothetical Polish washerwoman who has just arrived in the United States and is trying to make her way on eighty-five dollars a week. Should she feel guilty for slavery? What should she do to make amends? The frustrated Henry finally suggests that "she could kill herself, that's one real good thing she could do. She could not come here."

Henry is agitated, at moments almost coming unhinged. Further, he wears a massive ankh around his neck, suspended on something that looks like a swing-set chain, and he has two silent black security guards in military fatigues wearing Black Power amulets posted behind him throughout the program. They are unarmed, hands crossed sternly across their chests rather than hanging at the ready near holsters. Henry's complaints about the disempowerment of American blacks are earnest and passionate, and he aptly conveys why some, in frustration, had shifted gears from advocating integration to promoting separation, that is, black nationalism. But, set as he is on angry autopilot, his staccato rant is alarming and would be unlikely to convince anyone on the fence regarding Black Power. Still, it was an interesting conversation between two men who were unwilling to compromise but were nonetheless willing to hear each other out.

Buckley had declined to interview some whom he found too extreme, like LeRoi Jones and H. Rap Brown, but the Milton Henry episode alone shows the extent to which he was open to airing the opinions of radicals. Imagine the preproduction debate over the presence of Henry's bodyguards! Buckley could

Black nationalist Milton Henry has two silent black security guards in military fatigues posted behind him throughout the program; he proclaims, "I'm not interested in white people. I'm interested in the realization of freedom for black people, period. . . . I'm not worried about anything other than the elevation of black men, and if that means the fall of white men, fine. . . . If that meant even the slavery of white men, so be it."

CREDIT: *Hoover Institution*

not have been keen on the idea, but he was generally willing to make compromises in order to secure a guest—eight years later when lawyer Alan Dershowitz would only appear on the show to discuss obscenity if his client, *Deep Throat* star Harry Reems, could appear at his side, Buckley finally caved in, and even spoke a few contemptuous words to the porn star. (Responding to Reems's contention that pornographic films reflect women's new demands for rights: "Most porn movies remind most men who see them not that women would make good lawyers or good doctors, but [that] they make good sex.") Buckley neither introduced Henry's security men nor otherwise acknowledged their presence. An angry "good black racist," his mute guards, and the godfather of American conservatism, stuck seated in chairs on a half-lit minimalist stage debating for an hour whether American blacks should be given five or six southern states with which to form their own nation? It's a scenario teetering on the edge of the surreal, impossible to imagine on TV today.

By the time Huey P. Newton was on the show, five years after Henry's appearance, the Panthers were struggling. Newton and Cleaver had had a falling-out; Cleaver was still in exile; several leaders, such as Fred Hampton, had been killed; and the FBI's COINTELPRO had infiltrated the organization and planted seeds of dissension. A year later, Newton himself would flee to Cuba to escape a murder charge. On *Firing Line*, Newton was all smiles as he explained the Marxist dialectic, and Buckley was rhetorically flummoxed by his guest. At one point the host exclaims, "I'm attempting to pin down a point and I'm losing track of it. . . . It may be that one of the difficulties you have as chief spokesman for the Black Panther Party . . . is your total incoherence; that is to say, people don't understand what you're talking about. I don't understand what you're talking about, and I'm a very close listener."

Newton talked in a cheerful, steady stream of Maoist propaganda, barely coming up for air. Finally, Buckley performed the *Firing Line* version of throwing in the towel: he put down his clipboard, signaling that he realized the futility of attempting to tame his guest's logorrhea. For viewers already in sympathy with Newton's cause, his oration would likely not have seemed as incoherent as Buckley found it: Newton would have come across as a remarkably affable revolutionary. But those already inclined to be skeptical of the student radicals clutching Mao's Little Red Book to their breasts would certainly have found their doubts confirmed by Newton's performance.* A *Firing Line* viewer in Cambridge, Massachusetts, wrote Buckley, "I thought Huey Newton made a dialectic ASS out of himself without any help from you." Notably, there's no reason to think that this letter came from a dyed-in-the-wool conservative, as he added that he always enjoyed the program even though he didn't always agree with Buckley.[24]

Whether or not Newton made an ass of himself, there's no denying that he laid on the revolutionary shtick with a heavy hand.[25] The Black Power movement was spiraling, and this was one of the final *Firing Line* episodes to address the topic; later episodes of the 1970s that addressed race mostly centered on issues such as electoral politics and the legacy of the civil rights movement.

Watching network TV in the late 1960s, one received two very different pictures of America. In one, complacent white Americans populated pleasant small towns, suburbs, or perhaps even desert isles, their worries confined largely to interpersonal misunderstandings or intrafamily conflicts.[26] In the

---

* One of the best moments in the documentary *Berkeley in the Sixties* (Mark Kitchell, 1990) comes when Panther cofounder Bobby Seale describes how Newton revealed his plan for raising money to buy shotguns. Seale and Newton went to a Chinese bookstore, bought up a hundred copies of the Little Red Book for twenty cents each, quickly sold them for a dollar each on the Berkeley campus, then raced back for more books.

other, disgruntled blacks, students, and other "radicals" did not *populate* so much as *teem* in urban spaces, calling for shutdowns, revolution, and civil—or uncivil—disobedience.

In his classic book on media coverage of the New Left, Todd Gitlin observes that the latter picture was created within the strictures of dominant journalistic "frames" that required stories to feature "newsworthy" figures and dynamic action. With few exceptions, journalists emphasized sensationalism and violence, covering resistance to the Vietnam War, for example, as the story of angry protestors rather than conveying the protestors' complaints about the war itself. The 1965 *CBS Reports* episode "Watts: Riot or Revolt?" attempted some understanding of the black perspective, though media historians, looking back, tend to feel that it ultimately blamed black residents for their problems. That same year, *Hell in the City of Angels*, a documentary produced by local Los Angeles station KTLA, was even less sympathetic.[27]

By 1968, slogans like "Burn, baby, burn" and "Off the pigs" had largely displaced the "We shall overcome" rhetoric that King and others had promoted just a few years earlier.[28] As Hentoff had stated on the "Black Power" episode of *Firing Line*, by the late sixties there was a widespread feeling among blacks that the ending of "We shall overcome" would be endlessly deferred. The legislation King had advocated had been enacted, but it was not being enforced.

At the end of the day, *Firing Line* presents a picture of Black Power quite different than that created by the three television networks. Amazingly, a PBS public affairs program designed to convert Americans to conservatism shows us some of the most comprehensive representations of Black Power from this era outside of the underground press and other alternative media sources. As for the civil rights movement, the networks had gravitated to Dr. King as a spokesman. They had shown the most traumatic images of white-on-black violence, such as the police attack on the marchers on the Edmund Pettus Bridge in Selma and the turning of fire hoses on protestors in Birmingham. *Firing Line* took us away from such timely news events into the realm of contemplative discussion, and expanded the list of experts consulted beyond King, who never appeared on the show.

Remarkably, many years later Buckley would acknowledge his change of thinking regarding federalism and voting rights. In 2004 he told *Time*, "I once believed we could evolve our way up from Jim Crow. I was wrong: federal intervention was necessary."[29] The anti-racism, pro–states' rights advocate had come around. But by then *almost* everyone had, at least in theory. (In his twilight years, Jesse Helms would still maintain that the South should have been left alone with its race problem.) Buckley may have shifted his thoughts on federal intervention, but he certainly had not gone liberal in general where race was concerned. In fact, his interest in discussing racism, the civil rights movement, Black Power, and the implications of various strategies for improving the lot of American blacks had reached its apogee in the sixties and seventies. The topic of race was significantly less central on *Firing Line* in the 1980s. When it reappeared during the final ten years of the show, things really nosedived for liberal viewers as Buckley swiped at multiculturalism and "political correctness." The nadir came with *Firing Line*'s 1993 special two-hour debate titled, "Resolved: Political Correctness Is a Menace and a Bore."

It's a fascinating show on numerous counts. We find Buckley on the same side of the stage as Ira Glasser of the ACLU, since both opposed speech codes, though for rather different reasons. Robert Bork joins them as well. Cornel West, Mark Green, and others sit on the opposite side, and Michael Kinsley moderates. The opponents find themselves agreeing at numerous points that they have no use for the notion of "political correctness," with the liberals rejecting censorship as strongly as the conservatives and arguing that the whole notion of "political correctness" is a red herring (or a menace, if you will) to distract us from really debating the nature of inequality in American society. As Green notes, Buckley has, with his "political correctness is a menace and a bore" resolution, set up a "typically cunning, heads-they-win-tails-we-lose-scenario" for Green's side. Yet Green also notes in his opening comments that Buckley is sitting on the same side with the ACLU, so, really, the liberals have won from the get-go.

Buckley doesn't see it that way, though he does think that the civil rights activists (and feminists) have already gone as far as they need to go. Asked by Green how big a problem racial and gender discrimination are, Buckley responds, "I don't think it's a big problem . . . on the contrary, it seems to me plain that an enormous effort has been made to affirm and advance the rights of ethnic minorities, and I don't know of any woman at all, including the ones who rule my life, who are effectively discriminated against." The liberal debaters emphasize that more than half of the black children in America are born into poverty and that of the more than one hundred judges chosen for courts of appeal in the 1980s, only two were black. One of those two was Clarence Thomas.

Buckley sees these points as irrelevant. In fact, back in 1981 he had had the black conservative economist Thomas Sowell on the show, and he had been drawing on Sowell's arguments ever since. That there was only one woman in Congress in 1981 was not a symptom (much less proof) of sexism, Sowell and Buckley agreed: women chose to lead lives outside of politics. Blacks similarly made lifestyle choices that led them away from certain professions. That racism still *existed* was a fact that Buckley would acknowledge in the post–civil rights and Black

Power years, but that racial discrimination continued to be a serious *problem* he would deny throughout the remaining years of *Firing Line*'s history.

With Reagan in the White House, and the Republicans and the country veering right, affirmative action and political correctness became repeat targets for conservatives. Henceforth, for many of those marching in step with Buckley, anyone claiming that significant work remained to be done to cure America's racism, sexism, or other isms was simply a menace and a bore. As historian Nancy MacLean explains, the white "massive resistance" to desegregation in the post–*Brown v. Board of Education* years had been fully displaced by the 1980s by a notion of "color blindness" that allowed no room for strategies such as affirmative action.[30] Conservative movement strategists had pushed back (but never pushed out, she adds) the overtly bigoted politicians, and "their eclipse, in turn, enabled the right to appropriate the language of civil rights and racial justice, turning its power against its original bearers in a kind of political jujitsu."[31] Affirmative action, then, was not attacked by conservatives for helping blacks but for discriminating against whites. Having pioneered this line on the heels of JFK's initial use of the term *affirmative action* in 1961, Buckley would live to see his attacks on "quotas" and "reverse discrimination" become common parlance among conservatives.

Ultimately, Buckley both won and lost the *Firing Line* confrontation with civil rights and Black Power. He won to the extent that the "political jujitsu" described above ultimately gained—and continues to maintain—tremendous traction. He lost insofar as the federal government was ultimately responsible for the hard push to redress many of the repercussions of American racism. Further, he could not successfully drive home the case for a states' rights position devoid of racism. It was damn hard to find *Firing Line* guests who supported a notion of "states' rights" that was untainted by bigotry or by more submerged but still pernicious notions of the meaning of southern "customs." It was well and good for Buckley to tell an NAACP representative visiting *Firing Line* in 1966 that people should have the right to sell their homes to anyone they wanted, for example, but this individual preference existed nowhere without additional support lent by de facto segregation or redlining or unscrupulous real estate brokers unwilling to sell homes to blacks.

Of course, Buckley was not the only one arguing that one could oppose the Civil Rights Act, the Voting Rights Act, federal intervention in housing and schools, etc., on principled conservative grounds that were, theoretically, untainted by racism. Barry Goldwater argued that same thing, and the conservative movement that emerged in the wake of his 1964 defeat rode the wave of this argument. Looking back, critics on the left tend to assume that this was a shell game, that there was an inherently nonsensical dimension to the bait-and-switch of opposing desegregation on states' rights grounds while simultaneously opposing racism on ethical grounds. In his magazines and columns, Buckley could advance the argument on his own terms, but on his TV show it was more precarious because he had to defend attacks coming from both left and right. He held his own, but it was tricky.

He came closest to losing the argument in a 1998 *Firing Line* encounter with ACLU executive director Ira Glasser. Buckley twisted Glasser's arm for years to appear on a two-hour *Firing Line* debate titled, "Resolved: That the ACLU Is Full of Baloney." Glasser rightly saw it as a bit of a setup, but he finally consented to appear. Realizing that the ACLU was an old organization and that Buckley would be able to point to at least a few weak moves that they had made over the years, Glasser dug into the *National Review* archive to find question-

Buckley and Ira Glasser of the ACLU debate, while Michael Kinsley moderates.

CREDIT: *Hoover Institution*

able stuff Buckley had said about civil rights, and he read it aloud on the show.

Glasser describes this old *National Review* material as "completely unrespectable," and he says that Buckley knew it. Shortly thereafter, Glasser was at dinner at the Buckley residence, and Bill's wife Pat asked him, "Why are you so hard on my husband Bill on television?" Glasser said, "Well, Pat, he says so many terrible things! You have to do something about that in private." Needless to say, she did not.

This was just friendly dinner party banter. Off the air, the director of the ACLU and the architect of the postwar conservative movement got along smashingly. Glasser had taken Buckley to his first baseball game (he insisted they take the subway instead of Buckley's limo), and to Nathan's on Coney Island for hot dogs (this time Buckley won: they took the limo).[32] Buckley liked Glasser, not *despite* the fact that on several occasions he had backed him into a corner on *Firing Line* but precisely *because* of it. The price of advocating no-holds-barred TV debates was that sometimes you would lose, and your opponent would prove decisively that you had, at one point, really been full of baloney.

CHAPTER FOUR

CHIVALROUS PUGILISM

How *Firing Line* Tried to KO Women's Lib

William F. Buckley was not a feminist.

This hardly constitutes a shocking revelation. Yet he was not unsympathetic to all of feminism's goals, and he did not harbor the callous antipathy toward the movement that is typical of so many on the hard right. That said, the women's liberation movement was not a welcome cultural turn for him. By contrast, he could more fully understand the pressing concerns of the civil rights movement: he acknowledged that racism was a pernicious problem. Likewise, he understood that countercultural youth—antiwar activists, poets, musicians—were seeking a better world. He just disagreed about what made the world flawed and what would make it better.

Take the hippies. When Allen Ginsberg recited a very long poem on *Firing Line* in 1968, Buckley admitted with clear pleasure that he "kind of liked" it. He did not even seem to flinch at the obvious relish Ginsberg took in intoning the line "smelling the brown vagina-moist ground harmless." A conversation about drugs and poetry followed.

BUCKLEY: I enjoyed that. I think it's very beautiful [the poem]. Now, are you suggesting that because you wrote

that while you were under LSD you were able to
do it?

GINSBERG: Well, it's a natural thing. I cited Blake and
Wordsworth as having that natural vision. I think that the
LSD thing is not an unnatural vision as evidenced by the
particular details like "sheep speckled the mountain side"—

BUCKLEY: Yeah, yeah.

GINSBERG: —that you recognize, that are human things
that everybody has seen in nature. I think the LSD clarified
my mind and left it open to get that sense of giant, vast
consciousness. Specifically, the one thing I noticed and tried
to describe was the ocean of heaven, the atmosphere, is like
an ocean and at the bottom of that ocean of air are all sorts of
rivulets, and that those rivulets, like at the bottom of the fish
tank, move all the trees, move the people around, the hair,
the beards, the grass, the lamb's wool, the rain beating on the
grass. So that it's one system, like one giant being breathing.
One giant breathing being that we are all a part of. And which
we always forget, that we are together the God of the universe.

Ginsberg conveys all this with infectious enthusiasm. It's
fun to listen to him. As poetry, this kind of stuff obviously has
merit in Buckley's eyes. As philosophy or politics, he finds it
pretty lightweight, and he tells Ginsberg as much. As a wordsmith, Ginsberg was *interesting* to Buckley. His problem was
that Ginsberg's *analysis* was, like that of all the flower-power
crowd, merely "poetical," with ill-conceived "philosophical pre-
tensions."

For a conservative at the time, this was a relatively kind
judgment. The illiberal mainstream disparaged the hippies as
stinky spoiled brats. One irate *National Review* reader even declared, "The convincer in my decision to quit buying *NR* was
the disgusting appearance of Editor Bill Buckley on TV with

his seedy-looking Schickelgruber-Beatnik hairdo and sloppy-collared shirts, along with a retinue of whiney-snively-militant-Sodomite-looking punks."[1]

It's true that Buckley was occasionally rumpled on the show, and that he didn't particularly concern himself about Ginsberg's long hair and open devotion to buggery. Buckley didn't care if hippies were sloppy and—gasp!—different. He just wanted to decipher the sources of their alienation. In sum, many kinds of disaffected and rebellious liberals were, like the hippies, *comprehensible* to Buckley, and he was eager to debate them on *Firing Line*. But he just didn't *get* feminism.

Buckley believed in fair play and meritocracy. Yes, sexism and inequality existed. Yes, it was unfair for women not to get workplace promotions simply because they were women. But such problems were not insurmountable. The Equal Employment Opportunity Act of 1972 and the Equal Credit Opportunity Act of 1974, for example, provided legal recourse to women. Strange notions that women could stop shaving their legs, stop bearing primary responsibility for housework and child care, stop taking their husbands' last names, stop taking husbands at all—what on earth did this have to do with "equality"? On the whole, Buckley supported the notion of "equal rights" (as he defined them) but not of the "equal rights *movement*," which he felt had gone in an altogether too radical direction. True to form, he opposed the kinds of structural changes that many feminists called for—both the reformist liberals of the National Organization for Women and the more radical, revolutionary left-wing crowd.

Buckley maintained consistently on *Firing Line* that women were not "inferior" to men, but that they were simply "different" and worthy of male protection and respect. This did not mean that women should be legally disadvantaged, paid less than men, and so on. It was difficult for Buckley to grasp the scope of women's unequal status in some part, it is fair to surmise, because so many of the women in his own social and professional circles were highly accomplished, intelligent, and successful. His sister Priscilla, for instance, was managing editor of *National Review* from 1959 to 1986. And his friend Clare Boothe Luce had been a congressional representative, ambassador, and successful playwright. Strong and talented women rose to the top, he believed, just like strong and talented men.

Today, such ideas sound conservative, if not rabidly so. Taken in the context of the late 1960s and early 1970s, though, some of Buckley's notions about the fairer sex teetered on the edge of progressive. After all, he admired professionally successful women and did not declare that they were destroying the traditional home. Consider that in 1969 many right-wingers were absolutely livid that a female character on *Sesame Street* was employed outside the home as a nurse.[2] Antifeminists were really digging in their heels and did not like the changes they were seeing on TV, never mind the changes under way beyond the screen. In this climate, the fact that Buckley invited accomplished female lawyers, professors, and activists onto his TV show to debate political issues seems rather enlightened.

On the other hand, and on a somewhat ridiculous note, Buckley was also quite comfortable expressing the old male chauvinist platitude that women could hardly claim to be disempowered in light of how bossy they generally were. On an episode centered on freedom of expression he exclaimed to feminist lawyer and First Amendment advocate Harriet Pilpel, "God, the women I know aren't oppressed as regards their freedom of expression. . . . Supposing it were documented that women speak twice as much as men. Would that take care of the problem?" Pilpel firmly told him off and even iced the cake of her counterargument with a recent finding by a public interest group: "the amount of time available to women and for the discussion of women's issues is minuscule as far as television is concerned." She was completely right, though it was, of course, ironic to make this observation to a male chauvinist hosting one of the few shows that did provide reasonable time for such discussion.

The story of *Firing Line*'s engagement with women's lib is best told by examining Buckley's interaction with several key guests: on the left, Betty Friedan, Germaine Greer, and the lesser-known Harriet Pilpel; on the right, Phyllis Schlafly, Clare Boothe Luce, and even Margaret Thatcher. Via his conversations with these guests we see how *Firing Line* charted the ebb and flow of conservative reactions to and against feminism over a thirty-year period. Buckley was sometimes puzzled by feminism, wondering aloud on his TV show why women would want to eliminate chivalrous behavior, but his primary interest throughout the 1970s was in sparring with smart feminist guests, debating the very issue of patriarchal oppression, while also questioning the pros and cons of the Equal Rights Amendment.

By the 1990s, however, things had taken a turn, as *Firing Line* came to engage with feminism almost exclusively via the prism of multiculturalism and "political correctness," with guest conservative debaters such as David Horowitz taking a much harder (and meaner) line than Buckley, the old-school conservative who endlessly revisited the issue of "chivalry" at the expense of engaging with the hard realities of discrimination. As the country turned from left to right, from the sixties to the nineties, feminism seemed to have accomplished much, even as women endured the harsh cultural resistance identified by Susan Faludi in her 1991 bestseller, *Backlash*. In these same years, *Firing Line*'s take on feminism turned from curious and skeptical to bilious and hostile.

To be sure, Buckley's polite (if occasionally sarcastic) intellectual opposition to the women's liberation movement was in many ways unique. But then, there has never been an across-the-board homogeneous conservative stance on feminism and female empowerment. At the grassroots level we find, for example, conservative evangelical women's groups who seek personal (and sometimes political) empowerment in the biblical stance on womanhood even as many of them oppose "feminism" per se.[3] At the top, in terms of power and exposure, we find pundits like Pat Robertson equating feminism with witchcraft and Rush Limbaugh deriding "feminazis."

Or consider anti–Equal Rights Amendment activist Phyllis Schlafly, a powerful and successful political operative, lawyer, and mother of six who insists that legally mandated "equality" would unleash the natural male desire to exploit rather than protect women. As the women's liberationists of the 1970s enthusiastically noted that the ERA would efficiently invalidate hundreds of discriminatory laws regarding employment, property, and family relations, Schlafly predicted that the ERA would do nothing less than unleash a maelstrom of husbandly negligence, as men would no longer be legally required to support their wives: "Even though love may go out the window," she wrote in *The Power of the Positive Woman*, "the [financial] obligation should remain. ERA would eliminate that obligation."[4] Wives already had it great, she claimed, with housework requiring only a few hours each day, leaving a woman the opportunity to pursue full- or part-time work outside the home or time "to indulge to her heart's content in a wide variety of interesting educational or cultural or homemaking activities."[5] A typical American, middle-class, stay-at-home mom with one child might find this notion somewhat far-fetched. One with six would find it absolutely bonkers.

Making the first of six *Firing Line* appearances in 1973, Schlafly sat on the dais in a prim salmon-colored sweater, navy blue skirt discreetly covering her knees, hair swept up with more than a whisper of Final Net. She was the most gracious antifeminist imaginable—an alarming hybrid of Emily Post and some kind of Bizarro-World Susan B. Anthony. As was her

habit, Schlafly coyly mentioned that she wasn't mentioning lesbians: "I prefer to discuss and debate the thing [the ERA] on
the issues . . . but if you're going to bring it up . . . the National
Organization for Women [NOW], which is applying the most
intense pressure for this thing, at its recent convention passed
resolutions in behalf of lesbians and in behalf of prostitutes."[6]
Elsewhere she called feminists a "bunch of bitter women seeking a constitutional cure for their personal problems."[7] On *Firing Line* she was utterly composed; she never seemed to stop
smiling. This was the kind of person you could imagine taking
a conference call from Jesse Helms and Nancy Reagan while
frosting a Bundt cake.

Schlafly and Buckley were aligned on several fronts regarding women's issues. Neither was opposed to women working,
for example, and Buckley certainly had no problem with Schlafly's hard push to get Republican women more active in the
GOP, moving beyond being "merely doorbell pushers"[8] and

Always smiling while arguing, antifeminist Phyllis Schlafly was the
kind of person you could imagine taking a conference call from Jesse
Helms and Nancy Reagan while frosting a Bundt cake.
CREDIT: *Hoover Institution*

envelope stuffers to actively shaping the party platform. But in many ways Schlafly swung further right than Buckley. Looking back on the ERA in 2006, more than twenty years after the amendment's definitive defeat, Schlafly stated that she "simply didn't believe we needed a constitutional amendment to protect women's rights. . . . I knew of only one law that was discriminatory toward women, a law in North Dakota stipulating that a wife had to have her husband's permission to make wine."[9] Though not trained as a lawyer, and generally confident that the legal system could redress female complaints without recourse to a constitutional amendment, one suspects Buckley would have found it far-fetched to assert that the right to vinification was the single legal inequity facing women in the 1970s.

In sum, Buckley was skeptical, but still more sympathetic to feminist goals than Schlafly. One last example will drive the point home. In 1981 Schlafly stated before a Senate Labor Committee hearing on workplace sexual harassment, "Men hardly ever ask sexual favors of women from whom the certain answer is 'no.' Virtuous women are seldom accosted by unwelcome sexual propositions or familiarities, obscene talk or profane language."[10] Buckley was not so naïve as to believe that only the impure of heart were subjected to unwanted sexual come-ons from men.

Also more hard-line on feminist issues was journalist Midge Decter, an outspoken neocon who made two appearances on *Firing Line*. At the height of the women's movement in the 1970s, Decter had written that "the pursuit of orgasm for a woman is an entirely irrelevant undertaking." She later observed that women's libbers "were militant, angry, and in the grip of a curious but lethal combination of galloping self-pity and driving ambition. Almost overnight they succeeded in persuading an army of already fretful constituents that everything that troubled their lives was in essence political."[11]

Buckley would similarly bemoan the feminist notion that

"the personal is political," believing that the personal might be better described as informed by perfectly acceptable cultural norms fostered by valuable institutions such as the church and the family. The notion of disrupting such institutions was troubling to Buckley, but he was not venomous in his rhetoric; he would see no need to accuse women's libbers (at least publicly) of "self-pity and driving ambition," and he was about as likely to mention "the big O" as Phyllis Schlafly. (And much less likely to mention lesbians.) To put it rather conventionally, in attacking feminism on *Firing Line* in the 1970s, Buckley attempted—with uneven success—to be a perfect gentleman.

The program's presentation of women's lib was unique by virtue of the fact that Buckley had very specific worries, such as his near-obsessive concern about the potential impact of feminism on spoken and written language. *Firing Line* was also unique in that its host was interested not in sensationalism but, rather, in serious intellectual engagement with the other side. Elsewhere on TV, feminists were given much less time for thoughtful self-expression.

Take *Not for Women Only*, a patently misnamed morning talk show hosted by Barbara Walters. In 1973 NOW cofounder Betty Friedan and her daughter appeared on the program to answer hard-hitting questions like "Are you ever embarrassed by your mother?" It was utter pabulum. Friedan's *The Feminine Mystique* had been a major force in kicking off second-wave feminism in the United States in 1963. Ten years later, change had happened, but the goals of that movement were still very much a work in progress, and mainstream media discussion of feminism was typically slim, hostile, or dismissive. Walters was at least friendly, but this was not an interview that ran deep. And, to be fair, in the 1960s and '70s Walters had a hell of a time getting hard news assignments. She once had to cover "A Day in the Life of a Playboy Bunny."[12] So innocuous questions with Betty Friedan were a step up, but not exactly the feminist breakthrough in media coverage that either she or Friedan might have wished for.

In this context, *Firing Line* stood out for Buckley's genuine attempts to engage with, decipher, and debunk feminist goals, while allowing his feminist guests to have their say. For guests like Friedan who spoke best in sound bites or when reading from prepared texts, Buckley's approach was no blessing. Friedan appeared four times on the show. Invited initially in 1971, she managed to convey some of the aspirations of liberal feminism, but she spoke in a disjointed staccato. Listening to her felt rather like riding shotgun with someone still sorting out the subtleties of a manual transmission.

Buckley opened the show with a question that was truly pressing for him: "I should like to begin by asking Mrs. Friedan to comment on an observation of Sally Kempton, also of the movement [and Murray Kempton's daughter], who said of her, 'she misrepresents the case for feminism by making people believe that reform is the answer. The problem is more fundamental: the entire society has to be up-ended.' Is that so?"

In her peripatetic response Friedan said that Kempton's statement was "meaningless rhetoric," advocated for the radical restructuring of the family and against the "pseudo-radical rhetoric" of those in the movement who were "obsessed with rage," and noted that man was not "the enemy" and would also be liberated by the feminist movement. In other words, she was saying that reform *was* the answer, and that such reform would upend the entire society in a positive way that would be equally beneficial for men and women. She was calling for radical change, but not exactly revolution. The implication was that she was not a separatist, she was not a radical, she was not a man hater, she was not a lesbian.

Friedan had cofounded NOW and had been its leader from 1966 to 1970. This was the organization considered by many feminists to be home to "the squares" of the movement, as the president of the New York chapter, Jacqui Ceballos, had put it so aptly at a famous 1971 New York City debate on feminism moderated by Norman Mailer. The other women participating in that debate had promptly illustrated just how straitlaced the NOW folks really were. Jill Johnston of the *Village Voice* declared that "all women are lesbians except those who don't know it naturally; they are but don't know it yet." Then, she engaged in a three-way groping session with two other radical lesbians onstage.

In view of the fact that Friedan had referred to lesbians as a "lavender menace"[13] endangering the liberal feminist cause, this libidinous display was a real grapefruit-in-the-face to NOW. At this same debate, the Marxist Germaine Greer, author of the bestseller *The Female Eunuch*, favorably mentioned Mao Zedong's theorizing and bickered with Diana Trilling about how best to strategically deploy Freudian theory, all the while sporting a fetching feather boa. Greer was smart, articulate, and above all, cool.

Allowed the first question from the audience, Friedan could hardly compete with these extroverted vixens. She disjointedly suggested to the crowd that women had a right to speak publicly and to define their own ideologies. This was hardly breaking news. Elsewhere, NOW's spokespeople were widely seen, from the perspective of the "silent majority," as crazed bra burners. But here, surrounded by feminists further to the left, Friedan could be described at best as fuddy-duddy, at worst as incoherent.

Mailer cuts to the chase quite nicely: "Hmm. I simply don't know what you're talking about. Betty, you are just making speeches, you are appealing . . . to the lowest element in this audience. I've been on platforms with women all my life! My God! You act as if suddenly women are in public speaking. They've been, they've been doing that for a hundred years. We're not talking about that! What we're talking about is the extraordinary possibilities that exist in Women's Liberation. You're still talking about it as if I'm completely opposed to it, which I never was."

I hasten to add that at one point in the debate Mailer suggested he might put his "modest little Jewish dick on the table," only to fool people because it would really be a dildo, and he also referred to a heckler as "Cunty," which he used as a diminutive nickname rather than an adjective. So the point is not that Mailer was the voice of coherence and political reason at this event but that he did point precisely to the flaws in Friedan's self-presentation; her performance on Buckley's show had not been a deviation from the norm.

On *Firing Line*, Friedan would attempt to have her cake and eat it too, by showing the radical squareness of liberal feminism. It was extreme but good for everybody, even men.

FRIEDAN: I've found more and more men in the audience [at guest lectures], and they seem to feel that their liberation is entailed—why should men die ten years younger than women? And why should they have to live up to some stupid machismo that's obsolete when, you know, there are no bears to kill?! So, you know, to make every man think masculinity, the masculine mystique, you know—bear-killing, big-muscle, Ernest Hemingway would make every man to begin with feel so inadequate that then he has to defend himself, and you've got, you know, ten strikes against him before he begins. And this is almost as bad for men as the feminine mystique was in making women suppress their strength, or never even finding it in participation in society.

She added, as she had umpteen times before, that TV advertisers seemed to think that women should have an orgasm every time they used a vacuum cleaner—a formulation that she would repeat elsewhere by referencing floor wax or dishwashing soap. (Friedan had first introduced the notion of what we might call the "floorgasm" ten years earlier in the opening pages of *The Feminine Mystique*.[14]) Confusing? You bet. A transcript was produced of every *Firing Line* episode, available to viewers for a modest fee (a nice way to revisit a show that was virtually never repeated, in pre-VHS days), and one imagines a very frustrated stenographer pulling out her hair as she toiled over the 1971 Friedan episode. What kind of punctuation could possibly tame Friedan's "you know" mantra?

At one point, in debating abortion with Buckley, she seems to feel like she's got a real trump card.

> FRIEDAN: The reverence for life I share, and the reverence for this Jewish thing, you know, called humanity and, you know, the whole evolution of it. But you know—I think—you know, supposing that a uterus was implanted in you, and therefore you had to consider this in terms of an issue that was real for you, not just an abstract issue for someone else. I doubt that suddenly you would—you know, just as surely you don't consider yourself less important than all the sperm that might fertilize eggs that don't fertilize eggs, so you couldn't consider yourself as a person, you know, less important than an unborn fetus; you know.

What would William F. Buckley do if implanted with a uterus? This sounds like a setup for an elaborate off-color joke. Not taken aback for a second, Buckley responds that he would take care of a fetus with the same sense of responsibility as he would in caring for a senile father or mother. In sum, Friedan speechified on women's liberation without really engaging with Buckley. She was not invited back for twenty-three years.[15] It turns out that Friedan had actually given one of her best performances on the milquetoast *Not for Women Only*. Friedan simply didn't have the chops for TV. Buckley would have to look elsewhere for articulate experts on his favorite feminist topic, the Equal Rights Amendment.

The ERA came up quite often on *Firing Line*, and, really, the show offered the best available TV coverage. The rest of the mainstream electronic and print media tended simply to amplify women's internal disagreements about the amendment. The real action was taking place outside the spotlight, where lobbyists, activists, and politicians were duking it out, but that was of little interest to the mainstream media.[16] Buckley was largely disinterested in the typical "catfight" angle. He knew that some women disagreed about the ERA, but he had no desire to exploit this fact in particular. (Clare Boothe Luce similarly rejected such nonsense. At a 1971 public discussion following a screening of *The Women*—George Cukor's film based on Luce's very successful play—Luce and Gloria Steinem agreed on a surprising number of points, and Luce noted that even if they strongly disagreed they would not say so publicly lest they be accused of having a "hair-pulling contest."[17]) If *Firing Line* did often pair women against each other to discuss feminism, it did so not in the name of sensationalism but, rather, because they were the most informed and prominent experts on the topic. On the antifeminist side, of course, a frequent guest was the aforementioned Phyllis Schlafly.

Unlike Friedan, Schlafly was a media dynamo, a savvy activist who fully understood the nuances of style and spin. For instance, at a public debate with Schlafly in 1973 Friedan had notoriously blustered, "I'd like to burn you at the stake!" The line has often been repeated, though Schlafly's response is in many ways more interesting: "I'm glad you said that because it just shows the intemperate nature of proponents of ERA."[18] The retort perfectly illustrates Schlafly's capacity to craft a public image for the anti-ERA movement. As NOW members swung further left in the late 1970s, finally supporting lesbian rights and showing up at protests with signs saying things like "Lactators for ERA,"[19] Schlafly dressed her team in tasteful blouses, gave them advice about what makeup looked best on TV, and encouraged them to present homemade pies to legislators opposing ERA. A reviewer of one book on Schlafly observed that she was "ingratiating, intelligent, uncorrupted, energetic, determined, magnificently organized—conservatives tend to be gently bred, well mannered, splendidly educated, and perfectly groomed."[20]

Now, really, there are as many poorly groomed, uneducated, and rude conservatives in America as there are poorly groomed, uneducated, and rude liberals. But Schlafly managed to convey the impression—via her many media appearances on programs such as *The Phil Donahue Show* and *The Mike Douglas Show*, her CBS radio commentary, and her monthly newsletter— that she was a typical conservative. Comments about burning her at the stake, not to mention slights like Schlafly voodoo dolls (complete with pins), an incident in which a protestor smashed an apple pie into her face, and even a *Cagney & Lacey* TV episode about a prominent anti-ERA activist facing death threats—these things only made her stronger. As historian Donald Critchlow aptly concludes, the opposition actually worked to her advantage: "feminists helped make Schlafly into a national figure and perhaps even a cultural icon."[21] This prim activist—a delicate flower who had paid her way through college during World War II by working nights testing rifle and machine gun ammo[22]—was perfectly suited to expound upon the dangers of the ERA on *Firing Line*.

Firing Line's engagement with feminism runs parallel to wider cultural trends in that Buckley's conservative guests shared predictable concerns about the practical consequences of the ERA (the specter of military women engaged in combat loomed large) and, more generally, about the ways that the women's movement would potentially shake the very foundations of traditional interactions between the sexes. Indeed, there was a general sense of panic in the air in the years that feminists were advocating for ratification of the amendment. Growing up in Birmingham, Alabama, in the 1980s, the anxiety I most often heard voiced about the ERA was that it would mandate unisex bathrooms. Such panicky responses did not even come close to engaging with the real goals of the movement. Pro-ERA feminists were advocating for very basic rights in the 1970s and '80s: the right to receive equal pay for equal work, the right to be able to accuse your husband of rape, the right to receive proper insurance coverage for contraception. Gender-neutral access to toilets was simply not on the wish list.

While many liberal feminists focused on legal issues of equity, feminists further to the left like Germaine Greer advocated strongly for the disruption of conventional family relationships and structures. Or, as Buckley put it, on a 1973 program with Dr. Ann Scott from NOW, "[Y]our sister, Germaine Greer . . . feels that the family is really a very pernicious institution and that the genuine liberation of women won't come until after the family, the whole idea of the family—the molecular unit, she calls it—is destroyed." Clearly irked, Scott corrects him: "nuclear, nuclear unit." This rare rhetorical gaffe on Buckley's part revealed how strange the terms of the feminist movement were to him.

And what of the reference to Scott as Greer's sister? It is initially perplexing, as Scott looks nothing like Greer and doesn't speak in Greer's Oxbridge tones. Remarkably, Buckley was using *sister* in the broad feminist sense, without making even the slightest suggestion of sarcasm, though he would use scare quotes just moments later in referencing "woman power." This was one of his many moments of chivalrous pugilism. If feminists called each other "sister," he was willing to play along, up to a point.

The movement's oft-expressed desire to restructure or destroy the "molecular" family was a pressing concern for Buckley, but he seemed just as perturbed by the notion that matters of etiquette might be revised. Like Schlafly, he expressed anxiety that men would no longer graciously protect the weaker sex. This would go beyond mere violations of civility if women were allowed to engage in military combat. On a more mundane note, doors would no longer be opened for women, and moreover, they would be allowed to go down on sinking ships.

Buckley exhibited a particularly strong concern about the linguistic impact of feminism. When Friedan had appeared in 1971, he archly introduced her as the "founding father of the women's liberation movement." During the Q&A session of this episode, Lynne Williams, a regular on the questioning panel, suggested that she wanted "to do a little consciousness raising" with Buckley. She had recently married and had decided to keep her last name. Why then did Mr. Buckley continue to refer to her as "Miss Williams" instead of "Mrs. Williams"? Friedan interjected that "Ms." was the solution, but Williams rejected this as too difficult to pronounce. Buckley continued: "I would, of course, call you anything you like . . . Miss Millett, who is the author of *Sexual Politics*, I'm told won't come on this program unless I refer to her as 'Kate,' which I find . . . sort of decomposing, psychologically decomposing. I call some of my best friends on this program 'Mr. So-and-so,' and 'Miss So-and-so,' whatever, simply because I tend to feel that it observes a formality which is an act of respect for the audience. . . . I think notoriously the practice has been for people, who also have professional lives, to call themselves 'Miss So-and-so.' We called Miss Rosalyn Tureck here 'Miss,' and she's been married four times."

Williams asked if there was "something more serious" about "Miss," and Buckley interestingly replied, "The 'Miss' in effect says to your own constituency whether it's professional or artistic that they want very much to stress the fact of your being different from merely the connubial choice of your husband."

In effect, Buckley was positing that "Miss" established not unmarriedness, as many feminists claimed, but professional independence. There was no need for the acoustically jarring "Ms." neologism when a conventional word would suffice perfectly well. Of course, the feminists would ultimately win the battle for "Ms.," but what is interesting is that Buckley had thoroughly thought through the quandary and come up with a rhetorical solution he found quite reverential to the successful female professional. Again, chivalrous pugilism.

Buckley took particular pleasure in discussing the language of women's liberation with Germaine Greer on *Firing Line*. He opened the 1973 show by asking her opinion of new feminist-inflected rules about how the sexes should be referenced in textbooks. Greer was adamant that such questions were being addressed in entirely the wrong way:

GREER: The whole linguistic question of women's liberation is difficult because of the strange paradox of our position, which is the paradox which appears sometimes like a contradiction in my book. Are you to make "he" and "she" words equal in estimation or are you to screen out "she" as forever incapable of equaling "he" in estimation, grammatically?

BUCKLEY: Grammatically—

GREER: You could be anti-feminist, you see, by suppressing feminism, by suppressing the femaleness of a pronoun.

BUCKLEY: But there's no implied hierarchy, as far as I can see.

GREER: Oh, there is, because—

BUCKLEY: Well, now, [textbook publisher] Scott-Foresman says you should never refer to "early man." You should refer to "early humans," which means that you can't use a synecdoche.

GREER: But not only that. What it means is that the real attitude is going to be concealed by a form of primitive censorship, by a kind of ritual observance, whereas the actual situation won't change. It's like calling people "Ms." when in fact they're married. It doesn't change the character of their marriage, and I think it's a sort of hypocrisy.

BUCKLEY: In other words, you think that the emphasis on nomenclature is preposterous?

GREER: Well, I think it's such a trivial aspect of a real struggle that I think it's part of a general movement to co-opt a struggle for existence, really, and turn it into something futile.

Greer's radical structural analysis was spot-on. Changing language was meaningless if you couldn't address the foundational issues that made language biased in the first place. Buckley, conversely, felt that language was not biased, but that there must surely be elegant and reasonable ways to adjust our rhetoric in response to changing social conditions and norms. At base, he was delighted to converse with someone who was skeptical about the linguistic demands being made by mainstream liberal feminism. It must have been really exhilarating for contemporary viewers of an intellectual bent to witness this level of debate, with Buckley and Greer completely sidestepping the liberal feminist politics that appeared elsewhere in the mainstream media.

Needless to say, Buckley found much of Greer's analysis lunatic. She found great merit in communal childrearing, for example. But he was delighted to hear anyone speak critically of the feminist assault on everyday language, and, politics aside, this woman could really craft a sentence. With someone like Mailer, Buckley could rhetorically spar, but when Greer came on the show it was like a fencing match, more of a swashbuck-

ling "en garde!" than a pugilistic "sock-it-to-me!" affair. Greer
could certainly parry any highbrow literary thrust Buckley
might make, and she poked fun at him like a British schoolmarm for quoting Alcibiades: "Oh, come, come . . . we certainly
are flying high today."

Greer appeared only once on *Firing Line*, which is somewhat surprising, as Buckley shot some fifty episodes in the
United Kingdom, and he thought she had given a whiz-bang
performance. He tellingly included her in two later greatest-
hits episodes of *Firing Line*, and in his thank-you note to her
after the 1973 show he had written, "Goddamn it you are really
good."[23] A few weeks before her appearance on *Firing Line*, the
two of them had debated the motion "This House Supports the
Women's Liberation Movement" at Cambridge. Greer charmed
the pants off the crowd, even drawing laughter in the course
of mildly insulting them by suggesting they were "groupies"
assembled not out of a deep interest in the topic at hand but,
rather, to answer the question "How are these famous media
performers going to handle themselves?" She archly launches
her attack:

> GREER: Now, I am sorry to disappoint you, but I am not
> interested in delighting you with a song-and-dance routine
> with William Buckley, for whom I have rather more respect
> than you would be prepared to allow. I regard him as a man
> of intellectual probity, and part of my problem now is that
> I cannot understand altogether why Mr. Buckley is on the
> other side of the hall. Women's Liberation has always been
> historically a minority movement, something which again
> is not repugnant to Mr. Buckley, who is himself in favor, it
> seems to me, of minority movements of one sort or another.
> It strikes me as very strange that whereas Tennyson could
> support most of Mr. Buckley's propositions about free trade,
> and the private sector, and private enterprise, Tennyson found

no difficulty also in lending intellectual support to the idea
of Women's Liberation. And Mr. Buckley, whose general
political attitudes are about of the same vintage as Tennyson's,
apparently finds it impossible to follow him.

Buckley does not take the bait regarding Tennyson. Rather,
he opens with a slanted compliment, suggesting that Greer's
"brilliance is perhaps the principal asset of her movement,"
and adding that "I do not remember ever having opposed educational opportunities for women, or for that matter industrial
or political opportunities for women, and Miss Greer is quite
correct in her insight that it is inconsistent with my general
position to do anything of the sort."

He thereby affirms his support for women's liberation (allowing that the definition of "liberation" is open to debate), but
not for the women's liberation movement, which he rejects for
its revolutionary approach.

BUCKLEY: Those who do not allow an important distinction
between the two terms ["women's liberation" and "women's
liberation movement"] do not, for instance, allow a distinction
between a fight against poverty and a movement against
poverty that is led by representatives of an ideological creed.
Miss Greer moves on the assumption that the enslavement
of women is something that can only be dislodged by
revolutionary means. . . . Miss Greer [says] . . . we must have
communes. We must do away with religion. We must do
away with family. There is something of that comprehensive
concern of the worldmaker who says, "Because I do not choose
to marry, people ought not to marry. Because I do not choose
to rear a family, people ought not to rear a family." It is in the
name of that that we are being invited to consider a movement
toward the liberation of women, in the sense of giving them
rights to which, I think, most people feel they are obviously

entitled. This, ladies and gentlemen, is the fundamental issue before the House. Can we divorce women's liberation from the women's liberation movement? I say yes. Indeed we can. Can we assume that organic process can be made in your society—and in mine—without revolution? Yes, I do believe that it can.

Buckley's aversion to revolution was obviously conservative, but there was, too, a specifically libertarian angle expressed here, and this set him apart from the more conventional anti-ERA, "family values" crowd.[24] Buckley was not in favor of communal childrearing or the elimination of marriage, but his argument at Cambridge was that people had every right to make such lifestyle choices, just not to insist that they were mandatory for the entire culture. Both Greer and Buckley had been charming and articulate, and each had displayed genuine intellectual respect for the other. Still, Greer had won by a landslide vote of the students.

When Greer appeared on Buckley's show just a few weeks later, he seized the opportunity for a rematch. Greer held her own, though the small studio crowd was less in her corner than the rowdy Cantabrigians had been. Buckley, conversely, mustered more momentum than he had at Cambridge. Absent actual voting, the TV discussion had ended in a draw, although, arguably, Greer's entire argument about the exploitation of women was confirmed by the unexpected revelation on the show that Buckley had been paid three thousand dollars for his *Playboy* interview, whereas Greer had received not one thin dime for hers. "I had to sit for a whole week with a very obliging man [from *Playboy*]. The only people who made any money out of it were the peasants who had to dig his Fiat 1600 out of a field."

The small studio audience does not react in particular to this comment, though later there are audible gasps when a conservative questioner bemoans the fact that labor has become so expensive in Britain that middle-class professionals can no longer afford to hire servants. He even adds that he'd be quite happy not to have a wife to take care of him if he could only afford to eat out at a fine restaurant every night. This aristocratic whiner was not helping Buckley's side and, reading the transcript, Greer seems clearly ahead, but watching the show yields a different impression. Greer's tone is sour and exasperated. She is simply on edge. Buckley plays it cool, although, apparently unbeknownst to him, a disarming, atypical cowlick sprouting from the far side of his head bobs in and out of the frame throughout the episode, gently undermining his gravitas.

Discussing the exploitation of sex, Greer goes so far as to note that Buckley is "a very pretty man," which makes Buckley laugh but not the studio audience. The "very pretty man" moment is both uncomfortable and riveting. It's far-fetched to imagine that Greer was actually hitting on Buckley, and really, if you are debating feminism with a patriarch and you want to characterize him, *pretty* is one of the more emasculating word choices. Overall, it's an engaging episode precisely because Greer and Buckley are so finely matched in terms of wit and intellect, yet their personalities are so different, and it is never totally clear who is out-arguing whom. At one point, Buckley finds himself agreeing with Greer about the proper, compassionate treatment of rape victims. "If that's part of the women's liberation movement, I'm for it," he says somewhat unexpectedly. As if realizing he has gone over the edge in agreeing with sound feminist ideas, he changes the topic, asking abruptly, "Why do you want a communist state?"

The least successful *Firing Line* episodes were often those featuring conservative guests. One exception was the riveting Margaret Thatcher episode in 1975. Most of the conversation centered on economic policy and the ins and outs of governmental bureaucracy. Left to her own devices, Thatcher would

surely not have said anything for or against feminism. She
could not possibly have been less interested in the topic. But
during the Q&A session, Jeff Greenfield observed that there
had been an increased number of women running for public
office in the United States the preceding year and that "their
conservative ideology helps to overcome one of the stereotypical objections [to women who run for office] . . . there's a feeling
among the electorate . . . that women tend to think more emotionally, they're somehow less hardnosed."

Buckley interjects: "If you're going to run for office you're going to be like Bella Abzug." "Or Hubert Humphrey [would be]
more apt," Greenfield counters. He then remarks upon Thatcher's conservative reputation while serving in Edward Heath's
cabinet, when she was known as "Margaret Thatcher, Milk
Snatcher" for eliminating the free milk program for schoolchildren over seven years of age. Did her ideology help her overcome stereotypical objections to women holding office?

Thatcher takes immediate offense, irked by the notion that
her gender is of interest to anyone. There's no close-up to confirm, but early in the exchange one senses sweat breaking out
on Greenfield's upper lip.

THATCHER: No. Would you be so very surprised if I said
that at home on the whole we just look at the person and not
necessarily the sex?

BUCKLEY: Yes.

THATCHER: You would? Well, that's because you're a man,
you're limited. . . . Honestly, I regard these questions as very
trivial. You don't mind my saying so?

GREENFIELD: And if I did what would I do?

THATCHER: Look, we look at a person to see if they've got
the abilities. Now, I've heard this argument frequently, that
women are really rather more emotional than men. Really,

women are intensely practical. Again, I don't mean that flippantly. We are an intensely practical sex. We often get on with the job; we don't always talk about it as much as men; but we get on doing it.

BUCKLEY: But is—

THATCHER: Now you ask me—look, am I emotional? I don't know.

GREENFIELD: No, no, no, no. No. No. I think that is a misinterpretation.

THATCHER: You decided not. All right.

BUCKLEY: Excuse me, Mrs. Thatcher, but isn't a logical consequence of what you've just said that there are very few competent women in England?

THATCHER: No, not at all.

BUCKLEY: Because there are very few women politicians. And if everybody proceeds to elect people without any reference to sex, it must mean that they choose men ninety-nine percent of the time because they're superior. [audience laughter]

THATCHER: No, I'm afraid that women are—

GREENFIELD: *He* said that! [interrupting]

THATCHER: *Yes, I know.* —very much more modest in running for Parliament than men. Nothing like as many of them put up [run for office], you know. Now, that's not because the ability isn't there. Many of them are tied up with bringing up families, etc., and they're therefore out of the political scene for quite a time. We have far fewer women candidates than men candidates, and so it's not surprising that fewer get elected. There is an enormous ability there, an ability which could be tapped for both commerce and industry and for political life. We have far more in local affairs because it's not so difficult for them geographically to get to their local authority as it is to spend mid-week in London. But I wouldn't put anything like the stress on the question that you do.

GREENFIELD: It just interests me—

THATCHER: I mean, it *amazes* me that you regard it as a phenomenon. It really does.

GREENFIELD: But of course you are—

THATCHER: I'm just an ordinary politician.

GREENFIELD: No, no. That's not *amazing*. That's simple, objective *looking*. The first head of a major party in Britain who's a woman in its history is a *phenomenon*. Welcome, but a phenomenon. What's interested me is that it does not seem to have entered into the decision-making process when you took over the leadership of the Conservative Party. Whereas here, it is almost impossible for a woman to run for office and particularly an executive office . . . without that becoming almost a dominant issue. We've elected for the first time in America a woman governor, not elected on her husband's coattails, and it was almost the only issue against her.

THATCHER: But look. I was a cabinet minister. I was secretary of state for both education and science. It so happened that I was perhaps the only person in the cabinet at that time who had scientific qualifications. And all of the people who I worked with in the scientific field said, "Thank goodness we've got someone who speaks the same language." There was no question of "are you a man or woman holding that office?" It was a [question of the] person who was [most] suitable for the job.

Greenfield's questions are spot-on, and it is absolute non-sense for Thatcher to deny the uniqueness of her own position and to reject the opportunity to consider if it is, indeed, easier for conservative women to get ahead in politics than liberal women.

But Thatcher was not a particularly generous conversationalist; every response she made to Greenfield was delivered cordially but with a cutting undertone that would have made a lesser man wet his pants. Now, Buckley was the kind of person who would respectfully engage with virtually *anyone*. (When running for mayor in 1965, he had received a letter from a third grader asking for his opinions on busing; in his response, Buckley wrote that he was against it, and then he asked the boy to share *his* opinions on the subject.) Thatcher, conversely, had less-than-zero interest in this American what's-his-name, an unknown freelance writer. Four years later, Greenfield would be hired by CBS; his news career would take off, and he would publish a dozen books. But in 1975, he was just a very bright young man, giving it his all in a Q&A with Margaret-bloody-Thatcher, in front of a national TV audience. To his credit, Greenfield manages to keep it together, as Thatcher smiles and

Margaret Thatcher appeared twice on the show. Buckley seemed to have his most cogent thoughts about gender issues when he disagreed with conservative women.
CREDIT: *Hoover Institution*

politely tears him a new one. Indeed, interviewed some forty years later, Greenfield, who had appeared countless times on the show, understandably had few distinct memories of specific episodes. But he very clearly recalled this absolute thrashing by Thatcher.

Buckley knows that Greenfield is on the right track with his line of questioning, No sexism in British politics? Poppycock! Buckley pushes back, but, predictably, the Iron Lady does not give an inch. We see here, as we would time and time again, that Buckley seemed to have his most cogent thoughts about gender issues when he disagreed with conservative women. These were also the only women who could put him in his place. Particularly notable was the pummeling he received from Clare Boothe Luce.

Luce and Buckley were friends, and the two were politically aligned on numerous fronts. Like Buckley, she was passionately anticommunist, adamantly in favor of the free market, and tenaciously opposed to FDR's policies and their aftermath. However, she had been a booster for both the GOP, as it stood in the 1950s, and for Eisenhower, and this put her at variance with Buckley during the Cold War years; she was never quite as far to the right as Buckley. Buckley had supported McCarthyism, for example, though he had reservations about the man, while Luce had never been a booster for McCarthyism, complaining that all of the hullabaloo stirred up by McCarthy and HUAC was a ridiculous distraction from the real work of fighting communism. Further, she certainly wasn't as socially conservative as Buckley. In 1943, when the "Wayward Wives Bill" came before Congress, which would have eliminated government benefits for women who were unfaithful while their husbands fought the war, Congresswoman Luce suggested that an amendment be added "that if the *serviceman* is unfaithful overseas, the wife's allowance be doubled."[25] The bill died.

Novelist Wilfrid Sheed—who as a teenager had spent a

summer visiting with Luce, passing happy days fueled by good
conversation and a steady diet of steak and "icy shrimp salad"—
later wrote, "Legend to the contrary, I had never thought of her
as a label-bearing conservative before she started writing for
Buckley's *National Review* in the sixties."[26] Her work for *National
Review* and other publications in the years following the
Bay of Pigs invasion fiasco would, however, propel her to "her
emergence as an oracle of Republican conservatism."[27] Past the
prime of her career, Luce was drawn to Buckley seeking friendship and personal and political alliances, Sheed explains; writing for *National Review* "charge[d] Clare's batteries agreeably."[28]

Even though there generally wasn't much tension to propel their discussions, Buckley enjoyed having Luce on *Firing Line*. And, really, the shows weren't bad, because the two
had a strong rapport and Luce was quite articulate and interested in a number of issues that Buckley rarely engaged with,
such as overpopulation and environmentalism. Further, Luce
brought good energy to the table. She was a powerful woman
who exuded charm and confidence—though her most recent
biographer has unearthed quite a bit of underlying depression.
Unlike Buckley, she had not been born with a silver spoon in
her mouth or graced with a palatial family estate in Connecticut. Luce had been born in a humble home, out of wedlock,
in Spanish Harlem. Like Buckley, she was a devout Catholic
(though unlike him a convert) and outspoken about her faith,
and she was in possession of tremendous wealth and was a
cosmopolitan type, with a taste for the finer things. Notably,
though, Buckley had little flair for fashion and depended on
his wife to pick out his fine dress shirts. Luce had a distinctive
sense of style and a particular taste for bespoke dresses "with
deep, lined pockets for her spectacles, powder compact, lip-
stick, small notepad, and gold Cartier pen," all of which freed
her from the tyranny of the handbag.[29]

Luce pushed herself very hard in her work, often to the

breaking point. Buckley was similarly driven. He had a Ritalin habit that helped keep him afloat; Luce preferred Dexedrine, supplemented by an alarmingly diverse cocktail of pills for pain and sleep, including a suspicious concoction for "nervousness" known only as "#254764."[30] Although Buckley would eventually come around to supporting liberalization of drug laws, his drug of choice was alcohol, whereas Luce had turned to LSD experimentation in the late 1950s.

Further, unlike Buckley, she had pursued a political career, having been elected to the House of Representatives twice in the 1940s, and having been ambassador to Italy during the Eisenhower administration. She had several times been contemplated as a possible vice presidential candidate. In 1952 she quipped, "A woman on the ticket would be an asset to either party, if one could be found twice as good as the average male vice-presidential candidate. This shouldn't be too difficult."[31] She had also taken numerous lovers over the years—wealthy businessmen, dashing military men—before her dramatic turn to Catholicism tempered her infidelity. Buckley was adventurous, but Luce was an adventuress. Even while ostensibly walking the straight and narrow in her Catholic years, she had not hesitated to drop acid with her priest.

In sum, this was really a very *interesting* person, forceful with an occasionally flirtatious edge, a *Firing Line* guest who could definitively hold her own with Buckley. *Vogue* had once compared encountering Luce "to being dynamited by angel cake."[32]

In 1975, when Luce asked to appear (her fourth visit) specifically to discuss feminism, Buckley could hardly refuse her request. He opened with a spirited introduction.

BUCKLEY: The Equal Rights Amendment which, for a
while, appeared to be on the verge of adoption, appears
once again to be stalled, suggesting a subliminal resistance
to formal equality for women which surprises not at all

Mrs. Clare Boothe Luce, who, throughout her life, has given
her time equally to pleading the cause of female equality
and demonstrating the fact of female superiority. . . .
Clare Boothe Luce was never a failure, which is different
from saying she has never been unhappy. As a young
woman, she became very quickly the managing editor of
Vanity Fair. After an unsuccessful marriage, she became
Mrs. Henry Luce and began writing Broadway plays, mostly
successful. . . . She acted, from time to time, as a war
correspondent for her husband's magazines before entering
Congress as a representative from Fairfield County. She was
appointed ambassador to Italy by President Eisenhower and
subsequently ambassador to Brazil, a post she did not in fact
achieve because of the exercise of one of her most seductive
faculties, to wit her occasional inability to curb her tongue.
She is currently a member of the President's Advisory Board
on International Intelligence. . . . I should like to begin by
asking her whether she finds implicit condescension in the
rhetorical formulations with which men tend to introduce her.

There is so much to unpack in this oration. First, Buckley
pointedly opens by noting that the ERA has sputtered once
again, a fact of no small interest to Luce, who had lobbied for
the bill in Washington, DC, in 1923, and who had even dropped
pro-ERA leaflets from a plane over New York State.[33]
In response to the bait with which he had concluded his
introduction, Luce notes that Buckley had managed to get
through the whole thing with only one "masculine putdown":
he had referred to her inability to "hold her tongue." Had Buckley "been speaking of a man who spoke out and made enemies
for himself," she explains, he would have said of such a man
that he was "blunt" or "overly candid." But "hold her tongue"
is specifically "a phrase that men frequently use about children
and women."

Buckley inadvertently confirms that this is exactly what he had in mind when he responds, "Sort of comes out of *Taming of the Shrew*?" Luce bluntly rebuts: "No, it comes out of man's desire, highly successful, through the centuries to master women." Following this, Luce gives over much of the program to explaining exactly what made Jesus a feminist.

After much spirited discussion, Buckley seeks to tie things up, before moving to the final Q&A part of the program, by stating that "the notion of women's inferiority is something concerning which I have no original sin. That is to say, it never occurred to me that men are superior to women. That they are different is obvious, but that doesn't mean that I want to see a woman behind every Mack truck or think that she would sit there gracefully, and yet you would consider that a put-down, I think. Or would you?"

Smiling, flirtatious, and utterly in command of the conversation, Luce responds, "Bill, I'm much too fond of you to tell you what I really think about you." "Publicly," Buckley interjects almost bashfully, making any perceptive viewer understand that Luce has told him off privately on numerous occasions. (One imagines Luce scolding Buckley over a three-martini lunch at his favorite restaurant, Paone's.) Luce grins, shoots him an impossibly sexy septuagenarian look through her Coke-bottle glasses, and states categorically, "I think you're one of the most charming and subtle and sophisticated of male chauvinists." This was a knockout blow. The defeated Buckley escapes to the Q&A.

Betty Friedan, Germaine Greer, and Phyllis Schlafly were all famously for or against feminism, and one quite expects to see them appear on *Firing Line* debating the issue. But the feminist who appeared most often on the show was not a political celebrity but rather a relative unknown: Harriet Pilpel. Pilpel was general counsel for Planned Parenthood during the years when the Supreme Court ended bans on contraception and abortion.

Further, she had served on the national board of the American Civil Liberties Union and had chaired the ACLU's radio and television committee. Pilpel had "insisted, in 1964, that the ACLU defend women's reproductive rights and the civil liberties of homosexuals, two issues it had until then refused to touch."[34]

Pilpel had also been counsel to the Sexuality Information and Education Council of the United States (SEICUS), an organization favoring sex education in public schools. SEICUS was the target of numerous right-wing groups throughout the 1960s, and along with opposition to the ERA, abortion, and the banning of school prayer, the battle against SEICUS was pivotal (though on a smaller scale) to the shift of the conservative movement away from Cold War issues of military strength and toward the cultural concerns that would fuel the right in the 1960s and beyond.[35] Conservative activists simply *loathed* SEICUS. Viewed in this light, to be lead counsel for SEICUS was really something: Pilpel was the liberal's liberal. As the right extended its attack on sex education to attacking abortion, gay rights, and pornography, Pilpel confronted the same issues from the other side.

In addition to her strong support of reproductive freedom, Pilpel was a stalwart First Amendment advocate. Thus, she was a perfect foil to antipornography activist Andrea Dworkin on the 1985 *Firing Line* episode "Women Against Pornography." The radical feminist Dworkin—who understood all acts of heterosexual penetration as acts of rape—was unabashedly procensorship; she understood pornography not as expressive speech but as documentation of a crime. Pilpel would have none of it. Pilpel also ably debated the activist poet June Jordan on the 1976 episode "Should Books Like Little Black Sambo Be on Library Shelves?" Moreover, Buckley invited her three times to participate in his "turning-the-tables" episodes, in which he put himself on the firing line to square off against a panel of liberals.

Harriet Pilpel served as the show's feminist refrain for over a decade, and her low-key, businesslike approach to the topic offered the strongest antidote imaginable to the radical, bra-burner image.
CREDIT: *Hoover Institution*

Since she had appeared on *Firing Line* some thirty times, one might assume that Pilpel had some kind of flair for TV. To be sure, she was a skilled, articulate public speaker. She was very busy on the liberal, legal lecture circuit and regularly guested on shows such as *Good Morning America*, *Donahue*, and *The MacNeil/Lehrer Report*. Pilpel radiated competence and was always very well prepared, with pages and pages of hand-scrawled notes on her lap. On *Firing Line*, she was not the only guest to arrive with notes in hand. Indeed, one of the charms of the show was occasionally observing in long shot the piles of books and manila folders that both Buckley and his guests had assembled on their laps or at their feet.*

Pilpel fit right in with her own stack of notes, but she stood out in one notable way: she was not an entertainer. She was a very proficient lawyer who happened to be comfortable on TV, but her charisma was low-key, and she was not exactly

---

* Allen Ginsberg had not only notebooks of his poetry but also a harmonium at the ready.

glamorous. Pilpel was always perfectly accessorized with tasteful matching jewelry sets, full-coverage blouses suitable to *une femme d'un certain age*, and a borderline-alarming, bagel-shaped, pewter updo framing her face. Linen handkerchief firmly in hand, when she needed to read from her notes she would put on cat's-eye glasses with violet lenses. One yearns for a close-up.

Pilpel was capable with her *facts*, but her *quips* were few and far between. Pilpel was there because she was a liberal feminist, no-nonsense lawyer. She was not there to banter. On one episode, Pilpel did attempt a wisecrack, prompting a cranky professor of mathematics, one Henry E. Heatherly, to send a pedantic letter to Buckley, who forwarded it to Pilpel with a cover letter reading, "Sweet Harriet: Here's an instructive piece of fan mail for you! Love, Bill." Professor Heatherly complained that, "admidst [*sic*] a muddle-headed defense of the Supreme Court decision in *Roe v. Wade*," Pilpel had caused Buckley to be "momentarily taken aback when she replied to [his] statement about two plus two always being four with the counter that in the new math this need not be true. Let me assure you that unless one takes as contorted a view of the arithmetical statement as the female barrister does of the US Constitution, two plus two is indeed four."[36] Heatherly then proceeded to deliver a humorless lecture in abstract mathematics. Pilpel's attempt to poke fun at the new math had fallen quite flat. At least Heatherly was polite, unlike one unimaginative *Firing Line* viewer, "U.R. Fecal" of Brooklyn, who signed off his nasty postcard to Pilpel by wishing her a "happy coronary and/or fatal-mugging."[37]

One of Buckley's other democratic regulars, Mark Green, offers a striking contrast in style to Pilpel. The überliberal New York City political player—who served two terms as public advocate and was not-quite-elected to a number of offices, including mayor in 2001—was quite skilled at making humorous political comments on *Firing Line*, though one senses that some of his clever bits are more studied than off-the-cuff.* For example, Green wisecracks in the 1981 "William F. Buckley on the Firing Line" episode featuring him, Pilpel, and *National Review* writer Joseph Sobran that "Bill Rusher, your publisher at the *National Review,* the day after the November elections said, 'liberalism is dead.' At a conference last week he told a group of liberals, 'liberalism is dying.' Things are looking up, at least by his measure." Rather than teasing out Green's joke, Pilpel immediately responds by jumping in and asking Buckley about his present stance on the ERA. Buckley suggests that "the ERA is a flirtation whose time has passed. It's going into middle age and—" At this point Pilpel interjects, "I wasn't asking about its prospects," poking fun at Buckley's implication that the ERA was some kind of an old maid. But the quip did not get a laugh from the studio audience. Pilpel was always best when in "just the facts, ma'am" mode.

What was perhaps most interesting about Pilpel's repeat appearances on the show was not her articulate support of women's rights—which was indeed quite impressive—but what she inadvertently accomplished: showing that feminism was about as mainstream as your aunt Mildred. Sure, Buckley had hosted more radical types, like Andrea Dworkin, but Pilpel served as the show's feminist refrain for more than a decade, and her low-key, businesslike approach to the topic offered the strongest antidote imaginable to the radical, bra-burner image.

Buckley surely had not meant to present a "normal" image of feminism, but he had done exactly that. When "Miss Millett's"

---

* In his 1989 *Firing Line* book, Buckley describes Green as "unreconstructed: a lawyer who served for ten years at the right hand of Ralph Nader. He ran for Congress in Manhattan and lost; ran for senator in New York, succeeded in winning the Democratic nomination, but lost to Al D'Amato in 1986. He runs something called the Democracy Project, writes a book every six months or so, and is wittily and informatively engaged in furthering the cause of the Devil" (*On the Firing Line,* 172).

Sexual Politics emerged as a bestseller, Millett had been briefly crowned leader of the women's lib movement by the mass media; she was stereotyped as brawny and repellent, with dirty hair. *Time* printed a cartoon of her "saggy-breasted, beefy, and scowling."[38] Gloria Steinem, by contrast, was brimming with "emphatic sexuality," according to *Newsweek*.[39] She quickly displaced Millett as the mainstream media's iconic feminist.

If Steinem was the starlet and Millett was the ballbuster, Pilpel was the matron. Neither grotesque nor a sexpot, Pilpel was hidden away on PBS and known outside the ACLU and Planned Parenthood mainly for her monthly column in *Publishers Weekly*. She was doomed never to make a big splash—for better or for worse—in the pages of *Newsweek* or *Time*. But on the most long-running and important conservative TV show in American history, she argued again and again for the feminist cause.

When Pilpel passed away in 1991, Buckley lost his go-to feminist, and he never found an adequate replacement. He may not have looked very hard, for at this point Buckley was convinced that the feminist movement had really made a mess of things, and it was unclear if anything could really be done about it. By now Buckley was increasingly hosting large-scale formal *Firing Line* debates, with Michael Kinsley often pounding the gavel as moderator, and teams of debaters dissecting questions such as, in 1994, "Resolved: The Women's Movement Has Been Disastrous." Buckley would head the affirmative team, the question always being phrased so that the conservative response was yes. The 1994 debate included Arianna Huffington on Buckley's side and Betty Friedan and feminist cultural critic Camille Paglia on the other. With eight debaters—a number of them rather loud and bossy by nature—going at it for two hours, with no commercial break, it was pretty lively and dense stuff, with much time given over to fighting over abortion rights.

As was typical at these grand debates staged in the later years of the show, Buckley mostly sat back as an éminence grise. He did open the show, though, with a declaration that he saw as his trump card regarding the disastrousness of the feminist movement. Things had gotten so bad that even Phyllis Schlafly had slipped into the PC quagmire.

> BUCKLEY: Consider the far reaches of the women's movement and its effect on people as preternaturally normal as Mrs. Schlafly. In a published essay in *Current Events* last month, she used the following sentence: "Feminism has no happy role and can boast of almost no legislative victories. Its ideology is still and its spokespersons are bitter." Its *what* are bitter? Its spokespersons. Now, if you're not disrupted by the word "spokesperson" used in place of the simple word "spokesman," denoting someone whether male or female who speaks for a collectivity, then the assault on your ear is nothing less than disastrous. But no one is more eloquent on the subject of PC than Professor Paglia. If the search for so-called gender-neutral language causes you to refer to first-year college students as "freshpersons" and you bridle at the sentence "man is born to be free," then that is truly a disastrous turn against the laws of tradition and euphony. Yet it is so.

To be clear, Buckley raised some other concerns—about abortion, about women in the military—but he reserved his heaviest rhetoric for his attack on this nonsense language, which he saw, he would explain later in the debate, as "an index of a total perversion of taste and of a fanatical attention to details that are not only insignificant but absolutely unmusical in their consequences." Regardless of one's feelings about the laws of tradition and euphony, any sensible viewer, liberal or conservative, has to double-take at all of this, and finally circle back to what is actually important in Schlafly's declaration, her

notion that feminism could "boast of almost no legislative vic-
tories." Investigating this conceit should have been the meat
and potatoes of Buckley's commentary.

Over and over again in the 1994 debate, Buckley repeated
that the women's movement had gone in "the wrong direction,"
a neat bit of revisionism insofar as he had never really found it to
be going in the right direction. The quarreling was diffuse, the
rigorous focus of earlier Pilpel episodes sorely lacking. Indeed,
the 1994 episode made a striking contrast to a smaller-scale
Firing Line debate from 1982 that had included Pilpel debating
in the negative the proposition: "Resolved: That Women Have
It Just as Good as Men." Whipping out basic figures on domestic violence, rape, employment, poverty levels among American
women, and rates of child support payment by men, Pilpel's
side had easily trounced the opposition.

Much worse than the 1994 altercation about the disastrousness of the movement (at one point, Friedan slammed a book
on the table in anger, and Huffington had actually shouted,
"I'm sorry, Betty. Shut up, shut up! I'm talking!" eliciting laughter and applause), was a 1992 episode with Rush Limbaugh, in
which Buckley again complained about the wretched *freshper-
son* and bemoaned the "feminizing" of American culture. Limbaugh griped about the fact that it was increasingly difficult in
America's "politically correct" environment to complain about
feminist excesses.

Buckley was much smarter than Limbaugh, and the two
were not fully connecting conversationally, making it a weak
episode. But the show did cohere to the extent that it showed
how far *Firing Line* had drifted from its earlier, focused intellectual debates about this issue. The show's alarmist attacks on
feminism became meaner and meaner as the '90s progressed.
If feminists could no longer conceivably be seen as "ladies,"
men opposing feminism would simply take off the gloves and
no longer attempt to be gentlemen. For decades, Buckley had

tried to KO feminism on his show, but it had hung on and become a mainstream movement that brought about significant
social, legal, and (yes) linguistic change. By the '90s it seemed
that the only thing left to do on *Firing Line* was bemoan the
fallout.

Buckley has been mythologized as a hero of the conservative
movement, and even if you are opposed to that movement, it
is right to praise him for his thoughtful televisual interactions
with liberals. Sadly, this kind of reasoned political debate is
sorely lacking in today's TV landscape. Notwithstanding the
firecracker tempers that went off on some of the *Firing Line* debates of the 1990s, and the "bare knuckled intellectual brawls"
that were not uncommon in the earliest years of the show,
Buckley was consistently open to honest debate with his ideological opponents. One feels this openness strongly in most
of the episodes centered on feminism and the women's movement, where Buckley patiently engaged with ideas that seemed
particularly foreign to him. But despite his careful listening to
the opposition, it was very rare for him to change his mind on
any political issue. This is particularly clear in his interactions
with feminists on *Firing Line*. On this point, perhaps we should
give the last word to Margaret Thatcher: he was a man, he was
limited.

CHAPTER FIVE

TRIPPING OVER TRICKY DICK

*The greatest concentration of power
in the United States today is not the White House.
It isn't in the Congress and it isn't in the Supreme Court.
It's in the media. And it's too much.*

—RICHARD NIXON TO DAVID FROST, TV INTERVIEW,
APRIL 6, 1977

In the troubled years of the early 1970s, there was endless kin-
dling to feed the fires of fascination, despair, or sheer horror
inspired by the flaming collapse of the Nixon presidency. The
mainstream media presented a constant litany of indictments,
discoveries, gaffes, and denials. And what of the alternative
media? Left-wing underground newspapers found their disgust with Nixon confirmed by the Pentagon papers, My Lai,
Watergate, Laos, Cambodia. Right-wing newsletters had been
critical of Nixon for his liberal domestic policies (think welfare,
not Kent State) and for going to China, even as they tended to
support his policies in Southeast Asia—while also being suspicious of the foreign-born, Jewish Henry Kissinger. But per-
ceiving Nixon as under attack from the "liberal media" as his
political crises came to a head, much of the hard right rallied
to his defense.

Of course, by the time he resigned, it was hard for anyone to
defend Nixon. For the GOP, this was, obviously, quite a crisis.
For those like Buckley who wanted the party to move further

right, it was unclear if the situation was a total blowout. Yes, Republicans would obviously lose elections in the short term, as Nixon's defeat rippled outward. On the other hand, a cock-eyed optimist might see this as a scorched-earth type of opportunity. The party was in tatters. How would it rebuild? Perhaps it could pick up where Goldwater had left off. Perhaps Nixon's collapse was not an insurmountable crisis. After all, Senator McCarthy had presented a political—and public relations—problem for the right, yet it had soldiered on. Ditto Goldwater. *Firing Line* had defended McCarthy's legacy, and had helped stake a claim for the legitimacy of right-wing conservatism in those post-Goldwater years. If Buckley could use *Firing Line* to define a conservative response to civil rights, Black Power, and women's lib—all movements that did not augur well for his efforts to pull America rightward—he could certainly do the same in response to the Watergate crisis. Before Nixon finally stepped down, *Firing Line* had even stood up for the president. Well, sort of.

Now, if you didn't subscribe to those small scale, mail-order, Smith-Corona newsletter screeds spewing forth from both left and right—what we might call "primordial blogs"—you most likely followed Nixon's travails via mass-produced and distributed magazines, newspapers, radio, and TV. This was the mainstream media establishment that Nixon perceived as patently out to screw him. The fourth estate was, as far as he was concerned, putrid with liberal bias. A few years post-resignation, in his famous TV interviews with David Frost, he would go so far as to say, "The greatest concentration of power in the United States today is not the White House. It isn't in the Congress and it isn't in the Supreme Court. It's in the media. And it's too much." As on so many other fronts, Nixon's hatred of the press was more than a little bit tinged with paranoia and overreaction. In fact, there is ample evidence that the press tried hard to be objective in its Nixon coverage.[1]

Reading *All the President's Men* today, for example, one cannot help but be struck by how consistently *surprised* reporters Bob Woodward and Carl Bernstein are as their story gyroscopically spins closer and closer toward Nixon. At one point a source describes "ratfucking"—underhanded sabotage engaged in by Nixon campaigners against his opponents—as a "basic strategy that goes all the way to the top," even higher than former attorney general and Committee to Re-Elect the President campaign director John Mitchell. Who the hell was higher up than John Mitchell? *"Basic strategy that goes all the way to the top. The phrase unnerved Bernstein. For the first time he considered the possibility that the President of the United States was the head ratfucker."*[2] This disconcerting epiphany occurs more than one-third of the way into the book. No one could plausibly assert that Nixon and the media had a congenial relationship, but outside the pages of the *Washington Post*, the press underplayed the notion that Nixon might be engaged in a Watergate cover-up or other dirty tricks. As historian David Greenberg bluntly puts it, "It took reporters a while to label Nixon a liar."[3] But "the release of the damning tape transcripts on April 30, 1974, was the final straw."[4]

If the mainstream media was nonetheless, by all conservative accounts, riddled with liberal media bias, how would America's only unabashedly conservative public affairs TV talk show approach the Nixon crisis differently? And to what extent could *Firing Line* itself be legitimately described as part of that "mainstream media"? Sure, it was mainstream compared to niche media like the *Dan Smoot Report*, an ultraconservative newsletter from Texas mailed directly to subscribers, or to the *Oracle*, a psychedelic underground newspaper distributed to the Haight-Ashbury community in San Francisco. Clinging to the edge of the mainstream, insofar as it began as a small-scale syndicated public affairs show in 1966 before moving to PBS in 1971, and insofar as it tended to be aired late at night, or at least outside of prime time (pulling in even fewer viewers than the Sunday morning ghetto occupied by shows like *Meet the Press*), *Firing Line* still reached many more people than the homespun alternative press of the 1960s and early 1970s did. Yet Jeff Greenfield, who appeared on the show many, many times in the early years, before leaving for a career at CBS, ABC, and CNN, would later note that all that putative exposure rarely added up to even being recognized on the street: "Occasionally people would sort of squint and say, 'Oh, yeah, I've seen you on *Firing Line.*'"[5]

If the show could not compare to the *CBS Evening News* or the *New York Times* in terms of exposure, it was nonetheless obviously perceived by many guests as a program that was seen by *the right people*. Why else would someone like Nixon agree to appear on the 1967 episode "The Future of the GOP"? Buckley opened by noting that registration of Republicans had gone up a bit the previous year, and registration of Democrats had

Eager for right-wing votes, Nixon made a rather dull appearance on *Firing Line* in 1967.
CREDIT: *Hoover Institution*

gone down a little bit. Was this a sign that liberalism had not permanently trumped conservatism, which was the going line at the time? Or, as moderator C. Dickerman Williams put it to Nixon himself,

WILLIAMS: Is the Democratic Party running out of steam, or is it liberalism?

NIXON: Well, I would say first there are some technical reasons. Last year the Republicans had better candidates across the country generally than the Democrats had. They were better organized, more . . .

BUCKLEY: Wouldn't you say that of every year?

NIXON: Of course, I would tend to say that every year, but looking at it in retrospect, last year we just happened to come up with a very good crop, and they came up with a group of candidates who—well, just a bunch of turkeys, really. Now, under the circumstances—not all of them, of course, because some of them did win—I would say, too, that last year, in terms of the way the two parties presented their cases across the country to the people, the Democratic Party seemed to be the party of the past. They were applying the various programs of the thirties to the problems of the sixties; whereas the Republican Party seemed to be more in tune with what people believe in now.

BUCKLEY: What's an example of this, of the intuitions of the Republican Party that were communicated last year?

NIXON: Well, I think perhaps when we think of last year's election, many people tend to say the Republicans gained because of the war in Vietnam, or because of other issues. There was a tremendous disillusionment, for example, with the poverty program. The poverty program, of course, was a throwback to the programs of the thirties. And across the

country Republicans who stood up and pointed out that
these programs were costing a great deal of money, [and]
were not dealing with the problems of poverty, they were
taking what I think you might call a conservative line. They
won, and they won even though many political pundits said
they would lose, when they were in effect attacking Santa
Claus.

This analysis may be correct, but it seems like a Herculean
effort at spin. In 1967, the country tilted liberal, and it would
swing still further left—with the ascendency of Black Power,
women's lib, the New Left, the counterculture, etc.—before it
swung right, notwithstanding Nixon's narrow victory in 1968.
(And obviously, his landslide victory four years later would indicate an electorate definitively tilting right.) Liberals at the time
would have argued that the programs of the sixties were not
"throwbacks" because of their roots in the thirties but, rather,
a sign that liberal social programs continued to reign triumphant. Now, Nixon did point out on "The Future of the GOP"
that Reagan had recently won the governorship of California,
so it was clear that the seeds of change were actually in the
air. But viewed in the broader context of the Zeitgeist of the
late sixties, Nixon's "throwback" stuff could easily be seen as
wishful thinking.

The long and the short of it was, Nixon was gearing up to
run for president in 1968, and he needed Buckley more than
Buckley needed him. Or, at least, he needed Buckley's constituents. Nixon confided to Buckley, in the limo as they traveled
to tape the show, that in losing the 1962 California gubernatorial race he had learned that he couldn't win with *just* the right
wing behind him, but he also couldn't win *without* the right
wing.[6] He presumably did not bring up this additional concern
en route to the studio, but it must have already been on his
mind: if too many of the right-wingers voted for Wallace, he

would have been up a creek. And this is almost what happened. The 1968 election was a real squeaker.

National Review was very critical of Nixon, and Buckley was often hard on him in his nationally syndicated column. Nixon knew that support from Buckley and his contingent could never be taken for granted. Here's how Neal Freeman, Buckley protégé, board member of the Corporation for Public Broadcasting in the Nixon years, and a very successful PBS producer in his own right, described the situation:

> *Nixon always referred to Bill and those around him as "Buckleyites." . . . He knew that he had to have at least the low-key support of the conservatives because . . . in that '68 convention in Miami he was facing not only Nelson Rockefeller further to his left but potentially Governor Ronald Reagan to his right. And Nixon's view always was that you needed the base, you needed the conservative base, but you needed more than that. He was always looking to make accommodations to the right without fully embracing the right. And I think for him Buckley represented the intelligent right with whom he could reach accommodation rather than a full embrace of some kind.*[7]

Accommodation is the key, carefully chosen word here. Nixon and his team wanted to use Buckley strategically, and it worked to the extent that the *National Review* did finally endorse Nixon in 1968, having not done so in 1960. Notably, many at the magazine, including publisher Bill Rusher, were very negative about Nixon, and the 1968 endorsement had finally come at the urging of Buckley and *National Review* foreign policy guru James Burnham.[8]

Nixon must have seen this as a bit of a coup, in light of the fact that in 1965, commenting on Buckley's mayoral run, he had almost sabotaged his relationship with hard-right conservatives by declaring that "the Birchers could be handled,

but . . . the real menace to the Republican Party came from the
Buckleyites." The comment was forwarded to Rowland Evans
and Robert Novak, who published it in their column. Rusher
wrote three alarmed letters to Nixon asking him to confirm
whether he had indeed made this statement, but he received
no response, and Evans and Novak wrote of the scandal among
conservative Republicans that was growing out of Nixon's failure to respond to Rusher's queries.

Finally, in March 1966 Nixon aide Patrick Buchanan wrote
a long explanation addressed not to Rusher but to "the editor"
of *National Review*. It was a letter obviously intended as damage
control, for publication. Buchanan wrote that Nixon had spoken very positively of Buckley's repudiation of the John Birch
Society and indicated that Nixon felt conservatives should
work within the Republican Party, the implication being that
Nixon had merely been concerned that Buckley was running
for mayor on the Conservative ticket instead of the Republican ticket. Nixon's actual line about the Buckleyites being more
dangerous than Birchers was left unreferenced by Buchanan.

Strangely, Buckley bought the explanation, writing a memo
to Rusher saying that "it always seemed to me the obvious thing
to do, to interpret his statement as having meant that." But he
added, "it does make his long answer inexplicable."[9] Well, of
course it did, because the long answer was all nonsense, a classic Nixonite nondenial denial. Nixon had made the gaffe but
was not owning up to it.[10]

Buckley willed himself to believe the implausible Buchanan
letter to the editor. At this point, he seemed simply to want
to have faith that Nixon might be at least partially redeemable
for the right. Early in 1967, Nixon offered some additional
arm-twisting when he invited Buckley, Rusher, Freeman, and
a few other right-wing conservatives to spend an afternoon
at his Fifth Avenue townhouse, where he served South Afri-
can brandy to demonstrate his ideological alignment with his

guests—a classic "Nixonian touch," as Freeman described it. They spent the afternoon talking politics, and Buckley was won over.[11] But they were not friends. Following the *faux pas* about the Buckleyites, Nixon had begun to sporadically send Buckley short, almost-chummy letters suggesting he check out a transcript of a speech he had made. Notably, he addressed the letters "Dear Bill," but the return missives consistently opened, "Dear Mr. Nixon." Buckley was very comfortable writing to Charlton Heston as "Chuck," feeling real affection for him. And Reagan was "Ron" in private correspondence, until he was elected president. But Nixon could never be "Dick."

Once Nixon was in the White House, he would continue to court Buckley and his contingent, mainly via Kissinger's efforts. One of Buckley's early biographers, John Judis, emphasizes that Kissinger only pretended to seek advice from Buckley. Kissinger pointedly stated that, "as a type, Buckley is really an artist rather than a foreign policy thinker . . . he does not have any detailed strategic view of foreign policy."[12] The national security advisor invited the *National Review* editor to Washington more than twenty times, and, as Judis describes it, he used the same con on Buckley that he did on others. Former Young Americans for Freedom head and Agnew aide David Keene would later explain that Kissinger "had one line for liberals, one for conservatives, and all the time he'd swear you to secrecy—'What I'm about to tell you is the highest classified information'—and he'd give you some bullshit, and he'd give somebody else the opposite."[13] The idea was that the secret could not be confirmed, but you would feel special having heard it. Buckley was rather cynical about politicians, and it is quite possible that he was not as taken in as Judis implies. (Kissinger and Buckley did develop a genuine friendship over the years.) On the other hand, Kissinger was damn good at this game, and it's hard to believe Buckley was utterly immune to his "confidential" briefings.

On his TV show, Buckley sometimes attempted to justify Nixon's actions. At other times he redirected the discussion altogether to focus on issues of media spin, bias, and journalistic integrity. Overall, *Firing Line*'s Nixon coverage stumbled into a series of redirects. When White House officials responded to damning news stories about Nixon by calling them "unconfirmed" and "ridiculous," in effect they were denying that true stories were true without actually lying; the *Washington Post* came to refer to such statements as "nondenial denials." Without consciously seeking to mislead viewers, I believe, Buckley was issuing his own kind of nondenial denials throughout the Nixon (and, by extension, Vietnam and Watergate) *Firing Line* episodes. He wasn't being deliberately sneaky, and he openly rejected certain Nixon actions, but punches were also pulled, and the Nixon shows, though generally appearing logical and polished on the surface, were really tripping over the elephant in the room. There was almost always a way to frame the Nixon Problem other than in terms of Nixon's culpability. In fact, we might even say that the "denial" in play here was less about truth claims than about the more banal psychiatric notion of "being in denial."

To be clear, I am not arguing that Buckley was out of touch with his thoughts or feelings about Nixon but rather that *Firing Line* was a conflicted media space where the desire for conservative (and by extension Republican) political ascendancy was so strong that the pros and cons of Nixon could never quite be fully sorted out.

Buckley was hardly naïve about the machinations of politicians. Indeed, in the course of attacking Daniel Ellsberg on *Firing Line* in 1972, a frustrated and angry Buckley advocated for the practical, strategic necessity of lying. The commander in chief needed to lie in order to safeguard national security: "If one lives in the real world, one recognizes that when Nixon promises something, or McGovern, or Churchill or Roosevelt or whoever, there are no heroes. There are no heroes." This brings us to *Firing Line*'s nondenial denial number 1: If Nixon lied about Watergate, Laos, Cambodia, and innumerable other things, he did so because he had to in order to be an effective commander in chief; that's simply realpolitik. As the intellectual historian Martin Jay observes, "politics, however we [choose] to define its essence and limit its contours, will never be an entirely fib-free zone of authenticity, sincerity, integrity, transparency, and righteousness."[14]

If lying is simply business as usual for politicians, nondenial denial number 1 is pretty banal stuff. On the other hand, it would not be far-fetched to contend that Nixon lied too much, even for a politician, and that he was especially shameless about it. (If we take this up to the next level we have this infamous exchange. Frost to Nixon: "There are certain situations . . . where the president can decide that it's in the best interest of the nation . . . and do something illegal?" Nixon to Frost: "Well, when the president does it, that means that it is not illegal.") In any case, if it was okay to lie about Vietnam, it was okay to lie about an inconvenient public statement one had made about the Birchers versus the Buckleyites.

By far, *Firing Line*'s most important nondenial denial was number 2: the problem is not Nixon, it is the liberal media. *Firing Line* would function during the Watergate and Vietnam years as a kind of corrective to liberal media bias, a phrase that still rings in our ears today. Though Buckley did not invent the phrase (or even use these exact words very often), he definitely helped to mainstream the notion, pulling it from the penumbra of John Birch Society paranoia into the blinding light of mainstream conservatism. For example, questioning Edith Efron, on a 1971 *Firing Line* episode, about how she had proved in her book *The News Twisters* that the news was askew, he took a commonsensical, nonconspiratorial tone: "It is a little bit like how do you conclude there is gravity, isn't it? I mean, everybody knows . . . that it is biased."

Instead of wasting precious TV minutes griping about bias, Buckley was more likely to find an article supporting his point of view in, say, the *New York Times* and then use it as a sort of trump card against a liberal guest. This is exactly what he did in the very first episode of *Firing Line*, "Vietnam: Pull Out? Stay In? Escalate?" in which he sparred with socialist Norman Thomas, at one point citing facts he agreed with from "that *conservative* newspaper, the *New York Times*," by which, of course, Buckley meant exactly the opposite.[15] The unintended punch line here is that Thomas surely felt that the *Times* really was conservative, which from a socialist perspective it may be. I've never met a flaming left-winger *or* a flaming right-winger who didn't find the *Times* to be politically suspect.

We've already seen how, in *Firing Line*'s first year, Buckley devoted an entire episode to "the prevailing bias," inviting liberal talk show host David Susskind to debate the issue. Susskind failed to see a problem: "We have 598 TV stations, UHF and VHF . . . and 116 educational television stations . . . there are in this country 55,216,000 radio sets, AM and FM. . . . There are 1,763 daily newspapers. . . . And therefore the sheer pluralism, the sheer velocity and volume would suggest that there isn't a prevailing bias. It runs the gamut, in newspaper and magazine terms, for example, from the *Daily Worker* to the *National Review*. In television we have the John Birch Society broadcasting its peculiar messages on 103 stations in 30 states. We have reverend Billy Hargis, and we have, on the other hand, such sound men as Eric Sevareid, Howard Morgan, Huntley, Brinkley."

Susskind speaks, of course, at the peak of the pre-cable network era, when one might mistakenly assume that the dominance of NBC, CBS, and ABC meant that there was no diversity of political expression in the American mediascape. In referencing Hargis and the Birchers, Susskind points specifically to the right-wing broadcast movement that was thriving at the time, to some extent on TV, and to an even greater extent on

independently owned radio stations. This was a movement
helmed by conspiratorial nuts, whom Buckley did not take seriously. To him, such extremists didn't count as "conservatives,"
even though they agreed with him about a fair number of political issues. Like him, for example, they were strongly inspired
by anticommunist sentiments and opposed numerous federal
government programs and initiatives.[16] Unlike him, many
of them were quite overtly racist and anti-Semitic. Certainly,
Buckley resented the fact that the liberals in Susskind's disquisition were mainstream types like Huntley and Brinkley, while
the conservatives he listed were nut jobs.

How, then, would *Firing Line* combat what Buckley perceived
as hopelessly liberal media coverage of Nixon, Vietnam, and
Watergate without being lumped with the right-wing kooks? It
helped not to gripe *too* loudly about liberal bias. Such griping
inevitably gave off a whiff of the screwball. Interestingly, *Firing
Line*'s engagement with Vietnam and Nixon (the two becoming increasingly inseparable) remained consistently focused on
hard issues, even as mainstream press and network coverage
became increasingly distracted—distracted in such a way that
it would be a stretch to reduce the coverage to its putatively
liberal bias. As protest against the Nixon administration's military strategy became louder and louder, mainstream newspapers and electronic media (that is, the evening network news)
saw that high ratings would come less from talking about the
finer points of the war itself than from displaying the spec-
tacular protest against it.[17] Thus, a vast amount of reporting
centered on antiwar chaos in the streets, conveying the emotions of the antiwar movement more than the arguments of
that movement.

So, on the one hand, we have New Leftists, such as Todd
Gitlin, critiquing the mainstream media for its sensationalist orientation. On the other hand, we have conservatives
critiquing the media at the same time for almost the exact

same thing—the emphasis of emotion over substance. The difference between the two camps, of course, lay in their differing notions of what the "substance" of the coverage should be, with the left wishing that their antiwar sentiments would be more articulately conveyed and the right wishing that the media would more definitively attack the antiwar movement and support the war effort. Nixon's objectives were even more narrowly focused: he wanted the news media either to attack the protestors or, even better, to cease coverage of Vietnam protest altogether. PBS was seen as a particular offender, and in 1973 Nixon tried to cut off Corporation for Public Broadcasting funding for all the PBS public affairs shows. The *Washington Post* political cartoonist Herblock nicely summed it up as "Violence on Television."

In the early 1970s PBS featured political programming such as *This Week, Black Journal, The Advocates, The Great American Dream Machine,* and *World Press.* Nixon was not pleased: these shows were not toeing the line. In a confidential memo to Peter Flanigan, a special assistant to the president, White House Communications Office staffer Alvin Snyder complained about PBS. Snyder cited Bill Moyers's "scathing attack on our efforts to end the Vietnam war" on his show *This Week.* He also called attention to a particular episode of *The Great American Dream Machine* that had included "an anti-Establishment song and dance number by Jane Fonda." Nixon was rather obsessed with Fonda: "What Brezhnev and Jane Fonda said got about the same treatment," an aide noted later.[18] The episode also contained "a commentary by satirist Andy Rooney ridiculing the President's concept of an all-volunteer Army" and "an interview with [blacklisted] screenwriter Dalton Trumbo who pledged himself to work against the re-election of the President . . . [saying that] 'I sometimes think that since Mr. Nixon was on the committee that successfully sought to throw me out of my job, I perhaps owe him the favor of . . . a return engagement.'"[19]

Violence On Television

In 1973 Nixon tried to cut off Corporation for Public Broadcasting funding for all the PBS public affairs shows, whether liberal or conservative. *Washington Post* cartoonist Herblock nicely summed it up as "Violence on Television."

CREDIT: *A 1973 Herblock Cartoon,* © *The Herb Block Foundation*

Seeking to strike back, one of Nixon's strategies was to undercut PBS funding via the appointment of conservatives to the Corporation for Public Broadcasting, starting with Neal Freeman, *Firing Line's* first producer and a longtime associate of Buckley. One might presume that *Firing Line* would be immune to Nixon's attempted hatchet job. But no, Nixon wanted *all* the PBS public affairs shows canceled. Buckley did not seem too concerned (an issue that we will return to in discussing Reagan's later triumphant defunding of public broadcasting). In fact, having left the commercial syndicated market for PBS in 1971, Buckley had the nerve to label his very first PBS episode "Dump Nixon?" On this show, former Democratic congressman Allard Lowenstein and moderate Republican Pete McCloskey called for the impeachment of Nixon, long before the Watergate break-in, on the grounds that the Gulf of Tonkin Resolution had been revoked on January 1971, and Nixon therefore no longer had the legal authority to continue the war.

Of course, Buckley's stance was that we should *not* therefore dump Nixon. But it was an inflammatory title for *Firing Line's* PBS premiere—even if it was cribbed from Lowenstein, who had branched out from his earlier "Dump Johnson" initiative to launch a new "Dump Nixon" campaign. Nixon simply didn't want these kinds of thoughts expressed on the airwaves. Perhaps he was chafed by the fact that Buckley so often pulled for him on TV but gave him mixed reviews in *National Review* and in his newspaper column. With frenemies like this, who needed enemies?

While Nixon could make rigorous attempts to squeeze PBS financially,[20] attacking the Big Three networks was trickier, and this is where Vice President Spiro T. Agnew would come in handy. In a famous speech given on October 19, 1969, Agnew attacked both news coverage of Vietnam protestors and the protestors themselves. Describing the leaders of the antiwar movement, Agnew noted that "a spirit of national masochism prevails, encouraged by an effete corps of impudent snobs who characterize themselves as intellectuals."[21] The "liberal media" was nothing but a bunch of "nattering nabobs of negativism," he famously noted in a follow-up speech in September 1970. He would also refer to journalists as "pusillanimous pussy-footers" and even "hopeless, hysterical hypochondriacs of history." Agnew's speeches attacking American journalists were flowing freely in late 1969 and into 1970. It all added up to an alarming allocation of awkward adjectives. Reviewing Agnew's 1976 *roman à clef*, John Kenneth Galbraith would describe the former vice president's style as ranging "from bureaucratic to alliterative to a kind of technical baroque."[22]

Apparently, much of the so-called silent majority celebrated the impudent snobs speech. The White House claimed to have received some thirteen thousand wires, "overwhelmingly supporting him."[23] Agnew's approval numbers picked up considerably, and in the South, a Gallup poll revealed, he was almost as popular as George Wallace.[24] Agnew thus helped forward Nixon's ongoing Southern Strategy—to pull both regular conservative voters and hard-core right-wing voters toward the Republican Party (and, at a certain point, away from Wallace), and, of course, to maintain congressional support from die-hard old southerners like Strom Thurmond. With Agnew on the case, Nixon did not have to get his hands dirty by doing his own direct mudslinging at the war protestors and the "liberal media." Nixon had performed similar scut work as Eisenhower's vice president, and it was thus a most trenchant insult when some began to call Agnew "Nixon's Nixon."

The press reacted very negatively to Agnew's speeches, resenting his attack on their neutrality and sensing censorious undertones—or overtones. Of course, from Agnew and Nixon's perspective, this widespread negative reaction only confirmed the existence of liberal media bias, giving them more ammo for their complaints. Given that his speeches had *increased*

Agnew's popularity, implicitly helping Nixon, the administration's griping about negative mainstream media response
seemed more than a little disingenuous.

When Buchanan was on *Firing Line* in December 1973 (at
the height of Watergate, two months after Agnew had stepped
down as vice president in the wake of charges of income tax
evasion, and allegations of bribery and kickbacks), he was still
complaining that the press had been unfair to Agnew. On the
campaign trail in 1968, Agnew had made, Buchanan acknowledged, "a number of verbal missteps." Specifically, he had
made a "Polack comment" and a comment about a "fat Jap."[25]
Thereafter, Buchanan told Buckley, reporters had it in for him:
"The pens were just poised waiting, as it were, for the next image which would fit in with the current theme which was that
the Vice-President was Mr. Malaprop."

But let's face it, Agnew's "verbal missteps" did point to insensitivity and a lack of common sense. In its 1996 obituary,
the *New York Times* observed that during the 1968 campaign
Agnew had been "billed as the Nixon camp's urban expert,"
but that he "disdained visits to ghettos, saying, 'If you've seen
one slum, you've seen them all.'"[26] One need not be a nabob,
nattering or otherwise, to observe that such public comments
were both newsworthy and ill-mannered.

As for Buckley, it might seem predictable that he would be
on board with Agnew's attack on both protestors and liberally
biased media coverage of those protestors. It's true that Buckley was generally positive about Agnew, and Nixon's man had
every reason to be friendly with one of the few TV personalities besides Archie Bunker who actually stood up for the president. But Buckley did not immediately rally for Agnew in the
wake of his diatribes against the "impudent snobs" of the mass
media. Instead, he was incredulous that Agnew had delivered
such poorly written material. (Agnew's speechwriters included
Buchanan and William Safire, it is worth noting.)

Buckley was generally positive about Vice-President Agnew, and Nixon's man had every reason to be friendly with one of the few TV personalities besides Archie Bunker who actually stood up for the president.

CREDIT: *City News Bureau, Inc.*

In his nationally syndicated column Buckley let it rip. Of Agnew's "impudent snobs" speech he wrote, like a Yale instructor in freshman composition (which he was in fact, in the late 1990s*), "to begin with, the rhetorical arrangement is extremely unsatisfactory. The word 'snob' should rarely be preceded by an adjective, because it is a word that has to stand on its own two feet. An 'effete corps' has its stresses wrong, which

---

* In a 1997 article in the *Yale Alumni Magazine* Buckley writes, "the strategic design, in a strict-constructionist writing course, is to exact formal correctness while encouraging stylistic imagination." How disarming to hear Buckley use "strict-constructionist" outside of the context of a discussion of the Supreme Court!

is itself distracting. And then again, one doesn't think of people who are 'impudent' as being 'effete,' unless one is engaged in characterizations so subtle that they are better executed by Jane Austen than Spiro Agnew."[27]

This is one of those precious moments that succinctly illustrate why Buckley never actually entered politics or wrote political speeches for others: his standard for subtle characterization was Jane Austen. Buckley further lamented that Agnew had described Vietnam protestors as "ideological eunuchs." As he explained, "That kind of growling sounds awfully good, gruntwise. But it is spectacularly maladroit. The people Agnew is talking about are anything but eunuchs on the ideological scale. An ideological eunuch was, say, Eisenhower; or the Vicar of Bray. Never the protestors, who are ideological eunuchs only if Joan of Arc was an ideological eunuch."[28] Yes, of course, who doesn't think of the mythical, hypocritical seventeenth-century Vicar of Bray whenever Eisenhower comes up?

On *Firing Line*, Buckley held back on inveighing against Agnew's speech, and he even invited Nixon's director of communications, Herbert G. Klein, on the show. One could only really expect spin and public relations talk to ensue. Klein emphasized how "candid and honest" Nixon had been with the public about Vietnam and downplayed any negative interpretation of Agnew's speech. He was downright Pollyannaish: "Unless you set high goals and move toward them, take action toward high goals, uh, you're not gonna have the exciting chance we have in this decade to reach great peaks." While he thinks the press could be more balanced, he adds that "they're doing a far better job than has ever been done before. And they're the best in the world." Buckley can't help but quip, "I'll bet you say that to all the girls." Whether or not you agreed about the prevalence of liberal media bias, Klein's analysis was all puffery.

Buckley had been apoplectic about the publication of the Pentagon Papers, leaked to the *New York Times* by Daniel Ellsberg of the RAND Corporation in 1971, and you'd think this might translate into support for the censorious undercurrent of Agnew's speeches attacking the media; but Buckley was only selectively censorious. He had no qualms about the stifling of obscene speech or any speech that he judged as imperiling national security.* Outside of these two areas, he expressed little advocacy for media censorship, accepting, for example, that Katharine Graham of the *Washington Post* was "not inclined to install top editors who stray too far from her own liberal views."[29] She owned the paper, and this was her prerogative. What we needed then, from Buckley's perspective, was not the censorship that "Nixon's Nixon" implicitly favored but, rather, *more* media voices.

In this context, with the White House attacking both the antiwar movement and the mainstream media's coverage of that movement, and protestors themselves finding the coverage to be sorely lacking, *Firing Line* was really one of the best sources for learning about Vietnam. The show asked complicated questions and provided much more detailed information, though not from a "breaking news" angle, than the evening news.

Take the My Lai Massacre, which occurred in March 1968 and was revealed to the public in November 1969, when freelance journalist Seymour Hersh broke the story. In March 1971, platoon leader Lieutenant William Calley was convicted and sentenced to life in prison for his participation in the slaughter

---

* Setting aside the issue of censorship and national security issues, Buckley was generally more enthusiastic about the censorious impulse than about enacting censorship itself. In the 1980s, for example, the Moral Majority supported laws that stymied pornography and regulated people's sex lives. Buckley judged this kind of activism to be positive, though he would not have engaged in such activism himself. The loud disapproval of immorality seemed a healthy impulse to him, but he did not have the crusader's drive for such matters. Asked by Mark Green about laws against oral sex between consenting heterosexual adults on a 1981 *Firing Line* episode, Buckley voiced approval for the laws but disinterest regarding their rare enforcement.

of some five hundred unarmed Vietnamese men, women, and children; he served only three and a half years, part of that time being under house arrest. Hersh appeared on *Firing Line* in July 1971, in an episode titled "War Crimes: Part I." The other guest was Ernest van den Haag, a *National Review* contributor who was known for his support of segregation, the death penalty, and apartheid. At the time, he was researching a book that Buckley described as being centered on war crimes, though it would later emerge as more broadly about crime and punishment.[30]

A heated and chaotic discussion of the legal definition of "war crimes" ensues. One might presume that the conservative Van den Haag would defend military operations in Vietnam, and even defend Calley, as many conservatives did—"Free Calley" was even a popular bumper sticker at the time. Instead, Van den Haag acknowledges Calley's guilt and makes an unexpected recommendation.

VAN DEN HAAG: After trying Lieutenant Calley, we should have strung him up on the nearest tree in Song My, or the place where he committed his murders, and if we had done so, I think it would've been more effective than millions spent on psychological warfare, because we not only should do justice, we should also do it so that it can be seen. That, I think, is our big mistake. . . .

HERSH: When you talk about stringing up Calley, you know, you're not going to suggest that, certainly, Calley was unique in any way in what he did. And I think if you really look at—

VAN DEN HAAG: Oh—but I want to make him unique by stringing him up.

HERSH: But, uh, what—but [speechless]—

VAN DEN HAAG: That will deter some other people from imitating him.

HERSH: Let me just—

BUCKLEY: Are you using a metaphor?

VAN DEN HAAG: No, I'm not. I am quite seriously thinking—

BUCKLEY: Are you suggesting—

VAN DEN HAAG: —that a man who has been convicted of his monstrosities—

BUCKLEY: Well then, you're suggesting lynch justice—

VAN DEN HAAG: —should, at the very place that he committed them, be—

BUCKLEY: You're not suggesting lynch justice?

VAN DEN HAAG: No! I think he should be tried, and, if found guilty, strung up where I suggested he should be tried.

Hersh is flummoxed and steers the conversation back to war crimes, but he's already won (though he has no idea of his own victory) insofar as the conservatives are absolutely with him on one key front: war crimes are a serious and real problem in Vietnam.

Hersh is less concerned about the issue of punishment, though, than his conservative opponents. He says, let's end the war, stop the killing, and then worry about sorting out who did what. Meanwhile, aside from expressing concern that Van den Haag has gone off his nut in his passionate advocacy for stringing up Calley, Buckley mostly sits back and listens, not denying that the kinds of activities Hersh had exposed are indeed taking place. Hersh further points to systemic military problems:

HERSH: They've substituted something called the "rules of engagement" for international law. In essence . . . all commands have been ordered to issue very specific rules of engagement dealing with the way we operate in Vietnam.

That is, we have to get political clearance or military clearance
before we engage such-and-such and we do such-and-such.
And the—first of all, nobody pays any attention to them [the
rules of engagement]—and the other problem is that, lo and
behold, a two-star general is confronted with evidence that
indicates some of his helicopter pilots shot up a village and
killed twenty-five people, and he is sort of compelled to take
action, he can't duck, maybe because the Vietnamese civilians
and the local province people are excited. Otherwise, he would
duck. That's the obvious solution. "CYA" they call it—Cover
Your Ass in Vietnam. But he can't duck because of political
pressures, so he does something to the effect of maybe
issuing a letter of reprimand because, in his eyes, these
people are guilty of violating a rule, not murder. "Murder"
doesn't enter into this sort of situation.

If Hersh had extrapolated from My Lai that Nixon was a war
criminal, as other journalists had done at the time, this would
have become a program *explicitly* about Nixon. Instead, the
Nixon angle was submerged. Nixon himself had not slaughtered civilians in Vietnam, but all of this was happening on his
watch. In not denying the existence of such behavior, Buckley
was not attacking Nixon, but he was not standing up for him,
either.

"War Crimes: Part II" provided a completely different perspective. Three young marines who had served in Vietnam
were disturbed by what they saw as the biased picture of the
war painted by most media outlets, and they had been particularly shocked by the allegations made by Hersh on *Firing
Line*. They wrote a letter to Buckley asking to come on his program to convey their own experiences of war crimes—or lack
thereof—in Vietnam.

From the get-go this was unusual. Aside from the panel of
questioners, which typically included three students, profes-

sors, or journalists, *Firing Line* generally featured only well-known political or intellectual figures. You didn't *invite yourself* to be on the show unless you were pals with Buckley. And if this was the case there was a reasonably good chance that you also happened to be a well-known political or intellectual figure. But these young captains had had the temerity to offer their own account of what was going on in Vietnam, and now on the dais before us sat these three unknowns—John F. Bender, Donald B. Carpenter, and Oliver L. North. Yes, *that* Oliver North. Two of them appeared in uniform, one in a suit, and all three sported close haircuts and lean good looks that would not have been out of place in a World War II combat picture.

The earnest young men emphasized that they were appearing on *Firing Line* to describe their personal experiences in Vietnam, where they had never participated in or witnessed atrocities committed upon the civilian population. They took issue with a number of claims made by Hersh in the preceding episode, noting that they had never seen anyone culling ears from Vietnamese victims or lassoing civilians and dragging them with helicopters. North in particular objected to the comment Hersh had made about "CYA," the practice of military officers finding ways to hush up crimes. North suggests that any officer who dared to come forward and declare that he actually *had* followed proper procedures "would be massively disbelieved, because here is a man who, in the eye of the public because of the way this thing has been presented [by the media], is trying to cover his 'tail,' if I may use the vernacular, with paper [false reports]."

North was an arrow so straight he couldn't even quote someone saying "ass." He conveys total confidence in subservience to military procedure: marines follow orders, and the orders are just. As the show progresses, instead of learning about the issue of war crimes, we learn about the dental care that the United States is offering the Vietnamese, and about how our surgeons are saving both American and Viet Cong lives.

At first glance, this seems like exactly the kind of gung ho boosterism that Agnew, Nixon, and the rest would have loved to have seen on the tube all the time. The fly in the ointment is Buckley, who is incredulous. If *why* we were fighting the war had been at issue on "War Crimes" Part I or II, Buckley would have out-Nixoned Nixon with his anticommunist rhetoric. But Part I had been a dispute about what to do about war criminals, the assumption being that they actually existed. On Part II, the assumption that they did *not* exist was too much for Buckley to swallow.

North, Carpenter, and Bender insist that they are not disputing what others might have seen and that they are only speaking of their own experiences. In fact, they harp on this point like a broken record, always seeming on the cusp of saying that there have been no atrocities committed, then pulling back and saying, "We never saw such things." Buckley is increasingly vexed by this repetitious public relations spin. These young men may or may not be sincere, but they certainly seem heavily coached by military lawyers. By the end of the show, Buckley is fed up with all of this I-can't-discuss-the-veracity-of-My-Lai-because-I-wasn't-there rhetoric. What follows is, to my mind, one of the all-time great *Firing Line* take-downs.

BUCKLEY: Well, Captain Bender, let me ask you this. We've heard now for the last forty-five minutes what, in fact, is a flat repudiation of that which we have all been told is the case over there. Now, I know that you're not anxious to criticize anybody, but suppose you tell me how it is that you figure that what you insist is a myth has become so prevalent in America.

BENDER: Okay, you're putting words in my mouth.

BUCKLEY: Well, it's obviously a myth. If what you say is true, it's got to be a myth.

BENDER: It's—well, okay—as far as I'm concerned it [the existence of war crimes] is a myth. As far as my knowledge, and we talked about this before, the knowledge of my unit, and we can't go into discussing what happened at My Lai, because I wasn't there.

BUCKLEY: No, I think that's a cop-out. Look, if I live in New York City and I say I've never been mugged, therefore, there is no mugging in New York City, I'm intellectually irresponsible, right? Now, I don't ever go on saying, "I don't doubt the people who say they've been mugged"; but, in effect, if I invite myself onto a program or onto any situation in order to say, "Look, I've never been mugged and therefore, there is no mugging in New York City," I am actually urging a set of conclusions. Now, you asked to come on this program, and I welcome you on it, and you've done magnificently, but I ask you to be responsible enough to say why is it that you are right and they are wrong.

Buckley is agitated, almost cross. He compliments his war heroes ("You've done magnificently"), but he clearly resents their self-invitation in light of their self-serving performance. More to the point, he also gleans that they are full of shit. The two war crimes episodes were excellent examples of *Firing Line* combating liberal media bias not by grumbling about it but by simply providing a different take on Vietnam. On the other hand, one can hardly imagine Nixon approving of these episodes, since they not only gave airtime to Hersh and Van den Haag, with his *farkakte* ideas about public executions, but also raised doubts about the public relations capabilities of the US Marine Corps.

Buckley surely offended the Nixon administration even fur-

Offended by Seymour Hersh's discussion of war crimes on *Firing Line*, Marines John F. Bender, Donald B. Carpenter, and Oliver L. North appear to explain that they never witnessed any such crimes while serving in Vietnam. Buckley counters, "Look, if I live in New York City and I say I've never been mugged, therefore, there is no mugging in New York City, I'm intellectually irresponsible, right?" CREDIT: *Hoover Institution*

ther by inviting Woodward and Bernstein onto the show in 1973, shortly after the release of *All the President's Men*. Helping those sons of bitches to promote their book?!* Of course, Buckley's objective was hardly to give the journalists free publicity. And discussion would not center on Nixon's culpability, or lack thereof: the title of the episode was "The Limits of Journalistic Investigation," with Buckley questioning the reporters' politi-

---

* In 1977, Pat Nixon had suffered a stroke, allegedly after reading Woodward and Bernstein's bestseller *The Final Days*, which was, to say the least, unkind to the first couple. Nixon would not even speak their names to David Frost, but clearly referring to "Woodstein" he said, "I have nothing but utter contempt" for them, "and I will never forgive them. Never."

cal neutrality. In other words, the focus was on *their* culpability, or lack thereof.

Bernstein states, "I think we really prize our ability to detach ourselves in covering a story, very much as a juror does." Buckley responds, "Speaking of detachment, let me quote from your book where you came in with a piece of evidence and you presented it to the boss, Ben Bradlee. 'There was at least one witness,' the book says, 'who could do some damage to Mitchell, Colson, Ehrlichman, and Dean. Bradlee's eyes brightened. He did a little dance, holding an imaginary towel to his ass and wiggling it back and forth before walking off.' Is that typical detachment in the *Washington Post?*"

The line gets the laugh that Buckley hoped for from the studio audience, and Bernstein responds, "That has to do more with our *own* credibility than taking any joy in the guilt of others," but Buckley maintains that the whole book has "a certain prosecutorial feel." The episode does not definitively prove that "Woodstein" lack objectivity, though Buckley does provide some balance to the heroic narrative circulating around the journalists, even pointedly rejecting their willingness to discuss their personal lives: "I don't see that I have any right to ask you what you had for breakfast this morning. If I had a kooky curiosity about it, I should . . . be invited to suppress it, not to gratify it."

Buckley presses his guests throughout the show to admit that they would be disappointed to learn that Nixon was not guilty, and they, in response, maintain that they are neutral investigative journalists. In the final analysis, the show is not so much about guilt or innocence as it is about decorum. Buckley complains that journalists are revealing information that they should not, and that people like Daniel Ellsberg are being praised as heroes. It is all so *uncouth.*

BERNSTEIN: If you're talking now about espionage,
the espionage statutes—I don't think anybody's run into

the espionage statutes in Watergate, nothing close
to it.

BUCKLEY: No, but it's not the result of any obvious sense of
restraint.

BERNSTEIN: Oh, I think, you know, when it comes to
espionage, that there would be a tremendous sense of
restraint on the part of the press and on the part of people in
the security agencies. I don't think espionage is something
most people take very lightly.

BUCKLEY: I think it's a thing that most people take *extremely*
lightly. All kinds of operettas were written to the tribute of
people who committed or tried to commit espionage during
the Vietnam War. I think that the whole notion of the
individual conscience triumphant in matters of public policy
happens to be very fashionable right now so that I doubt that
there would be—what would you call it when you publish the
fallback position on SALT I, or what do you call it when you
publish the secret meetings of the National Security Council
during the Bangladesh-India confrontation?

WOODWARD: I call it disclosure and good reporting.

Obviously, Buckley does have real concerns about espionage,
but what the perceptive *Firing Line* viewer senses most keenly
here is a longing for the days of the gentleman reporter. The
notion of *restraint* was just shot to hell. Watergate was a crisis
on so many levels, reporters had run amok, and Nixon wasn't
doing much better himself. Buckley even argues that the president should have destroyed the tapes.

WOODWARD: Do you see the distinction between us not
disclosing our sources and the president not disclosing
what went on in those taped conversations in the White
House?

BUCKLEY: Well, I think he was an *ass* to disclose the taped conversations, and I think you probably do, too. And this is not an ethical judgment I'm making; it's a matter of taste [audience laughter]. I think that private conversations are awesomely private and ought to be. Besides, unless it's a soliloquy, you're involving somebody else, and to exercise dominion over somebody else's conversation and disclose it I simply find *heinous*.

BERNSTEIN: Do you question whether or not, when you have allegations of criminal activity, a court or a prosecutor has authority to obtain such information?

BUCKLEY: I think there is a hierarchy of considerations that all societies that choose to survive have got to attempt to construct, and one of them says, yes, under certain circumstances you can tape conversations; under certain circumstances, you can torture a guy who has the key to the H-bomb that's about to go off in central Philadelphia, that kind of stuff. But, by and large, it seems to me that to tape other people's conversations and to reveal them ought to be recognized by the law as what I judge it to be morally, a heinous offense.

WOODWARD: But, now, the tape recordings—

BUCKLEY: I think one of the worst things Nixon ever did was to reveal—I think that Nixon ought to have burned the tapes instantly and publicly—[on the] Fourth of July, preferably. [audience laughter]

Other supporters of the president had suggested that he should have destroyed the tapes to protect himself, but Buckley was indicating that it was outrageous to make the tapes in the first place because they harmed others and violated the protocols of civilized society. As is clear in so many episodes of *Firing Line*, but particularly in those centered on (or circling around) Nixon, Buckley's conservatism was married to a patrician notion of taste. A man of Nixon's temperament could never quite measure up, regardless of how conservative his policies might be.

On "The Limits of Journalistic Investigation," Buckley comes closest to actually defending Nixon—as opposed to criticizing his guests—when he argues that other presidents had behaved much more badly than Nixon.

BUCKLEY: As regards the American president, it seems to me that even pre–Woodward and Bernstein, there was enough investigative journalism to suggest an appropriate skepticism about a lot of presidents, at least a lot about some of the *crap* that they—

WOODWARD: Yes, but never in this magnitude.

BERNSTEIN: Yes, but again, it's never run into anything that I can think of like a criminal conspiracy to obstruct justice that occurred in the White House. I really can't think of any instance in history where that's happened.

WOODWARD: I can't either.

BUCKLEY: Well, what about a criminal conspiracy to suspend the Constitution? We've had several of those.

WOODWARD: Like?

BUCKLEY: Like suspending habeas corpus by Lincoln, like suspending the Constitution to buy the Louisiana Purchase, like suspending whatever the hell we had to suspend to move all those Japanese from California into Utah.

BERNSTEIN: There certainly have been isolated incidents, you know, throughout history.

BUCKLEY: Well, I'm glad they're isolated. I'm glad they're isolated, but it seems to me that they—

BERNSTEIN: But this has to do with something else.

BUCKLEY: —assume the proportions of Mount Rushmore compared to this kind of stuff.

WOODWARD: But does that mean that we shouldn't examine this with—

BERNSTEIN: I think that the proportions of this *are* comparable to Mount Rushmore.

BUCKLEY: No, not at all.

BERNSTEIN: That's the point of Watergate, that nothing has happened like this on this scale with this kind of intensity and scope.

BUCKLEY: My feeling is that Nixon contributed to this uniquely. What gives Watergate its proportions, my own judgment is, is the transfusion into it of that special self-serving moralistic rhetoric of the President of the United States. If he'd been a little bit more suave about it, a little bit less pompously innocent, it [Watergate] would have been accepted, I think, as pretty workaday.

Buckley had been rolling along, approaching a defense of Nixon, but then he swerved back to the issue of decorum. If Nixon had simply been more *suave*, Watergate would not have ballooned as it had. A retort to the liberal media had been provided on this episode to the extent that Buckley had, by example, rejected the glorification of Woodstein that was then in vogue. That said, he had not come up with any kind of truly spirited defense of Nixon. Taping and revealing private conversations was tasteless. Revealing governmental secrets (viz., the Pentagon Papers) was tasteless, and Nixon's self-defense, which would culminate in the infamous "I am not a crook!" declaration, was *particularly* tasteless. Nixon may have loathed the authors of *All the President's Men* only a bit more than Buck-

ley did, but Buckley was not really doing the president any favors with this episode.

Questions of taste and decorum aside, the bottom line was
that the Buckleyites were simply never satisfied with Nixon. As
John R. Coyne and Linda Bridges put it, "Always, always there
was the awareness that Nixon was not One of Us."[31] The chapter on Nixon in their Buckley book is fittingly titled "The Long
Detour." Nixon was, in other words, a detour on the way to Reagan, on the way to the triumph of right-wing conservatism. In
August 1971 Buckley and others from *National Review* had met
with a group of high-powered right-wing conservatives to issue "A Declaration" that they were suspending support of the
Nixon administration: "We consider that our defection is an act
of loyalty to the Nixon we supported in 1968."[32]

This was coy insofar as they had not been doing backflips
over the Nixon of 1968, and *NR*'s stance had long been that they
would support the "most electable" conservative candidate, operating under the assumption that such a person would not necessarily be as conservative as they would have liked. By late 1971,
National Review was officially supporting the nomination of
John Ashbrook for the Republican ticket. Buckley and his crew
were disappointed by Nixon on so many fronts. There was his
trip to China, his price and wage controls, his attitude toward
affirmative action ("racial quotas," the opposition maintained),
his attempt to set up a guaranteed minimum income (the Family Assistance Plan), his support of women's rights legislation,
and his creation of the Environmental Protection Agency.

One could reasonably contend that Nixon didn't really care
deeply about many of his reformist domestic efforts. One
Nixon historian has concluded that "Nixon chose to guide foreign policy himself and entrust the details of domestic policy
to subordinates since he did not consider the latter as critically important as the former."[33] Regardless of the sincerity of
his intentions, or his own personal, appalling attitudes about

women, racial minorities, or Jews, his progressive domestic policies added up to more federal government intervention than conservatives could stomach. This was all potentially bad for the future of conservatives within the Republican Party, quite apart from whatever harm Watergate and the resignation did to it. By the time Nixon stepped down in 1974, historian Donald Critchlow summarizes, "subscriptions to *National Review* were down and the magazine's deficits were the biggest ever, and the conservative movement as a whole was dispirited. . . . The Republican Right appeared to be in a state of rapid decline as a political force within the GOP and American politics."[34]

If the conservative movement was indeed "dispirited," what was *Firing Line*'s ideal response? Buckley didn't want to attack Nixon on the same grounds that the "liberal media" did, but he would still offer criticism. How far would he go? If Nixon was truly a detour on the way to a more conservative president, such as Reagan—this notion being but a glimmer in Buckley's eye at the time—it would not pay to be *too* negative about Nixon's presidency on *Firing Line*. How could one be critical without undermining the GOP? Or, more precisely, without undermining the conservative movement?

The difference between the two was important for Buckley, and one way to approach the Nixon Problem (that is, how to be in favor of a Republican in the White House, one who was clearly better than the last Republican, Eisenhower, but who was also a bitter disappointment to the right) was precisely to attempt to separate out the GOP from the conservative movement. And then to suggest that the two *could* actually converge . . . with the proper president in the White House. One could pull the GOP right rather than abandon the two-party system.

Buckley had run for New York City mayor in 1965 on the Conservative ticket as a symbolic act, knowing he would not win, to protest the almost comic notion that candidate John Lindsay was a Republican. But Buckley didn't want the Conservative Party to seriously challenge the GOP as a national party, notwithstanding the fact that his older brother James had been elected a senator for New York on the Conservative ticket in 1970—the first third-party candidate to win election to Congress since 1940. Appearing on "The Problems of a Conservative Legislator" in 1971, Senator Buckley told his brother that the role of third parties was to push the two-party system to improve itself (and implicitly, the fix was to push moderate Republicans out of the party). Third parties only appeared, in theory, if the two-party system offered candidates that were too similar.

Thus we have *Firing Line*'s nondenial denial number 3: Nixon's not the issue, the future of the Republican Party is the issue.

Nondenial denial number 3 is particularly in play in 1974's "The Nixon Experience and American Conservatism," featuring Senator Buckley in his third appearance on the show. As Bill Buckley would note repeatedly on *Firing Line*, Nixon's corruption was not specifically "conservative" or "Republican." He stated, and his brother agreed, that the typical corruption of the left came from the hunger for power (thus, machine politics in Chicago and socialist and communist dictators abroad), while the typical corruption of the right came from a desire for financial gain. Wait, Nixon wasn't power hungry? No, rewind the lesson: the *left* was power hungry, not the right, so there couldn't be a specifically "conservative" element underlying Nixon's corruption. Corrupt conservatives were motivated by greed. Thus, since Nixon did not gain financially from covering up Watergate (just the opposite), bugging the phones of those he saw as his enemies, breaking into the files of Daniel Ellsberg's psychiatrist, and so on, his misdeeds simply could not be seen as being of a specifically conservative nature. Hence, his ejection from office would not (or should not) harm either the GOP or the conservative movement in general.

On 1974's "The Republican Party and Mr. Nixon," with Republican national chairman George H. W. Bush, Buckley went so far as to say that "Agnew hurt conservatism more than Nixon in my judgment, in part because the traditional conservative political sin is greed. The traditional liberal sin is lust for power, so that Nixon's sins tend to be Democratic sins. . . ." Since Agnew left office amid financial scandal, he hurt conservatism more than Nixon? Yes. As Buckley would again put it on a 1973 *Firing Line* episode with Allard Lowenstein, "I think that the sins of Mr. Agnew are much more embarrassing than the sins of Mr. Nixon because the sins attributed to Mr. Nixon are much more of a left variant."

It was a perplexing formulation, a Hail Mary maneuver that did not become any more convincing with repetition. Buckley often stated on *Firing Line* that the difference between conservatives and liberals was that conservatives were "realists." They knew, for example, that you couldn't change the hearts of men by throwing federal government money at social problems. But the notion that Agnew's misdeeds hurt the conservative movement more than Nixon's could only be understood by most people not as a "realist" notion but as a flight of fancy.

In any case, on "The Nixon Experience and American Conservatism," Buckley and Buckley are quite sure of their analysis, though their confidence is visually undercut by some kind of technological gaffe whereby the TV studio is even more scorching than usual. The studio lights were always hot, and it was normal for a guest to begin to perspire only a few minutes into any *Firing Line* episode, but on this particular show rivulets of sweat flow freely. Our host is lucky enough to be wearing a light seersucker jacket, while his guest is dressed in cursedly heavy camel hair; alarming drops of sweat slowly descend his brow, on the cusp of stinging his eyes. Bill actually has to pause to reach off camera to borrow a handkerchief so that his poor sibling can blot himself. The perspiration crisis would be a mere footnote if not for the fact that the Brothers Buckley were discussing a man so often ridiculed for his five o'clock shadow and diaphoretic tendencies. Buckley and Buckley were clean-shaven, but sweating maniacally while indicating that Nixon had not betrayed the Republican Party could only seem like a bizarre, hysterical symptom of misguidedness. And the Buckleys *were* misguided, in that their discussion floated in some kind of platonic realm in which voters would understand that Nixon's sins had nothing to do with the fact that he happened to be a Republican, or a north-by-northwest conservative.

Obviously, actual voters did not intuit any of this, and the GOP was pummeled in the 1974 midterm elections, as predicted. Appearing on *Firing Line* six months before those elections—to analyze in advance what everyone assumed would be a royal ass-kicking—Bush bitterly complained about Democrats running campaigns largely on platforms that could be reduced to "I hate Watergate." He emphasized that Watergate was not the only issue on the table, conceding that many people would also vote for Democrats because of their concerns about the energy crisis and the economy. And though he did not say "read my lips," he was very emphatic that there was *no chance* that Nixon would resign. Meanwhile, Senator James Buckley had already called for Nixon's resignation on the floor of Congress, shortly before Bush's appearance on the show. As Freeman tells it, "Nixon knows that his presidency is finished when Senator James Buckley on the Senate floor calls for him to resign. . . . I happened to be in the White House that day, and the air went out of the balloon. They knew it was over."[35]

By this point, Bill Buckley himself was also clearly in favor of resignation. He had been blunt about this issue with Buchanan on the aptly titled "Views of a Nixonite," posing the question, "If the Republican Party does face a genocidal retribution in November of 1974 and if it were establishable by hypothetical polls that they would be spared this by the resignation of the president, does this add up in your mind to a good argument for his resigning?"

Answer: No. Buchanan preferred hypothetical genocidal retribution to his hero's defeat. With Bush, Buckley was more rhetorically diplomatic: "There has, of course, been a lot of talk about Mr. Nixon as an albatross. Is it your judgment that if Mr. Nixon were to decide tonight that he wanted to become a poet or whatever, and eliminate himself without any sort of residual stigma, under such circumstances as those would you project that the party would have an easier time in November?" Bush simply refused to consider the question: "You are not going to like this answer, because I know of your intellectual alacrity, but I am not going to get into these hypotheses because this is not going to happen."

Bush was intransigent: resignation was unthinkable. *Firing Line* viewers were informed otherwise by Buckley: resignation was highly thinkable, even if pondering an imaginary future for Nixon as a poet was ghastly. And thus we have nondenial denial number 4, closely related to number 3: It doesn't finally matter if Nixon is guilty (though he is); he must step down from office in the name of the greater good of America and of the GOP.

Many episodes of *Firing Line* circled around Nixon, displacing discussion of his missteps onto discussion of whether he was being treated fairly by the media, Congress, or the American people, but Nixon himself only guested once, on the aforementioned "Future of the GOP"—though he would also make cameo appearances later in compilation shows. On "Firing Line 1966–1986: World Leaders," a retrospective episode designed to celebrate the show's twenty-year anniversary, Buckley notes that the taping of Nixon's 1967 show had been unexpectedly delayed for three hours by a camera malfunction. During the delay, Buckley explains in 1986, he and Nixon had engaged in thoughtful conversation, and Nixon had demonstrated that he was "*cock*sure" that he would be nominated on the Republican ticket. Only Buckley could so confidently stress the first half of that word and not sound the slightest bit indecent.

"World Leaders" then cuts to a clip of less than two minutes in which Nixon emphasizes that Republicans—who, he pointedly takes pains to note, are the same as conservatives—need to find a way to make their policies "exciting."

NIXON: We have to recognize that politics is a great drama. And I will give credit to our Democratic friends, generally speaking, the Democratic politicians—the so-called liberal politicians—have been more exciting and more interesting. Now part of the reason for that is that they can be less responsible.

BUCKLEY: Uh-hum.

NIXON: Because whenever they have a problem they say, well, the government will do something. Whereas the Republican or the conservative has to recognize that it's a step-by-step process, and being responsible, cannot be the demagogue that the other side can be. But nevertheless I do think that the time has now come, at this particular juncture in our history—with all of the pat liberal ideas falling into disrepute, due to their failure—for us to make sound and, to use your term, *conservative* programs exciting, exciting because they will work. And that is the job, I think, of whoever is the next candidate on the Republican ticket.

Nixon didn't seem very excited about making conservative programs exciting, and the episode had been rather dull.

"World Leaders" next turns to clips of guests critiquing Nixon, with Hubert Humphrey capably overviewing the personalities of twentieth-century presidents, and Eugene McCarthy charming both Buckley and the studio audience with his humorous and clever attacks on Nixon's flouting of the law. Next up is Vice President Gerald Ford, a dynamic presence compared to Nixon, fervidly arguing that Nixon would not be impeached. Having shown four guests before Nixon (former and current British prime ministers Harold Macmillan and Margaret Thatcher; Robert Hawke, the Australian labor leader who would later become prime minister; and Philippines president Ferdinand Marcos sharing deep thoughts on Heraclitus), Buckley ends up making Nixon something of a centerpiece of the episode, while still keeping discussion of him relatively light and avoiding any vexing issues. (Even lighter was one of the show's other twenty-year anniversary episodes, hosted by Jeff Greenfield, with luminaries like John Kenneth Galbraith, Henry Kissinger, Tom Wolfe, and good ol' Harriet Pilpel "roasting" Buckley, the studio filled with balloons sporting some of the host's favorite vocabulary words.)

Finally, a full twenty minutes of "World Leaders" is devoted to an excerpt from the Panama Canal treaty debate staged on *Firing Line* in 1978 and featuring Buckley, George Will, and James Burnham arguing that the canal should be turned over to Panama, and Ronald Reagan, Pat Buchanan, and Roger Fontaine arguing the other side.

More on this debate shortly, when we turn all of our attention to Reagan. For now, it is instructive to reread this quintessentially Reagan moment as a strange sort of Nixon moment. That a full one-third of this 1986 greatest hits episode was given over to Reagan was, to some extent, simply a celebration of Reagan's triumphant presence in the White House. Given how very far-fetched such a triumph would have seemed to most when *Firing Line* premiered in 1966, it was reasonable to make him the shining star of the 1986 episode (though Buckley really does outdebate him on Panama). Thus, a look back at great world leaders would seem really, *on the surface*, to be mostly about Reagan.

Bill and *Firing Line* get "Roasted"

On one of the show's twenty-year anniversary episodes, hosted by Jeff Greenfield, luminaries such as John Kenneth Galbraith, Henry Kissinger, Tom Wolfe, and Harriet Pilpel "roast" Buckley, the studio filled with balloons sporting some of the host's favorite vocabulary words.
CREDIT: *Cartoonist, Walt Lardner/SCETV*

But Nixon was, arguably, the show's true spectral undercurrent. After all, his rise and fall was the meat of much of the episode; Reagan finally appeared at the end as a kind of exclamation point to emphasize that a "real conservative" had ultimately triumphed, the kind of man who would not be open to price and wage controls and who would not be enthusiastic about negotiations with Communist China.

Sam Ervin, who had been chairman of the Senate Watergate Committee, functioned as chair of the canal debate. His presence would surely evoke the ghostly presence of Nixon for many viewers. In fact, even before Watergate, in 1971, Ervin had held hearings on the Senate floor to address Nixon's attempts to curtail press coverage of his administration. Adding insult to injury, insofar as the end of "World Leaders" implicitly celebrates Reagan over Nixon, the debate clip even includes a cutaway shot of the packed house that prominently features Strom Thurmond.

Thurmond, of course, was the synecdochic figure par excellence of Nixon's Southern Strategy. And here Thurmond was, still a senator in 1978, still in the game four years after Nixon had left the White House in disgrace, watching Reagan and Buckley debate, sitting next to his wife, Nancy (forty-four years his junior), who here looks uncannily like Nixon's daughter Tricia. It's a fleeting moment that borders on the surreal. One can imagine Nixon watching the original *Firing Line* debate in his study in San Clemente, California, in 1978, a stiff drink in hand, feeling left out, sadly jotting down notes on the Panama Canal on a yellow legal pad. It is harder to imagine him responding to the 1986 clip episode in which his fall is referenced without malice but also without sympathy, and in which Reagan's rise—and the rise of right-wing conservatism—is simply a fait accompli.

By 1986, *Firing Line*'s nondenial denial number 3 could be retroactively revised: Nixon is not the issue, the future of the Republican Party is the issue, and Reagan is that future. Reagan's presence at the end of the "World Leaders" episode thus constituted a kind of victory lap for Buckley and his confederates. The long detour was over.

CHAPTER SIX

FROM THE MASHED POTATO CIRCUIT TO THE OVAL OFFICE

Ronald Reagan, *Firing Line*, and
the Triumph of the Right

Almost thirty years after completing his two terms as president, Ronald Reagan remains the left's archvillain and the right's shining hero. To many of those of a younger generation who did not live through the 1980s he is simply known, for better or for worse, as a tax-cutting cold warrior, the "great communicator" of the "greed-is-good" decade. The elements of the Reagan myth are easy enough to pinpoint. He was the smiling, mild-mannered, apple-pie guy, a fellow who, as Buckley pointed out in his commemorative column when Reagan left office, earnestly used words like *Hades* and *keister*. It was hard for interviewers to get past Reagan's G-rated surface. Buckley did not succeed where others had failed. That is, Reagan's *Firing Line* appearances did not reveal the man beneath the cold warrior. But then that was never Buckley's intention.

Journalist George Packer once observed, "It is notoriously hard to write about Reagan." Allowed "unprecedented access to the President while he was still in the White House," Packer continued, his biographer Edmund Morris "was so defeated by

Reagan's opacity and quips that he resorted to fictionalizing."[1] An uncharitable reader of Buckley's final (second posthumous) book, *The Reagan I Knew*, might also perceive some fictional elements therein—the product, arguably, not of imaginative spirit but of selective memory. But whether you come to the book as a friend or enemy of Reagan (or of Buckley, for that matter), there is no denying that Buckley never found it "notoriously hard" to write about his old chum.

Of course, Buckley was not interested in psychologizing. His Reagan book includes a bit of newly written material, but it is mostly a selection of correspondence revealing Reagan as personable and—more important—showing his political positions. We also see a bit of Buckley's flirtatious correspondence with Nancy Reagan, though this is kept on the tasteful up-and-up.* For the most part, *The Reagan I Knew* is a straight-up homage to the man who brought the right-wing conservatism that Buckley had been promoting for so many years—in his columns, in his speeches, in his books, on his TV show—to the White House. By the time Reagan left office, in fact, "right-wing conservatism" had become "conservatism" *tout court*.

Reagan himself appeared as a guest on *Firing Line* seven times over the years (and was featured in clip reels on four additional episodes). And, of course, Reaganism suffused the show throughout the 1980s.[2] Put another way, Buckleyism infused Reaganism, and Reaganism infused *Firing Line*; for let us not forget that Buckley liked to say he had been advocating "Reagan's" policies back when Reagan was still a liberal. On a 1981

---

* The originals held at Yale University are a bit more fun, revealing the correspondents' contrasting styles via the materiality of the letters. Buckley's letters are typed on no-nonsense plain paper, the closing signature their only flourish; Nancy's are scrawled on ladylike monogrammed stationery, and she had a penchant for drawing smiley faces (a disliked journalist was "in the pokey" for statutory rape) and frowny faces ("we had the Romney's [*sic*] for lunch!").

episode with John Kenneth Galbraith, the question is raised as to whether or not Buckley will approve of Reagan's plans to increase military spending. Buckley responds, with both humor and irritation, "Now the question is: will the Reagan administration agree with me? I started it all. . . . I came out for rearmament when Reagan was a member of the ADA [Americans for Democratic Action], so cut that out!" Buckley may have been conservative before Reagan, but Reagan obviously caught up—in part by being a charter subscriber to *National Review.*

Looking back, at first glance it seems to make sense that Reagan and Buckley would become friends. Reagan had once described himself as "a near-hopeless hemophiliac liberal," referring presumably to his early sympathy for FDR, his ADA membership, and his status as a registered Democrat until 1962.[3] He had never really been any kind of raging left-winger. But he had been a liberal who had gone right, and Buckley's circle was amply populated with such converts.

Reagan had been president of the Screen Actors Guild in the 1940s and '50s, and he had been a friendly HUAC witness, but the notion that he would become a full-time politician did not come into focus until a few years later. His movie career stalled, Reagan began doing more TV work in the 1950s. By 1954, Reagan was on General Electric's payroll, hosting their *General Electric Theater* TV series, appearing in GE advertisements, and giving speeches on free market conservatism to GE factory workers.

Lest it sound as if Reagan was floundering, I hasten to add that his GE salary was $125,000—that's worth $1,100,000 in 2015 dollars, though in the spirit of Reagan I should probably add that the 125K from GE was his pretax income. Soon, his audiences expanded to include Rotary club men, Elks club members, Chambers of Commerce, the National Association of Manufacturers, and so on.[4] As one historian sums it up, "Reagan went to General Electric as a failed movie actor tired of working the Las Vegas circuit. He left poised to begin his political career."[5] And, indeed, he would hit the big time with his half-hour "A Time for Choosing" TV speech for Goldwater in 1964, which positioned him to become governor of California a few years later. *National Review* assessed the speech as "probably the most successful single political broadcast since Mr. Nixon's Checkers speech of twelve years ago."[6]

Politically, Reagan and Buckley were an obvious match. As speakers and writers, though, they were something of an odd couple. Yes, each could, in his own way, charm the pants off an audience. But Buckley was an intellectual force, a wordsmith of an obviously intellectual bent, while Reagan was the square politician whose deeply conservative ideas were delivered in a cornpone wrapper. Perusing his letters to Buckley, one rarely spots a moment of rhetorical panache. At one point, Reagan references his fatigue with delivering after-dinner political speeches to the "mashed potato circuit." That seems like a mildly clever descriptor for the purgatory Reagan had once endured, until he uses it a second time in a letter to Buckley, and then during the *Firing Line* Panama Canal debate with Buckley in 1978, and even in the course of a milquetoast interview with Merv Griffin in 1983.

Reagan had made an awkward, stilted appearance on Milton Berle's TV show in 1953; he could not match pace with Berle's comic timing. But if he had one thing in common with "Mr. Television," it was a propensity to reuse crowd-pleasing material. Reagan had terrific timing and delivery, his emotional tone was pitch-perfect, and he knew how to read his audience. Although he had a knack for quick comebacks, he generally worked best off of prepared material. Pushed off-script, he would sometimes flounder until he found the canned anecdote that fit the occasion.[7]

Notwithstanding his reliance on prefabrication, Reagan could generally come up with quick retorts, crack hokey jokes that felt sincere, and keep his cool on TV, and specifically on *Firing Line*, better than most politicians. (In stark contrast, George H. W. Bush displayed his own rather short fuse on Buckley's show, though in 1988 this was no doubt purposeful, to show that the presidential contender was not a "wimp.")

Reagan was the consummate showman, but what was beneath the surface? After a campus visit in 1968, an article in the *Yale Alumni Magazine* remarked upon Reagan's "cordiality and vacuity." If he were to run for president, the authors speculated, "he would do better with the mass electorate than Barry Goldwater did, if only because he is the master of an electronic age while Goldwater was the relic of an oral one."[8] The authors further noted that "the governor makes you like him. He is one of the smoothest politicians on the hustings, with an All-American image of openness and sincerity."[9]

He was charming, and he was quick. But erudite he was not. Jessica Mitford's take-down profile, released in *Ramparts* magazine on the occasion of Reagan's 1965 autobiography, was as hard on Reagan's prose as it was on his political positions, and really, finding banality in this book was like shooting fish in a barrel.* Here's one painful zinger that Mitford highlighted: "Since my birth I have been particularly fond of . . . red, white and blue."[10] She even noted that an army buddy was astounded by Reagan's seemingly boundless passion for articles in the blandly conservative and middlebrow *Reader's Digest*.[11]

Obviously, Reagan's aw-shucks persona was a key part of his mass appeal, but this does not explain how he excelled on *Firing Line* or was befriended by Buckley. What drew Buckley to a

---

* The profile had been originally slated for *Esquire*, to the dismay of the Reagans. Buckley described Mitford in a letter to Nancy as a communist with "extreme political opinions" and gave editor Harold Hayes a ring from Switzerland. *Esquire* saw fit to let the story go, and it ended up at the definitively leftist *Ramparts* magazine. (Reagan correspondence, box 36, Buckley papers, Yale University.)

The Compleat Candida

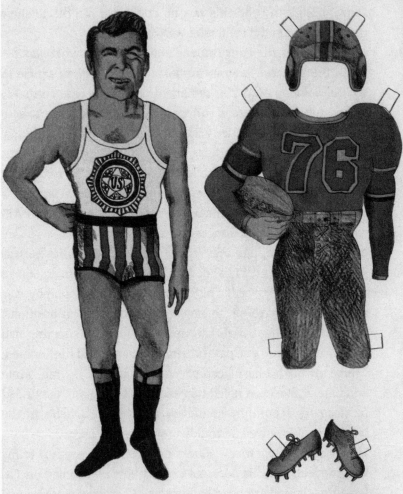

Be patriotic.
[*"Since my birth I have been particularly fond of . . . red, white and blue".**]

Don't shrink from competition.
[*"I had been lauded as a star in sports".**]

*From Ronald Reagan's autobiography, *Where's the Rest of Me?*   †From the official biography of Ronald Reagan published by

Jump right into the swim of things.
[Captain, college swimming team†]

Be a joiner.
[Lions Club, Friars Club,
Tau Kappa Epsilon Fraternity,
California Thoroughbred Breeders Association,
Screen Actors Guild,
American Federation Radio and Television Artists, etc.†]

Nancy Mitford's 1965 profile attacked the jingoistic patriot portrayed in Reagan's autobiography.

CREDIT: ©*1965 Seymour Chwast/Push Pin Studio*

man like Reagan, apart from his politics? Clearly, Buckley could
respect such a man from an ideological angle, but how could he
put up with his corny patriotism? His casual use of football references to explain politics? (On the need to wait before evaluating
Nixon's China initiative: "There are times in which you have to
get a good field position before you can throw the long pass."[12])
His goofball film references? (After thirty-nine American hostages were released in Lebanon, in 1985: "Boy, I saw *Rambo* last
night. . . . Now I know what to do the next time this happens."[13])

Part of the answer lies in Buckley's persistently practical
sense of the nature of realpolitik. He understood quite clearly
that what politicians said they would do, actually wanted to do,
and really could do were quite different things. Relatedly, he
understood that candidates had to *appeal* to the mass of voters,
and that the sesquipedalian discourse that appealed to Buckley
would not be effective in the down-and-dirty trenches of political campaigning or, later, when one was actually in office.
Reagan's style was crowd-pleasing, and the man himself was
patently telegenic. As "Draft Goldwater" strategist Clif White
succinctly put it on *Firing Line* in 1987, "Ronald Reagan talks
like the American people. That's why they like him."

Given his general approval of the conservative ethos behind
the cornball style, Buckley could not seriously object to Reagan's penchant for citing Mark Twain rather than, say, Edmund
Burke. Indeed, in his 1989 farewell newspaper column Buckley went so far as to note with appreciation that Reagan had told
60 Minutes that he was currently reading George Burns's book
on Gracie Allen. If Jimmy Carter had admitted to *60 Minutes*
that in his spare time he was busy poring over a book on peanut farming, one cannot imagine Buckley being so charmed,
notwithstanding his passion for peanut butter. What would
show thin intellect in one man revealed lack of pretension in
another. And, in fact, in 1967 Buckley had described Reagan's
mind as "very quick" and his wit as "mordant."[14]

Reagan's easygoing style, unencumbered by intellectual nuance, was also appealing to Buckley and his confreres because it helped to mark him as not-Goldwater. Goldwater was not an egghead, but he was blunt, and he had clearly lost not only because of his politics but also because of the manner in which he represented his politics. While liberals saw Goldwater's defeat as a referendum on right-wing conservatism, right-wing conservatives of Buckley's ilk were eager to spin the defeat as a first step toward the eventual victory of the right. What was needed was a candidate who did not draw so much support from the overt extremists and, just as important, a candidate who was a smooth talker likely to make fewer gaffes on the campaign trail and who could project a positive image. As Theodore White had observed in chronicling the 1964 campaign, Goldwater had been forced to fight a negative image coming right out of the gate: "Goldwater was cast as defendant. He was like a dog with a can tied to his tail—the faster he ran, the more the can clattered."[15] Reagan's record in California made him the darling of conservatives and the foe of liberals, and, to his great advantage, he did not have Goldwater's heavy "Doctor Strangewater" image to fight.*

Reagan's gubernatorial victory in California in 1966, then, signaled right-wing conservatism as a phoenix emerging from the embers of the Goldwater conflagration. Moreover, California was a huge state, with forty electoral votes, a complicated budget, and a history of campus upheaval. If a right-wing conservative could succeed as governor in such a state, he (and his handlers) could quite reasonably build a case for his qualifications to be president, needing only to prove that he had foreign

---

* Here are just a few of the cheery placards spotted by White at anti-Goldwater demonstrations: "Stamp out Peace—Vote Goldwater"; "Keep Your Atom Bomb in Arizona"; "Welcome Doctor Strangewater"; "Goldwater in 1864"; "Dulce et Decorum Est Pro Patria Mori."

policy chops. Here's where Buckley lent a hand, both in his journal of opinion and on his TV program.

Reagan appeared in 1967 and in 1971 on *Firing Line* episodes titled "Is It Possible to Be a Good Governor?" In both cases, Buckley's operating premise was that the federal government had such a tentacular grasp on the states that it was unclear what a governor could accomplish. The point was to lay the hypothesis out on the table and allow Reagan to show off his response, flexing his right-wing conservative muscles. Reagan obliged, arguing in the 1967 episode for changes to how the feds distributed income to the states and making the case for welfare reform. He also rather unexpectedly favored federal intervention in civil rights issues.

REAGAN: A great many of the violations in some of the states where the minorities have been abused, have been violations in which the federal government did have a right to intervene, because I believe—I'll say it as bluntly as I can—that where the constitutional rights of a human being in this country, the rights guaranteed by that document to all of us, where those are being violated, then I believe the federal government has a responsibility to go in and enforce those rights at the point of bayonet, if necessary. And a great many of the things that are being done against minorities in certain areas are violations of these constitutional rights, and there the federal government does have a responsibility.

This runs somewhat counter to the noninterventionist "states' rights" stance promoted by Buckley at the time. Rather than following that line of argument, however, Buckley makes a bit of a lane shift, pulling Reagan back to his position.

BUCKLEY: Well, Governor, surely one of the problems we all face is the constant enlargement of our "constitutional rights."

You and I live in a very progressive universe as far as this is concerned. When we die, we'll have four or five times as many constitutional rights as when we were born. Now, for instance, recently in California, I understand, the Federal Court told the prison authorities that they couldn't proceed with some executions that were required under California law. Was there a federal constitutional question involved there?

REAGAN: Well, I think there was a certain violation or something by way of the judicial process. As a matter of fact, I'm breathlessly waiting for that same judge now to pass an edict that there can't be any more crime or violence.

BUCKLEY: And I'm sure that he might be very tempted to oblige you. But the question that I'm raising is, still, have we seen an evolution in the whole notion of "constitutional rights" so that, you see, for instance, the Supreme Court today, as it recently did—[declared] that a labor union has the right to fine those of its members who don't follow its orders . . . when they're told to observe a picket line. This now becomes a federal constitutional guarantee question, and therefore can't we simply project that in the course of the next ten or fifteen or twenty or thirty or forty years, almost every right that you and I now consider to be a right that is primarily protected by the state, it's going to burgeon out into some sort of constitutional rights. . . .

REAGAN: Yeah, but Bill, will that be—will that really be an enlargement of our constitutional freedoms, or will that not be indeed an invasion of our constitutional rights? Did they not give the union, in that case [you just mentioned], a right to supersede the constitutional freedom of the individual?

BUCKLEY: Well, that would be my own notion, but I found myself—I find the Supreme Court proceeds without reference to my own ideas. . . .

REAGAN: Yes, well. If the Supreme Court goes any further, I'm going to ask them someday to rap on a rock with a stick and solve our [California] water problem. No, I think that they are violating—for example, these enlarged rights, these increased rights, you say—we have the freedom of speech—

BUCKLEY: Um-hmm.

REAGAN: —you and I. But if we continue in the policy that in the interpretation of the Court, I can expect someday that the Court will rule that you and I have the right to force these people to listen—

BUCKLEY: Um-hmm.

REAGAN: —and I don't think we do have that right.

Reagan has nailed his two jokes, about ending crime and the water shortage, but he has otherwise meandered a bit. He is just trying to follow Buckley's lead, and frankly, he can't quite keep up.

Still, having redirected from the issue of protecting minority rights, Buckley is now free to return to the question of what a governor can actually accomplish.

BUCKLEY: Have we reached the point where there is sufficient popular frustration with the incapacity of the states to maneuver as a result of all the obstacles thrown in their way by the federal government, that there will be a national protest which will be reflected in harmonious legislation by Congress and a certain feeling of self-inhibition exercised by the Supreme Court? Maybe *they* should be electrocuted.

REAGAN: I campaigned on the belief that the people are the best custodian of their own affairs, and I think we're proving it here in California, and I think some of the people who oppose this theory, who still—who want government by mystery, they don't want government by the people, they want

to keep alive the illusion that government is so complicated
that the people don't understand it and therefore just accept
what government does . . . I oppose this, and the only recourse
I've had in the few months I've been in office is, every once in
a while, when the issues grow hot, is to go to the people and
I go by way of television reports to the people, and it's been
pretty amazing.

Reagan's response is patently folksy. In this initial *Firing
Line* appearance, Reagan presents himself as a bit of a naïve
populist, but also as informed on the issues and canny about
how to use his showbiz background to his advantage.

The discussion conveys Reagan's political positions, while
also revealing him as a man of common sense rather than
intellectual prowess. In criticizing how federal grants work,
he comfortably uses phrases like, "I know I'm accused of over-
simplifying, but it doesn't make sense to me. . . ." At one point,
Reagan has listed budget cuts, and Buckley asks why there has
been such reform in California but not elsewhere. Reagan, a
twinkle in his eye, responds by citing Mark Twain: "Californians are a different breed . . . the easy and the slothful, the
lazy stayed home. . . . Californians have a way of dreaming
up vast projects and then carrying them out with dash and
daring."

The quotation is pure cheese, and also a bit improvised from
the original.* But Buckley likes it, and later, with characteristic

---

* In *Roughing It*, Twain writes: "It was a splendid population—for all the
slow, sleepy, sluggish-brained sloths stayed at home . . . you cannot build
pioneers out of that sort of material. It was that population that gave to California a name for getting up astounding enterprises and rushing them
through with a magnificent dash and daring and a recklessness of cost or
consequences, which she bears unto this day—and when she projects a new
surprise the grave world smiles as usual and says, 'Well, that is California
all over.'"

accuracy, he uncharacteristically cites Twain himself, noting
that "Mark Twain used to say the difference between the right
word and almost the right word is the difference between lightning and lightning bug." This is a sharp bit of phrasing—in
fact, "The Right Word" was the title of a collection of Buckley's
prose released in 1997—nicely illustrating that there was nothing cheesy about Twain's actual prose. It was only Reagan's
readjustment of the words and his velvety delivery that made
Twain seem a bit lightweight.

I could not help but flash back to this double-Twain moment
when watching British journalist Malcolm Muggeridge complaining about Margaret Thatcher on *Firing Line* in 1975. Over
the course of his career, Muggeridge appeared quite frequently
on the idiot box to share his opinions, chief among them that
TV was a perfectly dreadful medium. On this particular *Firing Line* appearance he contended that Thatcher defeated Edward Heath, becoming leader of Britain's Conservative Party in
1975, because she was good on the tube. She conveyed a sort of
"imbecile charm," Muggeridge claimed, while Heath suffered
from an "incoherent honesty" that did not play well electroni-
cally.

Buckley went along, concurring that politicians "have to be
'just-us-folksy'" to succeed in mass media. Muggeridge went so
far as to say that Thatcher owed her success to "that particular
flavor of the supermarket" that she exuded. At this, Buckley
gently observed that it was snobbish for Muggeridge to complain that Heath was displaced by a "suburban housewife," as
Muggeridge put it, but he was still on board with his guest's
contention that successful modern politicians have learned to
craft the persona of either clergyman or bookie. Buckley was
hard-pressed to push back against anything Muggeridge said,
so deep was his reverence for the man. Who else could get away
with being so snooty about Thatcher?

But Buckley was not simply nodding and being polite regarding Muggeridge's broad observations about what worked in televised politics. He agreed that TV generally dumbed down politics, and that the "just-us-folksy" clergyman types were abundant. Surely, Reagan was the epitome of the pious and earnest clergyman type who excelled on what certain Luddites of the sixties and seventies called "the boob tube." It is impossible to imagine Reagan reading Marshall McLuhan in his spare time (Nixon's spin doctors read McLuhan for him and reported back). But still, his soothing electronic presence did aptly convey McLuhan's "medium is the massage" ethos. And although Muggeridge's jabs about Thatcher could not be neatly transferred to Reagan insofar as they had a definite male chauvinist undercurrent, it is true that if you didn't buy in to Reagan's politics it was easy to perceive the "flavor of the supermarket" in the sterile fluorescence of his schmaltz. A failed movie star who became a mildly successful TV star and then a hugely successful politician? It was a scenario bolstering Muggeridge's claim that our humanist, media-saturated Western civilization was rapidly going down the drain like the Roman Empire.

No wonder Muggeridge had been a key British voice denouncing Monty Python's *Life of Brian* in 1979. One of the funniest films ever made was not merely too blasphemous for Muggeridge but also too *crude*. This was a man who, upon visiting Soviet Russia, conceded that it was a bleak society but found immensely soothing relief in the lack of sexed-up advertising. One spots a keen sense of humor in his writings, but he was often rather glum on *Firing Line*. It's rather a surprise when he actually succeeds in getting a big laugh from the studio audience upon noting that the Maharishi, with whom he had chatted on a radio show, "was just a *delectable* old Hindu con man."

In any case, Muggeridge did frequently revisit his own sense of the meaning of good and evil, and on this front—though he never mentions Reagan by name—one imagines him approv-

ing of the man's moral tenor. Reagan's tone did not change
significantly over the years, though his fluency and sophistication did go up several notches with the right speechwriter
on board: in his presidential years, he mastered the language
of American exceptionalism, offering a salve both soothing
and inspirational to many Americans still stinging from Vietnam, Watergate, and the Iranian hostage crisis.[16] Speaking off
the cuff in his second "Is It Possible to Be a Good Governor?"
Firing Line appearance, he reveals a politically more mature
persona than we saw in 1967. When he had first appeared on
the program only six months after being elected governor, a
"gosh-darn-it, government's not so complicated!" tone infused
his self-presentation. Now Reagan has been governor for four
years, and he sees how things really work, understanding the
gap between idealism and pragmatism.

For example, he began as governor opposing withholding
taxes as theoretically designed to help citizens but in reality an
unfair government imposition. (We are now so accustomed to
withholding that few will remember there was ever a debate on
the subject.) By 1971 he understands the simple reality that the
state needs constant revenue streams and cannot simply make
do until April 15 comes around. Most of the show's discussion
centers on welfare reform, with Reagan citing abuses of the
system and giving the impression that pretty much all welfare
recipients are in cahoots with local welfare workers helping
them to gouge the state.

REAGAN: Just the other day it broke in the paper here [in
Sacramento] that over in Richmond a young man went out on
the street, got a woman and child to come in the welfare office
with him and pose as his wife and child, and they [the county
welfare workers] put him on welfare. They never even made a
phone call. They never checked up on him. He was **a perfect**
stranger. They put him on at $190 [a month].

BUCKLEY: These [clerks] are federal or California employees?

REAGAN: These are county employees.

BUCKLEY: I see, yes.

REAGAN: And they put him on welfare. . . . And he not only got on welfare, he got on as totally disabled, just on his say-so. All he had to do was say, you know, "My back hurts," and he's down there listed officially as totally disabled. And then he met some buddies on welfare, who told him some of the other tricks—that you can buy a birth certificate in California for two dollars, and this one fellow had five, three of which he was working in three different counties; he's drawing welfare in three different counties under different names and birth certificates, and he's got—the other two he hasn't gotten around to getting to work for him yet, or he'll put those to work. And he said his biggest difficulty is to remember which office he's using [for] which birth certificate.

BUCKLEY: Like the Pill, huh? [audience laughter]

REAGAN: Yeah.

Buckley and his guest again agree on just about everything, though they still speak from opposite ends of the rhetorical spectrum, singing the same song of reform but in quite different tonal registers. Buckley prefers the theoretical (though he is not above throwing in an off-color joke), while Reagan's refrain is the anecdotal.

They do harmonize at the end, though, when the panel of examiners comes down hard on Reagan for, among other things, not having paid any federal income tax the preceding year. The three examiners understand the friendly welfare bureaucrat (a figure roundly vilified by the governor) who helps a poor person receive extra benefits as simply a downscale version of the helpful accountant who guides the wealthy in avoiding taxes.

REAGAN: Well, what is a loophole?

MISS KING: . . . What's a welfare loophole? That something within the law—

REAGAN: —well, I just described one.

MISS KING: —is something within the law that makes benefits available that you feel are, you know, inequitable, that—

REAGAN: —well, let me—

MISS KING: —that people don't deserve—

REAGAN: Yeah.

MISS KING: —these kind of benefits, even though they're perfectly legal. And there are those who believe that the same criteria would apply to people in higher income tax brackets who take advantage of benefits that are within the law.

California citizens all, the examiners are simply apoplectic over their governor's proposed welfare reforms, and it doesn't help at all when he adds that he paid $12,000 in property taxes, even if he paid no state income tax.[17] That's over $85,000 in 2015 dollars. You could argue, from a conservative perspective, that California property taxes were too high, but from a liberal perspective the huge amount of property tax that Reagan paid only suggested that he was a wealthy man who did not understand the problems of the poor. Buckley finally declares that the issue of Reagan's taxes "has become a great national bore," and they move on. This is a classic example of a *Firing Line* episode that seems a bit tame on the page, in transcript form, but that when viewed offers an unexpectedly charged experience. It's the difference between lightning bug and lightning. The bigger takeaway is that Reagan is a more polished politician than he had been in 1967. He no longer has to follow Buckley's lead.

Reagan's next TV appearance with Buckley was less notable than the first two. This time he participated in a panel making conservative predictions for 1972, and perhaps the most interesting thing about the episode is the opening proclamation from the producers: "A special note to all viewers: We announce tonight's program from the right of your television screen. No, there is nothing wrong with your television set . . . and at the danger of the broadcasting media's losing its liberal reputation, and receiving a special award from Spiro Agnew, SECA [Southern Educational Communications Association] presents the following program—a one hundred percent conservative view of the world."

In part this was a gag, clearly playing off of the goofy introduction to the sci-fi series *The Outer Limits*, which opened with a simulation of an out-of-tune TV and then cut to a throbbing white dot, and other menacing video effects, with an ominous voice-over saying, "There is nothing wrong with your television set. Do not attempt to adjust the picture. We are controlling transmission." The warning was SECA's pointed way of noting how unusual it was to hear an entire hour of conservative discussion on TV at the time. Reagan was, of course, a natural choice as guest, along with James Buckley, John Ashbrook, Daniel J. Mahoney, Clare Boothe Luce, and the icing on the cake, libertarian economist Milton Friedman. In this company, Luce emerges as the raging moderate in favoring Nixon's trip to China, and Reagan emerges, subtly, as the one most obviously gunning for higher office as he takes a gentle line on Nixon so as not to alienate Republican operatives.

In January 1980, Reagan appeared on a *Firing Line* episode titled "Presidential Hopeful: Ronald Reagan." Buckley *never* had his guests engage in the "pre-interview," the standard procedure for talk shows whereby guests and a staff member go over questions in advance. The pre-interview is exactly what makes so many chat shows feel canned, packed as they are with rehearsed shtick ("So, I hear something funny happened to you at the gym last week . . ."). Buckley insisted on spontaneity, and he also often had a very precise line of questioning meant to paint a liberal into a corner, so it would not do to reveal his cards—or brushstrokes, if you will—ahead of time. With Reagan's 1980 appearance Buckley sprung an unusual gimmick on his guest. He opened with the premise that Reagan had already been elected, and thus all the questions would go to *President* Reagan. It was a clever effort to illustrate that Reagan could extemporize rather than reverting to canned talking points.

More important, it was Buckley's opportunity to let Reagan show voters that he could tackle problems in foreign policy and other issues that would not have come up for a governor. Buckley opens with a softball question about how President Reagan would handle a race riot in Detroit. Answer: that's a local problem unless Detroit asks for federal assistance. Then Buckley gets more dramatic: "President Reagan, Tito is dead. The pro-Soviet faction in Yugoslavia has urged the Soviet Union, citing the Brezhnev Doctrine, to send its armies to restore order, and you are advised that in fact Soviet columns are on their way south." Reagan offers a tough-guy response, suggesting that the Soviet Union "would have received enough signals that a move of the kind you've just described would run the very serious risk of a direct confrontation with the United States. And I don't think the Soviet Union wants a direct confrontation with the United States."

The conversation continues in a predictable direction, with Reagan showing that he has done his homework, and then the exchange turns light again during the Q&A, which closes out with Buckley asking "President" Reagan his opinion of the current governor of California (the unnamed Jerry Brown), then in competition for nomination on the Democratic presidential ticket.

Reagan responds: "Well, he announced that it was all right to paddle a canoe—that he ran the government like paddling a canoe—you paddle a little while on the right and you paddle a little while on the left, and you kind of make your way down the middle. Well, I had canoes all my life, and I found out if you're a good canoeist, you can paddle on one side and keep on going straight."* It's cute stuff, he gets a good laugh, and Buckley closes out by breaking off the fantasy and thanking "Governor Reagan."

Of course, the fantasy became a reality, and Reagan's election symbolized the triumph of everything Buckley had been promoting for decades. Reagan was a right-wing conservative who had overcome the taint of extremism—not because it was impossible to see his policies as "extreme" but because they were presented in commonsense packages and were lacking in conspiratorial edge. Buckley had worked hard to forge a new kind of conservatism that was sophisticated, cool, intellectual, and, above all, not nutty. This level of sophistication worked well for Buckley, but voters were not looking for stump speeches in the Buckley rhetorical mode. Reagan's campaign manager John Sears had been responsible for propelling Reagan to a neck-and-neck race for the Republican ticket with Gerald Ford in 1976, and a notable aspect of this campaign had been Sears's toning down of Reagan's anticommunist rhetoric and his making the candidate seem more moderate to his detractors.

Reagan had claimed national attention twelve years earlier by supporting Goldwater; it was important that those outside of his base in 1976 understand that Reagan may have supported Goldwater in the past, but he was his own man, more moderate

---

* For the record, shortly after announcing liberal Republican Richard Schweiker as his would-be running mate in 1976, Reagan had taken Nancy for a ride in a canoe named "TRULOV," and the Associated Press photo documenting this nonevent clearly shows him paddling on the left.

than Goldwater and with a more positive message about America. Yet, Sears finally went too far, pairing Reagan up with a VP, Pennsylvania senator Richard Schweiker, who was tough on abortion and détente and in favor of capital punishment and school prayer, but who was liberal on other fronts, having ranked an 89 out of 100 on the ADA's voting record scale. As Buckley put it, "On the ADA scale, Senator Robert Taft would have come in at approximately 5 or 10, Senator Hubert Humphrey at 90 or 100."[18] Appearing on *Firing Line* in July 1976 to discuss "Who's More Electable?," Ford or Reagan, Sears had all the appeal of a warm, flat can of soda pop. Why did Reagan lose the New Hampshire primary to Ford? Because the weather had been unexpectedly good, Sears explained, which meant bigger voter turnout, and when voter turnout was up, incumbents did better. It wasn't necessarily inaccurate, but it was so *dull*. Sears was back in the picture as campaign manager in 1980, but was fired once Reagan won the New Hampshire primary.

Reagan would next appear on *Firing Line* to look back on his presidency, in a two-part 1990 episode with the hard-hitting title "Two Friends Talk." Both Reagan and his host paint those eight years as ragingly successful, although, they concede, Reagan could have accomplished more if he had been able to make use of line-item vetoes. Reagan is more modest than Buckley would like when it comes to taking credit for the decline of communism. Reagan even allows that Gorbachev has cleared the way for reforms in the Soviet Union and that he might not be an atheist! Nonetheless, an overall gung-ho tone of Americanism pervades the show. The not-so-subtle scent of impeachment that had hung in the air when the Iran-Contra scandal broke in late 1986 simply did not come up. Reagan would recede from public life a few years later, as Alzheimer's tightened its grip upon him. Years later, Buckley summed up his feelings about the former president as a public figure simply and eloquently in *The Reagan I Knew*: "The great heroes of the decade—Walesa, Solzhenitsyn, Sakharov—have earned their place in freedom's House of Lords; but the political leader was Ronald Reagan, who was trained as a movie actor. Only in America, one is tempted to say; except that Lech Walesa was trained as an electrician."[19] Thus was a long and fruitful personal and political relationship tied up with a bow.

So, could Reagan fairly be understood as an intellectually diluted, brilliantined, but politically aligned spin-off of Buckley? The relationship was not quite as tidy as one might think. On *Firing Line* and in the pages of *National Review* we see Buckley and Reagan disagree strongly on two issues: the Panama Canal treaty and the Intermediate-Range Nuclear Forces (INF) treaty. In brief, the proposed treaty (really two treaties, but usually referenced singly, for convenience) would turn over the Panama Canal to the Panamanians at the end of 1999, with the United States surrendering control of the waterway, which it had held since 1903. In his support for returning the canal to the Panamanians, Buckley stood virtually alone among conservatives. Oddly, he was joined by Barry Goldwater and John Wayne, who, Buckley noted, were excused by fellow conservatives "on the grounds of eccentricity."[20] Buckley felt that, as he put it, "Reagan's conspicuous position on the treaty, combined with the treaty's passage, combined to make possible his election as President four years later." It seems a bit much to position the Panama Canal Treaty as the make-or-break issue of the 1980 election, but Buckley's thesis was that "Reagan would not have been nominated if he had favored the Panama Canal Treaty, and that he wouldn't have been elected if it hadn't passed. He'd have lost the conservatives if he had backed the treaty, and lost the election if we'd subsequently faced, in Panama, insurrection, as in my opinion we would have."[21]

Setting aside such speculation, the importance of the Panama Canal Treaty to *Firing Line*, to Reagan's positioning of himself for the 1980 campaign, and to Buckley's relationship with Reagan is more clear-cut. Buckley had observed that Reagan had lost the New Hampshire and Florida primaries to Ford in 1976, but that he had won in North Carolina when he had amped up his opposition to the treaty.[22] Buckley invited Reagan to hash out their differences regarding the treaty in a two-hour *Firing Line* debate in 1978; for years to come, Buckley would point to this as a particularly important episode of the show. (In fact, the three episodes he seemed to cite the most were this one, the 1980 Muggeridge episode on faith that was aired in a shortened half-hour version every year around Christmastime, and the 1976 BBC interview with Solzhenitsyn, which had been aired shortly thereafter as a *Firing Line* episode, followed by commentary from Muggeridge and Bernard Levin.) Having already served two terms as governor of California, and having lost his bid to be the Republican presidential candidate in 1968 and 1976, Reagan, who had been born in 1911, could have easily faded into retirement at this point. But he kept himself in the public eye, or ear at least, via his *Ronald Reagan Radio Commentary* program, and the Panama Canal TV debate with Buckley was another opportunity to place himself in the media spotlight.

National Review publisher Bill Rusher observes that "who won the [TV] debate is still a matter of dispute, but there is very little doubt which side profited most in the long run from the controversy. The treaty was ultimately ratified. . . ." Rusher was on the other side of the fence from Buckley, but he agrees that the issue was key to Reagan's election. On the other hand, he puts a tellingly different spin on his explanation for how the controversy benefited Reagan: "The largest single net benefit to any of the warring parties, as a result of the whole affair, was undoubtedly the massive accretion of new names acquired by conservative mailing-list entrepreneurs like Richard Viguerie. Viguerie himself estimates that the campaign to petition the Senate not to ratify the treaties yielded the names and ad-

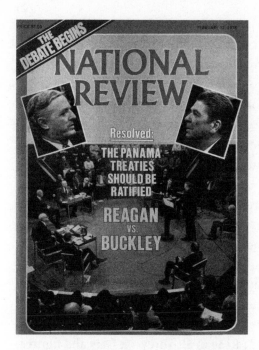

National Review trumpets the *Firing Line* debate over the Panama Canal. Buckley is in the minority among conservatives, heretically supporting the treaties.
CREDIT: ©*National Review Magazine*

dresses of some half million additional voters who could later be approached on behalf of related conservative causes (e.g., Reagan's 1980 presidential campaign). Of such defeats are brighter tomorrows born."[23]

The difference between Buckley's and Rusher's analyses is telling. Buckley was concerned with grand strategy, in the Kissinger mode. Politics to him was like a chess match, where one player's moves impacted another's, you anticipated moves, you tried to come up with unanticipated tactics. Debate worked in a similar manner. Buckley was not a politician himself, but on his TV show he played out this kind of my-knight-takes-your-pawn thinking in confronting the left, or, in the case of the Panama Canal, the right. The on-the-ground kind of stuff that Viguerie specialized in—organizing, fundraising, door-bell ringing, envelope licking—was not quite on Buckley's radar, though he would, of course, acknowledge the importance of such activities had anyone directly asked him.

And yet it seems not unlikely that the 500,000 fundraising addresses that the anti–Panama Canal Treaty campaign yielded ultimately did more for Reagan's successful 1980 presidential run than Reagan's two-hour appearance on *Firing Line*, even if the studio audience for the event was packed with high-power politicians and political operatives who would end up fighting in Reagan's corner a few years later.

Describing the Panama Canal debate, liberal Buckley biographer John Judis rightly observes that "Buckley's performance . . . was masterful and largely defused Reagan's jingoistic appeals."[24] Reagan wasn't strictly jingoistic, but it wasn't an unfair assessment on Judis's part—he did draw on some of his favorite old chestnuts. ("In the days ahead, we're going to be treated to fireside chats from the Oval Office [from President Carter, supporting the treaty]. Members of the Cabinet will barnstorm across the country, playing one-night stands on the mashed potato circuit.") Reagan also drew on facts and figures, a number of which Buckley contested.

Through it all, a sense of earnest goodwill was maintained. Reagan's first question to Buckley, for example, after opening arguments from both sides was, "Why haven't you already rushed across the room here to tell me that you've seen the light?" Buckley responds, "I'm afraid that if I came any closer to you the force of my illumination would blind you." Buckley even opened the event, after Chairman Ervin's introduction, by emphasizing his ideological alignment with his momentary adversary: "If Lloyds of London had been asked to give odds that I would be disagreeing with Ronald Reagan on a matter of public policy [audience laughter] I doubt they could have flogged a quotation out of their swingingest betting man, because judging from Governor Reagan's impeccable record, the statisticians would have reasoned that it was inconceivable that he should make a mistake [audience laughter]. But, of course, it happens to everyone. I fully expect that someday I'll be wrong about something [laughter]." That the crowd starts laughing early, even before Buckley reaches his first punch line, indicates how primed they are for a lively event.

What follows is a two-hour debate that is not, actually, consistently entertaining, but things definitely pick up steam in the second half, and Buckley strikes his strongest rhetorical blows toward the end.

> BUCKLEY: Well, let me ask you to give me the answer to a question which you cannot document, but which I permit you to consult only your insight [to answer]. Would you guess that the Panamanian people would prefer or not prefer to exercise sovereignty over their own territory? Take as long as you want to answer that. [audience laughter and applause]

> REAGAN: I was just sitting here wishing that I had with me the transcript of the impassioned plea that was made to United States senators at a meeting of the Civic Council a week or so ago in Panama . . . the speaker was a black, a Panamanian, not an American, second generation. His father, a West Indian, worked on the canal, in building the canal. He has worked all his life on the canal, and his impassioned plea was, even though he was a Panamanian, "Don't! Don't do this! Don't ratify those treaties." I could quote the *Chicago Tribune* reporter who did a man-on-the-street thing in Panama and how many of the Panamanians, some refuse to give their names, but they answered, but many of them were so outraged they didn't care. They gave their names even though their relatives and friends were pulling at their sleeves and saying, "Don't answer. You'll go to jail."

> BUCKLEY: If what you're saying, Governor, is that [Panamanian leader Omar] Torrijos has enemies, it seems to me that you do not need to say that at any length, because I can see that he does. Among his enemies are yourself and

myself and anybody who has any respect for human freedom, but it is a worldwide phenomenon that irrespective of the ugly character of their ruler, people do desire independence. They do desire sovereignty. There were Russians who fought even under Stalin and fought to the death to defend their territory. Why is it that those impulses which you so liberally recognize as beating in the breasts of people all over the world should suddenly stop beating in Panama because of Torrijos?

REAGAN: Well, I have to ask, Bill, whether this is all that strong on the part of people. As I said before, we deal with a government that does not represent the will of the people. The people never had a chance to express their will, and—

BUCKLEY: But it was before Torrijos became the dictator that the initial riots took place demanding an assertion of that sovereignty. How do you account for that?

REAGAN: I think the first time that it was expressed was in 1932 in the charter of the new Communist Party of Panama that they put as one of their top objectives the taking over of the canal.

BUCKLEY: Are you saying that the communists invented patriotism in Panama?

REAGAN: No, no.

BUCKLEY: Yes. Well, you really tried to say that.

REAGAN: No. [audience laughter and applause] No, Bill, I really didn't, but I also have to point out something else about this. The canal and Panama are Siamese twins. Neither one could have been born without the other, and ninety percent of all of the industry and the population of Panama is on one side of that canal. We have the right to sovereignty. . . . Let me just read something. . . . We had the worst riots of all in 1964. More than a score of people were killed. Yet not one move was made to attempt to sabotage the canal. Business didn't stop for one second, and this statement was made about those riots that said, "Led by persons trained in communist countries for political action of the type that took place, the government of Panama, instead of attempting to restore order, was, through a controlled press, TV, and radio, inciting the people to attack and violence."

BUCKLEY: Who was it who taught the people who did the Boston Tea Party how to exercise violence?

REAGAN: Well, the gentleman who said this was Mr. [Ellsworth] Bunker [on hand at the debate as a technical expert for both sides], and I think it's a very eloquent statement and description of what took place in 1964. [audience applause]

BUCKLEY: In making that statement, Mr. Bunker was reiterating a statement made at some length by Professor James Burnham [at the debate on Buckley's side] in his book *The Struggle for the World*, showing exactly how the Soviet Union would attempt to take over patriotic movements, but to attempt to take them over does not mean necessarily to contaminate them, and the notion that someone who wants freedom for Panama wants freedom for Panama because he is being manipulated by the communists is the kind of talk that belongs in Belmont, Massachusetts [home base of the John Birch Society], but not at the University of South Carolina [host of the debate]. [applause]

Buckley was not going to let Reagan get away with what he saw as crowd-pleasing conspiratorial nonsense.

In fact, later Reagan gets big applause with a line about how we should tell the Panamanians, "We don't negotiate with anyone under threats." Buckley counters, "He says we, in fact, don't negotiate under threats, and everybody here bursts out in applause. The trouble with that is that it's not true. We *do* negotiate under threats. Ninety-nine percent of all the negotiations that have gone on from the beginning of this world have gone on as a result of threats [audience applause]." At this point, with both sides eliciting strong audience reactions, this event is teetering on the edge of being a personality contest, but that is not what Buckley is striving for. He wants to make a point about threats and negotiations that he sees as patently realistic; Reagan's line, conversely, is crafted to show the bravura of someone who would soon be a presidential candidate.

As per Judis, Buckley won the TV debate, if you approached the whole thing objectively. But if you approached it more emotionally, you would find that the jingoistic appeals had been very well executed, and that Reagan, the earnest clergyman-style politician (as per Muggeridge), had emerged ahead of Buckley, the clever Oxbridge-style debater. Buckley seemed to see the episode as ending in a draw, given that he had staked a claim for the position he found to be correct and Reagan had done exactly what he needed to do to be perceived as a highly electable conservative candidate. Buckley's only regret was that the reception after the debate "was chilled by (a) our host the governor's teetotalism, and (b) the sad news . . . that Hubert Humphrey had died."[25] This was classic Buckley: he had mixed things up by staging a ripping TV debate between *conservatives*, eschewing his usual left-versus-right format; he had taken a position bound to upset his peers, but he was a journalist and public intellectual, not a politician, and he had no problem rocking the boat; he had expressed sadness at the passing of a liberal, a typical moment for a man of the right so comfortable with having friends on the other side; and, at the end of the day, he was ready for a cocktail, goddammit.*

If the *Firing Line* Panama Canal debate helped to rev up

---

* "The consensus is that a dry martini in the evening is a straightforward invitation for instant relief from the vicissitudes of a long day" (*Athwart History*, 195).

enthusiasm for Reagan shortly before he declared his 1980 candidacy, it also did some damage to Buckley's relationship with his right-wing compatriots. Reagan himself never seemed to hold it against Buckley that he had supported the Panama Canal "giveback." He even teased him by inviting him over to his house and decorating his driveway with a series of three hand-drawn signs reading "we built it . . . we paid for it . . . it's ours!" But those flying the New Right, Christian Right, and neoconservative banners were less forgiving. Howard Phillips of the Conservative Caucus went so far as to write off Buckley completely: "Buckley, for all the good work he has done, is simply not on the cutting edge of American politics anymore. His positions on legalizing marijuana and passage of the Panama Canal treaties were a great disappointment. He really isn't with us anymore."[26]

Buckley had made a career out of not only attacking liberalism but also out of staking a claim for ways that different kinds of conservatives could get along and get things done. He may have not quite wrapped his head around the indispensability of the envelope-licking and fundraising side of the conservative movement, but he had fostered the fusionism that the fractious old Cold War extremists had found simply unthinkable. That in 1978 some would now reject him as no longer on the team because they disagreed with two of his political opinions was an indicator of how precarious the "fusion" Buckley had fostered could really be. It was one thing to display a variety of conservative opinions within the pages of *National Review*, but it was quite another to make such variety work on the ground.

As for the INF, a 1987 arms reduction treaty that Reagan had spent years negotiating, Buckley was comfortable with all manner of arms buildup, but not of arms reductions. The INF treaty specified that the United States and Soviet Union would eliminate both their short-range and intermediate-range missiles, but not their sea-launched missiles. Buckley might have stood apart from the majority of his ideological allies in supporting the Panama Canal treaties, but they were all on the same page in rejecting the INF. He and his confederates had decisively rejected the Nixon-Kissinger détente efforts, and the notion that Reagan would reach out to Gorbachev—would even call him "Gorby"—this skirted along the edge of danger, even if at the same time Reagan was building up the military and pursuing his Strategic Defense Initiative ("Star Wars") program.

Buckley did not belabor the point in *The Reagan I Knew*, but he did observe that during the eight years Reagan was in office, "there were times . . . particularly over the Intermediate-Range Nuclear Forces Treaty . . . when President Reagan seemed to me and to many conservatives to come perilously close to trusting the Soviet Union."[27] Clearly, Reagan was not soft on the "evil empire" and was himself dubious of détente efforts, but Buckley was uncomfortable with any signs of America letting its guard down.

He was, of course, deeply inspired by Solzhenitsyn, who had stated, in the BBC interview replayed on *Firing Line*, that détente was a "thin crust" that could easily crumble away. It was, in effect, a fantasy on the part of the West to imagine that the Soviet Union was easing up on its military preparedness; they had a wartime economy in place and could strike at any time. Any impression otherwise was just wishful thinking, according to Buckley's hero. In his introductory comments before airing the interview, Buckley had gone so far as to describe Solzhenitsyn's words in visceral terms as "a blow at the solar plexus of the kind that first numbs and then revives and conceivably transfigures. . . ." In an article on the dissident in 1974, Buckley had observed, "His indictment is universal: an indictment of totalitarian society. Brezhnev can no more convincingly denounce Stalin than he can denounce his own aorta."[28] That Reagan engaged in disarmament negotiations with this totalitarian society was too much for Buckley, even if the president simultaneously engaged in heavy military spending and made it abundantly clear that he was as much hawk as Jimmy Carter had been dove.

Of course, when conversing with liberals on *Firing Line*, Buckley did not go out of his way to display his differences with Reagan, but when directly questioned about possible points of disagreement, he responded with candor. In a 1988 two-hour *Firing Line* debate, "Resolved: The Right Is Better Able to Deal with the Soviets than the Left," Senator Gary Hart asked Buckley, "In all honesty now, when Ronald Reagan went to the Kremlin and threw his arms around the general secretary of the Communist Party, didn't you just twang—" Buckley interrupted with an alarmed, "Oh, yes! He thought he was back in Hollywood." Hart asked, "Well, doesn't that worry you?" To which Buckley replied, "Oh, it does, yes," and Hart asked what was to be done about it. Buckley then cut short his own alarmism by noting that this was just how politics played out as theater: "That's what people do at summit conferences, which is one of the reasons I am less enthusiastic than some people are about them."

If his opponents had done better research to prepare for this debate, Buckley would not have been able to retreat so easily. In May 1987 the cover of *National Review* had actually read "Reagan's Suicide Pact."* All the liberal *Firing Line* guests had really needed to do to nail Buckley in the 1988 debate was to have prepared by reading his magazine's attack on the INF treaty. Instead, Congresswoman Pat Schroeder wondered aloud how

---

* Buckley sent Reagan an advance copy, and Reagan took it in stride. He was *much* more angered by a scathing attack that Hugh Kenner made on him earlier in the pages of *NR*, attacking his actions, as governor, against the University of California, as anti-intellectual, anti-research, and superficial. Reagan sent Buckley a furious, detailed response to Kenner's piece, but he declined to have his rebuttal published in the magazine. Reagan correspondence, box 53, Buckley papers, Yale University.

Buckley would have responded differently to a Democrat going to China than he had responded to Nixon's trip, almost impossibly ignorant of how disgusted Buckley and his camp had been by the whole thing.

Firing Line viewers were probably surprised to see Buckley disagree with Reagan about the INF and the Panama Canal, but there was virtually perfect alignment between the two of them on the domestic front, particularly in terms of economic policy, in theory, if not always in practice. Moderator Michael Kinsley noted in his introductory comments to the two-hour 1992 *Firing Line* debate, "Resolved: That Reducing the National Deficit in the Next Four Years Is a Top Priority," that Reagan had observed when he was sworn into office that a deficit of almost $80 billion was unacceptable; at the end of the Reagan/ Bush years, in 1992, the deficit stood at over $300 billion, and the national debt at over $4 trillion. Kinsley gets a big laugh from the Bard College audience by asking, "Was Reagan wrong in what he said about the deficit twelve years ago, or was he wrong in what he did about it?"

Kinsley was not alone in making these kinds of cracks; liberal *Firing Line* guests repeatedly pointed out in the course of the 1980s that the national debt was increasing dramatically under Reagan's watch. When confronted with this datum, Buckley admitted that he was in favor of military spending, though generally disappointed by the rising debt, but he also deflected criticism by noting that Reagan could not accomplish all that he wanted through no fault of his own: he did not have the full congressional support that he needed, and he had to contend with the legacy of years of Democratic congressional domination. He would follow with a redirect. The problem, for example, was not Reagan's fiscal plans but that companies were still forced to spend money on health care for employees. Or, yes, Reagan made cuts, but tax dollars were, against Reagan's wishes, still going toward ridiculous endeavors like restoring Lawrence Welk's childhood home and funding SETI, the Search for Extraterrestrial Intelligence organization.

Faced with a question from a liberal *Firing Line* guest regarding any issue where Reagan might *seem* not to agree 100 percent with Buckley, Buckley would remain composed, often noting that we couldn't be sure what politicians were really up to: the nature of politics was subterfuge. He even rather imperiously told John Kenneth Galbraith in 1981, "I'm in favor of the Reagan administration when it pleases me to be so." A Buckley debate with Galbraith on Reagan's policies was relatively predictable. If Galbraith were to argue for a higher tax rate for the wealthy, for example, Buckley would argue against it, in line with Reagan's reductions. Here the surprises for a *Firing Line* viewer would lie not so much in the specific opinions as in how elegantly (or sarcastically) they were expressed. Buckley was more likely to voice dissatisfaction with Reagan when confronted by a *Firing Line* guest positioned politically closer to himself.

This made Congressman Ron Paul's 1988 appearance particularly interesting. Buckley opens by noting that he had never received more viewer mail requesting the appearance of a particular guest than he had for Paul, who was running for president on the Libertarian Party ticket at the time. Paul was in favor of eliminating the CIA and FBI, a position that was obviously intolerable to Buckley. Still, Buckley sometimes described himself as a libertarian, and he was in sympathy with many of Paul's criticisms of taxation and government spending. Buckley even says, "I was as disgusted as you were by his [Reagan's] campaigning in 1986 about all the farm subsidies he had been responsible for. That was an unhappy day in his life." Further, both found Reagan's actions on Social Security in 1984 (presumably referring to the Social Security Disability Benefits Reform Act) to be "terrible." Paul laments the fact that "with the most conservative president ever" in office, we still end up with a $220 billion deficit and an additional 140,000 federal government employees, and Buckley says, "I couldn't agree with you more."

He could not, conversely, agree with Paul's opinions on foreign policy. To put it succinctly, Paul thinks the United States should mind its own business. Vietnam, for example, was "a worthless adventure," in Paul's estimation, and very, very expensive. Still, Buckley's moments of agreement with his guest are revealing. Buckley agrees with Paul that Reagan had spent too much on entitlements, though he also notes that there are practical issues here in that a president could not single-handedly eliminate entitlements and Reagan had had his hands tied by virtue of not having access to the line-item veto. Paul is opposed to the line-item veto on the grounds that a liberal in office would use it to his or her advantage, whereas Buckley feels it would simply improve the system overall. Paul's *Firing Line* visit clarified the limits of Buckley's libertarian inclinations and underscored how in tune he was with Reagan, even if they differed on a few points.

At the end of the day, Buckley and Reagan agreed on a very long checklist. They were for: economics à la Milton Friedman, deregulation, reduced taxation, budget cuts for social welfare programs of all sorts, and budget increases for military spending of all sorts. They were against: communism, abortion, and the ERA. Both maintained an astonishing indifference to the HIV/AIDS crisis, and both were avowed Christians, although the nature of their connections with the Religious Right differed markedly.

Reagan was unique not only as a right-wing conservative but also as a president with strong support from the emergent new Christian Right.[29] Certainly, it is true that Jimmy Carter had been backed by evangelicals on the campaign trail and was the first high-profile born-again Christian elected president in the years that the Christian Right was emerging. Carter had let

that constituency down, however. In his first nationally televised appearance, on *Firing Line* in 1973, Governor Carter may
have come across as relatively conservative on welfare, but as
president he did not enact the right-wing agenda that many
of his evangelical supporters would have hoped for. The born-
agains imagined that Reagan would succeed where Carter had
failed, in particular by finding a way to ban abortion. This he
did not do, though federal funding cuts, the gag order (prevent-
ing international organizations that received US government
funding from providing abortions or abortion counseling), and
other actions undeniably struck a blow for the pro-life side.

Reagan's very presence in the White House invigorated groups
such as Operation Rescue. As Jerry Falwell's Moral Majority
gained traction in the 1980s, and James Dobson's Focus on the
Family started to slowly creep into mainstream news coverage,
it seemed more obvious than ever that the Reagan Revolution
represented an advance for the Christian Right. As a candidate
in 1980, Reagan had addressed an audience of fifteen thousand
conservative Christians at an event sponsored by the Religious
Roundtable, where he expressed support for the teaching of
creationism and said, famously, to the cheering crowd, "I know
you can't endorse me because this is a non-partisan meeting,
but I endorse you."[30] In 1983 he spoke before the National Association of Evangelicals, homing in on issues such as abortion,
school prayer, and anticommunism. In fact, it was here that he
had famously referred to the Soviet Union as an "evil empire."
And as he launched his 1984 campaign he addressed the National Religious Broadcasters, again focusing on moral issues.

As historian Allan Lichtman summed it up, "No prior president had given such eloquent voice to the right's moral concerns, making anyone but Reagan unthinkable for Christian
conservative voters."[31] It is worth adding, of course, that Reagan
offered more "eloquent voice" than anything else to the right's
battle over moral issues. Social concerns were pivotal to getting

out the GOP vote; once elected, Reagan's conservative agenda was aligned with Buckley's, particularly when it came to economics and foreign policy, but he did not deliver all that the evangelicals had expected on the social policy front. The point remains, though, that he effectively courted the evangelicals and his election was seen as a victory for the Christian Right in a way that Carter's clearly was not, even if Carter was the one who wore his born-again beliefs more plainly on his sleeve.

Firing Line responded not at all to the importance of evangelical support to Reagan's success. That is, Buckley kept his laser focus on the conservative movement as conceptualized and crafted by himself and his cohort, beginning in the postwar years, coming to an initial climax with Goldwater's nomination, and finally culminating with Reagan. The fact that Christian Right and New Right folks like Jerry Falwell, Pat Robertson, James Dobson, and Richard Viguerie were important players was peripheral to his narrative of the triumph of conservatism.

Falwell appeared three times on the show: for a debate over drug legalization (with Buckley opposite him, on the pro side) in 1991; for a 1988 discussion of Falwell's suit against *Hustler* magazine, featuring liberal feminist Harriet Pilpel taking her typical First Amendment line and Buckley and Falwell aligned in their support of their own notions of decency; and for a one-on-one discussion of the Moral Majority in 1981, when Buckley was courteous but ultimately irked by Falwell's attempts to appear quite moderate, spinning a picture of religious pluralism rather different from that promoted in his own literature. On this program he noted no discomfort with specific political positions held by Falwell, but just one year earlier in his *60 Minutes* profile Buckley had tellingly observed that if "the John Birch Society or the Moral Majority or whatever were actually to threaten the United States with oppression, you would find an instantly galvanized conservative body of opinion opposing them." Here, Buckley had not only staked a claim for the sensible nonextremism of conservatives but had also let it slip that Falwell's organization might reasonably (or at least rhetorically) be lumped together with Robert Welch's.

Those in Buckley's coterie whom I queried suggested that he was quite comfortable with the Religious Right. *National Review* staffer Linda Bridges noted immediately Buckley's strong Catholicism and the numerous Jews who wrote for the magazine—accurate, but not getting at the kernel of his somewhat distanced relationship with the Christian Right.[32] Buckley defended conservative evangelicalism on *Firing Line* as a force that should not be feared, and he was generally comfortable with evangelical positions on issues such as school prayer and abortion. Further, he often had a redirect at the ready, to the effect that: nothing the Christian Right advocates is as alarming as what liberals advocate. Still, if one looks at the roster of conservative guests on *Firing Line*, it was the politicians and the economists—the elected officials and the intellectuals—who dominated, with only cameos by the Religious Right and what one might call the more populist side of the conservative movement.

In the years following the 1925 Scopes Trial, which had been fought over the teaching of evolution in Tennessee public schools, fundamentalist Christians had been separatist by nature, and separatists are not big voters. The newly emergent, modernized conservative evangelical, by contrast, was a demographic that could be lured into worldly action.[33] The populist political strategists (Viguerie, Paul Weyrich) insisted that it was the moral and cultural issues that were going to get conservative Christians to the voting booth in the 1980s.[34] And they were absolutely correct. Buckley cared deeply about these issues, but he always defaulted to economics, foreign policy, and other less "marketable" issues that meant a lot to the policy wonks but were harder to promote via emotionally resonant slogans and bumper sticker proclamations. Certainly, a strong part of Reagan's appeal to Team Buckley was that his economics and foreign policy recommendations were almost exactly what they were going for, while they were also aligned with his moral/cultural values, values that also resonated strongly with the anti-intellectual bumper sticker crowd.

Asked about Buckley's thoughts on populist-versus-intellectual conservatism, Neal Freeman explains that "he saw himself as a synthesizer" drawn to "what Frank Meyer called fusionism, a coalitional view of conservatism. . . . He was for building the coalition constantly, but he was always aware of the basic political arithmetic. You needed them all . . . he spent a lot of time keeping everybody on board. He of course was a fervent Catholic himself." The fusionism embodied by the bringing together of the anticommunists, libertarians, and traditionalists under a large conservative umbrella (and in the pages of *National Review* and on the *Firing Line* dais) was clear, but wasn't the Christian Right always a bit on the outside of Buckley's circle?

Freeman responds, "No, not at all. I think for a while one manifestation of the CR, what you might call the Falwell-Robertson Christian Right, there was initially with the movement a stylistic problem [for Buckley]. Because they came out of the South, they came out of a more expressive religious tradition; they were from a different culture, if you will. But Bill made extraordinary and extraordinarily effective efforts to bring them into the coalition. What he always wanted to do was maintain some balance in the coalition. In other words, for instance, he wanted the neoconservatives inside the coalition, but he didn't want them to dominate the coalition. When I say traditional conservatives, what I mean is people of religious faith. The Christian Right was just a new manifestation of a part of the coalition that had been there from day one." Finally, he adds, "The real connection Bill makes with the Christian Right initially is with Pat Robertson. And why is that? Because Pat Robertson, unlike Jerry Falwell, was the son of a US senator, Willis Robertson, one of the most elegant, learned members of the US Senate in the twentieth century. Pat Robertson had multiple degrees, one of them from Yale. Pat Robertson had worked at a major US corporation, W. R. Grace, all of this *before* he gets the call and becomes a full-time minister of the church. So that was an easier bridge to cross perhaps than with Jerry Falwell."

This is an apt analysis, but I would also emphasize that representatives of the Christian Right were relatively scarce on *Firing Line*—and were only on the fringes of Buckley's circle—because many of them were simply not intellectual enough for him. Take James C. Dobson and Tim LaHaye. Dobson was founder of Focus on the Family, was a member of the Meese Commission on Pornography, set up the Family Research Council, with Gary Bauer at the helm, and would later be credited for getting out the evangelical vote for George W. Bush in 2004. He was a serious *player*. But he also ran a Christian self-help empire, and his breakthrough 1970 bestseller was *Dare to Discipline*, a sort of right-wing Dr. Spock book. LaHaye was one of the masterminds of the Moral Majority, but he first hit the scene with a Christian sex manual (PG-rated) that he coauthored with his wife, and in 1995 he struck publishing gold with the *Left Behind* book series of right-wing apocalyptic potboilers about the Antichrist. Dobson and LaHaye were never on *Firing Line*, and I think it is fair to speculate that Buckley was publicly in favor of their activities but must have privately found them to be a bit tacky. Further, as a devout Catholic so old-school that after Vatican II he found a priest willing to deliver the mass in Latin to him for years, Buckley must have found the faith practices of the conservative evangelicals somewhat alien. He was comfortable with faith-based political advocacy, but one suspects he found a certain inelegance and lack of mystery in the theology and worship practices of contemporary born-agains. And even if he agreed with what they were fighting for—the ending of legalized abortion, for example—there was a crude reductionism in the dictum issued by Christian Right leaders to the effect that "if you are a Christian you must vote against pro-choice candidates."

Malcolm Muggeridge, visiting *Firing Line* once again in 1980, offers this critique, without explicitly using the words "Christian Right": "The Christian of modern times believes that a table of conduct can be derived, and you say, 'this is the Christian program. Vote for it. I'm in favor/I'm not in favor.' There's no such thing [as a 'Christian program']. This life we have to live between the earthly city and the City of God, between time and eternity, between ourselves and our Creator; and we have to deal with the circumstances that arise in our individual life and in our collective lives on that basis."

There were certainly some evangelicals who would have been on board with these sentiments and who would have been befuddled by the notion that there was such a thing as a "Christian program." But the public image of evangelicalism in the 1980s and '90s was embodied in figures such as Pat Robertson, Jerry Falwell, James Dobson, Ralph Reed, Gary Bauer, and Tim LaHaye, all of whom were very clear that there was such a thing as a "Christian program" that could be voted for. Such activism struck Buckley as entirely appropriate, but the theology was flat-footed.[35]

Another New Right player underrepresented on *Firing Line* in the Reagan years was Richard Viguerie, the direct-mail guru regularly tagged as the "funding father" of the New Right. Viguerie's career really took off in the post-Goldwater years, so he was not technically a newcomer when Falwell and

Robertson burst onto the national scene in the 1980s. Still, he had been (with others such as Weyrich and LaHaye) in on the ground floor of the founding of Falwell's Moral Majority, and he is strongly associated with that movement.

Viguerie was on three *Firing Line* episodes, and Buckley simply did not seem very keen on him. In the two-parter "1979: A Conservative View," Buckley offers this arch introduction: "Richard Viguerie has figured more conspicuously in journalistic accounts of the ascendency of the New Right than anyone else in the country because, you see, it was he who more or less invented political financing by direct mail. As president of Richard Viguerie Associates and publisher of the *Conservative Digest*, his smiles on individual candidates are legal tender." Discussing Milton Friedman, Keynesian vocabulary, and the Steiger Amendment (reducing capital gains taxes) a few minutes into the show, Buckley observes that this stuff is tough to popularize because it is so complicated, and he asks "How would someone like Richard Viguerie package something that requires that sophistication? Necessarily, you deal in the art of sloganizing, don't you?" He adds that he had read something on the Panama Canal issued by Viguerie's office and noted, "I had difficulty distinguishing myself from Fidel Castro."

This gets a laugh, but two serious points have implicitly been made. First, Viguerie is, to Buckley, more crass marketer than political strategist. And second, Viguerie does not play well with others who are, theoretically, on his side. It was one thing to disagree with Buckley about the canal (most conservatives did), quite another to convey the notion that Buckley was some kind of lefty for disagreeing with his cohort. Buckley was a fusionist by nature, and he wasn't going to go out of his way to disparage Viguerie publicly, but that didn't mean that on his TV show he had to treat him as a crucial figure in the conservative movement. It is probably worth adding that Viguerie had not "smiled" on Reagan in 1976, having promoted Texas governor John Connally instead, and in 1980 he had also pushed for Connally early on.[36]

There is no doubt that Buckley saw it as a healthy sign for the conservative movement as a whole that the New Right and Christian Right gained momentum in the 1980s. But he was not going to give them too much credit for crafting the movement, being more likely to see them as riding the Reagan wave than as having participated in its creation. What Buckley slighted here, though, was the absolute centrality of the *social* issues that Viguerie and his clan sloganized for over and over again in terms of building the strength of that wave and getting out the vote. For Buckley, foreign policy and economics were the most important things about Reagan; the issues so imperative to the Christian Right (abortion, opposition to gay rights and the ERA, and so on) were also important, but free market economics and anticommunist foreign policy remained the backbone of the Reagan endeavor. Neither Buckley nor Reagan was, at heart, really a "social issues" conservative.

In sum, the 1980s were victorious years for *Firing Line*, and for the American conservative movement, and Reagan, of course, was the centerpiece of that victory. His presence would linger in the show's final decade on the air. In fact, the two-hour formal *Firing Line* debates of the 1990s were often siren songs for the Reagan years, with those on Buckley's team as standard-bearers for the Gipper asserting the total success of 1980s economic policies and the need to complete whatever work Reagan had not finished.

To give just one example, in 1995 Buckley hosted a riveting two-hour slugfest on the debate topic "Resolved: That the Flat Tax is Better than the Income Tax." Buckley argued in his opening statement that higher taxes on the wealthy penalized economic productivity. MIT economist Lester Thurow, captain of the opposing team, argued that those who got the most out of the system should put the most back in. As the show moves along, Thurow gets pretty steamed at former Delaware governor Pete du Pont, and George McGovern charms the audience with an anecdote about his preacher father telling his congregation not to complain about the progressive income tax: "'Brother Jones, what that means is that you're making a lot of money. Praise the Lord!' And that's why I came to Texas [for the debate with Buckley]. I want to try to convert you." To which Buckley replies with understated disgust, also getting a big laugh from the studio audience, "Yes, that's terribly pleasant and very folksy."

On a practical note, the liberal team repeatedly suggests that if capital gains were no longer taxed, as per the flat tax scheme, the wealthiest would find clever ways to be paid in stock options, and so forth, reducing dramatically what counted as "income." The Reagan years served as a refrain throughout, with the conservatives celebrating tax cuts and the liberals elaborating the negative fallout of Reaganomics. Robert Kuttner of the *American Prospect*, for example, summarizes thusly: "The statement that your side made about everybody gaining during the eighties, that's shameful. I mean, every single reputable study has shown that the bottom half of the income distribution has lost income in real terms for the past nineteen years. So you can deny the fact, but those are the facts."

It seems to me that nobody clearly wins this debate. A viewer would have to have a full-on conversion from liberal to conservative, or vice versa, to change his or her perspective. But one does clearly see that the implicit winner over the long term is Buckley's side insofar as Reagan popularized and mainstreamed a right-wing conservative approach to economics that had been simply unthinkable to those outside movement politics just a few years before his 1980 election. In other words, the flat tax notion did not emerge for wide discussion until the 1990s, but it was Reaganomics that paved the way for this turn of events.

Buckley concludes *The Reagan I Knew* by describing the 1980s as a "triumphant decade . . . a decade that began with the election of Ronald Reagan and ended with a Soviet offer of aid to tranquilize Rumania after the execution of its Communist tyrant."[37] He further notes that "the 1980s are most certainly the decade in which Communism ceased to be a creed, surviving only as a threat. And Ronald Reagan has more to do with this than any other statesman in the world."[38]

Viewed through a conservative anticommunist lens, of course, the 1980s was indeed a glorious decade in which we fought the good fight. For liberals, conversely, it was a most alarming time. It was a decade when women's reproductive rights were under assault. When billions were spent on a missile defense system the mechanics of which had been far-fetched from the get-go. When the Christian Right gained tremendous visibility, and built an infrastructure that would only get stronger in the Clinton years. When the Mental Health Systems Act was repealed and spending on mental health programs was cut by some 25 percent, resulting in deinstitutionalized mentally ill on the streets, and a homelessness rate that ticked upward. When radical cuts to the Department of Housing and Urban Development had a similar effect. When the Environmental Protection Agency was gutted by a president who had actually said, in 1981, that "trees cause more pollution than automobiles do." And when a national health crisis—AIDS—was quite shockingly ignored by the nation's commander in chief, even as his own Surgeon General C. Everett Koop, a confirmed conservative, advocated for education and, in order of preference, for abstinence, monogamy, and condoms. Until Rock Hudson died, Reagan thought of AIDS, according to his own White House physician, as if "it was measles and it would go away."[39]

For a TV show engaged deeply with major social movements such as feminism, civil rights, and Black Power, the disinterest in the gay rights movement as a *Firing Line* discussion topic was a notable lacuna.[40] In a 1986 op-ed, Buckley had even alarmingly suggested that anyone infected with HIV should be tattooed with warnings on one forearm and one buttock. What would the buttock inscription be? A *National Review* office contest was held, and Joe Sobran (later ejected for anti-Semitism) won with "Abandon hope all ye who enter here."[41]

One could come up with a longer list of liberal complaints from these years. Iran-Contra comes to mind, as well as the Bitburg cemetery fiasco. But the point is not to argue, contra Buckley, that Reagan was actually a terrible president, but rather that the zeitgeist of the era was radically different depending on where you were standing, how you defined your sympathies and interests, or to put it more crudely, how much money you earned. When Friedrich von Hayek appeared on the show in 1977, questioner Jeff Greenfield had staked a claim for understanding the plight of the poor and for the value of taxing those with more discretionary income in order to help those with less. Buckley contended that we cannot really understand and compare the suffering of others with our own suffering: "Mr. Bertrand de Jouvenel in his book *The Ethics of Redistribution* said that it is the height of arrogance—and I agree with him—for anybody to presume to know what deprivations mean to individual people. For an individual who loses his *Mona Lisa*, let us say, we are simply not in a position to say that he is less anguished than the person who has to sleep under a bridge at night."

Buckley thinks he has made a whiz-bang argument and tops it off by telling Greenfield, "I think it's very important for you to meditate [on] that. In fact, if you want to take a few minutes off, you may." Greenfield is taken aback by what amounts to, in his mind, a rejection of empathy and of a sense of duty to the impoverished. For if the man who has lost his precious painting is just as devastated as the destitute man without a roof over his head, what obligation do we have to the destitute? Greenfield feels that the horrific implications of Buckley's statement are so self-evident that rebuttal would be superfluous: "No, no. I must say I think that statement ought to go absolutely unchallenged. Let it just sit there for a moment for what it is," he says with more than a hint of sarcasm.

Buckley was a charitable man not personally disinclined to helping the underdog. In fact, he strongly believed that Reaganomics would reduce inflation and unemployment and was the best possible thing for the poor. The crucial takeaway here is not that Buckley and fellow conservatives were intentionally seeking to increase the population of those sleeping under bridges but that the *Mona Lisa* line and the exchange with Greenfield so fully encapsulated the rift between conservative and liberal worldviews, a rift that would be exacerbated in the Reagan years.

So, as per Buckley, was the 1980s truly "a triumphant decade"? It depended on where you were standing—on top of the bridge, beneath the bridge, or far from the bridge in a fancy penthouse, wary of art thieves.

* * *

In considering *Firing Line* and the Reagan years, there is one final matter to address: the president's drive to defund PBS.

The Reagan administration deregulated the telecommunications industry, resulting in the elimination of any officially recognized notion of "public service" on the airwaves. Explicitly rejecting the paternalism he identified in FCC chairman Newton Minow's famous 1961 "vast wasteland" speech, Reagan's FCC chairman Mark Fowler had infamously stated that "television is just another appliance. It's a toaster with pictures." Nixon had put pressure on public broadcasting from the very beginning, but it was Reagan who really succeeded in tightening the thumbscrews. A *Firing Line* guest observed **that one of** the first items on Reagan's agenda after being sworn into office in 1981, for instance, was asking for a 25 percent reduction in National Public Radio funding.[42] Journalist James Ledbetter explains that, "although conservative hostility toward PBS in the eighties was essentially the same is it had been under Nixon, Reagan's methods were subtler—he did not issue edicts to shut the system down—and ultimately more effective." Reagan played "budgetary hardball" and used his CPB appointees as "ideological enforcers," Ledbetter argues.[43] Buckley was pleased to see the federal monies recede, though he had an obvious personal investment in his PBS enterprise continuing, albeit with support from private revenue streams.

To tell the full story of how loss of federal support for PBS in the Reagan years impacted *Firing Line*, we need to briefly back up twenty years, to see how *Firing Line*, and PBS as well, were subject to the market in the pre-Reagan years. *Firing Line* was a great public affairs show (arguably the greatest), yet it was a small fish in a big pond of more profitable fare. As a venue exhibiting confrontations between intelligent and entertaining conservatives and liberals, the show was an unequivocal success. But as a product competing in the American media marketplace, it was for the most part a bomb.

It did, however, find advertisers in the early years, and, Buckley was pleased to note, not just right-wing ones: "Beer companies, deodorant manufacturers, gas and oil companies, etc." were all willing to advertise, he told a San Francisco businessman interested in sponsoring the show in his town, adding that "it strikes me that the people in San Francisco are slightly more terrified than those elsewhere."[44] The ads were sold on a city-by-city basis, not nationally, and it was an uphill battle in the late 1960s, when for most potential advertisers "conservative media" meant fundamentalist, anti–civil rights radio shows, and John Birch Society propaganda, not the kind of stuff that upright conservative businessmen necessarily wanted associated with their products.

Granted, *Firing Line* often featured advertising for *National Review*, and even when it did not it indirectly functioned as a sixty-minute ad for the magazine (which also turned no profit), so the TV show helped keep Buckley's other venture afloat and was not lacking in practical financial value even in the early syndicated years. But if PBS had not served as lifeboat in 1971, *Firing Line* might well have sunk rather early on. You might say that *Firing Line* was, in some respects, saved *from* the free market by PBS, and then when PBS was eviscerated by the Reagan administration's budget cuts, *Firing Line* was saved *by* the free market, in the form of underwriting corporate and individual sponsors.

Interestingly, even in its early commercial years, *Firing Line* did make the rounds of some National Educational Television (NET) stations, the not-for-profit stations that would become PBS member stations in 1970. In 1968, a New Orleans NET station aired *Firing Line* against NBC's popular *Laugh-In* on Monday at 7 p.m., but then they moved Buckley's show and replaced it with Julia Child's *The French Chef*, a show so popular it was sometimes shown three times a week. It's unlikely that Julia Child, wielding a meat cleaver on her cooking show, could have seriously competed with Goldie Hawn, wielding bikini power on *Laugh-In*, for high numbers of viewers. But both femmes fatales had the popular edge over Buckley, armed only with a slightly rumpled dress shirt and rapier wit.

In sum, in the commercial TV market, *Firing Line* garnered a small niche audience. And in the noncommercial TV market, *Firing Line* also garnered a small niche audience. The irony was patently obvious: for thirty-three years Buckley promoted the free market on a TV show that could not cut it in the free market. It would never have survived if its life had depended solely on ratings numbers generated by A. C. Nielsen.

In a 1971 interview, Buckley explained the fallout from *Firing Line*'s abysmal ratings in the strangest possible way: "It seems

Before the jump to PBS, Buckley had to court local markets individually to find sponsors. A public relations firm working for him wooed a Washington, DC, station with a TV-shaped cake.
CREDIT: *Photographer, Eddie Loreiro/courtesy of Vic Gold*

to me, if you live in a free society, you say what it is you believe
in and how you think the society ought to be organized, but if
people decline to take your advice, you simply make do with
what you have left. For instance, if I voted, let's say, against a
bond issue for a new gymnasium for a local school, I wouldn't
therefore forbid my son to use the gymnasium if I lost the particular vote."[45]

Buckley seemed to be wondering why low ratings meant
that the small number of people who *did* like his show couldn't
watch it. He next seems to break character for a moment, saying "it seems to me that . . . the big villains in this particular
piece are the capitalists, not the government. . . ." What? Here's
what he means: "It is the capitalists who prevented pay TV from
taking hold. I think that would have been the ideal solution—
wedding individual consumers to the kind of programs they
wanted to see."[46]

There is a very interesting progression here. First, Buckley has quite rightly implied that programming decisions are
not necessarily fair or democratic, per se. They represent, in
fact, a quite concrete manifestation of the tyranny not of the
majority but of the measured audience desired by advertisers.
In fact, this was part of the rationale behind creating PBS in
the first place. When Buckley blames "the capitalists," what
he really means is "the networks," who were already lobbying
strongly (and successfully) against cable—what Buckley refers
to as "pay TV"—in the early 1970s. The answer was to jump
ship from the commercial TV market, though of course, PBS
was strapped for cash from day one, and the search for outside
sponsorship was always in play, for all kinds of PBS programs.
So while we often think of the Reagan years as the moment
when PBS took its biggest knockout punch, public broadcasting took a steady pummeling, in terms of federal funding,
from the earliest days.[47]

Government funding for public broadcasting has steadily

decreased since the Reagan years, making the recurring Republican threat to the CPB budget—an easy go-to talking point during presidential election debates—increasingly symbolic. In 2012 Mitt Romney made a wisecrack about loving Big Bird but nonetheless wanting to cut off all funding for public TV and radio. By this point, public TV and radio received $445 million from the government, a grand total of about 0.014 percent of the federal budget. PBS received 15 percent of its budget from the federal government, while NPR received 2 percent.[48]

Whether or not this is money well spent is a whole separate question, and at the risk of being branded heretical by my fellow liberals, I would venture my own opinion that PBS was simply much more necessary, relevant, and valuable in the network-era three channel TV environment than it is today. Even then, in large part because of endless funding crises, it only, unfortunately, fulfilled its promises unevenly. Locally produced public affairs shows targeting community-minded urban blacks, for example, quickly lost ground to British imports such as *Masterpiece Theater*, clearly targeting an upper-crust, affluent white audience. In our own post-network, YouTube era, voluminous content does not inherently guarantee diversity and quality. But the notion that we still desperately need a noncommercial venue to provide alternatives to viewers who otherwise would not have access to specialized content simply cannot hold up.

Now, given that PBS received federal government funding via the CPB, and given Buckley's opposition to federal spending on most things unrelated to defense, one cannot help but wonder how he justified his presence on PBS. James Ledbetter explains that *Firing Line* was distributed by "a regional network called the Southern Educational Communications Association (SECA). The shell-game financial arrangement . . . allowed Buckley, after nearly thirty seasons on the public broadcasting dial, to mouth the politically convenient canard that he receive[d] no federal funds; instead, his distributor, SECA, receive[d] the federal funds."[49] That sounds about right, except that I've not encountered Buckley mouthing any such thing. Though he advocated for cable over and over again, he only sporadically advocated against public broadcasting. In fact, it's worth adding that even SECA had to promote itself to keep its head above water, and Buckley was useful in this regard.[50]

That is, he was willing to travel to promote SECA, and PBS in general, squeezing in the taping of promos for local PBS stations after his *Firing Line* road shows.[51] In the 1980s and '90s, producer Warren Steibel became increasingly interested in organizing large-scale two-hour *Firing Line* debates, and these were hosted by various college campuses, often by the University of South Carolina, on SECA's stomping ground. The popular special events (such as the Panama Canal debate) were obviously designed to provide a boost for SECA, and, at the same time, they brought a boost to the show, and SECA and the local campuses promoted them heavily. In fact, the local hosts paid $400,000 to fund these events,[52] so they had every reason to publicize the hell out of them.

There were hundreds of audience members in attendance at these shows, while in the same years *Firing Line*'s New York studio audiences got smaller and smaller, regardless of program quality. A zippy John Kenneth Galbraith show from 1996 is attended by a small audience culled from a senior citizens' center. And a damn good 1985 episode featuring Norman Mailer and Kurt Vonnegut has fewer than a dozen audience members, scattered sadly between empty metal folding chairs. The flashy, high-profile two-hour debates, shot on the road with all-star political panels (George McGovern, Henry Kissinger), made for a stark contrast. These were the shows illustrating that *Firing Line* was still vibrant and alive in the years following Reagan's election. The shows did much to promote Buckley's show and PBS itself, though public broadcasting remained a desperately underfunded enterprise.

When the Reagan administration began to gut PBS in the early 1980s, Buckley sent out exuberant letters to potential sponsors, explaining that he needed private support to stay on the air. Buckley's fundraising letters, the subtext of which was the possibility of his imminent cancellation, are extraordinarily triumphant. Indeed, he had nothing to worry about. For one thing, the show was relatively inexpensive to produce. Numbers from the early years reveal *Firing Line* as a particularly frugal production by PBS standards. The Emmy Award–winning *VD Blues*, an hourlong 1972 special starring talk show host Dick Cavett, cost $105,000. That same year, the children's show *Zoom* cost $35,000 per half hour. Backed up by an extraordinary research budget, *Sesame Street* budgets ran much higher. In 1973, by contrast, *Firing Line* had cost $13,153 per hour.[53]

Why so cheap? There were studio costs, labor costs, and fees to performers, but there was no script, no set to speak of, no costumes, no visual aids. So raising enough to fund the show in the wake of reduced CPB funding was not truly arduous, although individual stations still needed to survive financially in order to actually broadcast the show, which is a whole separate story.

That corporations were eager to support the show in the wake of Reagan's PBS defunding is hardly surprising. Naturally, successful capitalists could be found to support a show voicing support for the successes of capitalism. Eventually the John M. Olin Foundation would become one of *Firing Line*'s central supporters, up until Buckley chose to close up shop in 1999, but there was also a slew of others: Dow Chemical, Kellogg, Mobil, Pfizer, Tandy/Radio Shack, Sundstrand, Chevron, Mary Kay, PaineWebber, the list goes on and on.

Notwithstanding the successful two-hour traveling debates, the half-hour episodes (a format change put in place in mid-1988) were quite uneven, and there is no denying that the program was declining in its final ten years. When you consider how many TV series, like *Firefly* and *Freaks and Geeks*, are of very high quality and have fanatically devoted cult audiences yet barely survive a season due to weak ratings, it's rather amazing that a PBS show of inconsistent quality and increasingly thin viewer interest could soldier on for an entire decade past its prime. By the nineties, the show was fully funded by underwriters, and PBS outlets were no longer even charged for it. The promotional letters sent by Steibel to secure contracts from local PBS stations became increasingly desperate in tone, noting repeatedly, "It's free!" Buckley's program undoubtedly continued to find space for itself on PBS not only because it was self-funding but also because of the culture wars of the Reagan decade and beyond: the show was handy proof that PBS spokespeople could whip out over the years to illustrate that they were not in the liberal propaganda business. As Jeff Greenfield put it, "To have *Firing Line* on was a nice way to say, 'Well, wait a minute, how can you call us a lefty station when we feature the most prominent conservative in America an hour a week?!'"[54]

In fact, Nixon and his cronies had occasionally referred to *Firing Line* as PBS's conservative "fig leaf," and there was much truth to this. Newton Minow was chairman of PBS in the late 1970s, and one day he noticed that the programmers had dropped *Firing Line* from their projected schedule. He phoned to ask what was going on, and the response was that viewer numbers were low and there was no underwriter, and therefore they were canceling the show. Minow's response was, "'Oh no you're not! That's the one conservative point of view that sticks out importantly in our schedule, and we can't drop it.' And . . . I called Walter Annenberg, who was a big supporter of ours . . . and he said 'I'll give you some money.' Which he did. And we continued *Firing Line*, which I was very pleased about. . . ."[55] Minow adds that in the years he was chairman of PBS (1978–80), Annenberg was the single largest individual contributor to public broadcasting, pledging $150 million, a sum that he delivered on in 1981.

Annenberg was a wealthy philanthropist, and a conservative to boot, so his stay of execution for *Firing Line* is not really too surprising. What is lovely in this tale, though, is, first, Minow, the consummate liberal, absolutely insisting that *Firing Line* could not be canceled and second, Annenberg, the consummate conservative, saving not just a show he was inherently in sympathy with but also helping to sustain a whole roster of politically variable (sometimes liberal, often neutral) programming. Both men had a sense that public TV provided a valuable service to citizens.

This sort of thinking was quite alien to the Reagan years. As Reagan's FCC commissioner Mark Fowler had so bluntly put it in a 1981 speech to broadcasters, "The FCC has no business trying to influence by raised eyebrow or by raised voice for that matter. I confess that there was a romance bordering on chivalry when a Chairman [Minow] might declare television to be a wasteland. Those kinds of pronouncements, as I see my job, are not mine to make. You are not my flock, and I am not your shepherd."[56]

Nixon had tried to exert influence on PBS by appointing conservatives sympathetic to his administration such as Thomas Curtis and Henry Loomis to the CPB board.[57] Reagan did the same. In fact, over the years a number of Buckleyites have appeared on the CPB board, such as Richard Brookhiser and Neal Freeman, who were both on the *National Review* masthead. In addition, a number of conservatives linked with *NR* were involved in PBS over the years, even if they did not sit on the CPB board. John McLaughlin of *The McLaughlin Group* was an *NR* author, and the magazine's publisher, Bill Rusher, was a regular on a PBS show called *The Advocates*.[58] With SECA president Henry Cauthen appointed to the CPB by President George H. W. Bush in 1990—and reappointed by President Bill Clinton in 1994—it seemed increasingly improbable that the defund-ing fallout from the Reagan years was going to harm *Firing Line*. Indeed, the program kept going and going, until Buckley himself finally pulled the plug in 1999.

In that year, the last substantive episode aired was a two-hour debate, "Resolved: The Federal Government Should Not Impose a Tax on Electronic Commerce." Guests included Jack Kemp, Christopher Hitchens, and Robert Kuttner. Kemp and Kuttner had been on the show many times, and they put on their usual fine performances, the former again offering a smooth political performance, the latter asking tough professo-rial questions about economics intended to test the very compe-tence of the conservatives. Kuttner was always fun because he kept his facts together even as he became angry and you sensed his neck veins popping out. (On another debate episode, Kutt-ner had almost lost it when Buckley had said, explaining how sometimes we must accept our fate, "Faute de mieux, il faut se coucher avec sa femme." [For lack of better options, one must sleep with one's wife.]) On the electronic commerce debate, Hitchens was extremely clever and British, drawing peals of laughter with relatively simple but expertly timed lines such as, to a debater he thinks has gone off track, "I will be gentle, but I must be firm. And I must recall you to—tough but tender—I must recall you to my question." There had been better epi-sodes twenty years earlier, but this one reminded you what all the fuss was about regarding *Firing Line*'s imminent departure.

The truly final episode was a two-parter titled "The End of *Firing Line*," featuring conservatives Richard Brookhiser, Rich Lowry, William Kristol, and Peter Robinson, and liberals Mi-chael Kinsley and Mark Green. The guests were great, but this was little more than a meandering elegy for the program, and there was no real conflict or tension to drive the show forward. There were some fun clips from earlier shows, but even so, and even with such clever guests, one had the impression of a series teetering along on life support. Following the taping, champagne was served, and *Nightline* interviewed Buckley. At the end, host Ted Koppel said, "You've got a few seconds left. Are you capable of summing up in ten seconds?"

Let's pause here for a moment to recollect that for some years Buckley had bucked the notion that *Firing Line* needed to change with the times. Snappy graphics were out. A new theme song was out. Any kind of format tweak was out. (The two-hour debate format inaugurated by Steibel in 1988 had, if anything, demanded a *longer* attention span than the regular half-hour format.) PBS had even asked Neal Freeman to dine with Buckley, and, presumably on the heels of a martini or three, to broach the notion that Buckley might update the show.

At that point in the late 1980s or early 1990s, Freeman seemed like the perfect choice for the task: he was the largest single public affairs producer at PBS, had won a Peabody and an Emmy, and was an old friend of Bill. Buckley had "rebuffed all other overtures" to update what was, as Freeman put it, "a radio show with a TV camera pointed at it." Yet Freeman valiantly agreed to "try to edge him toward modernity." As Freeman tells it, he made his overtures, at which point Bill dramatically whipped a letter out of his pocket, a letter supposedly received that very day. "It is a love letter from Solzhenitsyn to the host of *Firing Line*. '*Firing Line* is an oasis of intelligent thought in a sea of banality.' . . . So Bill says, 'Well, Neal, if it's good enough for Solzhenitsyn it's good enough for the rest of us.'"[59] Case closed.

So, back to Ted Koppel. How exactly could a man who had hosted a radio-show-with-a-TV-camera-pointed-at-it for thirty-three years, a man whose ideal viewer was Aleksandr Solzhenitsyn, how could such a man "sum up in ten seconds"? With pitch-perfect timing, Buckley answered Koppel's query literally: "No."

CONCLUSION: IN PRAISE OF HONEST INTELLECTUAL COMBAT

> *You weren't just debating liberals.*
> *You were debating actual radicals. You were debating people*
> *all across the spectrum. . . . How often does anyone*
> *with an intelligent opinion get an hour of television?*
> *We just finished three series of presidential debates.*
> *We have men who want to be the most powerful man in*
> *the world having to utter haiku and slip them into forty-five*
> *second slots, and that's the level of discourse. . . .*

—RICHARD BROOKHISER TO WILLIAM F. BUCKLEY, FINAL
EPISODE OF *FIRING LINE*, 1999

> *This is not a hospitable moment for serious-minded*
> *intellectuals on the right. The place once claimed in the*
> *culture by [Irving] Kristol and William F. Buckley Jr. is now*
> *inhabited by Fox News hosts and Rush Limbaugh and the*
> *radio host Laura Ingraham.*

—SAM TANENHAUS, "CAN THE GOP BE A PARTY OF IDEAS?,"
NEW YORK TIMES MAGAZINE, JULY 2, 2014

In the *National Review*'s 1955 mission statement, Buckley declared the magazine's devotion to "honest intellectual combat (rather than conformity)." He and his comrades proceeded to forge a new brand of right-wing conservatism that was modern, mainstream, and nonconspiratorial. *NR* writers attacked liberalism, but the journal was also a space for conservatives to debate and refine their own credos—a space where different strains of conservatism could duke it out.

Firing Line continued this mission but also took it in a new tactical direction. While conservatives did sometimes gather on the show to sort out their own questions—how could the Republican Party rally from Watergate, for example—Buckley's program was more often a space for liberalism to meet conservatism, for the left wing to meet the right wing. The result was no-holds-barred, honest intellectual combat, a space that both liberal and conservative viewers could turn to have their ideas confirmed, but also challenged. Buckley hoped to convert viewers, but there was more to it than that. You could actually learn about other points of view, and thereby become a *better* liberal or a *better* conservative from watching the show.

There is simply no equivalent on TV today. Conservatives have Fox News, liberals have MSNBC, and in more neutral territory we find C-SPAN. Overall, politically oriented broadcasting has become a vast echo chamber (especially on talk radio), with many tuning in largely to have their views confirmed and to hear the other side vilified. This is not a scenario that encourages dialogue between those holding different political convictions. Concluding their study of Rush Limbaugh and other conservative media players, communications scholars Kathleen Hall Jamieson and Joseph N. Cappella observe that "it was for good reason that Thomas Jefferson's rules for the House of Representatives created sanctions for language that impugned the good will and integrity of others on the floor of that body. A person tagged as a liar or a traitor or both is no longer a person with whom one can productively talk, in part because the attacks undercut any assumption of mutual trust and in part because no one so characterized is likely to want to continue the discussion."[1]

Civility has never been firmly in place in American politics, Jefferson's rules notwithstanding, and if things look worse today we can't put all the blame on cable news and talk radio. The stuff survives because it is profitable, and it is profitable because people like it. It's the triumph of the "free market of ideas" writ large.

It is easy to pine for the days when news and public affairs were (theoretically) smarter, before the rise of cable news, but this is nostalgia plain and simple. *Firing Line* mostly stood alone in a TV news and public affairs environment that was not particularly cerebral. In the 1950s and into the early 1960s, the nightly news consisted of fifteen minutes of anchors mostly reading Associated Press wire stories; this was expanded to a whole half hour by the mid-1960s. The fifteen-minute format was a carryover from radio, but it was also a sign of how much the networks valued such programming: not much. In this environment, newscasters were supposed to convey trustworthy reliability, not rhetorical panache or—even worse—their own opinions.

The Huntley-Brinkley Report was a rare standout in that it featured serious newscasters who nonetheless radiated a bit of personality.[2] And there was *Meet the Press*, which strove for extreme objectivity, and tended (and continues) to be a rather dull affair. "Just soporific!" *National Review* editor Richard Brookhiser declares.[3] *Washington Week in Review* (1967–) and *The MacNeil/Lehrer Report* (1975–83) were similarly earnest and informative and mostly lacking in intellectual oomph. Today, *60 Minutes* (1968–) has managed a balance of investigative reporting, profiles, interviews, and sensationalism that has kept it going, and has kept ratings high, but it is more about exposés than enlightened discussion. When *60 Minutes* profiled Buckley in 1981, Morley Safer asked why he used so many big words.

If TV news has historically strived for objectivity, and more often than not has sought to provide neutral public service and avoid controversy,[4] there are nonetheless two remarkable moments that we might identify as golden ages. First, there was coverage of civil rights in the 1950s and into the early 1960s. It would be difficult to overemphasize the importance of the presence of news cameras in raising national consciousness of the civil rights movement. Go to the Birmingham Civil Rights Institute and you will see displayed both eyewitness and national news accounts that flatly contradict the stories told by local news sources. It was the national media that most often got the true stories out, framing civil rights as an American crisis rather than a local, southern problem.

Second, there was the explosion of network news documentary that followed on the heels of Newton Minow's 1961 "vast wasteland" speech. These heavily researched and decidedly liberal New Frontier documentaries reported on hunger, health care, banking scandals, and so on. In 1962 alone, the three networks produced more than four hundred documentaries.[5] Edward R. Murrow, the reporter behind a number of Cold War liberal productions, had forged a place for the smart and articulate presentation of TV news in the 1950s (and before that on radio, during World War II). His work persisted as a model for high-quality network documentary into the 1960s, but he had always been menaced by the specter of cancellation. Murrow is remembered for his hard-hitting *See It Now* series (1951–58), but CBS was generally uncomfortable with Murrow's pursuit of controversial topics (McCarthyism, school integration) and pushed him to do a fluffy celebrity interview show—*Person to Person* (1953–59)—in order to earn his keep. When *See It Now* was finally canceled, CBS chairman William Paley told Murrow, "I don't want this constant stomach ache every time you do a controversial subject."[6] Thus was the shining light of network news snuffed out by management.

During the network era, news shows at their worst had no budgets and were thin enterprises. At their best, they were expensive, because reporters actually went out in the field and did real in-depth reporting. Such programs did not make money.

Rather, they were loss leaders providing public service. All of which is to say, in remarking upon the depressing one-sided, echo-chamber turn in much of today's cable news and public affairs programming, we should take care not to romanticize the past by overstating the high quality of pre–cable era news. True, it had some great moments, and some great reporters. Further, it performed a service by conveying breaking news such as the Kennedy assassination, the moon landing, and election results. But the networks always saw entertainment shows as their bread and butter; news and public affairs were the green vegetables they were required to provide in order to keep their FCC licenses secure.

Of course, *Firing Line* was about political talk more than breaking news per se. So where did Buckley fit in this context? Who were the other big talkers on TV in the pre-cable era? From 1957 to 1960 there was *The Mike Wallace Interview,* sponsored by Philip Morris (a voice intoned over the opening of a number of episodes, "Probably the best natural smoke you ever tasted!"). The shows were carefully researched, but in the main they were designed to entertain and to shock. Looking back, *Nation* editor Victor Navasky summarized, "Mike Wallace was there to embarrass his guests, whereas Buckley was there to joust with them."[7]

In the sixties and seventies, there were also talk show personalities like David Susskind and Dick Cavett. Cavett was liberal and clever and generally stuck to entertainment rather than politics in his exchanges with guests. It would be reasonable to describe him as the thinking man's Johnny Carson.[8] Predictably, he was scheduled late at night and had low ratings. Also a liberal, Susskind leaned toward more political guests than Cavett did, but he was a showbiz guy underneath it all. He had Buckley on one of his shows in 1964 and, expressing confusion when his guest used the word *irenic,* he demanded an explanation for why a simpler word would not be better. Gore Vidal was on hand and said, "You know, the trouble with you, David, is that you don't learn anything, ever."9 This may literally have been the only point on which Vidal and Buckley ever agreed.

There were real talk show talents on the air in the network years, and a few of them even had a political edge, but there was nobody to match Buckley. All of which is to say, as frustrating as the cable news environment is today, we must not pretend that TV news, talk, and public affairs used to be a shining beacon of intelligent, thoughtful reporting and conversation.10 *Firing Line* was utterly anomalous. Today, *Charlie Rose* (1992–) stands virtually alone on TV in allowing uninterrupted, long-form discussion. His show is terrific, though Rose never quite hits those Buckley high notes; Rose is a great *interviewer*, whereas Buckley was more of a conversationalist and debater.

Getting back to the question of "How did we get from there to here?," deregulation and the collapse of the Fairness Doctrine are a key part of the story. There *was* one-sided political broadcasting before the demise of the doctrine, but it was a risky endeavor because it violated FCC policy. It was mostly right-wing stuff: John Birch Society members attacking Earl Warren, fundamentalists preaching against desegregation, and White Citizens' Council representatives delivering anti-integration editorials. Such programming tended to stay beneath the FCC's radar by remaining local instead of national. One-sided news and public affairs blatantly violated the Fairness Doctrine and thus, obviously, sought to avoid FCC attention. The Reagan administration eliminated the doctrine in 1987, and it is no coincidence that Rush Limbaugh became a national radio star shortly thereafter.

The rationale of the doctrine had always been scarcity: there was limited spectrum space for broadcasters, and if you had a TV or radio license, you had to serve the public with this scarce resource. Thus, the doctrine proclaimed, broadcasters were expected to cover controversial issues of public importance, and, when they did so, they were to provide contrasting points of view on those issues. With deregulation came the rise of cable in the 1980s, and TV stopped being so scarce. The "pay TV" for which Buckley had longed for so many years had become a reality. Today, of course, we also have satellite radio, the Internet, podcasts, and so on. We've gone from a diet of scarcity to one of gluttony.

The rise of cable in the Reagan years and beyond brought with it highly specialized programming. If today many conservatives gravitate to Fox News, then this should be understood within the wider context of a radically subdivided entertainment environment in which liberals gravitate to MSNBC, men to ESPN, women to Oxygen, children to Nickelodeon, homeowners to HGTV, movie lovers to AMC, pet owners to Animal Planet, ad infinitum. The odds are not in favor of truly "fair and balanced" news thriving in a deregulated and fragmented communications marketplace in which serving a "mass audience" is not a realistic objective outside of a few special events, like the Oscars and the Super Bowl. News and public affairs programs targeting everybody, like in the Walter Cronkite days, simply have a tough time surviving. It is likewise increasingly rare to find sitcoms or dramas targeting everybody. Further, the rise of twenty-four-hour news channels has created a need for huge amounts of content. As one media scholar concludes, this has led to "the elevation of talk over reporting . . . talk on television is literally cheap."[11] The result is that twenty-four-hour news is never really twenty-four-hour news. It is a bit of news recycled constantly, and surrounded by a lot of opinion-oriented programming. "The cable networks have demonstrated how to craft endless hours of talk *about* the news more than the reporting *of* it."[12]

Although cable news has, I believe, done much damage in undercutting civility in political discourse—a civility to which more journalists and newscasters aspired in the pre-cable era—it is insufficient to simply single out blowhards like Bill O'Reilly, or Fox News overlord Roger Ailes, or on the left, Chris Matthews and Keith Olbermann, formerly of MSNBC. The problem is partly that there's money in staging the televisual equivalent of cockfighting. But it is also worth emphasizing the insufficiency of describing the current environment of rabidly competitive niche TV as simply a "post-network" symptom. We are beyond "post-network" at this point. It is only a slight exaggeration to say that we live in "post-TV" days.

Variations on the old genres are still produced—sitcoms, dramas, talk shows, news, game shows—but Americans are no longer watching these programs play out inside big square boxes perched on tables, and many don't even watch them on big flat rectangles hung on walls. We watch TV on our computers, on mobile devices, on the go, whenever we want, and often without advertisements. TV used to be known as a "push" medium—you took what you were given. Now it is a "pull" medium—you take what you want (even if recommendation engines seem to endlessly extrapolate from whatever you've consumed in the past and inform you what music, TV, or films you should like in the future).

Scripted content has gotten better than ever in order to compete. Unscripted content, to a large extent, has gone in the other direction, also to compete. In other words, to put it bluntly, class and trash are the two poles of today's TV content. Further, many people spend as much or more time engaging with social media or reading and watching "not-TV" content (blogs, news aggregation sites, YouTube videos, etc.) than they do watching actual TV shows. If cable has helped news devolve into one-sided opinionmongering and shouting matches between political opponents, it has done so because the competition for eyeballs has never been fiercer, and because content must be very specifically branded to stand out from all the noise.

In light of all this, it is not enough (though it can be self-satisfying) to be a crank and declare the death of civility in the public sphere, taking cable news skirmishes as proof of your grand declaration. The problem of grandstanding newscaster personalities is real, but the disintegration of network TV domination is the bigger, structural issue with which we must contend.

Given this environment, one has to wonder how *Firing Line* chugged along until 1999. Clearly, it had been out of place for years—a sort of network-era time capsule. As both the New Deal and the Great Society went down in flames on Reagan's watch, *Firing Line* gradually became less compelling. In 1967, Buckley had debated left-wing activist Noam Chomsky on Vietnam. In 1990, Buckley debated right-wing economist Milton Friedman on how to best make American youngsters feel a stronger sense of gratitude toward their country. Interesting idea for a show, but not exactly *pressing*.

Drifting away from the animated, two-sided debate that had been compelling to all political camps during the show's first two decades on the air, *Firing Line* increasingly became an inspirational program for many youngsters who would later constitute the New Right. The show had probably always functioned as a kind of gateway drug to conservatism, offering a two-sided intellectual kerfuffle that led some viewers to *National Review*'s more one-sided analysis, but in its later years it felt like it was increasingly preaching to the choir. Recounting his political development as a young man, *National Review* editor Rich Lowry recalls thinking, "Reagan was a conservative; I'd like to be a conservative; what the heck is a conservative? I had to find out. I went in search of explanations and defenses of conservatism. My first stop was William F. Buckley's program *Firing Line*."[13]

Of course, there were some good episodes in the Reagan years and beyond, but really, unless you were a brainiac young conservative looking for role models, *Firing Line* was simply not as exciting as it had been in earlier years. All of which is to say, for twenty years *Firing Line* was perhaps the smartest show on American television. And for ten years, it was just okay. Overall, that's a pretty strong track record. By the 1990s, Buckley had passed from movement builder to grand old man of the right. A *New York Times* trivia game went so far as to feature Buckley, with his photo on one side of a playing card and numbskull political questions on the other side. Buckley's contributions had never been trivial, but his persona had passed into the realm of trivia.

Buckley's son, Christopher, explains, "As the final years of *Firing Line* were proceeding apace or, as he would say, *pari passu*, with the rise of cable TV's Aristophanean cacophony of chattering, nattering nabobs . . . [my father] never spoke invidiously about other TV programs and fora; he was happy to keep going with what he viewed as a certain golden standard in televised rational discourse."[14]

Even before Fox News had appeared in 1996, there had been signs that *Firing Line* was going the way of the Studebaker. *National Review* editor and Buckley protégé Richard Brookhiser observes, "*The McLaughlin Group* was really the death knell for *Firing Line*." The program, which premiered in 1982, lowered political discussion, he contends, to a kind of sitcom level. "The guests were *characters*, and that's why they were on. Now, of course Bill himself was a character. He played himself. But Bill was also truly interested in what people thought and in arguing with them. He was on the Yale debate team, and that was kind of part of his training. . . . He liked to see where he could take a person in a discussion and what might ensue, and that's not at all the way *McLaughlin Group* worked."[15] The show is hosted by conservative John McLaughlin, a *National Review* columnist and former Nixon speechwriter, and in addition to the host it features two conservatives and two liberals in a political shouting match. The *New York Times* described the show in 1992

Pictured: William F. Buckley
"Does baloney fear the grinder?"

By the 1990s, Buckley had passed from movement-builder to grand-old-man of the right. A *New York Times* trivia game went so far as to feature Buckley, with his photo on one side of a playing card and numbskull political questions on the other side. Buckley's contributions had never been trivial, but his persona had passed into the realm of trivia.

CREDIT: *Game card, NYTimes Trivia Game, photo courtesy of Nancy Rose.*

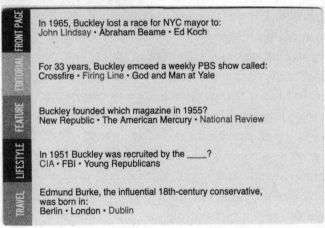

FRONT PAGE

In 1965, Buckley lost a race for NYC mayor to:
John Lindsay • Abraham Beame • Ed Koch

EDITORIAL

For 33 years, Buckley emceed a weekly PBS show called:
Crossfire • Firing Line • God and Man at Yale

FEATURE

Buckley founded which magazine in 1955?
New Republic • The American Mercury • National Review

LIFESTYLE

In 1951 Buckley was recruited by the ____?
CIA • FBI • Young Republicans

TRAVEL

Edmund Burke, the influential 18th-century conservative, was born in:
Berlin • London • Dublin

as a "circus" in which "five barking, squawking, ideologically split pundits . . . argue national and foreign affairs in a go-to-hell fashion that would have made Walter Lippmann, the patrician columnist of an earlier, gentler age, weep at the loss of any last shred of political gentility."[16]

This kind of stuff drives home the point that the problem with cable-era news is not just that it skews toward one-sided harangues but that, simultaneously, two-sided debate is built

into the system in order to amp up the volume of the drama, or
rather, the circus. It's not enough for liberal and conservative
opinionmongers to state their perspectives; they have to attack
each other on-air and escalate their animosity, all grist for the
sausage grinder that is news-about-news. In this toxic environment, liberal Mark Shields and conservative David Brooks,
making ten-minute weekly appearances on *PBS NewsHour*, offer nothing short of an oasis of gentility. The effect is positively
irenic.

Buckley advocated for pay TV for many years, and one has
to wonder if he actually consumed the one-sided stuff that ultimately emerged thanks to deregulation and the rise of cable.
According to Christopher Buckley, he watched a wide range
of political programming, from Fox News to the network evening news. "He was ecumenical in his TV watching. He enjoyed very much *Crossfire* . . . where Michael Kinsley made a
very great impression." Christopher adds, "I never heard him
deride Fox News or any of the others. If someone was making
an ass of him or herself on one of the shows he'd roll his eyes
and say, 'Honestly!'" Buckley also remembers "being puzzled when [he] expressed a favorable opinion of journalist Bill
Press, who was one of the early combatants on *Crossfire*, but a
ferocious liberal. And I said, 'Oh, really?' And he said, 'Yeah,
I think he's a terrific polemicist.' He evaluated people's performances very evenhandedly and not in the least according
to ideology."[17]

Buckley *père* found clever moments in the post–*Firing Line*
TV landscape, but this wasn't easy, requiring eclectic viewing,
not tunnel-vision selection of exclusively conservative content.
It is reasonable to assume that he would be appalled by the
ongoing downward spiral in televised political debate since his
passing, although it is also prudent to add that he would not
have been overly nostalgic about the putative "good old days"
of civil political discussion. In the Fairness Doctrine years, TV

was generally more polite, but that doesn't mean it was consistently more substantive.

While there is clearly no TV host today who brings together Buckley's unique style, erudition, and sense of humor, I did sometimes see a glimmer of *Firing Line* in the *Colbert Report* (2005–14). Perhaps this sounds far-fetched, but stay with me. On the *Report*, host Stephen Colbert was, like Buckley, interested in hearing what the other side had to say, tremendously sharp and entertaining, and inclined to see the humor in politics. Like Buckley, he was even a devout Catholic. No one did a better job of putting the chattering, nattering nabobs on the firing line. On the other hand, he was a satirist, playing a truly outrageous version of Fox News' Bill O'Reilly (he mockingly celebrated O'Reilly as "poppa bear"), and Colbert's guests never got more than five to eight minutes to exchange ideas. It was terrific stuff, but it was finely crafted comedy, with politics coming in sound bites rather than via slowly unfurled disquisition.

Jon Stewart did similar work in the sixteen years that he hosted *The Daily Show*, also exhibiting a liberal tilt coupled with a willingness to be skeptical of foolish public figures of any political persuasion, but without the benefit of playing an outrageous character. Stewart likewise allowed his guests more than a few seconds to talk about their newest book or political campaign. As Brookhiser puts it, "half an hour of Jon Stewart . . . it's like sitting down to read *In Search of Lost Time*, because everyone's on Twitter."[18]

The self-described "fake news" shows are chopped into segments targeting a short-attention span viewer, and to that extent, *The Daily Show with Jon Stewart* and *The Colbert Report* were nothing like *Firing Line*, but these days one appreciates what one can get. Alarmists who attack "fake news" as a denigration of public discourse miss two points. First, Stewart and Colbert were not "objective," but they also were not making stuff up. They were often more hard-hitting and thoughtful than more conventional TV news sources. It was not on the *CBS Evening News* but on *The Daily Show* where politicians making abrupt about-faces were likely to see aired earlier clips of themselves voicing opposite views. Second, these shows should not be dismissed as a sign of the collapse of serious discourse about current events. Rather, they should be embraced for exposing the comedy inherent in many news stories. As *Firing Line* regular Michael Kinsley once wrote, "[H]umor is not only valuable for its own sake. It also efficiently makes the point that much of what goes on is perfectly ridiculous. This is a point that serious political punditry often suppresses."[19]

In his tribute to *Firing Line* the day after Buckley died, Colbert cross-cut shots of Buckley debating Noam Chomsky with Bill O'Reilly croaking "Shut up!" When guest Brookhiser explained to Colbert that on *Firing Line* Buckley attacked people for their *ideas*, not for their personal qualities, Colbert responded cannily, "This is what I didn't like about him. It's that he didn't get personal. He was all about ideas and arguments, and today," he added with put-on puffery, "we have emotion and volume." In his *60 Minutes* profile, Buckley had declared, "There's nothing better or more amusing than a theatrical pomposity. It's an art form. People who don't have a sense of humor have a very hard time with *National Review*." It would be hard to name a politically oriented TV host more masterful in his theatrical pomposity than Colbert.

The Colbert Report was very much a product of its time. TV programming has become so niche compared to the old network days that not only is there a station just for comedy, but within that there is a sub-niche of news comedy, with a liberal host offering a satirical portrayal of a right-wing news pundit from a different niche channel. If Walter Cronkite were alive today, his head would be spinning.

And there is yet another issue to contend with in our "post-TV" news world: the current revival of conspiratorial thinking, a situation exacerbated by the maelstrom of social media. In the old days, any nut could stand on a street corner pontificating against fluoridation as a communist plot. He could even write a pamphlet on the topic for the John Birch Society to distribute in its American Opinion bookstores. This was free speech in action, but how many actually heard it? Today such a person can reach an exponentially larger audience on Facebook, Twitter, and YouTube. There will always be grassy knoll types; they just seem particularly shrill at the moment, and they are an easy go-to story for cable news. In the Cold War years, Buckley did much to push the conspiratorial elements out of right-wing conservatism, and *Firing Line* consistently helped him in this endeavor. By the time the show went off the air in 1999, the Birchers would have been little more than a distant memory for fans of the show.

But by 2008, there was a new conspiratorial force on the right, the Birthers. And following Obama's election, the roar of conspiracy theorists only became more earsplitting. Glenn Beck, for example, promoted his conspiracy theories on Fox News for two and a half years, until he was finally canceled— not because his ratings were low, but because it was increasingly difficult to find advertisers willing to associate themselves with him. There was only so much ad time that could go to gold and silver merchants (helpful hint: if you are anxious about a Marxist dystopian future, apparently hoarding precious metals is a good way to prepare). Undeterred, Beck launched his own channel on the Internet, and in 2015 he was picked up by Cablevision, which has three million subscribers in the New Jersey–New York–Connecticut area. Beck is the perfect example of the post-TV conspiracy-theorist-cum-entertainer. He can thrive on TV or off it, thanks in large part to social media.

Although the Tea Party is not exclusively a conspiratorial force, it has become a synecdoche for the newest incarnation of the conspiratorial ethos. Certainly, there are many notions promoted by Tea Partiers that are strongly approved of by the conventional far right, as epitomized by *National Review*. There's nothing inherently conspiratorial in wanting to radically cut taxation and government spending.* Asked about their eccentricities, *NR* editor Rich Lowry responds that the Tea Party is simply a new manifestation of conservative Republicanism, adding, "I reject any notion that they're similar to the John Birch Society, which is a group devoted to crankery and conspiracy theories." Both left and right have their kooks, he notes: "If you take any crowd you're going to get people holding crazy signs or saying idiotic things. . . ."[20]

It's true that there are conspiracy theorists on all sides. The 9/11-was-an-inside-job nuts are not doing any favors for the legitimate left. But since Obama's election, there has been a surge on the right of a kind of neo–John Birch Society mentality, and the kookiness that Buckley helped push way out to the fringes has moved closer in. To offer the most obvious example, consider how tenaciously Tea Party boosters clung to the notion that Barack Obama is not a US citizen.

In the Cold War years, Robert Welch, founder of the John Birch Society, had with similarly intense fervor contended that President Eisenhower was "a conscious agent of the Communist conspiracy." And *Firing Line* offered an analysis of Welch's tactics that still holds water today. In the 1971 episode that I discussed earlier, Buckley and former JBS recruiter Gerald Schomp discuss how Welch wove his conspiratorial narratives. Welch would come up with a thesis about how the communist conspiracy was functioning in the United States, and then he would hire a researcher to come up with facts supporting

---

* Neal Freeman states categorically, "There is no analogy to be drawn between the John Birch Society and the Tea Party. These are people who have real lives. In other words, they're not political junkies. . . . It is not a political organization; it is a genuine citizen uprising." Neal Freeman, interview with the author, July 15, 2014.

the thesis. Facts that might refute the thesis were ignored. As Schomp perfectly summarizes, "He overwhelms you, he blitzes you with information, you know; only the information he wants you to have; he does not analyze the information, look at both sides, present both sides and then draw conclusions. He makes up his mind in advance." The facts are almost relentlessly correct, but they are also relentlessly selective. This approach remains the meat and potatoes of contemporary conspiracy theorists.

It would be historically sloppy to say that we've gone back to the Birch Society days, but you'd have to bury your head in the sand not to observe that we live in neo-conspiratorial times. All of which is to say, Bill Buckley may have famously pushed out the conspiracy theorists, but they never really went away, and now they are back with a vengeance. In this climate, both left and right would profit from the kind of reasoned debate that dominated on *Firing Line*. But would it be feasible to produce a new program in the Buckley tradition? What would it look like?

Here's my fantasy version of what I will tentatively call *Firing Line 2.0*. Such a program would provide a full hour of uninterrupted political talk, most often between political opponents. It would be relatively cheap to produce, and would require a charismatic and wildly smart host willing to book not just big-name politicians but also intellectuals. It would be a brainiac show with brainiac guests, oriented toward *discussion* rather than *interview*. When a host asks all the questions and then waits for answers, we are in interview mode. When both host and guest participate equally in a conversation or debate (even as host perhaps provides prompts), we are in Buckleyite discussion mode.

Such a program, without splashy graphics and music, without the intense degree of "emotion and volume" that Colbert pointed to, without personal attacks, and without the nasty conspiratorial edge that characterizes so much personality-driven cable news programming, would not stand much of a chance on Fox News, even if the right host could be found. That kind of show is simply not a match for the Fox News "brand." It's not the kind of thing Fox viewers are going for, and it's not the kind of thing that would easily draw advertising revenue. The same would hold for MSNBC, if my show had a liberal host.* In fact, I wouldn't advocate for a show like this on Fox News or CNN because these two channels have the highest viewer numbers of the news channels. C-SPAN or CNBC, with lower numbers, would be better cable news homes. A cable news channel with a higher profit margin would be less willing to risk making room for an intellectual show with predictably not-stellar ratings. In point of fact, the smartest home for the show would probably be HBO, a cable channel not branded as a place for news but as a place for "quality." For almost thirty years, *Firing Line* was shot in HBO studios in New York. How fitting it would be to have things come full circle and to find *Firing Line 2.0* not just shot at HBO but also shown on HBO.

If I have learned anything as a liberal watching hundreds of hours of *Firing Line*, it is the value of testing political ideas against each other, hashing them out, and finding a way to disagree (usually, if not always) without animosity. This kind of discussion demands long, uninterrupted blocks of time. Thus, on the hypothetical *Firing Line 2.0* our host and guest would sit and talk, engaging in honest intellectual combat without clips and cutaways, without interruptions for advertisements, and far away from the sound bite culture of the tweetosphere. We don't have to pretend to go back in time—*Firing Line 2.0* could have its own website, which might include discussion spaces, links to material mentioned on the show, etc. Our updated *Fir-*

---

* It may seem heretical, but I believe that the host of *Firing Line 2.0* could be conservative or liberal. Some may yearn for the existence of a show in the *Firing Line* tradition out of a feeling that we need more conservative public intellectuals. My own feeling is that we need more public intellectuals, period.

ing Line could even be promoted via social media. But on the show itself, what we would get is simply one hour of smart talk.

In the *Firing Line* tradition, episodes would not be required to respond in a flat-footed manner to current events. For example, let's say there were an obnoxious billionaire running for president, with no actual political qualifications, and a propensity for making disparaging comments about women and racial and ethnic minorities. Buckley would have been unlikely to have conceived an episode responding directly to this guy's latest shenanigans. Instead, he would have had a journalist or political philosopher on the show to discuss a topic along the lines of, "What's up with outsider political candidates?" Discussion would center on debating the desirability of such candidates and wondering if they represented democracy at its apex or nadir. (Note the subtitle of *Road Show*, Roger Simon's book on the 1988 presidential election: "In America, Anyone Can Become President. It's One of the Risks We Take.") Rather than responding to the candidate's latest ignominious outbursts, *Firing Line 2.0* would shelve sensationalism in favor of illumination.

After all, we already have plenty of shows, both good and bad, that review "what happened in the news this week." Part of what made *Firing Line* unique was that it was responsive to current events, but also tried to get at the bigger picture. The shows were very rarely repeated, but many of them could have been, which is untrue of most episodes of today's political programs. Certainly, a *Firing Line* like 1976's "The New Spiro T. Agnew" is distinctly of its time, a frozen historical moment. On the other hand, Mortimer Adler speaking graciously on "How to Speak, How to Listen" is timeless, as is Rosalyn Tureck on "Why Do They Fear Bach?" *Firing Line* always vacillated between evergreen and amber, and at its best it was a little bit of both.

If a long-attention-span type of show in the *Firing Line* tradition could be launched today, in a venue besides HBO that required sponsorship beyond subscriber support, it would be ideal for it to have underwriters rather than advertisers so as to avoid commercial breaks. And what if the underwriters for my hypothetical show were not exclusively associated with one side of the political spectrum? In the wake of PBS's defunding, *Firing Line* had conservative underwriters like Mobil Oil and Dow Chemical. They didn't influence content, but they didn't have to: Buckley was unlikely to say much that the chieftains of such companies would disagree with.* Imagine a political show with underwriting support from, say, Apple, IBM, the National Review Institute, the Nation Institute, the ACLU, the Ford Foundation, the Heritage Foundation, and Ben and Jerry's. Like the original, *Firing Line 2.0* would not turn a profit. It wouldn't have to, though, because it would be relatively cheap to produce, and it would simply have to be seen as worthy by the companies underwriting it, like *Firing Line* was for the last twenty years of its existence.

The host of such a show would need to be very smart and well-read, a political junkie who also has other interests, not necessarily trained as a journalist but trained (or at least practiced) in the fine art of debate. Above all, he or she would need a sharp sense of humor coupled with a basic sense of civic-minded courtesy. Energetic humor without a "gotcha" kind of sarcasm is, I think, key. One immediately thinks back to all the moderators, questioners, and other emcee types that Buckley had on the show over the years. Who are today's young Michael Kinsleys, Jeff Greenfields, or Mark Greens? Can we find a more intellectual Stephen Colbert type?

---

* Anomalously, Chase Bank balked about underwriting a 1983 *Firing Line* debate on Reaganomics at Harvard if it would only feature Buckley and John Kenneth Galbraith. The show *had* to have Milton Friedman, too. What, Buckley wasn't conservative enough?! Friedman declined, and Chase was out. William F. Buckley, *Overdrive: A Personal Documentary* (Garden City, NY: Doubleday, 1983), 239–40.

Pondering possible contenders, one easily ends up with a list of people who would be great guests but might not have the range of background interests or conversational skills to carry the show as a host over the long haul. It's possible that no one out there has the right temperament, skill set, and catholic interests, and, indeed, *Firing Line 2.0* might well be a pie-in-the-sky notion. But even thinking about such an idea helps us to see what kind of political discourse is lacking from the TV (or, if you will, post-TV) landscape, and this in itself is a salutary exercise. There will never be a show just like *Firing Line*, but that's okay. It doesn't mean we shouldn't *try* to improve the quality of political discussion on TV, and to increase the amount of honest intellectual combat. There will never be an author just like James Joyce, either, or a director like Preston Sturges, and yet novelists and filmmakers keep plugging away nonetheless.

There are many lessons to be learned from *Firing Line*. Some of them are quite literally lessons: watch enough of the show, and you will know much more than you ever imagined about topics such as civil rights, feminism, the Republican Party, the Democratic Party, libertarianism, the death penalty, the blacklist, the New Journalism, the conservative movement, the counterculture, Vietnam, Bach, China, the Soviet Union, the UN, Watergate, the US Postal Service, and even meat prices and agricultural policy. On the other hand, while the view on the ground reveals all these varied topics, the helicopter view of the show's thirty-three-year run reveals—as the preceding pages have sought to convey—a country turning from left to right, from the Great Society to the Reagan Revolution and beyond. You see an America that weathered massive civil unrest in the 1960s, the collapse of the presidency in the 1970s, and the rise of conservative approaches to economics and foreign policy in the 1980s: an America that, by the 1990s, had emerged as a society in which certain key cultural values had shifted left, even as the Republican Party had continued its rightward shift, pulling the Democratic Party along in its wake.

You will also learn that political discussion is at its best when it brings with it a strong sense of humor and a willingness not to vilify the opposition as the Enemy. Politics is serious business, but rage doesn't improve the quality of your debating any more than pimped out graphics and set design do.

Consider the great exchanges that Bill Kristol had with Jon Stewart on *The Daily Show* over the years. A 2009 discussion on Sarah Palin's candidacy and on health care reform was so good that, while a truncated version aired on the show, you could watch the extended version online. Liberal outposts like the *Huffington Post* felt Stewart had backed Kristol into a corner. But *National Review* linked up the extended footage on its website, which would seem to indicate satisfaction with the exchange. I encourage you to try this exercise. First, check out the fifteen-minute version of the 2009 exchange between Stewart and Kristol. What you see is entertaining and idea-driven, two people sitting at a desk sorting through their differences. Granted, it's not hugely informative, but it is an engaging and thoughtful conversation. Then check out the half-hour *Crossfire* episode with Kristol and Cornel West debating health care in 2013. The show features two hosts, multiple video screens in the background, a rolling scroll at the bottom of the screen giving updates on unrelated issues, excessive use of split screen, and quite a bit of shouting. It's a diffuse bells-and-whistles show, not lacking in substance, but not measuring up to *The Daily Show* exchange. Like so much of today's news and public affairs programming, it is rhetorically aggressive, absurdly overproduced, and largely humorless.

With its carpeted dais, a few chairs, the occasional ashtray, and perhaps a luxurious glass of water, *Firing Line* proved definitively that less is more. Looking back, it is clear that the 1960s and '70s were the show's golden age insofar as Buckley was

The spare *Firing Line* set and format never budged. Buckley seemed to have been sitting next to the same table and glass of water for thirty years.
CREDIT: *Hoover Institution*

the voice of an embattled minority, the right-wing conservative, and this lent an urgency and energy to his encounters with the left. Following Reagan's election, and in the years to come, the show had many exceptional moments, but there was also a pervasive sense of "we won . . . now how do we bring our victory to full fruition?" The show mostly fired on all pistons until it went to the half-hour format in 1988, starting with "Dirty Rock Lyrics" with guest Tipper Gore. A half hour was never enough time to really get a solid discussion going, though in today's world in which three or four minutes constitutes an "interview," these half-hour episodes seem like Russian novels in their complexity. Luckily, in those same years there were also two-hour *Firing Line* special debates, which did often require a Herculean attention span, but usually paid off.

Even as the show lost the urgency that had characterized it in the 1960s and '70s, Buckley continued to stake a claim for

Flashy all-star two-hour debates in the late years of *Firing Line* were quite successful. Here, Buckley debates George McGovern, with Henry Kissinger, Jean Kirkpatrick, Pat Schroeder, et al.
CREDIT: *Hoover Institution*

the value of honest conversation. In the 1983 episode "How to Speak, How to Listen," guest Mortimer Adler asked, "Don't you think that the whole purpose of conversation is the meeting of minds?" Buckley responded, "Either that, or the crystallization of differences." To which Adler replied, "Either understood agreement or understood disagreement, but understanding comes first. People who disagree with what they don't understand are impertinent, and people who agree with what they don't understand are inane. And inanity and impertinence rules the roost most of the time, I think."

For three decades, Buckley had battled such inanity and impertinence. But on the very last episode he asked liberal Mark Green, with a flourish of impertinence that was suitable to the occasion, "Tell us . . . what impression you carry off about your one hundred appearances on *Firing Line*. Did you learn *anything*?" Green had. We all had.

NOTES

PREFACE: THE MAKING OF WILLIAM F. BUCKLEY JR.

1. Judis reports 12,000 copies sold in November 1951 and 35,000 copies by spring 1952. Dwight Macdonald reports 12,000 in October and 23,000 in the spring, with ongoing sales of 1,000 per month. John B. Judis, *William F. Buckley, Jr.: Patron Saint of the Conservatives* (New York: Simon & Schuster, 1988), 92; Dwight Macdonald, "God and Buckley at Yale," *Reporter*, May 27, 1952, 35.

2. William F. Buckley Jr., "Just to Say Thanks," *National Review*, March 26, 1981, accessed December 26, 2015, http://www.nationalreview.com/article /211344/just-say-thanks-william-f-buckley-jr .

3. Judis, *William F. Buckley, Jr.*, 48.

4. Ibid., 50.

5. Kevin M. Schultz, *Buckley and Mailer: The Difficult Friendship That Shaped the Sixties* (New York: Norton, 2015), 138.

6. William F. Buckley Jr., *The Unmaking of a Mayor* (New York: Viking, 1966), 147.

7. William F. Meehan III, ed., *Conversations with William F. Buckley* (Jackson: University Press of Mississippi, 2009), 29, 45.

8. Norman Mailer, "Lindsay and the City," October 28, 1965, reprinted in *The Village Voice Anthology (1956–1980): Twenty-Five Years of Writing from the Village Voice*, ed. Geoffrey Stokes (New York: Quill, 1982), 114.

9. Neal B. Freeman, "William F. Buckley Jr.'s Run for Mayor: Fifty Years Later," *National Review*, October 24, 2015, accessed December 28, 2015, http:// www.nationalreview.com/article/425998/william-f-buckley-jrs-run-mayor-fifty-years-later-neal-b-freeman.

10. Roy S. Durstine Inc., "Memorandum to Mr. William F. Buckley, Jr., the Hon. Frederic R. Coudert, Jr., Mr. James L. Buckley, and Mr. Neal B. Freeman for the 1965 Campaign for Mayor of New York City," box 296, folder 42, Buckley mayoral papers, Yale University.

11. *Les Vampires* idea from Lewis L. Lloyd, letter to Buckley, September 20, 1965; "pixilated" response from Buckley to Lloyd, September 25, 1965, box 296, folder 42, Buckley mayoral papers, Yale University.

12. Letter from Kathleen Bradley to Buckley, September 24, 1965, box 296, folder 40, Buckley mayoral papers, Yale University.

13. Buckley, *The Unmaking of a Mayor*, 83.

14. Ibid., 65.

15. Letter from Ken Auletta to Buckley, October 31, 1965, box 296, folder 43, Buckley mayoral papers, Yale University.

16. Neal Freeman, unpublished interview with John B. Judis, July 12, 1985.

17. Quotations from *Firing Line*, here and throughout, are the product of my own transcription or are drawn from transcripts of the program held at the Hoover Institution. Copyright for the programs and transcripts is held by Stanford University.

18. Christopher Buckley, interview with the author, April 7, 2015.

19. Christopher Buckley, "Postscript: Christopher Hitchens, 1949–2011," *New Yorker*, December 15, 2011, accessed January 7, 2016, http://www.new yorker.com/news/news-desk/postscript-christopher-hitchens-1949-2011.

20. The Reliable Source [pseud.], "Morton Kondracke, Pioneering Telepundit, Recalls the 'McLaughlin Group' Years at Retirement Party," *Washington Post*, April 12, 2011, accessed April 9, 2016. https://www.washingtonpost.com/blogs/reliable-source/post/morton-kondracke-pioneering-telepundit/2011/04/12/AF08zaSD_blog.html.

INTRODUCTION: THE MAKING OF *FIRING LINE*: A "BARE-KNUCKLED INTELLECTUAL BRAWL" WITH "NO PRODUCTION VALUES"

1. Neal Freeman, interview with the author, July 15, 2014.

2. Rich Lowry, "I Was a Teenage Conservative," in *Why I Turned Right: Leading Baby Boom Conservatives Chronicle Their Political Journeys*, ed. Mary Eberstadt (New York: Threshold Editions, 2007), 272.

3. Peggy Noonan, *What I Saw at the Revolution: A Political Life in the Reagan Era* (New York: Random House, 1990), 14–15.

4. The Fairness Doctrine specified that broadcasters were obliged to cover controversial issues of public importance and that, when they did so, they were required to air multiple opinions (two sides were generally assumed). Though the doctrine never functioned as well as intended, it was an earnest attempt to keep demagoguery at bay, in the wake of Father Coughlin's success in the 1930s and '40s. The doctrine was undergirded by the notion of spectrum scarcity: there were only so many radio and TV channels available, and the public interest would not be served by broadcasters promoting only one political point of

view. The Federal Communications Commission under Reagan killed the doctrine in 1987. Heather Hendershot, *What's Fair on the Air? Cold War Right-Wing Broadcasting and the Public Interest* (Chicago: University of Chicago Press, 2011).

5. Warren Steibel, unpublished interview with John B. Judis, c. 1987.

6. Buckley quoting a letter from Harold Berliner in memo to Steibel, March 18, 1976, box 13, "Wm. F. Buckley Jr. Correspondence, Steibel, Warren" folder, *Firing Line* collection, Hoover Institution, Stanford University.

7. Hugh Kenner to William F. Buckley, July 25, 1967, box 11, "Television Program *Firing Line* Apr–Oct 1967" folder, *Firing Line* collection, Hoover Institution, Stanford University.

8. William F. Buckley, *On the Firing Line: The Public Life of Our Public Figures* (New York: Random House, 1989), xxxi, 9.

9. Ibid., 10.

10. Quotation from William F. Buckley, *Cruising Speed: A Documentary* (New York: Putnam, 1971), 210. For the Beatles, see 14.

11. Meehan, ed., *Conversations with William F. Buckley*, 92. In an alternate version of the story, Buckley sadly has to miss the show to arrive at Rockefeller's dinner on time, only to find himself seated next to Archie Bunker himself, Carroll O'Connor. William F. Buckley Jr., *Overdrive: A Personal Documentary* (New York: Doubleday, 1981), 55.

12. *Firing Line*, "Final Program—WOR TV," March 2, 1971.

13. Jabba the Hutt from Christopher Buckley, *Losing Mum and Pup: A Memoir* (New York: Twelve, 2010); pro football from *Firing Line*, "Final Program—WOR TV," March 2, 1971; Mickey Mantle from Neal Freeman, unpublished interview with John B. Judis, November 7, 1985.

14. On wine with peanut butter and bacon, see Linda Bridges and John R. Coyne Jr., *Strictly Right: William F. Buckley and the American Conservative Movement* (Hoboken, NJ: Wiley, 2007), 133.

15. Buckley, *On the Firing Line*, xxxi.

16. William F. Buckley Jr., *The Reagan I Knew* (New York: Basic Books, 2008), 90.

17. Memo from WFB to James Buckley, October 22, 1970, box 293, "Buckley, James for Senate," folder, Buckley mayoral papers, Yale University.

18. Eric Hoyt, *Hollywood Vault: Film Libraries Before Home Video* (Berkeley: University of California Press, 2014), chapter 5.

19. Matty Fox's nephew claimed that it was Fox who brought O'Neil in and brokered the deal with Hughes, whereas O'Neil's family claims that it was all O'Neil's doing. See ibid., 165.

20. October 25, 1967, memo from Howard Carter to Frank Boehm, box 11, "TV Program *Firing Line* Viewer Comments, News Clippings, 1967" folder, *Firing Line* collection, Hoover Institution, Stanford University.

21. All figures from "CPB/Focus on Research #4," March 10, 1975, box 12, "WM. F. Buckley, Jr., Important Business, 1976" folder, *Firing Line* collection, Hoover Institution, Stanford University.

22. Buckley quoted in Bridges and Coyne, *Strictly Right*, 55.

23. Letter from Buckley to Thomas O'Neil and John B. Poor, RKO Features, August 28, 1969, box 12, "Wm. F. Buckley Jr. Correspondence, I–M" folder, *Firing Line* collection, Hoover Institution, Stanford University.

24. On the other hand, one must also note, first, that the free market may not be able to sustain certain kinds of content many would consider desirable, such as news that is genuinely "fair and balanced," and, second, that with its financing and syndication rules in the early 1970s the FCC had made a genuine, initially successful effort to improve the lot of independent TV producers, paving the way for innovative producers like Tandem Productions (Norman Lear) and MTM Enterprises (Mary Tyler Moore and Grant Tinker).

25. As Eric Hoyt explains, "Zenith's Phonevision, Paramount's Telemeter, and Skiatron's Subscribervision all represented different variations on the same basic concept. To purchase home access to a movie, consumers inserted a Skiatron computer punch card into a slot atop the television, dropped coins into a set-top Telemeter box, or called a telephone operator. The set-top box then correctly interpreted a scrambled TV signal and the movie appeared on-screen." Hoyt, *Hollywood Vault*, 147. Hoyt is here drawing on Michele Hilmes, *Hollywood and Broadcasting: From Radio to Cable* (Champaign: University of Illinois Press, 1999). O'Neil himself had attempted to profit from a set-top descrambling box, in which viewers inserted four quarters to view a film. But this primordial pay-per-view system was a failed venture. "Thomas F. O'Neil, 82; Brought Movies to TV," *Los Angeles Times*, March 18, 1998. O'Neil had also hoped to charge viewers to watch sports, spurring an FCC investigation. "The $6,000,000 Question," *Sports Illustrated*, December 26, 1960.

26. Buckley, *The Reagan I Knew*, 89.

27. Jeff Greenfield, interview with the author, July 3, 2014.

28. Buckley, *On the Firing Line*, 171.

29. Steibel interview.

30. *Firing Line*, "Bill Buckley and Firing Line Get Roasted," taped January 14, 1986.

31. Richard Hofstadter, "The Paranoid Style in American Politics," *Harper's Magazine*, November 1964, 77–86.

CHAPTER ONE: FORGING A NEW IMAGE FOR THE RIGHT: GOLDWATER, EXTREMISM, AND STYLISH CONSERVATISM

1. Neal Freeman, unpublished interview with John B. Judis, July 12, 1985.

2. Heather Hendershot, *What's Fair on the Air? Cold War Right-Wing Broadcasting and the Public Interest* (Chicago: University of Chicago Press, 2011), 100.

3. Hugh Kenner cited in obituary by Douglas Martin, "William F. Buckley Jr. Is Dead at 82," *New York Times*, February 27, 2008. Kenner himself had passed away before Buckley, in 2003.

4. Arnold Forster and Benjamin R. Epstein, *Danger on the Right: The Attitudes, Personnel, and Influence of the Radical Right and Extreme Conservatives* (New York: Random House, 1964), 62.

5. Ibid., 63.

6. Ibid., 53–54.

7. Ibid., 256.

8. Lisa McGirr rejects terms like "Radical Right," "ultraconservatism," and "Far Right" as overly broad and "fraught with psychological overtones and dismissive connotations." She is quite correct. I use the terms not because they are precise descriptors but because they are the language in use in the 1960s. The point is not to discern whether Buckley was "really" an extremist but that this was the language floating around him and that he reacted against in his column, in the pages of *National Review*, and on *Firing Line*. McGirr, *Suburban Warriors: The Origins of the New American Right* (Princeton, NJ: Princeton University Press, 2001), 9.

9. Forster and Epstein, *Danger on the Right*, 257.

10. Hendershot, *What's Fair on the Air?*, 100.

11. Dan Carter, *The Politics of Rage: George Wallace, the Origins of the New Conservatism, and the Transformation of American Politics*, 2nd ed. (Baton Rouge: Louisiana State University Press, 2000), 366.

12. Victor S. Navasky, *A Matter of Opinion* (New York: Farrar, Straus & Giroux, 2005), 74.

13. Linda Bridges and John R. Coyne Jr., *Strictly Right: William F. Buckley and the American Conservative Movement* (Hoboken, NJ: Wiley, 2007), 41.

14. Cited in Carl T. Bogus, *Buckley: William F. Buckley Jr. and the Rise of American Conservatism* (New York: Bloomsbury Press, 2011), 158.

15. Ibid., 162.

16. Buckley was deeply offended by accusations of racism and anti-Semitism, but that doesn't mean that he always got it right. See, for example, Diane McWhorter, "Dangerous Minds: William F. Buckley Soft-Pedals the Legacy of Journalist Westbrook Pegler in *The New Yorker*," *Slate*, March 4, 2004, accessed October 1, 2015, http://www.slate.com/articles/arts/culture-box/2004/03/dangerous_minds.html.

17. Ted Humes quoted in Jonathan M. Schoenwald, *A Time for Choosing: The Rise of Modern American Conservatism* (New York: Oxford University Press, 2001), 161.

18. Cited in Joe McGinniss, *The Selling of the President 1968* (New York: Trident, 1969), 21.

19. Theodore H. White, *The Making of the President 1960* (New York: Atheneum House, 1961), 348.

20. Ibid., 345–46.

21. Ibid., 353.

22. Ailes cited in McGinniss, *The Selling of the President 1968*, 64.

23. October 1965 memo to Buckley, box 297, folder 47, Buckley mayoral papers, Yale University.

24. Buckley, *The Unmaking of a Mayor*, 76.

25. William F. Buckley Jr., *Flying High: Remembering Barry Goldwater* (New York: Basic Books, 2008), 153–54.

26. Karl Hess, *In a Cause That Will Triumph: The Goldwater Campaign and the Future of Conservatism* (New York: Doubleday, 1967), 57.

27. Ibid., 49.

28. Theodore H. White, *The Making of the President 1964* (New York: Harper, 2010), 211.

29. Richard A. Viguerie and David Franke, *America's Right Turn: How Conservatives Used New and Alternative Media to Take Power* (Chicago: Bonus Books, 2004), 101.

30. White, *The Making of the President 1964*, 112.

31. Rick Perlstein, *Before the Storm: Barry Goldwater and the Unmaking of the American Consensus* (New York: Hill & Wang, 2001), 515.

32. Michael Murphy, "Conservative Pioneer Became an Outcast," *Arizona Republic*, May 31, 1998, accessed August 14, 2014, http://archive.azcentral.com/specials/special25/articles/0531goldwater2.html.

33. "Goldwater Had a Way with Words," *Arizona Republic*, May 29, 1998, accessed August 14, 2014, http://archive.azcentral.com/specials/special25/articles/0529goldwater2.html.

CHAPTER TWO: "APODICTIC ALL THE WAY THROUGH": FIRING LINE TAKES ON COMMUNISM

1. Christopher Buckley, interview with the author, April 7, 2015.

2. Michael Kackman, *Citizen Spy: Television, Espionage, and Cold War Culture* (Minneapolis: University of Minnesota Press, 2005); J. Fred MacDonald, *Television and the Red Menace: The Video Road to Vietnam* (New York: Praeger, 1985).

3. Cited in Heather Hendershot, *What's Fair on the Air? Cold War Right-Wing Broadcasting and the Public Interest* (Chicago: University of Chicago Press, 2011), 30.

4. William F. Buckley Jr. and L. Brent Bozell, *McCarthy and His Enemies: The Record and Its Meaning* (1954; reprint New Rochelle, NY: Arlington House, 1970), xiv.

5. Thomas Doherty, *Cold War, Cool Medium: Television, McCarthyism, and American Culture* (New York: Columbia University Press, 2003), 260.

6. John B. Judis, *William F. Buckley, Jr.: Patron Saint of the Conservatives* (New York: Simon & Schuster, 1988), 108.

7. William F. Buckley, "Standing Athwart History," in *Athwart History: Half a Century of Polemics, Animadversions, and Illuminations*, ed. Linda Bridges and Roger Kimball (New York: Encounter Books, 2010), 7.

8. Victor S. Navasky, *A Matter of Opinion* (New York: Farrar, Straus & Giroux, 2005), 71.

9. William F. Buckley Jr., *On the Firing Line: The Public Life of Our Public Figures* (New York: Random House, 1989), 221–27.

10. James C. Goodale, "Forced Union Membership, The First Amendment and the Buckley-Evans Case," "Media and the Law" column, *New York Law Journal*, February 23, 1978.

11. Buckley, *On the Firing Line*, 306.

12. Cited in Herbert Mitgang, "Michael Harrington, Socialist and Author, Is Dead," *New York Times*, August 2, 1989, accessed January 12, 2016, http://

www.nytimes.com/1989/08/02/obituaries/michael-harrington-socialist-and-author-is-dead.html.

13. Buckley, *On the Firing Line*, 424.

14. Ibid., 428.

15. Buckley cited in a review of his *United Nations Journal: A Delegate's Odyssey*. Eric Redman, "William Buckley Reports on a Tour of Duty," *New York Times*, October 6, 1974, accessed January 12, 2016, http://www.nytimes.com/books/00/07/16/specials/buckley-un.html.

16. Murray Kempton, "My Last Mugging," *Playboy*, December 1971, reprinted in *Rebellions, Perversities, and Main Events* (New York: Times Books, 1994), 221.

17. Murray Kempton cited in David Remnick, "Prince of the City," *New Yorker*, March 1, 1993, 49.

18. Buckley cited in John Avlon, "Genius for Friendship," *National Review*, July 1, 2013.

19. Buckley cited in James K. Galbraith, "James K. Galbraith on Bill Buckley," *New Republic*, February 28, 2008.

20. Ibid.

21. I have not ascertained with certainty their very first media co-appearance, but it may have been on one of David Susskind's talk shows, in 1965, when Buckley appeared with Galbraith, Billy Rose, and (if "memory serves," WFB wrote three years later) Dick Gregory. William F. Buckley, "Is There a Last Straw?," in *Athwart History*, 183.

22. It is not clear that Galbraith originated this phrase; he may have repeated it from his hosts at the Polish Economic Society, where he visited in the 1950s. John Kenneth Galbraith, *A Life in Our Times* (New York: Ballantine, 1981), 351–52.

23. William F. Buckley, "Theodore White, R.I.P.," in *Athwart History*, 315.

24. Ibid.

25. Theodore H. White letter to Buckley, December 2, 1965, box 296, folder 38, Buckley mayoral papers, Yale University.

26. Christopher Buckley, *Losing Mum and Pup: A Memoir* (New York: Twelve, 2009), 107.

27. William F. Buckley Jr., *Atlantic High: A Celebration* (New York: Doubleday, 1982), 32.

28. Victor S. Navasky, *Naming Names* (New York: Penguin, 1981), 78.

29. Stander cited in Patrick McGilligan and Paul Buhle, *Tender Comrades: A Backstory of the Hollywood Blacklist* (Minneapolis: University of Minnesota Press, 2012), 612.

30. On *Mission to Moscow*, see Clayton R. Koppes and Gregory D. Black, *Hollywood Goes to War: How Politics, Profits, and Propaganda Shaped World War II Movies* (New York: Free Press, 1987), 191–208. Unnoticed by HUAC were more subtle radical moments in film noir and other low-budget postwar productions. As Thomas Doherty notes, "the on-screen evidence persuasively debunks the notion that left-of-center content was totally erased from Hollywood cinema—even in the depths of the Cold War and the blacklist." Review of *Red Hollywood* in *Cineaste* (Winter 2014): 46.

31. Blacklisted American director Jules Dassin points to the idea that members of the Screen Writers Guild were actually writing "subversive stuff" as "howlingly funny." To his mind, the real problem was that the guild was "demanding rights and better financial arrangements," and "this was impossible for management to accept." Dassin cited in *Tender Comrades*, 211.

32. Christopher Buckley, interview.

33. Victor Navasky, interview with the author, May 4, 2012.

34. Excerpt from Roy M. Cohn, *McCarthy*, reproduced in "Roy Cohn: 'He Was Right in Essentials,'" in *Joseph R. McCarthy*, ed. Allen J. Matusow (Englewood Cliffs, NJ: Prentice-Hall, 1970), 111–17.

35. Nicholas von Hoffman, *Citizen Cohn* (New York: Doubleday, 1988), 398–404, 422.

36. Judis, *William F. Buckley, Jr.*, 376.

37. Buckley, *On the Firing Line*, 409.

38. Cited by Alonzo L. Hamby, "Reds Under the Bed," review of *Joseph McCarthy: Reexamining the Life and Legacy of America's Most Hated Senator*, by Arthur Herman, *New York Times*, December 12, 1999, accessed April 7, 2015, http://www.nytimes.com/books/99/12/12/reviews/991212.12hambyt.html.

39. *Leaving Cleaver: Henry Louis Gates Jr. Remembers Eldridge Cleaver*, PBS Home Video, 2008.

CHAPTER THREE: FROM "WE SHALL OVERCOME" TO "SHOOT, DON'T LOOT": FIRING LINE CONFRONTS CIVIL RIGHTS AND BLACK POWER

1. Nixon had never fully won Buckley over, yet he suggested, at the height of the Watergate scandal, that the administration could get Buckley to write a positive newspaper column about Howard Hunt. James Reston Jr., *The Con-*

viction of Richard Nixon: The Untold Story of the Frost/Nixon Interviews (New York: Three Rivers Press, 2007), 194.

2. William F. Buckley, "Who Did What? Covert Questions," *National Review*, November 1, 2005, accessed February 2, 2015, http://www.nationalreview .com/articles/215833/who-did-what/william-f-buckley-jr.

3. Beverly Gage, "What an Uncensored Letter to M.L.K. Reveals," *New York Times Magazine*, November 11, 2014, accessed February 4, 2015, http://www .nytimes.com/2014/11/16/magazine/what-an-uncensored-letter-to-mlk-re veals.html.

4. Dan T. Carter, *The Politics of Rage: George Wallace, the Origins of the New Conservatism, and the Transformation of American Politics* (Baton Rouge: Louisiana State University Press, 2000), 306.

5. Carl T. Bogus, *Buckley: William F. Buckley Jr. and the Rise of American Conservatism* (New York: Bloomsbury Press, 2011), 162. Setting aside the 1957 editorial, Bogus points mostly to other authors in the pages of the magazine, not to Buckley himself

6. Ibid., 169.

7. Sam Tanenhaus, "Q&A on William F. Buckley," *New York Times*, February 27, 2008, accessed February 9, 2015, http://artsbeat.blogs.nytimes.com /2008/02/27/qa-with-sam-tanenhaus-on-william-f-buckley/.

8. Kevin M. Kruse, *White Flight: Atlanta and the Making of Modern Conservatism* (Princeton, NJ: Princeton University Press, 2005), 6.

9. Diane McWhorter, *Carry Me Home: Birmingham, Alabama: The Climactic Battle of the Civil Rights Revolution* (New York: Touchstone, 2001), 455.

10. Joseph Crespino, *Strom Thurmond's America* (New York: Hill & Wang, 2012), 51–54.

11. Christine Acham, *Revolution Televised: Prime Time and the Struggle for Black Power* (Minneapolis: University of Minnesota Press, 2004), 25; Aniko Bodroghkozy, *Equal Time: Television and the Civil Rights Movement* (Urbana: University of Illinois Press, 2012).

12. Devorah Heitner, *Black Power TV* (Durham, NC: Duke University Press, 2013).

13. Acham, *Revolution Televised*, 48. See also Peniel E. Joseph, *Stokely: A Life* (New York: Basic Books, 2014), 135.

14. William F. Buckley, "Why We Need a Black President," in *Athwart History: Half a Century of Polemics, Animadversions, and Illuminations*, ed. Linda Bridges and Roger Kimball (New York: Encounter Books, 2010), 80.

15. Lawrence Chickering, interview with the author, February 18, 2015. Senator James L. Buckley references how Chickering influenced his thinking on Black Power and black empowerment in *Gleanings from an Unplanned Life: An Annotated Oral History* (Wilmington, DE: Intercollegiate Studies Institute, 2006), 113. His takeaway was that he should find ways to help black entrepreneurs, while opposing "well-meaning social programs and race-based preferences that implied that blacks couldn't hack it on their own."

16. Todd Gitlin citing Edward Jay Epstein in *The Whole World Is Watching: Mass Media in the Making and Unmaking of the New Left* (Berkeley: University of California Press, 1980), 213.

17. Notably, Baldwin's *The Fire Next Time* was highly regarded by almost everyone but Buckley. Joseph notes that "even its detractors" hailed the book "as an important piece of social criticism." Peniel E. Joseph, *Waiting 'Til the Midnight Hour: A Narrative History of Black Power in America* (New York: Henry Holt, 2006), 72.

18. Joseph, *Stokely*, 176.

19. David M. Stone, *Nixon and the Politics of Public Television* (New York: Garland, 1985), 234.

20. Laurie Ouellette, *Viewers Like You? How Public TV Failed the People* (New York: Columbia University Press, 2002), 180–81.

21. At the opposite side of the political spectrum from Buckley, journalist Nora Sayre also noted the high level of white support for the Panthers. At a three-day Panther gathering in Oakland in 1969, 80 percent of attendees were white. Nora Sayre, *Sixties Going on Seventies* (New York: Arbor House, 1973), 57.

22. Joseph, *Waiting 'Til the Midnight Hour*, xviii.

23. Buchanan cited in Angela D. Dillard, *Guess Who's Coming to Dinner Now? Multicultural Conservatism in America* (New York: New York University Press, 2001), 59.

24. Undated letter from Everett C. Shores to William F. Buckley, box 13, "Wm. F. Buckley Jr. Correspondence, possible cancellation of program" folder, *Firing Line* collection, Hoover Institution, Stanford University.

25. Even those on the left utterly sympathetic to the Panther cause, like journalist Nora Sayre, could reach a rhetorical burnout point: "When the word 'revolution' is flying around like an old Frisbee," she wrote in 1969, "when 'fascism' twangs like a wornout rubber band, even 'racism' may become too familiar—a word and a concept that may already have ceased to shock a numbed society." She continues: "This fascist tablecloth, that racist tree,

those imperialist soap flakes—you start entreating others in the movement to preserve their ammunition, to allow language to keep its force." Sayre, *Sixties Going on Seventies*, 62.

26. This is not to trivialize the conflicts expressed in mainstream entertainment of the era. See Nina C. Leibman, *Living Room Lectures: The Fifties Family in Film and Television* (Austin: University of Texas Press, 1995); Erin Lee Mock, "The Horror of 'Honey, I'm Home!': The Perils of Postwar Family Love in the Domestic Sitcom," *Film & History* 41, no. 2 (Fall 2011): 29–50; and Walter Metz, *Bewitched* (Detroit: Wayne State University Press, 2007).

27. Samantha N. Sheppard, "Persistently Displaced: Situated Knowledges and Interrelated Histories in *The Spook Who Sat by the Door*," *Cinema Journal* 52, no. 2 (Winter 2012): 86.

28. Bodroghkozy, *Equal Time*, 180.

29. Cited in Bogus, *Buckley*, 173.

30. Nancy MacLean, *Freedom Is Not Enough: The Opening of the American Workplace* (New York: Russell Sage Foundation, 2006).

31. Ibid., 226.

32. Ira Glasser, interview with the author, November 21, 2014.

CHAPTER FOUR: CHIVALROUS PUGILISM: HOW *FIRING LINE* TRIED TO KO WOMEN'S LIB

1. John Owen cited in Daniel Oliver, "Bill Buckley: A Life on the Right," *Insider*, Summer 2008, 6.

2. Heather Hendershot, *Saturday Morning Censors: Television Regulation before the V-Chip* (Durham, NC: Duke University Press, 1998).

3. R. Marie Griffith, *God's Daughters: Evangelical Women and the Power of Submission* (Berkeley: University of California Press, 1997); Brenda E. Brasher, *Godly Women: Fundamentalism and Female Power* (New Brunswick, NJ: Rutgers University Press, 1998).

4. Schlafly cited in Barbara Ehrenreich, *The Hearts of Men: American Dreams and the Flight from Commitment* (New York: Doubleday, 1983), 148.

5. Schlafly cited in ibid., 149.

6. On a 1977 ABC special, Schlafly said, "I don't spend my time going around telling you all the lesbian organizations that are pushing ERA, although I could. I like to argue on the merits of the question." Cited in Susan Douglas, *Where the Girls Are: Growing Up Female with the Mass Media* (New York: Random House, 1994), 235.

7. Cited in ibid., 221.

8. Schlafly cited in Donald T. Critchlow, *Phyllis Schlafly and Grassroots Conservatism: A Woman's Crusade* (Princeton, NJ: Princeton University Press, 2005), 139.

9. Cited in Ginia Bellafante, "At Home with: Phyllis Schlafly. A Feminine Mystique All Her Own," *New York Times*, March 30, 2006, accessed October 4, 2015, http://www.nytimes.com/2006/03/30/garden/30phyllis.html?pagewanted=print.

10. "The Mud Slinger," *New York Times*, April 26, 1981, accessed October 4, 2015, http://www.nytimes.com/1981/04/26/opinion/the-mud-slinger.html.

11. Midge Decter, "Farewell to the Woman Question," *First Things*, March 2010, accessed September 28, 2014, http://www.firstthings.com/article/2010/03/a-farewell-to-the-woman-question.

12. Christina Pazzanese, "Answers from Walters," *Harvard Gazette*, October 8, 2014, accessed October 12, 2014, http://news.harvard.edu/gazette/story/2014/10/answers-from-walters.

13. Historian Alice Echols notes that, "until mid-1971 when NOW finally passed a resolution supporting lesbianism 'legally and morally,' anyone within the organization who advocated lesbian rights was vulnerable." In the 1970–71 period, "the movement was convulsed by the gay-straight split." Echols, *Daring to Be Bad: Radical Feminism in America 1967–1975* (Minneapolis: University of Minnesota Press, 1989), 220.

14. "What kind of a woman was she if she did not feel this mysterious fulfillment waxing the kitchen floor?" Betty Friedan, *The Feminine Mystique* (New York: Norton, 2001), 62. This line comes on the fifth page of the book itself, following new introductions, etc. for the 2001 edition.

15. A few years later, she shot a pilot for a New York City cable access series, *At Home with Betty Friedan*, in which friends visited her in her apartment to engage in short, awkward conversations. She berates one for not bringing a copy of her new book so that she can promote it to viewers, and she cuts off another friend for talking too slowly. Mercifully, the episode apparently never aired.

16. Douglas, *Where the Girls Are*, 226.

17. Sylvia Jukes Morris, *Price of Fame: The Honorable Clare Boothe Luce* (New York: Random House, 2014), 570.

18. Cited in Critchlow, *Phyllis Schlafly and Grassroots Conservatism*, 226–27.

19. Ibid., 236.

20. Elaine Kindall cited in ibid., 279.

21. Ibid., 227.

22. Ibid., 23.

23. Letter from Buckley to Greer, March 8, 1973, box 12, "Wm. F. Buckley Jr. correspondence, *Firing Line* F–H" folder, *Firing Line* collection, Hoover Institution, Stanford University.

24. "Family values" is a bit of an anachronism here, as the term would only gain wide traction in the 1980s, as right-wing Christian activists such as Jerry Falwell and Pat Robertson gained power and prominence.

25. Morris, *Price of Fame*, 35.

26. Wilfrid Sheed, *Clare Boothe Luce* (New York: Dutton, 1982), 132. Sheed was a guest literary critic discussing *Brideshead Revisited* with Buckley when it initially aired on PBS in 1982.

27. Morris, *Price of Fame*, 532.

28. Sheed, *Clare Boothe Luce*, 133.

29. Morris, *Price of Fame*, 416.

30. Ibid., 385.

31. Ibid., 252.

32. Ibid., 87.

33. Ibid., 29.

34. Josh Lambert, "How Harriet Pilpel Took Obscenity off the Map," *Lilith* 38, no. 4 (Winter 2013/2014): 48.

35. Heather Hendershot, *What's Fair on the Air? Cold War Right-Wing Broadcasting and the Public Interest* (Chicago: University of Chicago Press, 2011), 195–96; Lisa McGirr, *Suburban Warriors: The Origins of the New American Right* (Princeton, NJ: Princeton University Press, 2001), 227–31.

36. February 11, 1980, letter to Buckley forwarded to Pilpel, "January 3, 1980, *Firing Line*" file, carton 2, 82-M123, Harriet Pilpel papers, Schlesinger Library, Harvard University.

37. Postcard from January 1980, "January 3, 1980, *Firing Line*" file, carton 2, 82-M123, Harriet Pilpel papers, Schlesinger Library, Harvard University.

38. Douglas, *Where the Girls Are*, 228.

39. *Newsweek* article cited in ibid., 228.

CHAPTER FIVE: TRIPPING OVER TRICKY DICK

1. David Greenberg, *Nixon's Shadow: The History of an Image* (New York: Norton, 2003).

2. Carl Bernstein and Bob Woodward, *All the President's Men* (New York: Simon & Schuster, 2012), 129.

3. Greenberg, *Nixon's Shadow*, 166.

4. Ibid., 167.

5. Jeff Greenfield, interview with the author, July 3, 2014.

6. William F. Buckley, "Richard Nixon, RIP," in *Athwart History: Half a Century of Polemics, Animadversions, and Illuminations*, ed. Linda Bridges and Roger Kimball (New York: Encounter Books, 2010), 321; John R. Coyne and Linda Bridges, *Strictly Right: William F. Buckley Jr. and the American Conservative Movement* (Hoboken, NJ: Wiley, 2007), 113.

7. Neal Freeman, interview with the author, July 15, 2014.

8. Carl T. Bogus, *Buckley: William F. Buckley Jr., and the Rise of American Conservatism* (New York: Bloomsbury, 2011), 338.

9. Letters to Nixon from Rusher, box 36, Buckley papers, Yale University; letter from Buchanan to *National Review* and memo from Buckley to Rusher, box 40, Buckley papers, Yale University.

10. Buchanan had been the perfect choice to write the letter. In his three-hour job interview, Nixon had asked Buchanan, "you're not as conservative as William F. Buckley, are you—or am I wrong?" As Rick Perlstein tells it, "Buchanan, who was *more* conservative than Buckley (his specialty as an editorial writer for the right-wing *St. Louis Globe-Democrat* was disseminating smears about civil rights leaders passed on by J. Edgar Hoover), artfully dodged the question: 'I have a tremendous admiration for Bill Buckley.'" Rick Perlstein, *Nixonland: The Rise of a President and the Fracturing of America* (New York: Simon & Schuster, 2008), 84.

11. John B. Judis, *William F. Buckley, Jr.: Patron Saint of the Conservatives* (New York: Simon & Schuster, 1988), 280; Neal Freeman, interview.

12. Judis, *William F. Buckley, Jr.*, 302.

13. Ibid., 304.

14. Martin Jay, *The Virtues of Mendacity: On Lying in Politics* (Charlottesville: University of Virginia Press, 2010), 180.

15. The Thomas program was the third episode of *Firing Line* that was shot, but it was the first to air.

16. Heather Hendershot, *What's Fair on the Air? Cold War Right-Wing Broadcasting and the Public Interest* (Chicago: University of Chicago Press, 2011).

17. Todd Gitlin, *The Whole World Is Watching: Mass Media in the Making and Unmaking of the New Left* (Berkeley: University of California Press, 1980).

18. Aide cited in Perlstein, *Nixonland,* 517.

19. David M. Stone, *Nixon and the Politics of Public Television* (New York: Garland, 1985), 116.

20. The story is told in great detail in both Stone, *Nixon and the Politics of Public Television,* and James Day, *The Vanishing Vision: The Inside Story of Public Television* (Berkeley: University of California Press, 1995).

21. Box 81, "Herbert Klein" folder, *Firing Line* collection, Hoover Institution, Stanford University, 7.

22. Galbraith cited in "Spiro T. Agnew, Ex–Vice President, Dies at 77," *New York Times,* September 18, 1996, accessed October 9, 2015, http://www.nytimes.com/1996/09/18/us/spiro-t-agnew-ex-vice-president-dies-at-77.html?pagewanted=all.

23. Herb Klein gave this number on *Face the Nation,* November 16, 1969, transcription included in research file for Klein's *Firing Line* appearance, box 81, "Herbert Klein" folder, *Firing Line* collection, Hoover Institution, Stanford University, 8.

24. Box 81, "Herbert Klein" folder, *Firing Line* collection, Hoover Institution, Stanford University, 9.

25. According to James Keogh, Agnew was referring to a Japanese-American journalist whose nickname among his friends was "the fat Jap." Keogh, *President Nixon and the Press* (New York: Funk & Wagnalls, 1972), 134–35. Agnew thought his comment had been misrepresented, but it came shortly on the heels of his having referred to Polish-Americans as "Polacks," and he had already earned a reputation for racial and ethnic insensitivity.

26. "Spiro T. Agnew, Ex–Vice President, Dies at 77," *New York Times,* September 18, 1996.

27. Buckley, *On the Right* column, "Mr. Agnew and the Demonstrators," October 23, 1969, box 81, "Herbert Klein" folder, *Firing Line* collection, Hoover Institution, Stanford University

28. Buckley, *On the Right* column, "The Role of Agnew," November 25, 1969, box 81, "Herbert Klein" folder, *Firing Line* collection, Hoover Institution, Stanford University.

29. Box 81, "Herbert Klein" folder, *Firing Line* collection, Hoover Institution, Stanford University. This appears to be a comment made by *Firing Line* researcher Agatha Schmidt (Dowd), but seems to aptly convey Buckley's own feelings.

30. Ernest van den Haag, *Punishing Criminals: Concerning a Very Old and Painful Question* (New York: Basic Books, 1975).

31. Coyne and Bridges, *Strictly Right*, 126.

32. Ibid., 139.

33. Dean J. Kotlowski, *Nixon's Civil Rights: Politics, Principle, and Policy* (Cambridge, MA: Harvard University Press, 2001), 12.

34. Donald T. Critchlow, *Phyllis Schlafly and Grassroots Conservatism: A Woman's Crusade* (Princeton, NJ: Princeton University Press, 2005), 209.

35. Neal Freeman, interview. David Greenberg notes that Senator Buckley's call for resignation made it "safe for the far right to break with the president" (*Nixon's Shadow*, 201); it had been difficult for the right to break with Nixon, in part, because liberals were calling so loudly for his resignation.

CHAPTER SIX: FROM THE MASHED POTATO CIRCUIT TO THE OVAL OFFICE: RONALD REAGAN, *FIRING LINE*, AND THE TRIUMPH OF THE RIGHT

1. George Packer, "The Uses of Division: Rick Perlstein Chronicles the Fall of the American Consensus and the Rise of the Right," *New Yorker*, August 11, 2014, accessed May 19, 2015, http://www.newyorker.com/magazine/2014/08/11/uses-division.

2. His final appearance in 1990 was a two-parter, "Two Friends Talk: Reagan and Buckley," which was taped in one sitting. I count this as two episodes, as they aired separately. Also, I have counted "Conservatives Confront 1972," which was a PBS show that was not technically a *Firing Line* episode, but Buckley always considered it as such.

3. Reagan cited in Frances FitzGerald, *Way Out There in the Blue: Reagan, Star Wars, and the End of the Cold War* (New York: Simon & Schuster, 2001), 49.

4. Kim Phillips-Fein, *Invisible Hands: The Making of the Conservative Movement from the New Deal to Reagan* (New York: Norton, 2009), 114.

5. Ibid., 111.

6. Cited in Jessica Mitford, "The Rest of Ronald Reagan," *Ramparts*, November 1965, 33.

7. "Reagan would hear a particularly persuasive story told by a constituent about governmental red tape, commit it to memory, and then simply recall it whenever he wanted to illustrate the evils of big government. As one biographer [Lou Cannon] put it, 'It was as if someone had hit the "play" button on a tape cassette recorder.'" Jonathan M. Schoenwald, *A Time for Choosing: The Rise of Modern American Conservatism* (New York: Oxford University Press, 2001), 195.

8. Douglas W. Rae and Peter A. Lupsha, "Politics as Theater: Ronald Reagan at Yale," *Yale Alumni Magazine*, January 1968, 43.

9. Ibid., 42.

10. Mitford, "The Rest of Ronald Reagan," unpaginated. This text accompanies a cutout paper doll of Reagan, and it is actually a slightly altered gloss on the opening of the book. Buckley cited the opening in an article in 1967 and acknowledged how "disastrous" it was as prose: "The story begins with the close-up of a bottom. My face was blue . . . my bottom was red . . . and my father claimed afterward that he was white . . . Ever since . . . I have been particularly fond of the colors that were exhibited—red, white, and blue." Buckley blamed the ghostwriter, but what politician does not sign off on first-person prose that he knows will be attributed to him?

11. Ibid., 36.

12. SECA special, *American Conservatives Confront 1972.*

13. Cited in Michael Rogin, *Ronald Reagan, the Movie and Other Episodes in Political Demonology* (Berkeley: University of California Press, 1987), 7.

14. William F. Buckley, "A Relaxing View of Ronald Reagan" in *Athwart History: Half a Century of Polemics, Animadversions, and Illuminations,* ed. Linda Bridges and Roger Kimball (New York: Encounter Books, 2010), 299.

15. Theodore H. White, *The Making of the President 1964* (New York: HarperCollins, 2010), 346.

16. FitzGerald, *Way Out There in the Blue.* On the earlier years, see also Rick Perlstein, *The Invisible Bridge: The Fall of Nixon and the Rise of Reagan* (New York: Simon & Schuster, 2014).

17. On Reagan and California welfare reform, see Perlstein, *The Invisible Bridge,* 411–13.

18. William F. Buckley Jr., *The Reagan I Knew* (New York: Basic Books, 2008), 75.

19. Ibid., 241.

20. William F. Buckley Jr., *On the Firing Line* (New York: Random House, 1989), 364.

21. William F. Buckley Jr., *Overdrive: A Personal Documentary* (New York: Doubleday, 1981), 119.

22. Buckley, *On the Firing Line*, 363. It was Senator Jesse Helms who had engineered Reagan's push on the canal issue in North Carolina.

23. William A. Rusher, *The Rise of the Right* (New York: William Morrow, 1984), 300. See also Richard A. Viguerie and David Franke, *America's Right Turn: How Conservatives Used New and Alternative Media to Take Power* (Lanham, MD: Taylor Trade Publishing, 2004).

24. John B. Judis, *William F. Buckley, Jr.: Patron Saint of the Conservatives* (New York: Simon & Schuster, 1988), 400.

25. Buckley, *On the Firing Line*, 385.

26. Howard Phillips cited in Judis, *William F. Buckley, Jr.,* 401.

27. Buckley, *The Reagan I Knew*, 118

28. William F. Buckley, "Solzhenitsyn at Bay," in *Athwart History*, 144.

29. I will refer to the conservative evangelical political movement that emerged in the 1970s and 1980s, helmed by figures such as Jerry Falwell and Pat Robertson, as "the Christian Right," but historians tend to identify this group as the "new" Christian Right. The "old" Christian Right was composed of anti-Semitic extremists, such as Gerald L. K. Smith and Gerald P. Winrod, who emerged during the Great Depression. See Leo P. Ribuffo, *The Old Christian Right: The Protestant Far Right from the Depression to the Cold War* (Philadelphia: Temple University Press, 1983).

30. Cited in Allan J. Lichtman, *White Protestant Nation: The Rise of the American Conservative Movement* (New York: Grove Press, 2008), 344.

31. Ibid., 376.

32. Linda Bridges, interview with the author, July 9, 2014. The response is useful insofar as it points to Buckley's distance from the old anti-Semitic, anti-Catholic American right wing. Notably, "to keep the magazine from being pigeonholed as a Catholic publication and to avoid any hint of anti-Semitism, Buckley consciously sought out Jewish conservatives to counterbalance the disproportionate number of Catholics on the masthead. But despite his attention to religious parity within the leadership, the *National Review* published strikingly few articles on religion between 1955 and 1960." K. Healan Gaston, "The Cold War Romance of Religious Authenticity: Will Herberg, William F. Buckley Jr., and the Rise of the New Right," *Journal of American History* 99, no. 4 (March 2013): 1152.

33. Heather Hendershot, *Shaking the World for Jesus: Media and Conservative Evangelical Culture* (Chicago: University of Chicago Press, 2004).

34. Buckley seemed to hold Weyrich in higher regard than he did Viguerie, and Weyrich appeared on *Firing Line* three times to discuss strategy in the episodes: "Who Should Reagan Pick as Vice-President?" (1980), "Debates and Politics" (1987), and "What Should Conservatives Look for in President Reagan's State of the Union Address?" (1987).

35. You might assume that a 1990 *Firing Line* episode titled "What's Up with Evangelical Christianity?" would involve Buckley arguing through the ins and outs of the Christian Right, and, indeed, the show opens with emcee Michael Kinsley referencing the Jim Bakker scandal and the "image problems" of televangelists, but Buckley's discussion with R. C. Sproul immediately turns apolitical and theological.

36. In *The Rise of the Right*, Bill Rusher remarks upon Viguerie's support for Connally in the course of his discussion of the "elaborate litany of complaints" against Reagan issued by the New Right. Rusher, *The Rise of the Right*, 314.

37. Buckley, *The Reagan I Knew*, 239.

38. Ibid., 240.

39. Lou Cannon, *President Reagan: The Role of a Lifetime* (New York: Simon & Schuster, 1991), 814.

40. Buckley invited Alan Dershowitz to discuss "AIDS: The Rights of the Patient, the Rights of the Public" in late 1985. Buckley had in 1981 hosted a *Firing Line* episode on "The Question of Gay Rights," and he would host "The Problems of Gay Life" in 1997. In all of these, Buckley is particularly concerned with what he sees as the problem of gay promiscuity.

41. Buckley writes in a 1986 letter to Reagan that it was Sobran who suggested this line. Buckley, *The Reagan I Knew*, 196. Dinesh D'Souza claims in 2008 that Dartmouth professor and *National Review* book reviewer Jeffrey Hart was the contest winner. Dinesh D'Souza, "Unforgettable William F. Buckley," Townhall.com, March 3, 2008, accessed June 9, 2015, http://townhall.com/columnists/dineshdsouza/2008/03/03/unforgettable_william_f_buckley/page/full.

42. *Firing Line* episode with Anthony Lewis, "President Reagan: A Preliminary Evaluation," 1981.

43. James Ledbetter, *Made Possible By . . . The Death of Public Broadcasting in the United States* (New York: Verso, 1997), 170.

44. Letter from Buckley to Sam H. Husbands Jr., December 13, 1966, box 11, "Television Program—*Firing Line* Viewer Comments, 1966" folder, *Firing Line* collection, Hoover Institution, Stanford University.

45. Buckley interview with Nancy Dickerson, excerpted in PBS press release,

April 1, 1971, box 5, "PBS" folder, *Firing Line* collection, Hoover Institution, Stanford University.

46. Ibid.

47. The text from a fundraising slide show directed to potential underwriters, which was sent to SECA president Henry Cauthen by the Corporation for Public Broadcasting (CPB) in 1973, is quite telling in this regard: "3M's funding of *VD Blues* represents 3M's concern for the vital area of health. The McDonald Corporation's co-funding of *ZOOM* indicates McDonald's concern for the nation's youngsters in a positive way." This early, somewhat desperate call for support was an early sign of the underwriting mandate that was to come. According to the CPB document, total PBS funds—for station expenses, program production, distribution costs, the whole enchilada—for the 1971–72 fiscal year came to $141 million, of which 17 percent came from the federal government, mostly via the CPB. Another 54 percent came from state and local governments, boards of education, state- or university-run public TV systems, etc. A further 16 percent came from viewers, and 13 percent came from corporate and foundation underwriters. What we see here is more than half of a budget coming from local/state government sources. All 1973 information from slide show text enclosed with letter from George Page (PBS) to Henry Cauthen (SECA), September 28, 1973, box 6, *Firing Line* collection, Hoover Institution, Stanford University.

48. Brad Plumer, "Why Exactly Should the Government Fund PBS and NPR?," *Washington Post*, accessed May 28, 2015, http://www.washingtonpost .com/blogs/wonkblog/wp/2012/10/10/why-exactly-should-the-government-fund-pbs-and-npr/.

49. Ledbetter, *Made Possible By . . .* , 89.

50. A 1970 SECA-NAEB (National Association of Educational Broadcasters) convention featured two main events, a *Firing Line* taping by Buckley and luncheon with Marshall McLuhan. The flashy orange promotional flier asked "Watch ya doin' Marshall McLuhan?" A cartoon head of McLuhan answers: "I'm looking forward to meeting you at the NOW frontier to explore new concepts for involving today's turned-on youth in the process of learning." The event organizers have the good sense not to try to portray Buckley as such a hepcat, but they do promise attendees "a reserved seat at ringside to see the sesquipedalian Mr. Buckley in action with headline-making guests! Two fast-moving sessions are followed by reception."

51. Buckley, *Overdrive*, 152.

52. This was the cost to the University of Mississippi in 1999. Contract between *Firing Line* and University of Mississippi, August 2, 1999, box 6, "War-

ren Steibel" folder, *Firing Line* collection, Hoover Institution, Stanford University. The funding qualified for 501(c)3 tax exemption.

53. Memo "To All Concerned," probably from Warren Steibel, "Re: Firing Line, and the cost of it to local stations," September 1977, box 6, "William F. Buckley Jr. Correspondence, Miscellaneous Memoranda, Pamphlets" folder, *Firing Line* collection, Hoover Institution, Stanford University.

54. Jeff Greenfield, interview with the author, July 3, 2014.

55. Newton Minow, interview with the author, January 28, 2015.

56. Fowler cited in Heather Hendershot, *Saturday Morning Censors: Television Regulation before the V-Chip* (Durham, NC: Duke University Press, 1998), 110.

57. David M. Stone, *Nixon and the Politics of Public Television* (New York: Garland, 1985), 190–202.

58. Ledbetter, *Made Possible By . . .* , 178–79.

59. Neal Freeman, interview with the author, July 15, 2014.

CONCLUSION: IN PRAISE OF HONEST INTELLECTUAL COMBAT

1. Kathleen Hall Jamieson and Joseph N. Cappella, *Echo Chamber: Rush Limbaugh and the Conservative Media Establishment* (New York: Oxford University Press, 2008), 246.

2. The show was even profitable, bringing in $21,000 per minute of advertising in 1965. Top-rated *Bonanza*, by contrast, racked up $63,000 per minute. But the *Huntley-Brinkley Report* ran five days a week, 52 weeks a year. "Television: Huntley-Brinkley's Chunk of Crinkly," *Time*, April 2, 1965, accessed August 3, 2015, http://content.time.com/time/magazine/article/0,9171,941023,00.html.

3. Richard Brookhiser, interview with the author, September 4, 2014.

4. Right-wing monitoring organizations have long claimed bias on TV news, but, then, so have those on the left. On Vietnam, for example, see Daniel C. Hallin, *The Uncensored War: The Media and Vietnam* (Oxford, U.K.: Oxford University Press, 1986).

5. Chad Raphael, *Investigated Reporting: Muckrakers, Regulators, and the Struggle over Television Documentary* (Champaign: University of Illinois Press, 2005); Michael Curtin, *Redeeming the Wasteland: Television Documentary and Cold War Politics* (New Brunswick, NJ: Rutgers University Press, 1995). Curtin seeks to complicate the "golden age" notion by unearthing the ways that the Kennedy-era productions supported the administration and fostered notions of how TV could be used as a weapon to contain communism.

6. William S. Paley cited in Fred W. Friendly, *Due to Circumstances Beyond Our Control . . .* (New York: Random House, 1967), 92.

7. Victor Navasky, interview with the author, May 4, 2012.

8. Heather Hendershot, "Fame Is a Bee: On Dick Cavett," *Nation*, November 4, 2010, accessed August 5, 2015, http://www.thenation.com/article/fame-bee-dick-cavett/.

9. Buckley interviewed by Sam Vaughan, *Paris Review*, 146 (Spring 1998), accessed August 5, 2015, http://www.theparisreview.org/interviews/1395/the-art-of-fiction-no-146-william-f-buckley-jr.

10. It is worth adding that there have been a variety of cable access programs that tapped into the political and practical needs of local communities. Deirdre Boyle, *Subject to Change: Guerrilla Television Revisited* (New York: Oxford University Press, 1997).

11. Jeffrey Jones, "Rethinking Television's Relationship to Politics in the Post-Network Era" in *iPolitics: Citizens, Elections, and Governing in the New Media Era,* ed. Richard L. Fox and Jennifer M. Ramos (Cambridge, U.K.: Cambridge University Press, 2012), 55.

12. Ibid.

13. Rich Lowry, "I Was a Teenage Conservative," in *Why I Turned Right: Leading Baby Boom Conservatives Chronicle Their Political Journeys,* ed. Mary Eberstadt (New York: Threshold Editions, 2007), 272.

14. Christopher Buckley, interview with the author, April 7, 2015.

15. Brookhiser, interview.

16. Richard Sandomir, "At Lunch with: *The McLaughlin Group;* Just Another Talk Show? Wronnnggg!," December 16, 1992, accessed August 3, 2015, http://www.nytimes.com/1992/12/16/garden/at-lunch-with-the-mclaughlin-group-just-another-talk-show-wronnnggg.html?sec=&spon=&pagewanted=1.

17. Christopher Buckley, interview.

18. Brookhiser, interview.

19. Michael Kinsley, *Big Babies* (New York: William Morrow, 1995), xii.

20. Rich Lowry, interview with the author, July 10, 2014.

Catholicism
Buckley and, xii, xxviii, 269–71
Clare Boothe Luce and, 175, 176
National Review and, 333n32
Stephen Colbert and, 303
Caute, David, 74–75
Cauthen, Henry, 287
Cavett, Dick, 295
Ceballos, Jacqui, 157
Central Intelligence Agency (CIA),
50, 88, 89, 92, 265
Chamberlain, John, xii
Chambers, Whittaker, xii, liv, 40, 81
Chapin, Harry, 49
Charlie Rose (TV program), 296
Cherne, Leo, 72
Chiang Kai-shek, 63–64
Chickering, Lawrence, 119
China, 62, 63–66
Chinese famine
of 1942–1943, 65
of 1958–1961, 62
Chomsky, Noam, xlii, 59–62, 60n,
60f, 68, 299, 304
Chou En-lai, 64
Christian Right, 31, 261, 270–72,
274, 276. *See also* Catholicism;
evangelicals
abortion and, 267, 269, 272, 274
defined, 333n29
new vs. old, 333n29
Reagan and, 266–68
Citizens' Councils. *See* White Citizens' Councils
civil disobedience, 96, 100
civil rights, xv–xvi, xxvi, lii, 49,
99–101, 105, 108, 109, 131, 143
National Review and, 102–3, 144–45
Reagan and, 240
Civil Rights Act of 1964, 132
civil rights legislation, communists
and, 98
civil rights movement, 12, 87–89, 93,
99, 120, 125, 126, 135, 139. *See
also specific topics*
Allard Lowenstein and, 48
Buckley's shift in stance on, 14, 141
communism and, 94, 97
conspirational right wing on, 93, 98
liberalism and, 135
media coverage of, 293–94
modern conservatism and, 105
Pat Buchanan on, 135

civil rights organizations, 125. *See also
specific organizations*
network news and, 115, 140–41,
294
Civil War, 107n
Clark, Kenneth, 128–30
Cleaver, Eldridge, 86, 123, 130–31
Buckley and, 85, 86, 116, 123,
132–35
on democracy, 85, 86
in exile, 85, 138
on *Firing Line*, xlii, 85, 116
Huey Newton and, 136
on Julian Bond, 129, 131–32
on Marxism, 85–86
on Nixon, 85, 130
on Republican Party, 132, 134
on Vietnam War, 129, 131f, 133
Coffin, William Sloane, l–lii, lxiii
Cohn, Roy M.
Buckley on, 80–81
communism and, 76–78
as guest on "How Should Ex-
Communists Cooperate?"
(1980), 75–80
as guest on "Subversion and the
Law" (1976), 80–81
as guest on "The Ghost of the
Army-McCarthy Hearings Part
I" (1968), 72, 73f
Mark Felt and, 93, 97
Martin Luther King surveillance
and, 97
McCarthy, McCarthyism, and, 72,
73f, 75, 78, 79, 82
personality, 79–80
Victor Navasky and, 75–80
Colbert, Stephen, 303–4
Colbert Report, The (TV program),
304
Cold War, 34–36, 61, 77, 82
collectivism, 36, 47
communism
and the American left, 62
labor unions and, 41–44
Communist Party USA (CPUSA), 46,
68–71, 93
actors who joined, 74
compared with KKK, 69
Henry Wallace presidential cam-
paign and, 93
Martin Luther King and, 91
Victor Navasky on, 69–71

ABOUT THE AUTHOR

Heather Hendershot is a professor of film and media at the Massachusetts Institute of Technology and the author of *Saturday Morning Censors*, *Shaking the World for Jesus*, and *What's Fair on the Air?* She has held fellowships at Harvard University, New York University, Princeton University, and Vassar College, and has also been a Guggenheim Fellow. She lives in Cambridge, Massachusetts.